THE PAN-AFRICAN NATION

THE PAN-AFRICAN NATION

Oil and the Spectacle of Culture in Nigeria

Andrew Apter

Ch. 7 & 2

21 - 83

The University of Chicago Press   *Chicago and London*

ANDREW APTER is professor of history and anthropology at the University of California, Los Angeles, and chair of the interdepartmental program in African studies. His previous book, *Black Critics and Kings: The Hermeneutics of Power in Yoruba Society,* was published by the University of Chicago Press.

The University of Chicago Press, Chicago 60637
The University of Chicago Press, Ltd., London
© 2005 by The University of Chicago
All rights reserved. Published 2005
Printed in the United States of America

14 13 12 11 10 09 08   2 3 4 5

ISBN: 0-226-02354-0   (cloth)
ISBN: 0-226-02355-9   (paper)

Library of Congress Cataloging-in-Publication Data
Apter, Andrew H. (Andrew Herman)
   The Pan-African nation : oil and the spectacle of culture in Nigeria / Andrew Apter.
      p.   cm.
   Includes bibliographical references and index.
      ISBN 0-226-02354-0 (hardcover : alk. paper) — ISBN 0-226-02355-9 (pbk. : alk. paper)
      1. Petroleum industry and trade—Nigeria.   2. Revenue—Nigeria.   3. Nigeria—
   Cultural policy.   4. Africa—Civilization.   5. World Black and African Festival of Arts
   and Culture (2nd : 1977 : Lagos, Nigeria).   I. Title.
      HD9577.N52A68 2005
      305.896—dc22   2004014638

CONTENTS

Acknowledgments   vii

Introduction   1

LA MISE EN SCÈNE

1   Rebirth of a Nation   21
2   Nigeria at Large   52

THE SPECTACLE OF CULTURE

3   Producing the People   87
4   War Canoes and Their Magic   121
5   A Genealogy of the Durbar   167
6   The Mirror of Cultural Production   200

LA MISE EN ABÎME

7   The Politics of Illusion   223
8   Death and the King's Henchmen   258

Conclusion   278
Notes   285
References   309
Index   323

ACKNOWLEDGMENTS

MANY FRIENDS, students, and colleagues have accompanied this study, which began as a projected five-year plan that ineluctably evolved into a ten-year odyssey. Intellectual, logistical, and financial support has come from a variety of people and institutions, for which I remain deeply grateful.

Fieldwork and archival research in Lagos from June through December 1993 was funded by a Fulbright–Council for the International Exchange of Scholars fellowship (92-67755) that arranged my double affiliation in Nigeria with the Centre for Black and African Arts and Civilization (CBAAC) and the Department of Cultural Studies at the University of Lagos. Given the turbulence of this six-month period, starting with the abrogation of the June 12 elections followed by riots, strikes, and the fateful coup of the violent and repressive Abacha regime, these were interesting times; and my thanks extend to my official Nigerian hosts at that time, Dr. Union Edebiri of CBAAC, and Dele Jegede at the University of Lagos, who stood up for me when my presence became a potential liability. Many Nigerians assisted me with legendary hospitality, and their names would fill many pages; particular thanks, however, go to Professor Jacob Ade Ajayi and his wife, Christie Ajayi, Segun Ojewuyi, Dan Awodoye, Ogoni activist James Nalley, Yusuf Adebayo Grillo, the late Bola Ige, Dr. Garba Ashiwaju, Dr. Judith Asuni, Lari Williams, Babalola Lanade, Uche N. Abalogu, Mrs. Y. Fowosire, Dr. Chibogu, and Lieutenant General Olusegun Obasanjo, former head of state and Grand Patron of FESTAC, who reminisced with me on two occasions and would be wrongfully imprisoned by Abacha before winning two presidential elections. In addition to extended interviews, I further benefited from the special collections of the Cultural Library at the National Theatre and the extraordinary press file at the Nigerian Institute of International Affairs. With the (then) British high commissioner, Sir Christopher MacRae, and his wife, Lady Mette, I acknowledge a special friendship and rewarding reciprocation—access to Nigerian VIPs in exchange for entry into Yemoja's shrine (*ipara*) during the annual festival in Ayede-Ekiti. To Olusanya Ibitoye, my principal research assistant during this and my previous projects in Nigeria, I can only say "A kìí dúpé ará eni, omo ìyá ni wa" [We don't thank ourselves, we are children of one mother].

If a Fulbright-CIES fellowship launched this study of cultural production during the oil boom in Nigeria, a National Endowment for the Humanities fellowship (FA-36156) helped bring it to a close, supporting final research at the Rhodes House Library in Oxford, an affiliation with St. Antony's College in 2000, and a year of much-needed sabbatical. At Oxford I benefited greatly from Alan Lodge's archival logic and magic, Anthony Kirk-Greene's legendary assistance and unparalleled knowledge of colonial Nigeria, William Beinart's lively seminars and colloquia, and the stimulating Africanist community around them, which included the late Helen Callaway. Other centers of Africanist scholarship where I have presented various chapters and drafts over the years include the Center for West African Studies in Birmingham, with Karin Barber, Paolo Moraes de Farias, and Tom McCaskie; University College London and the School of Oriental and African Studies, with Murray Last and Chris Pinney, Akin Oyetade, Richard Fardon, Richard Rathbone, and Donal Cruise O'Brien; and the University of Manchester, with Richard Werbner, all of whom provided rigorous and valuable feedback. I have also benefited greatly from Northwestern University's Africana Library collection, and many seminars (in which I first encountered the influential work of Michael Watts, the grounded iconoclasm of Ed Wilmsen, and the challenging criticisms of Agbo Folarin) held at the Program for African Studies when directed by David William Cohen and then Jane Guyer.

At the University of Chicago, my intellectual home for fourteen years, and where passion and scholarship are impossible to separate, words threaten to fail me . . . except to acknowledge that my study developed dialogically and dialectically, in many a challenge and riposte, with a critical spirit amplified throughout seminars, meetings, conferences, and colloquia, most notably the African Studies Workshop. My thanks extend to Beth Ann Buggenhagen, Alex Dent, Vicki Brennan, Nicole Castor, Robert Blunt, Jesse Shipley, Anne-Marie Makhulu, Frank Romagosa, Paul Ryer, Brian Brazeal, Ralph Austen, Carol Breckenridge, Constanze Weise, Anne Ch'ien, the late Barney Cohn, Jennifer Cole, Jim Fernandez, Ray Smith, Ray Fogelson, William Hanks, Marshall Sahlins, Terry Turner, William Sewell, Arjun Appadurai, John Kelly, Jackie Bhabha, David Laitin, Claudio Lomnitz, John MacAloon (who also arranged an invaluable interview with Andrew Young), William Mazzarella, Robert Nelson, Tom Mitchell, Moishe Postone, Manuela Carneiro da Cunha, Michel-Rolph Trouillot, Michael Silverstein, George Steinmetz, George Stocking, Salikoko Mufwene, Lisa Wedeen, and especially John and Jean Comaroff—leaders in the historical ethnography of Africa, comrades in the broader struggle of decolonizing Africanist discourse. With David Brent, my patient yet demanding editor at University of Chicago Press, the deep history of this text bespeaks an unbreakable friendship. To 'Dayo Laoye, whose art and wisdom continue to inspire, "may you live longer than your forefathers."

At UCLA, where I have since become an anthropologist among the historians, I received a final volley of inputs and arrows through the valuable comments of Ned Alpers, Bobby Hill, Richard Sklar, Emily Musil, Don Cosentino, Teo Ruiz, Chris Waterman, and Allen Roberts, who, as director of the James S. Coleman African Studies Center, offered moral, intellectual, and institutional support during the final stretch of the writing process.

Finally, I thank my better half, Robin Derby, for sharing my love of Nigeria, and for opening my eyes and expanding my vistas to the Caribbean.

VERSIONS OF several chapters have appeared in edited volumes. Chapter 5 appeared as "The Subvention of Tradition: A Genealogy of the Nigerian Durbar," in *State/Culture: State-Formation after the Cultural Turn,* ed. George Steinmetz, 213–252 (Ithaca, NY: Cornell University Press, 1999). Copyright © 1999 by Cornell University. Used by permission of the publisher, Cornell University Press. Chapter 7 appeared as "IBB = 419: Nigerian Democracy and the Politics of Illusion," in *Civil Society and the Political Imagination in Africa,* ed. John and Jean Comaroff, 267–

307 (Chicago: University of Chicago Press, 1999). Copyright © 1999 by The University of Chicago. Chapter 8 appeared as "Death and the King's Henchmen: Ken Saro-Wiwa and the Political Ecology of Citizenship in Nigeria," in *Ogoni's Agonies: Ken Saro-Wiwa and the Crisis in Nigeria,* ed. Abdul-Rasheed Na'Allah, 121–160 (Trenton, NJ: AWP, 1998). Permission to reprint them is gratefully acknowledged.

INTRODUCTION

I BEGIN this book on a personal note, because its genesis dates back to my first visit to Nigeria in the summer of 1977. Jimmy Carter was president, OPEC ruled the West, the American economy was in the throes of "stagflation," the killings in Soweto were revealing the horrors of apartheid, and Yale—where I was an undergraduate philosophy major—was leading its critical retreat into semiotics and deconstruction. I identified strongly with this exciting if somewhat escapist intellectual moment, moving between what Needham (1983) has called "the tranquility of axioms" in logic and syntax, on the one hand, and the disruptive textual strategies of rhetorical theory, on the other—looking for meaning and tracking its slippery tropes. In those days, the alliance between linguistics and structuralism was still viable, and outstanding problems in semiotics could still be solved. And it was in this particular milieu that I formulated my first research project on Yoruba talking drums.

The linguistic principles of Yoruba drum language and the multiple meanings of drummed proverbs and utterances proved far too difficult an area to penetrate for the novice that I was, and if ever I return to the challenge, I will rely on Akin Euba's ethnomusicological foundations (Euba 1990). However above my head at the time, it was the project that first took me to Nigeria, one strangely suited to the high modernism of the black world's fair called FESTAC '77. FESTAC had ended five months earlier when I arrived in Lagos in mid-July, but its echoes were literally still audible on the airwaves, its discourse still alive in the streets. "Ah, you are a cultural!" was the frequent response to my self-presentation as a would-be anthropologist. For in FESTAC, culture made money and sense, ratifying the role of visitors like myself. Spanning out from the University of Lagos, my first hosts and advisors included Akin Euba, Peggy Harper, Laz Ekwueme, and Wale Ogunwale, each of whom had been involved with FESTAC in various capacities. During that summer they helped me explore the formal dimensions of Yoruba music, language, and dance; invited me to their dance dramas in the National Theatre; and sent me into the "interior," where I would find in situ performances of talking drums in ritual contexts.

I embarked on a typical *Oyinbo* (European) tour—to Oshogbo, where I met Twins Seven-Seven and his artistic entourage, bought a mask from Suzanne Wenger, saw the Oshun Festival, and stayed for several weeks; and beyond to Iwo, where I first met the Egungun spirits, and then east to Ogidi in the Akoko hills. I was, to use Diamond's incriminating phrase, "in search of the primitive," the authentic, precolonial culture "code" of which drum language was literally paradigmatic. According to this colonial touring model (also ratified by FESTAC), the deeper into the bush one went, the more authentic the culture one found. Extravaganzas like FESTAC's staged performances counted for little in this anthropological scheme, removed from village life as they were and "compromised" by the cosmopolitanism and prosperity of Lagos. Nonetheless, even if closed to its significance at the time, I was deeply struck by the oil boom and the cultural fantasia that FESTAC had fueled. I rode in the controversial FESTAC buses, felt the barrage of arts traders and vendors doing business in the streets, experienced the notorious Lagos "go-slows," and listened to King Sunny Ade's hit FESTAC theme song with its opening welcome to overseas visitors. I was thus touched by FESTAC and the spirit of the oil boom, disoriented by the generosity and affluence that I encountered, and inspired by the sheer speed of a nation kicking into high developmental gear.

Having grown up in an academic family where "Forward ever, backward never!" and "We shall never rest content, 'till we have self-government" were standard exhortations of my Africanist father, I was no stranger to modern African realities. Nonetheless, I was totally unprepared for the spectacle of opulence that Nigeria presented as a major oil producer on the international scene. It was a spectacle that would haunt me for many years before its significance began to claim my attention.

I mention these autobiographical beginnings in order to frame a historical project within an attenuated ethnographic present. Many years have gone by since this first foray into Nigeria, including extended fieldwork on Yoruba ritual and politics; and it was only after producing a relatively "standard" monograph (Apter 1992) and teaching African Civilization to University of Chicago undergraduates that I envisioned FESTAC during the oil boom as an interesting ethnographic study. A new kind of ethnography, to be sure, focusing on cultural production and class formation in a nation "awash in petrodollars" (Watts 1992, 26), one that extended a developing literature on world's fairs and expositions to postcolonial Africa; engaged new debates on translocal and transnational forms of community; confronted the state; and addressed the mysterious relationship between nationalism, modernity, money, and value. Quite a busy if fertile set of interests to begin with, but they coalesced around a few key issues and arguments as the project took shape.

The idea for a study of FESTAC '77, otherwise known as the Second World Black and African Festival of Arts and Culture, germinated in a lecture I had quickly sketched in the spring of 1990. I wanted to investigate the colonial conventions of representation in Africanist scholarship without losing sight of what lay beyond its ideological distortions and horizons. FESTAC provided good material for this approach because it involved cultural representations produced by Africans in a postcolonial context of exceptional prosperity, bringing visions of cosmopolitan Lagos and its upbeat modernity into critical dialogue with its colonial past. At the very least, the lecture challenged undergraduate stereotypes of the Dark Continent with a sense of what African states, scholars, and artists were doing, while capturing the unbridled optimism of Nigeria's oil economy. FESTAC further revealed how the national recuperation of cultural traditions was by no means limited to local festivals and village dances, but involved the Economic Organisation of West African States (ECOWAS) and the Organisation of African Unity (OAU), thus remaking the local within a modern framework of regional, national, and global "communities." Moreover, in remapping the African diaspora, FESTAC produced a Nigerian vision of the black and African world —self-centered, to be sure—that reflected the global circuits of oil in an expansive model of racial equivalence and inclusion. In this respect, FESTAC broke from the earlier discourses of negritude and Pan-Africanism by placing their essentially oppositional strategies within an emerging black world that shaded into lighter hues at its edges. As its theme song proclaimed, if FESTAC was "for black people," it was also "for everybody." Backed by oil and petrodollars, FESTAC's culture and associated idioms of blackness seemed to be less about politics than money and value.

My interest in FESTAC could have ended there, as a fifty-minute lecture to a sea of students, but it echoed provocatively with exciting new work in cultural history and anthropology, and developed further. The first body of scholarship that it addressed directly was the emerging literature on European and American world's fairs and exhibitions—on those "carnivals of the industrial age" (Hinsley 1991, 334) that combined the sobriety of science with the erotics of desire. Beginning with London's Crystal Palace Exhibition in 1851, this great tradition of imperial spectacles included Queen Victoria's Jubilee of 1897, France's Exposition Universelle of 1889 and Exposition Coloniale of 1931, and America's Columbian Exposition of 1893 and Panama Pacific Exposition of 1915 among its illustrious highlights while informing conventions of museum display, knowledge production, racial classification, and gender stereotyping more generally.[1] As studies of such cultural productions revealed profound connections between empire and knowledge—mapping the wealth of nations onto racial hierarchies in idealized models of imperial order—they moved from marginal scholarly status to center stage, providing windows into the generative politics of colonial representation and objectification. No longer seen as secondary reflections of underlying political and economic forces, imperial spectacles and colonial expositions were dynamically recast as primary shapers of these forces through images, hierarchies, models, and plans. In many ways, the secondary representation—the simulacrum—transcended the referent in official truth-value and effect, performing a profound if implicit symbolic reversal. As Mitchell's *Colonising Egypt* so elegantly reveals, the idealized Egypt of the 1889 Universal Exhibition became more real and authentic than the Egypt visited by travelers and tourists, corrupted as it was by empirical chaos in relation to the purified principles through which it was perceived (Mitchell 1991).

The significance of such symbolic reversals in the postcolonial fantasia of FESTAC '77 would emerge gradually as I worked through its events and materials. At the beginning, my interest was more comparative and dialectical: how did an explicitly black world's fair in a former British colony compare with the exhibitionary conventions from which it descended? In many ways, FESTAC inverted the conventions of imperial expositions by transforming the gaze of othering into one of collective self-apprehension. Blacks from Uganda, Belize, even Papua New Guinea represented not inferior stages of colonized races but the self-conscious unity of the black and African world. Whereas the natives of the imperial world's fairs were corralled into fairgrounds and "primitive villages" to be seen, those of FESTAC returned to the homeland, housed in the ultramodern FESTAC Village as a base from which to see. Thus it appeared that a study of FESTAC would contribute to the wider literature on world's fairs and expositions through a series of significant contrasts and reversals, further illuminating "the exhibitionary complex" (Bennett 1996) by throwing its mechanisms into bold relief.

Like its imperial predecessors, FESTAC invoked heroic narratives of progress and modernity—both explicitly, in venues like the FESTAC Colloquium, where black contributions to civilization were presented and discussed by university scholars, and implicitly, in the formal architecture of cultural representation and display, which included dioramas, showcases, and a National Theatre equipped with the latest technology that oil money could buy (Apter 1996, 444–49). But unlike its imperial forebears, FESTAC rejected the opposition between civilization and barbarism that had sustained colonial overrule. Chief among its celebrated themes and objectives was the emergence of a distinctive black and African modernity from the collective wellsprings of traditional culture, a culture that it would recuperate and reinforce as the foundation of industrial development. In FESTAC's programmatic terms, this culture was explicitly precolonial, manifesting an original power and authenticity that had been undermined and degraded by imperial domination. Drawing on the discourse of anticolonial struggle in the neocolonial context of the 1970s, a "return to origins" was the only way toward final emancipation and self-determination. In this sense, FESTAC performed a cultural exorcism, casting out the colonial ghosts and demons that continued to afflict African hearts and minds. Although Wole Soyinka (1977) flirted with the idea of promoting Swahili as an African lingua franca, few proposals would go as far as Ngugi (1986) in rejecting all former colonial languages to decolonize the mind. Nonetheless, the recuperation of an African voice was high on the ideological agenda, expressible in principle through the entire range of indigenous languages that were subsumed by Nigeria's master narrative of progressive development. And as with language, so with culture. Shifting between particular and general forms, traditional cultures associated with specific ethnic groups and historic kingdoms would return within the elevated framework of the modern African nation. FESTAC's path from tradition to modernity was one of progressive abstraction and singularity, building upon a culturally differentiated past to unite the black and African world.

Thus even in terms of its official rhetoric, FESTAC addressed a number of broader issues in the anthropology and cultural history of the early 1990s. Nigeria's black and African world was clearly an imagined community, national in idiom yet Pan-African in proportion, with a racialized sense of shared history, blood, and culture. Artistic directors and cultural officers invented traditions with precolonial pedigrees. How did such inventions illuminate postcolonial nation building and the colonial situations from which it derived? FESTAC's diasporic community was further animated by Nigerian oil, throwing the processes of cultural production and commodification into bold relief. To what extent did the commodity form serve as the general—that is, fetishized—form of culture itself?

Gradually, such questions coalesced around more focused themes, each of which bears upon the anthropology of world's fairs from different directions. The first concerns the historical context of the colonial culture from which FESTAC emerged; not just the imperial ontology of what Mitchell (1991, 222), following Heidegger, calls the "world-as-exhibition," but the culture coproduced by Europeans and Africans throughout the continent. In her landmark study of European women in colonial Nigeria, Callaway (1987), following Ranger's approach in Northern Rhodesia (1980), explored the ritual foundations of colonial hegemony, arguing that durbars, installation ceremonies, Empire Day parades, staged arrivals and departures, as well as more quotidian routines of dining and dressing, were just as important as Maxim guns in sustaining "the thin white line" of colonial domination. Such formalized arenas of ceremonial interaction not only established important distinctions between Europeans in the colonies, but incorporated Africans into indirect rule through symbolic negotiations of relative place (Apter 2002). If colonial culture emerged as the "synthesis" of such dialectical encounters, it also reinforced lines of separation between not only whites and blacks but also the rationalized "tribes" of native administration. Such colonial legacies were central to FESTAC's forms of exhibition and display, both concretely, in the reproduction of durbars, march-pasts, and ceremonial dances, and implicitly, through the very forms and categories of representing "native" peoples. Moreover, as the Comaroffs (1991, 212) have shown in South Africa, and Ranger (1983) in East Africa, the very dialectics of the colonial encounter codified European and African traditions into opposed domains. Thus in a fundamental sense, the customary culture which FESTAC resurrected was always already mediated by the colonial encounter, and in some degree was produced by it. To what degree, and through what modes of production?

I pose this question heuristically, not to provide a literal answer (even if such an answer were possible), but to identify a central problematic that FESTAC's cultural material brings to light. My interest was not to extract an authentic tradition from its "fictive" colonial and postcolonial forms, but rather to focus on those very transformations which "culture" undergoes when produced and consumed. Thus the second major theme that this study engages is the production of national culture and tradition, a process that converts cultural objects and materials into icons of a "higher" symbolic order—a sanctified regime of national value and spectacle.

The literature on nationalism and national culture is vast and interdisciplinary, spanning the philosophical idealism of Hegel and Herder, the reified psychologism of Margaret Mead and Ruth Benedict, the unilinear developmentalism of modernization theory, and more recently, the imagined communities of Benedict Anderson ([1983] 1991). Anderson's seminal study signaled a critical paradigm shift, rejecting the mythic bedrock of primordial affiliations that were both extended and transcended by the modern nation-state and historicizing the rise of a collective imaginary in relation to the development of print capital. He thereby de-essentialized nationalism as an entity or "variable" in favor of a phantasm with no fixed or stable referent. Key studies that followed in its wake include Ivy's study of national phantasm in Japan (1995), Handler's ethnography (1988) of cultural production in Quebec, and Fox's edited volume (1990) on nationalist ideologies and the production of national cultures. These studies emphasize the processes over the products of cultural production, political insofar as they involve contests over identity formation, but also "economic" in their modes of objectification and reification. Whereas Handler's attention to spectacle suggests important affinities with commodity fetishism, Fox's focus on the fuzziness of categories—ranging between ethnic, national, and racial forms—identifies a critical indeterminacy of cultural production which his own appeal to public identity politics does not fully resolve. By what logic does cultural production shift ethnic, national, and racial horizons, narrowing its referential domain in some contexts, universalizing it in others? I was interested not merely in the structural logic of segmentary opposition and hierarchical inclusion that always applies within a political field (M. G. Smith 1956), but in the transpositions between the cultural forms themselves. My intuitions suggested that print capital, spectacle, and cultural reification were not just contingently associated, but represented a fundamental relationship between the commodity form and the nation form, an emerging hypothesis which brought the phenomenology of value to the center of cultural production. To anticipate, what FESTAC reveals through its multiple mediations is the ultimate transposition of money into blood; or more precisely, the "general equivalent" of the money form (Goux 1990, 3) into the "invariant substance" of the nation form (Balibar 1991, 86).

Thus the claim of this study is not one of causal influence or historical determination, in that FESTAC changed the course of Nigerian history, the shape of the state, or even the black consciousness movement in lasting ways.[2] The cultural agendas that it set into motion evolved slowly if at all, without the national mobilization that FESTAC envisioned. If there is a prime mover in this study, it is Nigerian oil and its fluctuating cycles, which—as we shall see—did transform the shape of the state and the character of Nigerian class formation. Rather, FESTAC is significant for what it reveals about the forms of valuation in cultural production precisely because it was funded by an oil-rich state with its own specific contradictions.

Briefly stated, Nigeria's goal as a developing country, to build an efficient and productive industrial economy, was implemented from above, by a state that swelled the civil service, imported expensive technology, yet promoted relatively little domestic production. If new wealth flowed into private hands, little was invested in private industry, since it was mainly acquired through patronage networks that provided coveted access to state resources and revenues. The Nigerian ruling class was primarily a state class, based less on the exploitation of wage labor and more on the exploitation of political connections, through a de facto market of government contracts, licenses, and offices (Berry 1985, 13–14). Moreover, it was a growing class financed by exceptionally high-grade oil. As the state expanded the public sector, forestalling organized assaults on its position by absorbing whole sectors of the economy together with their internal class divisions and tensions, it internalized the entire process of class formation (ibid.), bringing new recruits into the civil service while providing free education and medicine for the masses. It was a dizzy time, as administrative structures, civil servants, and employment opportunities proliferated, as cash and commodities accelerated in complementary flows, and fortunes appeared overnight without any apparent relation to capital investment or hard work. The magic of Nigeria's nascent modernity was based on unproductive accumulation that was controlled by the state. It was only a matter of time before the growing demands on Nigeria's oil revenues would outstrip their mysterious value.

It was thus within the dialectic of a self-consuming state—a rapidly expanding public sphere that was simultaneously privatized by kickbacks and subsidies (Watts 1992, 37)—that FESTAC's commodification of culture made ideological sense, masking divisive ethnic cleavages and the *lack* of indigenous production through the production of Indigenous Culture. As a dramaturgy of power, FESTAC obscured the growing class divisions that were absorbed by the state, reproduced by its clients, and objectified by the fetishism of both "traditional" culture and imported commodities. Through FESTAC's forum of public culture, ethnic difference and class formation were subsumed by the inclusive horizons of blackness. Within Nigeria's spectacle of culture, the contradictions of the oil economy were nowhere to be seen.

But if FESTAC represented an idealized vision of ethnic equality and harmony in Nigeria and beyond, it also provided a significant contrast to the ethnically framed realpolitik that operated behind the scenes, a drama of considerable import given the country's scheduled return to civilian rule in 1979. FESTAC's discourse of black global citizenship, substantiated by identity cards issued for participants, mirrored a discourse of Nigerian citizenship often discussed in terms of ethnicity and oil. Was a representative vote possible where the winner would take all, "chopping" the spoils of victory for his inner circle while distributing the rest along ethnic lines? Was corruption so endemic that basic interest articulation would be undermined? Was there a national bourgeoisie? Was the goal of politics simply access to the "national cake"? Using FESTAC as a mirror of the broader political economy of oil, I examine the nexus of class, ethnicity, and the state in Nigeria within the mediating framework of the public sphere. I had already experienced the predatory violence of the 1983 presidential and gubernatorial elections from a local perspective (Apter 1987), and was familiar with the intimidation and rigging that ultimately served Hausa-Fulani domination; but I wanted to understand the method of the madness, framing the problem not in terms of bad leadership and moral failure but rather of rational investments in different forms of capital. Hence it was my desire and goal that a study of FESTAC would illuminate the anthropology of the state in Africa.

That was how my research agenda evolved. In the summer of 1993 I returned to conduct fieldwork and archival research in Lagos. My wife and I landed two days before the results of the 1993 elections were annulled and all hell broke loose.

FIELDWORK

During my six months of archival and field research from June to December, 1993, Nigeria went through a prolonged crisis spanning President Babangida's desperate final days, Shonekan's ephemeral transitional regime, and the fateful coup of Sani Abacha, who sent the country into an unprecedented tailspin. Between popular protests, crippling petrol shortages, military crackdowns, and several general strikes, these were interesting if unpredictable times. Rumors circulated of secret payoffs and deals between various political and military factions, with sacks of naira and barrels of oil disappearing into the shadow economy. But facts and evidence remained elusive, both in the courts and on the street. The one defining touchstone of the real was that for whatever reasons and with whatever hidden backing or pressure, Babangida pulled the plug on the June 12 elections to prevent Moshood Abiola from his imminent victory over Bashir Tofa, the virtually unknown northerner. Through a series of illegal decrees and frantic maneuvers, Babangida abrogated the election results, aborted the Third Republic, and gradually lost control of the state, alienating his various clients and constituencies until pressured out of office.

I discuss these events at some length in chapter 7 to show how the hidden costs and instabilities of oil prosperity precipitated a crisis of value by the 1990s. I mention them here to illuminate some of the extenuating circumstances that limited my research in terms of access and mobility. At the outset, research on FESTAC looked to be largely self-organized by a dedicated archive in the Centre for Black and African Arts and Civilization (CBAAC) built by the government as a storehouse of cultural knowledge. This archive is an extraordinary resource and achievement, containing meticulous minutes of the International Festival Committee, film, video, and tape recordings of hundreds of FESTAC performances and events, internal reports, special publications, photographs, schedules, plans, identity cards . . . enough to keep a scholar happily buried for years. My plan was to work this archive as judiciously as possible and pursue interviews with FESTAC organizers and participants in Lagos, Ibadan, and beyond. I soon learned, however, that CBAAC was no ordinary archive but doubled as a national shrine. Housed in the monumental National Theatre, this sanctified storehouse of cultural knowledge contained the cultural patrimony not only of Nigeria but of the black and African world, as per FESTAC's spirit. Furthermore, these double functions were structurally at odds: if the national resource was open to scholars, as sacred patrimony it remained a closed book, valorized by its status as an inalienable possession (Weiner 1992) and thus effectively removed from circulation.

When I first arrived, one of the archivists assured me that everything I needed to know for my project could be found in the ten-volume published compendium of papers presented at the FESTAC Colloquium, and that I need not bother myself with restricted material in the stacks.

I did of course gain access to extraordinary materials, but always within shifting limits. Initially, I was allowed to walk freely throughout the stacks and sift and sort through the amazing array of boxes and folders, but after two weeks was banished to the front room, where I could submit requests without the assistance of a catalog or index. I could watch films on 35 mm, but the low-band video machine, like the photocopier, was never repaired. On two occasions, I was told by the guards not to enter CBAAC at all, but to report to a variety of authorities whose job, it seemed, was to keep me waiting. I began to give up hope, planning another research topic altogether on Lagos markets.

The problem of politics—indeed of witchcraft—in the archives was of course exacerbated by the political crisis raging outside; and my sponsor, CBAAC's director, who was a fellow academic, later explained that a special meeting was held to determine whether I was a political liability. What I had experienced as simple obstructionism was complicated by the deterioration of U.S.-Nigerian relations over the abrogation of the June 12 elections. Eventually, a working truce developed and I regained access to the stacks, immersed myself in committee reports and correspondence, and discovered the joys of tracking paper trails. One of the comparisons that this highly focused body of documentation provided was between those plans that developed and eventually materialized in FESTAC and those that failed, revealing significant initiatives and struggles in the politics of cultural production that could not be inferred from the final events and performances. These trajectories could furthermore be plotted within different temporalities, ranging from rehearsals, performances, and the hurried schedules of the planning committees to the broader history of exhibitionary conventions that were consciously and unconsciously reworked. Even with the wider holdings and clip files of the less sanctified National Theatre Library and the more efficient Nigerian Institute of International Affairs, however, I remained wary of the tunnel vision that a strictly archival project could produce, and sought out participants, European expatriates, and Nigerians from all walks of life whose experiences and memories of FESTAC would provide a better sense of its national significance and reception.

And here again, the political crisis intervened. With the chronic petrol shortages, periodic protests and strikes, and general climate of uncertainty, I was more or less limited to Lagos and Ibadan, daunted by the prospects of traveling throughout Nigeria's many states and hot spots, which included the Andoni and Ogoni conflicts of the Niger Delta and a new round of riots in Kano and Kaduna. In addition to skittish police and soldiers unsure of whose orders to follow from day to day, the no-torious gangs of armed robbers were on the rise, trained in the arts of refined dissimulation. Known colloquially as "the 419," after the penal code statute outlawing the impersonation of officials for personal gain, the con game or confidence trick developed in the early 1990s into a significant way of life, characterizing the ethos of those unstable and uncertain times. Days after the Abacha coup, I found myself the target of such an orchestrated scheme—one which emptied my wallet and opened my eyes.

I had just boarded a taxi on Ikorodu Road en route to the National Theatre when an unmarked police van cut us off and several uniformed men jumped out, waving identity cards and shouting with intimidating urgency, "We are sss from Alagbon Close! Do not be alarmed! This is a routine check! Please enter the van!" Since I had been similarly appre-hended and released after Buhari's 1983 New Year's coup, I figured that this was indeed a basic routine check. I was legal, with papers and con-nections via Fulbright-cies to the U.S. Embassy, and was confident that all would be sorted out at the station. But I was also holding a lot of cash, since on that day I had planned to buy the festac compendium of Col-loquium papers on the black and African world. As the van speeded off, everybody began shouting—the driver, his associates, even those youth in the back posing as usual suspects picked up from the streets. "Where is your passport! Give us your cocaine! Bring your particulars!" In an in-stant, invisible hands removed my waist pouch with its fat wad of naira while I was given paper and pencil and told to write down everything: my name, address, and life history. Sudden outrage ensued when my pouch yielded only a photocopy of my passport. "Where is the original!? Why do you carry only photocopy!?" "Because of thief, and 419!" I yelled back, while announcing my official connections and bringing forth some impressive vip cards, including those of former (and once again current) Nigerian Head of State, General Olusegun Obasanjo. Although the driver cracked a smile, more outrage followed: "You are not even begging us!" said the man at my ribs, so I replied in Yoruba, "Ẹ Jọ́ọ́, Mo bẹ̀ yin, Ẹ jẹ́ kin lọ sòkalè" [Please, I beg you, let me get down]. "He is speaking Yoruba!" another tout (hustler) exclaimed. "Why don't you speak Ibo!" So these were Ibo thugs, I surmised, silently assured by my Yoruba chauvinism that I was indeed at the mercy of savvy imitators. Af-ter that they slowed down, returned my pouch, opened the van, and pushed me onto the tarmac. As the van sped off I looked for the license plate, but it was obstructed by the back engine cover. I opened my pouch and found a wad of newspaper in place of my bills. I had been success-fully duped. They had had me in their power. But why this final act of deception—the newspaper masquerading as money inside my pouch? They had scored a big hit—nearly two hundred dollars' worth of naira. Why the extra trouble to maintain appearances?

The question still intrigues me, since it draws attention to the art of the 419: no mere coercive or instrumental crime but a skillful cultural performance with costumes, props, and a mobile stage of suspended disbelief. As such, it was transitive, generating an economy of images and appearances that produced value from floating signifiers. Nor did I remain a passive victim, but unwittingly deployed similar if less premeditated tactics to get something back.

Perhaps as a matter of personal madness, I went to file a police report. Partly for insurance purposes and partly just to document my foray into what Fanon (1997, 645) has called, in another context, "this zone of occult instability," I made two trips to the station, but to no immediate avail. The form I was told to fill out and bring back turned out to be the wrong one. Without the license plate number, I was wasting my time. The presiding officer was unimpressed by my visits and VIP business cards. But on my third and final attempt I brought a U.S.-Nigeria friendship pin that one of the Embassy officers had given me—standard diplomatic fare, with a Nigerian flag on one side and an American flag on the other. I asked the police officer, "Excuse me, Oga (boss, uncle), but have you ever seen this?" I pulled the pin from my pocket and cupped it in my hand. "Do you know what this is?" "Eh," he replied, showing interest for the first time, "I think so." "Do you know what this is?" I reiterated for dramatic effect. "With this pin," I declared, "it means you are a member." "Eh?" he replied, "You mean it?" "It means you are a member," I replied.

Of course, I never specified of what I was a member, and he never asked. It was clear, implicit in the Nigerian popular imagination, that hidden mafias and cults ran things behind the scenes, from the low-level gang that literally took me for a ride to the power brokers in hidden corridors of Nigerian and foreign governments. Nor, I should add, were such conspiratorial images merely Taussig's marginated fantasies of the center, given the machinations of Babangida and the murder of journalist Dele Giwa discussed in chapter 7. From my hands, the pin became a fetish of political power, a sign of restricted access to an inner circle that would grant its wearer a visa. The exchange was immediate: one pin for one police report, one fetish for another—equally valuable in the shifting economy of official signs and appearances.

I mention this minidrama because it opened my eyes to the cultural phenomenology of the 419, one which gradually informed the broader theoretical issues raised by FESTAC '77 and its relationship to oil.

On the surface, the oil boom of the 1970s and the extended economic crisis of the 1990s could not appear more diametrically opposed: the one, a time of exhilarating optimism and expanding opportunity, the other, of pervasive cynicism and austerity. During the boom, when Nigerian hospitality reached unprecedented heights, naira flowed freely as the good times rolled, whereas after the bust, when funds became scarce, the very foundations of civil society began to crumble. Perhaps the greatest single contrast was in the Nigerian naira itself, once a robust currency set at $1.60 US in 1976, having plummeted by 1993 to a shadow of its former glory, hovering somewhere between one and two cents. To be sure, part of this dramatic drop followed the relaxing of currency regulations by the Central Bank, bringing the official and black markets for foreign exchange into neoliberal alignment. The drop in the world price of oil also contributed to the devaluation of the naira and the inflation of domestic prices. But the structural contradictions of the oil economy and the pattern of class involution that it produced explain the crisis of the 1990s as one of systemic collapse, in which the illusions of a state expanding through an inverted form of negative production could no longer be sustained.

As Coronil (1997) has shown in his masterful study of the Venezuelan petro-state, oil created both this illusion of growth and a specific phenomenology of national development that gave rise to an empire of signs.[3] The initial spectacle generated by Nigerian oil was that of economic takeoff, visible in the material effects of windfall revenues distributed formally and unofficially from the center.[4] Following Debord (1994), Nigeria was reborn as a society of the spectacle, with oil money serving as its dominant form of value. But the source of this value was fundamentally different from those of full-fledged capitalist systems, based not on the accumulation of surplus value but on the circulation of a specific form of excess—one of oil rents and revenues that underwrote the importation of staples and luxury goods, as well as various white elephant projects that produced only negative returns. As I argue in chapter 1, the credibility of the oil-rich Nigeria was ratified by signs of material development masquerading as its substance, purveying a "seeing-is-believing" ontology that disguised the absence of a productive base.[5] If the oil economy was somehow dubious—with its invisible and mysterious sources of wealth fueling a nation on the move—FESTAC was designed as a stabilizing force, anchoring the signs of sudden prosperity in the bedrock of tradition and culture.[6]

Backed by petro-naira, the value of this culture was confirmed by the spectacular scale of the festival itself. As the new Nigeria assumed central roles in OPEC, ECOWAS, and the OAU, it emerged—I argue in chapter 2—as the preeminent Pan-African nation, projecting itself throughout the black and African world while drawing representatives into its center. Reflecting the global circuits of petrodollars in its ever-widening span of influence and control, Nigeria's wealth-cum-cultural patrimony established a profound correspondence between sign-value and commodity-value, one that fixed the locus of truth to a convertible system of exchange values. On the domestic front, organized by the national participation committee, Nigeria's vast tapestry of local ethnicities and regional cultures became equivalent expressions of national tradition—one that extended to the black and African world through its visiting contingents in Lagos. Through FESTAC, Nigeria's empire of signs was pegged to petroleum. During this high point of oil politics and prosperity, money became the measure of cultural value.

What manner of commodity, then, was the culture produced by FESTAC?[7]

To answer this question, I focus on FESTAC as a mode of cultural production. In chapter 3, I examine the making of national culture out of local and regional artifacts and performances, a process fraught with political competition over forms and pathways of symbolic capital. If in practical terms this involved bringing artifacts to Lagos and "grooming" representative dance and drama troupes, symbolically it entailed their transformation into icons of a "higher" national heritage, a process of condensation and ultimate assimilation to a sanctified—indeed bloodlike—order of value. As cultural officers, traditional rulers, and local government officials jockeyed for influence and political recognition, "the people" produced by FESTAC's national spectacle were disconnected from Nigerians themselves, who were clamoring at the entrance gates, unable to participate. There is of course nothing surprising in this general process of national typecasting, which is built into the very logic of world's fairs and expositions; but in the context of Nigeria's oil-fueled development—directed from above and dispersed from the center—it became a model of mystification and false historical consciousness.

Chapters 4 and 5 focus on the longer *durée* of historical amnesia in the Regatta and the Durbar, two major events showcasing the riverine peoples of the east and the equestrian emirates of the northern savanna. Here I investigate the politics of Nigerian regionalism as it developed through European contact and indirect rule. Contra FESTAC's claims of resurrecting a precolonial tradition through its "staged creation of a mythic, detemporalized past" (Guss 2000, 14), I show that the Regatta and Durbar historically emerged as central mechanisms of colonial interaction—the first, between European traders and Africans on the coast and up the inland waterways; the second, between British officials and northern emirs during the consolidation of the northern protectorate. My point is not to correct FESTAC's historiography with a more detailed and accurate historical account, but to identify the conversion of colonial culture into indigenous idioms of national tradition. In effect, colonial culture was nationalized and indigenized by FESTAC—revalued as Nigerian and projected back into a precolonial past. If FESTAC's work of cultural production concealed the material relations of Nigeria's oil prosperity, it also congealed an entire colonial heritage under the sign of its displacement and disavowal; that is, through the explicit project of cultural recuperation as a way of exorcising the ghosts of colonial domination.

Chapter 6 returns to the phenomenology of the oil boom through the mirror of cultural production itself, examining its inflated costs, hidden fiscal pathways, and mercurial money forms. FESTAC represented not only the waste and excess of the oil economy but a peculiar form of deficit production disguised by the appearance of material progress. Here I focus on the role of copyright in transforming FESTAC's culture into legal property, a technical instrument of commodification that authorized a commercialized sphere of reproductions and souvenirs.[8] Within this secondary sphere of economic circulation, the FESTAC emblem doubled as a trademark generating value and franchise fees through symbolic association with Nigeria's cultural patrimony. That actual returns never even remotely approached expectations only underscores the illusion of what was a symbolic mode of production all along—an illusion that lasted as long as oil remained king.

Hence the relevance of the Babangida and Abacha regimes, when the contradictions of the oil economy erupted into full view. As the world price of oil tumbled, as revenues retreated further into private hands, and as the Nigerian petro-state withered away, a crisis of representation and social credibility eroded the very foundations of civil society. No longer backed by petrodollars, Nigeria's currency and associated money forms lost their purchasing power and material value, giving rise to the era of the 419 and its arts of dissimulation. As oil retreated from the body politic, the symbolic foundations of inverted production rose up like a chimera of capitalist culture, destabilizing domestic and international markets with signs stripped free from their material moorings. In chapter 7, I analyze the 1993 elections as a politically choreographed "419," representing not simply government corruption and fraud but a more systematic disconnection between a simulated vote and its popular base. Chapter 8, written in anger and disbelief over the brazen hanging of Ken Saro-Wiwa, examines how and when the Ogoni struggle became a rallying cry for a dispossessed citizenry, representing the destruction not only of Delta creeks and waterways but of civil society itself.

Exactly what, then, is this book about? Although it examines FESTAC '77 as an oil-fueled engine of cultural production, it does so not as an extended event but, following Walter Benjamin, as a form of historicity—one that illuminates Nigeria's colonial past, its national economy, and its postcolonial predicaments. As an anthropological work, it engages the problem of value in its temporal, material, and symbolic modalities.[9] If, echoing Baudrillard (1981), it offers a critique of the political economy of the sign in postcolonial Nigeria, I will be satisfied.

LA MISE EN SCÈNE

CHAPTER ONE

Rebirth of a Nation

We are no longer the third world. We are the first world.
—Commander O. P. Fingesi

IN PERHAPS the most famous passage of *Capital,* Marx (1978, 319) wrote, "A commodity appears at first sight, a very trivial thing, and easily understood. Its analysis shows that it is, in reality, a very queer thing, abounding in metaphysical subtleties and theological niceties." Thus opens the section on the fetishism of commodities, introducing a specific argument about the mystification of productive relations and a more general phenomenology of value forms that moves from external appearances to underlying levels of contradiction and determination. Marx's dialectical reversals are of course well traveled today, standing Hegel, political economy, even chairs and tables—not to mention class relations—on their heads. My own invocation of commodity fetishism concerns the reversal of fortunes during the early 1970s known as the energy crisis among Western powers, otherwise experienced as an oil boom among those third world countries allied with OPEC and endowed with precious petroleum.

I start, then, with the momentous impact of oil on Nigeria, a nation emerging from the bloody civil war between the central government and the eastern region, the former secessionist state of Biafra (1967–70), and catapulted into what Watts (1992) has called "fast capitalism" and rapid development. After nearly four years of armed struggle, infra-structural deterioration, and imminent political fragmentation as Biafra attempted to secede, Nigeria's deposits of high-quality crude—com-bined with a fourfold leap in world market price—was received as a blessing from Providence. Nigeria's newly found "God-given" wealth re-united the nation with unprecedented prosperity, portending a state-directed industrial revolution that would be lubricated by oil. As pe-troleum revenues poured in, an ambitious national development plan invested in parastatal industries, education, hospitals, and mass me-dia, matched by a boom of imported commodities ranging from staple foods and raw materials to expensive technology and luxury goods. An ever expanding public sector bringing schools, clinics, piped water, and electricity to the rural areas developed the national landscape from "above" while well-connected contractors amassed private fortunes through business deals. Nigeria's oil bonanza was literally sensational. Lavish parties, fleets of new Mercedes-Benzes and Peugeot 504s, and the congested "go-slows" of Lagos traffic reflected the dizzy excitement of new wealth and opportunity, celebrated by popular Juju and Fuji mu-sicians exhorting their patrons to live up to their good fortunes (Water-man 1990). The clutter and cacophony of new construction intensified as sports stadiums, national monuments, bridges, highways, and pala-tial hotels modernized the nation. Nigeria's oil boom was a spectacle to behold.

The blessings of oil were mixed, however, and would eventually be-come a curse. A highly fetishized commodity in Nigeria's national economy, oil concealed, within its natural forms, the social and political contradictions of its money-generating powers. These are not easily re-duced to the classic opposition between labor and capital, or even use-value and exchange-value, given the global and deterritorialized charac-ter of transnational oil, but embrace a wider range of structural features that developed out of the colonial economy and into the postcolonial African state.[1] In the most basic sense, the oil-based wealth of the Ni-gerian nation derived not from domestic labor or commodity produc-tion but from royalties and revenues appropriated from such companies as Shell-BP, Elf, Agip, and Chevron. Although never fully nationalized, the state gained increasing control over production and marketing, giv-ing rise to the proverbial goose that laid the golden egg, as the oil bo-nanza was called in the popular media. Serving the nation as a natural resource beneath the ground, oil was technically owned by the federal government, which underwrote domestic production and national development within its own grand narrative of a manifest destiny.

In addition to money and commodities, the opening act of Nigeria's dramatic boom featured new forms of state-fetishism. These involved not merely the majestic trappings of power that the federal military government could suddenly afford but the reification of the rentier state itself as a centralized organ of economic and political disbursement, suspended above society and penetrating into the circulatory system of a revitalized national body (see Watts 1994, 418; Coronil 1997). Moving from the logic of state power and planning to the apparently boundless wealth of the nation, this chapter will trace the circulation of value during the formative years of the oil economy, focusing on its "paradoxes of prosperity" (Watts 1994, 418) and associated value forms. These involve a specific contradiction between state-controlled capital and private patronage (prebendalism) that was intensified and mystified by the emergence of oil as a general form of value. As Nigeria's "black gold" revitalized the economy, coursing quickly but unevenly throughout the body politic, the Nigerian nation was literally remade in the image of a highly valued commodity form. Backed by petrodollars, the convertible petro-naira, as Nigeria's new and powerful currency came to be known, represented a nation reborn into "natural" wealth. If in concrete terms this meant higher buildings and per-capita income, more abstractly it assimilated the nation form to the dazzling image of the money form. Nigerians may have been divided by region and ethnicity, but they were dramatically united by the "blessings" of oil, which circulated, like blood, through the national body.

As we shall see, the transmutations of oil into money and blood were not automatic phantasms of an imagined community, but took shape through specific technologies of cultural production. Building on a history of local and regional festivals of art and culture, including rituals of colonial rule such as northern durbars and riverine regattas, FESTAC '77 fashioned the Nigerian nation into an autonomous object of vision and reflection that could be separated from the state and thrown back into the precolonial past. To be sure, the boundaries of the new nation form were fluid and variable, narrowing into local icons of cultural tradition and fanning out into global expressions of Pan-African unity, thereby mirroring the very commodity that underwrote the festival's exorbitant costs. But underlying the nation's shifting horizons was a general "substance" of intrinsic value, differentially articulated in ethnic, cultural, and racial terms, convertible into money and commodities, and endowed with a mysterious life of its own. We will thus examine

FESTAC "post festum" (Marx 1978, 324), not merely as a celebration of Nigeria's oil wealth, but as the midwife of the nation's historic renewal.

THE RISE OF THE PETRO-STATE

On September 26, 1975, Gulf Oil Company Nigeria Limited concluded the fourth Nigerian oil seminar, part of a series about the oil industry held to educate the general public about the nation's sudden wealth. The working sessions on oil law, exploration, production, and global marketing were supplemented by a televised visit to the Escravos Oil field, where the participants were flown in helicopters to the company's offshore drilling rigs. But the crowning event that stole the show was Mr. Emmanuel Omatshola's Magic Barrel, a public relations conjuring trick that featured the countless commodities generated by oil. Out of the Magic Barrel came "gasoline and diesel oil to drive your cars and tractors; greases to lubricate the moving parts of machines; kerosene for lighting your cooking stoves and hurricane lanterns; gas for cooking." The dance of commodities then moved on to the "miracles" of the petrochemical industry: insecticides to save the cattle, which "provide milk and steak for man"; cellophane and polyethylene for wrapping "carrots, frozen poultry, fish and meat"; Freon 12 in refrigerators and freezers "to make food keep"; and a wide range of materials used to improve homes and bodies, including asphalt shingles, paint and varnish, "perfumes, face creams, lipstick, rouge, eye shadow, wave lotion, nail polish removers and other beauty aids." To conclude with his Magic Barrel, Mr. Omatshola pulled out rubber heels and soles of shoes, nylon stretch socks, shoe polish, plastic buttons, nylon zippers, neckties, polyester shirts, and plastic bags.[2]

Mr. Omatshola's public relations gimmick illustrated the magical qualities of oil through its alchemical transmutations into "one thousand-plus" commodities, a mysterious process clearly witnessed if not well understood during Nigeria's boom in imported goods. The Magic Barrel yielded distinctly modern commodities: fuels and lubricants for cars and industry, fertilizers and insecticides for the new agro-industry that would nourish the nation, new building materials for hotels and housing projects, synthetic clothes and cosmetics for refashioning the national body. Small wonder that amidst the technical papers and reports delivered by experts and disseminated by journalists, the Magic Barrel seemed to capture the essence of the boom. Nigerian oil meant money and modernity; it was revitalizing and glamorous. As one journalist in the oil-producing area of Port Harcourt reported, "You have to tell a woman you are an oil worker or a contractor to oil companies to be in favour with girls."³ At two million barrels of daily production, the petroleum industry brought international political influence, national pride, and an intensified hustle for money and profits. But if the magic barrel inaugurated an era of prosperity, it also prefigured unspoken anxieties about the questionable properties of conjured wealth. Popular idioms of money-magic generating instant cash from human blood and body parts would come to characterize the hidden evils of oil (Barber 1982, 438). In the early days of the boom, however, such anxieties were easily allayed by the tidal wave of wealth and opportunity.

Aggregate statistics of government revenues from oil reveal windfall profits boosted by OPEC's price hikes and augmented by the state's growing participation in production. Between 1972 and January of 1974, Nigeria raised the posted price from $3.56 to $14.96 US per barrel and assumed 55% participatory shares in the oil companies through the Nigerian National Oil Corporation.⁴ Up from the previous 35%, Nigeria's controlling interest formed part of a general policy of indigenization that increased Nigerian access to foreign capital but avoided total nationalization of the oil industry. While the oil companies continued to finance exploration and production, the government expanded its share of the take by raising royalties from 12% to 20% and profit taxes from 50% to 61%. As oil flowed into the global market and money flowed into the government purse, the nation's money supply more than doubled, rising 57.4% from November 1975 to June 1976 alone, further boosted by a climbing gross domestic product that reached $25.2 billion in 1975 and $27.2 billion in 1976 (fig. 1.1).⁵

Maintaining control of the commanding heights of the nation's growing oil economy, the federal military government embarked on a variety of prestigious projects and structural reforms designed to lift Nigeria out of postwar poverty and into mainstream industrial production and development. Over 30 billion petrodollars were budgeted in the utopian Third National Development Plan (1975–80). In addition to modernizing the "traditional" agricultural sector, overhauling national health and education, building roads and power plants, and improving mail delivery and telecommunications, the Third Plan would invest the profits of oil in a mighty engine of industrial production. Addressing the nation in the formal launching of the plan on March 29, 1975, Head of State Yakubu Gowon declared, "The nation is now on the threshold of an industrial revolution which will be characterized by the production of consumer durables such as motor cars, and capital goods such as trucks, iron and steel, and petrochemicals." Featured among the new initiatives was the mighty Ajaokuta steel mill that would become a notorious white elephant scheme, and two petroleum refineries in Warri and Kaduna

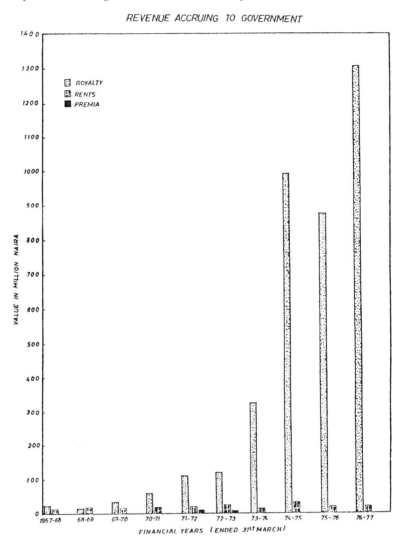

designed to break the nation's dependency on foreign processing while developing a network of pipelines and flow stations that would bring petrol to the people. We will examine the economic realities of implementation in due course, addressing what Watts (1992, 27) calls the "spasm of state-led investment and industrial development" which followed. Indeed, Gowon's grandiose government-by-largesse was soon cut short by the bloodless coup of Murtala Mohammed on July 29, 1975, calling for greater fiscal responsibility and stronger measures against corruption. But as the personnel of government continued to change—Murtala was assassinated six months later on February 13, 1976, in a failed coup attempt that put Lieutenant-General Olusegun Obasanjo in charge—the Nigerian petro-state continued to take shape, carrying many of the earlier initiatives forward while transforming the body politic in fundamental ways. Following Watts (1992, 1994) and Joseph (1987), I will highlight political centralization, bureaucratic expansion, and what I call the *involution* of class formation in a preliminary structural sketch of the Nigerian petro-state.

There is no question that as Nigeria's enclave economy developed, the state grew increasingly dependent on oil as source of export earnings and foreign exchange. During the boom years, oil accounted for over 80% of government revenue, a figure which reached over 95% in the 1990s. Like other oil and "monocrop" economies, such dependency rendered the rentier state highly vulnerable to fluctuations in the global market while systematically eroding traditional productive sectors in agriculture and manufacturing. In Nigeria's version of what economists call the Dutch Disease—referring to how overperformance in North Sea gas production caused distress and underproduction in other sectors (Karl 1997, 5)—oil overwhelmed the regional bases of agricultural production, which declined in prestige and output.[6] Whereas earlier, state marketing boards had served as mechanisms of peasant surplus extraction for regional elites, oil provided greater and immediate wealth disbursed directly from the center, deepening what Watts (1992, 35), following Hirschmann (1976), calls fiscal linkages to the federal purse. In the historical context of Nigeria's federal structure, the political consequences of centralized disbursement were dramatic.

According to the Richards (1945) and Macpherson (1951) constitutions, the British—with increased Nigerian participation—established the Northern, Western, and Eastern Regions, with separate budgets and Houses of Assembly that were weakly federated in what would soon become a parliamentary model of self-government. As political entities of a "consociational" democracy from 1959 to 1966, these regions became increasingly ethnicized into Hausa-Fulani (Northern), Yoruba (Western), and Ibo (Eastern) sections within a fragile union that nearly broke apart during the Biafran war. In an effort to stabilize the federation and recognize the interests of ethnic minorities (some of which formed the Mid-West Region in 1963), the Gowon regime restructured the regional system into twelve states (1967) that increased to nineteen under Murtala. Through this process of "states creation," which would continue to develop under Babangida and Abacha, the politics of oil patronage was consolidated at the center of what became an increasingly unitary government.

The rhetoric of minorities notwithstanding, the creation of more states broke up regional power blocs—including the venal governors' fiefdoms that had formed under Gowon—to disburse petro-naira more directly from the center. In formal terms, the Supreme Military Council assumed executive, legislative, and economic functions as it directed development from above, ruled by decree, and bought off rival interests and initiatives. The convenient marriage of oil and politics is, in fact, well represented by their coterminous centralization within the corridors of power. It was in government's interest to reorganize the control of oil from several ministries and committees into one self-contained and self-policing body that became the Nigerian National Petroleum Corporation in 1976, designed to integrate all sectors of the oil industry while domesticating foreign capital. In addition to exploration and production, the federal military government also assumed total control of petroleum licensing in domestic marketing and distribution, taking allocative authority away from the states to further undercut their autonomy. In an arrangement of "internal dependency," top-down fiscal control was politically secured by a new statutory formula that siphoned off oil from the Delta states for equitable revenue redistribution throughout the nation. In the accelerated excitement of the 1970s boom, however, the patrimonial (if not praetorian) politics of oil were second to the imperatives of national development. The military governments from 1974 to 1979 meant well and had the money to prove it. Combining the discipline and efficiency of a top-down chain of command with a revitalized infrastructure, they would pave the way for a return to civilian rule.

Of the nation-building projects that followed, including Universal Primary Education (UPE), Operation Feed the Nation (OFN), and improved communications, hospitals, and housing, none captured the state's vertical intrusion into civil society more effectively than Local Government Reform (LGR). Conceived as "the third tier of government activity" after the federal government and its "second tier" of states, the new local government authorities (LGAS) were organized nationally to promote even and rapid development throughout the country. In principle, the new councils would bring local initiative to government projects, receiving input from the people while pumping resources from the center. Effectively, they extended the arm of government beneath and beyond the larger administrative units of the states, providing robust budgets that would insulate LGAS "from the encroachments on their functions by state governments."[7] Just what these functions were remained unclear at the local level, as conflicts between traditional rulers, LGA chairmen, and chief executive secretaries erupted over respective jurisdictions and even housing privileges.[8] In some states, traditional rulers were told to keep out of politics and mind their festivals and ceremonies, whereas Benue State appeared to incorporate traditional councils within the LGA system itself, giving rise to a postcolonial version of indirect rule.[9] In the broader context of national renewal, however, local government reform meant money and votes. Following a financing formula combining demographics with the equality of states, the federal government provided direct funds to local government bodies to the tune of 250 million naira in 1977.[10] Moreover, access to the new wealth was opened up by preliminary elections (open in some states, indirect in others) of local government chairmen and councilors, who were subject to confirmation by the governor. These would introduce representatives at the local level who, in turn, would elect members of the Constituent Assembly to approve the final draft of the constitution in preparation for the Second Republic.

If local government reform meant more easy money, it also shows how the state produced locality from above, "harmonizing" its features and functions—including LGA salaries—with the administrative armature of the civil service. As oil centralized political power it underwrote a growing administrative machine that *standardized* the national framework of Nigerian society to forge solid foundations of citizenship. Harmony was quite literally the order of the day, as government "harmonized" university salaries and admission policies and conditions of service; built new schools and universities; and assumed the costs of an ambitious program of universal primary education. To manage and staff these nation-building projects, the state financed what Joseph (1987, 82) has called "a 'revolutionary' expansion of the public sector," swelling the ranks of the civil bureaucracy and the rising number of parastatal agencies. In the famous Udoji Commission reforms of October 1974, all government employees received salary increases of 30%–100% that included nine months of tax-exempt arrears, creating instant elation throughout the cities and countryside (Cosentino 1991, 246–50).[11]

The impact of centralized state spending and civil service expansion and reform was complex and multisectorial. If euphoria was tempered by rising inflation, growing income differentials, legendary port congestion in Lagos, and incomprehensible fuel shortages, the oil sector provided the model of modernization itself, combining big capital investments and sophisticated technology with centralized planning and control. In its effort to revitalize the agricultural sector, which lagged from the rural exodus to the cities and a growing preference for imported foods, Operation Feed the Nation resembled the distributive arm of the oil industry. The government bought tractors and fertilizers for agroindustry to boost production, provided trucks and vans to facilitate transportation, and even built storage facilities for food surpluses that would be "streamed" into circulation. The failures of such schemes would soon become apparent, and as we shall see were attributed by the state to the indiscipline and profiteering of unpatriotic Nigerians and saboteurs. Seeing like a petro-state (J. Scott 1998), national development meant vertical integration. The body politic would be rationalized, standardized, and harmonized into an oil-burning engine of prosperity and growth. What the state refused to see from its commanding heights was how the shifting basis of class formation and the prebendalization of public office eroded the armature of the state from within and threw the wheels of progress off track.

As Joseph's (1987) penetrating study of the Second Republic reveals, prebendalism, combined with ethnic patronage and political clientelism, were well established under the First Republic, when political coalitions and pacts formed around elite access to the regional governments and their marketing boards. Defining the Weberian notion of prebendal politics as "an unremitting and unconstrained struggle for possession and access to state offices, with the chief aim of procuring direct material benefits to oneself, and one's acknowledged communal or other sectional groups," Joseph (1987, 75) has argued that the oil boom shifted the spoils system from regional surpluses to a "national cake" while simultaneously changing the basis of accumulation away from peasant production and into oil-based returns (see also Watts 1984). Among the many consequences of this shift, including the reification and centralization of the state already discussed, were (1) the creation of the nouveaux riches embedded in the military or attached as clients, bypassing the first generation of colonial civil servants trained by the British; (2) the rise of an interstitial category of "contractors" who brokered deals with government and industry that involved substantial kickbacks and private gains; (3) the reinvigoration of ethnic competition for control of the state; and (4) the privatization of the state apparatus in the general struggle for a piece of the action. What successive civilian and military regimes have decried as the moral failings of corruption and bad leadership has actually been the modus operandi of politics itself. For the purposes of our preliminary sketch of the bureaucratic petro-state, the mixture of oil with prebendalism explains two general trends that it set into motion. The first concerns the clear association in the minds of many Nigerians of ethnic clientelism with oil wealth, whether as beneficiaries of a valuable "long leg" or as victims of expropriation and exclusion by others. Beyond the access to resources which it indeed provided, ethnicity in a sense became commodified as a value form infused with naira. Second, as later chapters will further discuss, the prebendalization of the rentier state produced a pattern of *class involution* by which the state absorbed within itself the contradictions of oil capital. To examine these contradictions in various guises, we turn to the circulation of petroleum—and its associated value forms —throughout the nation.

THE CIRCULATION OF VALUE

In March of 1977 in Benin City, a man was burned to death and two others critically injured when the gasoline they were storing in cans caught fire and exploded. According to witnesses, the man "was pouring some petrol from the drum inside the store into a container when fire from a nearby kitchen caught the vapour." The gruesome event ignited outrage and controversy over the crippling fuel shortages afflicting the nation even as new records in daily production were announced. The "magic barrel" of unlimited commodities that the Lagos oil seminar had so successfully contrived was now revealing its deadly secrets and exacting hidden costs. Cycles of shortages in a time of plenty came to represent a host of problems and anxieties associated with oil wealth: "Fuel shortage . . . long queues at petrol filling stations, illegal roadside one-naira-one-gallon roadside dumps, storing petrol in drums have become too frequent that tragedies like the Benin fire incident only dramatised the double irony that the black gold had brought to Nigeria."[12] Even as oil was rebuilding the nation, it was not getting to the people. In many ways it was destroying the people. Political scientist Claude Ake warned that oil boom was making "every Nigerian a spoilt child" while production was declining in other sectors of the economy.[13] Meanwhile, the first reports of ecological devastation from oil spills and gas flares in Rivers State were beginning to break, although nearly twenty years would pass before Ken Saro-Wiwa could mobilize the crisis into a global *cause célèbre* (as we shall see in chapter 8), for which he sacrificed his life.[14]

To solve Nigeria's immediate domestic fuel shortages, the government began importing super petrol (high-octane gasoline) from overseas. Like hauling proverbial coals to Newcastle, the Nigerian postcolony—in a classic model of underdevelopment—produced and exported its high-grade crude through multinational companies, only to buy back refined fuel to meet rising domestic demand. Given congested ports, bad roads, limited storage capability, and inadequate telecommunications, the distribution network frequently broke down, causing the long queues, fights, and stampedes at the petrol stations that came to mark the fits and spasms of development during the oil boom. Official statistics report that from 1975 to 1976, total consumption of "super petrol" alone increased 46%, matched by a 56% increase—from 620 million to 968 million liters—in imported fuel.[15] To develop long-term solutions to these periodic shortages and render Nigeria self-reliant in its energy needs, the government appointed a special commission to investigate the root causes of the problem. On the basis of the Oputa Inquiry report, the government took characteristically strong measures and bold steps, issuing new decrees and investing in new projects. As we shall see, government policy toward petroleum distribution mistook symptoms for causes, developing into a struggle for control over the flow of value itself as congestion, hoarding, profiteering, and even industrial sabotage registered the more systemic diversion of oil wealth from its intended national targets.

The government's first step to ensure the flow of oil to the people was the promulgation of the Petroleum Anti-Sabotage Decree of 1975, sentencing to death by hanging or firing squad any person guilty of disrupting "the production, procurement or distribution of petroleum products in any part of the country."[16] The main targets of this decree were the tanker drivers who had withdrawn their vehicles from the roads to protest the introduction of "mobile courts" earlier in the year, but who would also crash their vehicles to collect insurance, littering the highways with the burning carcasses of their trade. But the decree extended to all those who "tampered" with the mechanisms of petroleum distribution, either directly or by association. In this respect, government's image shifted from benevolent provider to vigilant protector of the nation, cleansing the body politic of bad elements within, ranging from unscrupulous hoarders and smugglers to villagers who "poached" on the oil companies themselves. If the former category of criminals were guilty of private gain at the expense of the public good, stockpiling and hoarding oil to drive up its price on the black market, it was the latter category that inspired the newly formed army mobile patrols— known as "kill and go"—"to shoot and kill on sight any person tampering with flowline pipes or any equipment in oilfield installations."[17] The main targets of these army raids were the increasingly militant indigenes of the oil producing areas who received token, if any, compensation for the pollution and destruction of their farms and waterways.

One of the first incidents of local resistance was a major blowout in Shell-BP's "Afam-18" oil well, attributed to industrial sabotage that caused over one million naira in damages as well as fourteen hundred barrels of lost production per day.[18] In a coordinated spin, both the government and the oil company explained the loss in terms of property rather than politics, highlighting the growing theft of pipelines by unscrupulous villagers in search of illicit profits and building materials. As one progovernment newspaper reported,

> In the case of Nigeria, investigations have proved that, although there may be a few cases of industrial sabotage, the main factor responsible for recent oil well blow-outs is the activity of thieves. It has been discovered that the flowline pipes which are solely imported by oil companies and used exclusively in their operation is (sic) in high demand as building materials, mainly as pillars. What thieves do is to exhume, hacksaw-cut and remove the pipes for commercial purposes.[19]

What is significant in this discourse of pipeline theft is not merely its empirical implausibility—even if isolated cases occurred, they could hardly have *caused* the blowouts and losses—but its transposition of larceny into crimes against the nation. Likened to the universally despised armed robber, who, as the modern witch of Nigerian society, accumulates illicit wealth by taking (or by threatening to take) human life, the pipeline thief undermined the flow of value throughout the national body and its circulatory system. In both cases, therefore, the penalty must be death. The report concluded,

> The case of a flowline pipe theft is, to some extent, similar to that of an armed robber. There is the danger to life in both cases. If protection of the oilfield is to be ensured, the penalty applicable to armed robbery should equally apply to flowline pipe theft. For example, any person who has stolen a pipe from an oilfield or engaged in any act of sabotage likely to cause a blow-out is guilty of a most serious crime against the economy of the country and should be executed publicly. The same penalty should be meted out to any person who knowingly deals in stolen flowline pipes.[20]

In this statist formula of blaming the victim, the nation's vigor and economic well-being would be restored by eliminating the internal parasites that fed upon its vascular tissue. Not that the problem ended with unpatriotic thieves. Weaknesses within the formal distribution sector also were dealt with by decree. To prevent hoarding by the oil marketing companies, which retained exclusive reserves for staff members and middlemen who would resell to buyers at inflated prices during shortages, a penalty of five thousand naira would be imposed on any company registering nil or nonpumpable stock in its underground tanks.[21]

And to ensure that adequate supplies would be available, the government promised faster delivery of the Kaduna and Warri refineries under construction, as well as storage depot installations in all state capitals. Guided by government, a national distribution system not only took shape but was also set into motion. Planned from above, oil would be refined in the different regions of the nation, stored in each state, and transported from tank farms to individual selling stations by one of the 114 brand-new tankers which the government provided, allocating eight vehicles to each state free of charge.[22] To guarantee an even supply to the remote and marginal areas of the country, where fewer cars traveled the dilapidated roads, the government built gas stations with fixed fuel prices that were also harmonized by decree to one uniform rate throughout the nation. By "rescuing" the distribution network from private "profiteers," the oil economy was thus protected from exposure to "uncertainty and the possibility of sabotage," even when this meant fluctuating prices governed by supply and demand.[23] As the rising petro-state took control, unpredictable global market forces—which caused a production slump in 1975—were projected within the nation, where the private sector of distribution itself was compromised by "the unscrupulous and unpatriotic capitalist character of the Nigerian distributor" (Usoro 1977, 69). To further consolidate control over the flow of oil throughout the body politic, the government took over major shares of all marketing companies, nationalizing Esso-Standard outright into Unipetrol while assuming 60% control of Shell Oil Marketing Company, renaming it National. One petrol to serve one nation.

The government's measures to solve the fuel shortages by protecting domestic distribution from thieves and hoarders effectively removed it from the market. By selling oil overseas in order to subsidize its consumption at home—at low 1967 price levels in spite of inflation—government was underwriting the public good, including other utilities such as electricity and water. Cheap fuel, it was argued, would lower transportation costs, stimulate trade and industry, and prime the pump for economic takeoff.[24] It also increased demand for petrol itself, creating the very shortages which government sought to alleviate. But in more symbolic terms, by protecting domestic petrol distribution from the vicissitudes of the global market, government protected the nation itself, investing its form with a substance of value that would revitalize the body politic to achieve rapid and even development. By fixing its price and regulating its sale, the state privileged petrol in relation to all other commodities, reducing—in Marx's terms—its relative value in the sphere of circulation while expanding its equivalent value as the underlying standard in relation to which other commodities could be bought and sold. The effect not only sealed Nigeria's borders, since "pirates" could sell their fuel to Niger and Benin Republic for enormous profit at the Nigerian government's expense, but also rendered equivalent all Nigerians from every "tribe" and state throughout the nation. Increased policing of Nigeria's black gold along its borders combined with calls for greater national security from foreign enemies and oil-hungry superpowers.[25] Market forces notwithstanding, government would bring Nigerian oil to the Nigerian people, whatever the transportation and distribution costs.

The extent of government's commitment toward this end is illustrated by the spectacular if misguided construction of its own crude-oil supertanker. Built at a cost of 28 million naira, the *M.V. Oloibiri,* as it was called—to commemorate the first commercial oilfield discovered in Nigeria—joined the ranks of supertankers crossing the seas, but differed in one crucial respect. Whereas most supertankers carried their cargo for profit, the *Oloibiri* carried at a loss, in that the 2 million barrels of Nigerian crude which it loaded in Port Harcourt was taken to Curacao, where it was refined and reloaded for a return trip home. Hailed as an important step toward self-sufficiency, since now it was Nigerian oil that was refined abroad and carried in a Nigerian ship, the scheme only replaced one form of dependency with another, relying upon overseas industry rather than foreign oil, and underwriting the compounded costs of shipping, refining, and "marketing" with the royalties and revenues from the multinational companies in Nigeria. The big issue for the petro-state, however, was not profit but control. By the end of 1976, the public sector of the oil industry was reconsolidated into the Nigerian National Petroleum Corporation (NNPC), merging the former Nigerian National Oil Corporation (NNOC) with the Ministry of Petroleum Resources and further coordinating government involvement in exploration, production, refining, and marketing. A new decree shored up further control by establishing exclusive federal government authority over the issuing of licenses, formerly delegated to state and local governments, for dealing in petroleum products.

The NNPC thus presided over an empire of oil, one that exported its crude for the petrodollars that would reunite and revitalize the nation. As the lifeblood of the new Nigeria, oil became a general form or "substance" of value, the king of all commodities, refined for domestic consumption and stabilized by the state for equal access by all. *Regulated and controlled from above, oil was removed from the domestic market of commodity circulation because it served as its precondition, standardizing the relative values in terms of which other commodities were bought and sold, and thus approaching the general equivalent of the money form itself.* From cer-

FIGURE I.2 The circulatory system of the nation. Source: 1977 Annual Report, Petroleum Inspectorate of the Nigerian National Petroleum Corporation.

tain standpoints, the barrel of oil became a money form, as the terms *petrodollar* and *petro-naira* suggest, measuring value and standardizing price both abroad and at home. In this more phenomenological light, the government's preoccupation with domestic petrol shortages was indeed about keeping the economy—not just automobiles—in motion. Nigeria's three refineries, linked by a vast network of depots, pump stations, and pipelines, shaped the anatomy of the national economy, uniting regions, states, and ethnic groups into one sovereign nation through which money and commodities, like petrol, began to flow (fig. 1.2). That the depots and pipelines fetishized the flow of commodity value more generally, and its state-dominated relations of production and distribution, accounts for the inverted causal relations attributed by government to shortages in a land of plenty. If petrol crises came to represent the paradoxes of oil prosperity, they did so as consequences, not causes. The draconian sanctions against pipe stealing and hoarding were misdirected attacks against the general dialectics of prebendalism and the privatization of the public sector at large. Similarly, government preoccupation with the national grid countered ethnic competition for the national cake. To see how the underlying contradictions of the oil economy sabotaged directed development from within, we can step back from the filling stations and flow lines to survey the movement of oil money and capital as it was systematically indigenized and diverted into private hands.

Indigenization by decree began in 1972, stipulating increased Nigerian staffing in management positions to reduce the "earnings leakage" (Biersteker 1987, 81) exacted by expatriates and thus promote what Gowon would call "the new Nigerian businessman."[26] Greater Nigerian participation, however, not only was directed toward the local private sector, but promoted state expansion into the fastest-growing enterprises in the economy, particularly industry and mining, as well as commercial banking, by acquisition or in the form of joint ventures (ibid., 75). Prior to the mushrooming of parastatal industries that became the sign if not symptom of Nigeria's state-led development, foreign businesses were required to sell off 40% of their equity shares to Nigerian entrepreneurs, who formed joint-venture partnerships. If in principle foreign business would be at least proportionally "indigenized," in practice the shares were privately distributed to connected partners who would tow management's line with their dividends. The result was less the active involvement of Nigerians in management and more the rise of a new connected elite, known as "the Mr. 40 percenters," who formed a tight circle of comprador cronies around foreign capital according to ethnoregional patterns of stratification—traditional rulers in the north, Lagosian businessmen in the west, and fewer entrepreneurs from the midwest and east. Concentrated, by one estimate, in the hands of twelve families—mainly in the west—the indigenized shares of the first decree are significant not for the scale of capital involved but for the pattern of inequality and spending which they established.[27] First, it is clear that the shares of joint ventures were not widely distributed throughout the nation, but were tightly consolidated by regional elites along political and ethnic lines. Second, dividends from the shares were not productively invested, but favored patterns of conspicuous consumption. On the basis of interviews with indigenous entrepreneurs and joint-venture partners, Biersteker (1987, 148) reports,

> Nearly all listed consumption as the first use of the proceeds from joint-venture operations (consumption of imported consumer items, acquisition of a Mercedes, taking a new wife, or throwing a big party). Building a large home in the home village or meeting expenses for extended family members were other common forms of immediate consumption. After consumption, investment in real estate (either land or the acquisition or construction of

new buildings) was the most common activity for local capital. Expansion of commercial and service ventures came third, followed by investment in industry.

The logic of conspicuous consumption can be recast as a conversion into forms of symbolic capital in order to illuminate not the "irrationality" of Nigerian business practices but their historically specific, political rationale. Of significance at this point, however, is the diversion of proceeds away from industrial production in favor of social capital and the commercial and service sectors, along kinship and ethnic lines. This pattern would intensify as the oil economy boomed into high gear, accentuating the structures of inequality and ethnic patronage while frustrating the state's efforts to foster Nigerian industry.

If the first indigenization decree set the precedent for increased state involvement in domesticating foreign capital, the second such decree of January 1977 went much further, providing a blueprint for public sector leadership of the economy by extending indigenization to finance, petroleum production and services, steel, cement, and even food products (ibid., 175). Designed in part to break the cronyism and corruption of the Gowon regime, the second indigenization decree signaled a more populist commitment to centralized planning and equitable allocation, a heightened spirit of economic nationalism, and a new guard within the army and civil service promoting policy reforms. Ironically, part of the pressure for reform came from northerners against what they perceived as the regional imbalances of the first decree, which favored Lagos-based entrepreneurs. With oil money filling the coffers of the rising petro-state, the second decree provided greater economic access to northern powerbrokers, financing a powerful alliance between the old elites of the emirates and the rising group of younger, more educated officers and entrepreneurs who became known as the Kaduna Mafia. The state-financed Kaduna refinery and miles of pipeline illustrate the north's reconsolidation of political and economic control as it regained the lion's share of the national cake under the guise of greater regional equality. In general, however, the second decree extended indigenization to virtually every foreign enterprise operating in Nigeria, boosting equity levels to 60% while providing for more equitable allocation of shares. Designed to promote Nigerian entrepreneurs and local capital, instead it enabled the public sector to absorb the private sector, acquiring banks, major manufacturing firms, and mining ventures in addition to its holdings in petroleum.[28] When local capitalists sought market advantage, they were accused of unpatriotic profiteering. Private gain in this model of state capitalism was seen at the expense of a public good that was underwritten by petro-naira.

The shifting boundary between public and private sectors which the expanding petro-state set into motion was offset by the counterappropriation of the state, or prebendalism, as public resources flowed back into private hands. These flows took many forms: kickbacks to officials granting inflated contracts, mobilization fees to construction companies for starting—and in many cases finishing—their projects, graft for securing licenses for importing goods and marketing petroleum products, sinecures, padded expense accounts for shopping trips to London, defaulting on government loans, nepotistic recruitment to inflated payrolls, and the legendary spending on lavish parties and mansions that secured social status within a highly volatile prestige economy.[29] Often characterized as the wasteful spending of a wasting asset (oil), the diversion of public resources and funds was at the core of the Nigerian career trajectory, which required powerful patrons, loyal clients, and a "long leg." The appropriation of public funds, however, was not strictly motivated by personal greed but served as a form of rational investment in symbolic and social capital. By this I do not mean conspicuous consumption as such, but rather investment in a mobile fund of favors, obligations, and networks organized around influential men and women who could "manage" the state by helping friends and obstructing rivals and enemies. Corruption, then, was not a matter of moral compromise but of survival, obligation, and advancement. Diverted funds were expended as gifts and countergifts to build alliances and enhance reputations of "bigness" and generosity. No better example of such investments can compare with the "spraying" of cash to musicians and dancers on the floor of *ariya* parties, celebrating the new oil prosperity with style and largesse (Waterman 1990, 180–212). These social arenas established sensitive playing fields for the negotiation of status, choreographing the exchange of money for the enhancement of one's name. Nor were the results of such events a foregone conclusion. During these social displays one could always be outdone by rivals, as implied by the popular saying "there is danger on the dance floor."

Despite the Murtala regime's purge of the civil service and the issuance of more stringent regulations and decrees, the privatization of the public sector could not be legislated away. To be sure, it could be projected onto the images of the pipeline thief and the merchant hoarder, much like the Venezuelan *pirata* discussed by Coronil (1997, 319), but the contradiction was not thereby resolved. The parceling up of the national cake was, after all, the normalized vision of effective government, even if the channels of distribution remained somewhat obscure. To cement the bonds of complicity, a muted 50% rule prevailed, glossed by the euphemism "let's keep our secret secret," according to which half of an official's bribe or kickback ("dash") would be sent up to his or her superior, who would take a cut and send the remainder on up the ranks to the very top. By this distributive mechanism, everybody gained by the institution of the "dash," and also by keeping quiet. When I once asked a customs officer why some of his coworkers were dismissed for graft (and in effect, how he survived the purge), he explained that they had violated the 50% rule, pocketing the share that should have gone up the ladder.[30] Their crime was not in taking the bribes but rather in not disposing them correctly. Such inclusive webs of mutual implication explain why government probes into financial mismanagement were so ineffective, seeking political scapegoats without changing the system.

The expansion of the petro-state at its own expense, in which "the very offices of bureaucracy were highly desired spoils of the system" (Joseph 1987, 84), reconfigured ethnic relations as well. Just as the concept of "ethnic balancing" informed civil service appointments and promotions, so it extended beyond the armature of the state and into the informal constituencies that appropriated the public sector. As one ex–civil servant complained, "The various ethnic groups forming the state . . . clamour for all manner of posts for their respective sons of the soil in the various arms of the public services," adding that "their primary consideration in any bargaining process is the extent to which the members of their ethnic or cultural group stand to gain or lose in the societal allocation of scarce resources" (Sani 1976; quoted in Joseph 1987, 84). Whereas at least officially, the state sought to subsume ethnic differences within the overarching framework of national integration, competition for the rising national cake intensified ethnic sectionalism and parochialism, extending the logic of legitimate ethnic bargaining into the gray areas and black markets of "extraordinary" business as usual. Distributing the public good throughout one nation, the state itself was distributed along ethnic lines.

Thus sketched, the diversion of oil money as it circulated throughout the national economy was more "structural" than the military government could afford to understand. And as long as its oil wells kept pumping and its customers kept paying, the government could afford not to see. Throwing good money after bad, the petro-state kept covering its losses while waiting for the miracle of economic takeoff to occur. Punishing "unpatriotic elements" with draconian sanctions and Band-Aid reforms, the state absorbed the real contradictions of expansion-without-development within itself. These contradictions, moreover, were difficult to grasp because of the accelerated flow of money and commodities that they generated and sustained.

Macroeconomic indicators reveal what economists call a "circulation economy" (Watts 1992, 38) in the oil-rich 1970s, when the consumption of imports far outstripped domestic production, and when all manner of materials and expertise could be bought. If oil money paid for the goods, it did so through state channels that privatized access to import licenses and foreign exchange, giving rise to dense patronage networks extending from the highest ministries and government officials who juggled enormous sums of cash to the market women and street vendors operating on the lowest margins of profit and loss. While the nation's circulatory system expanded, everyone seemed to get a piece of the action. The tangible signs of progress and abundance, moreover, ratified the new prosperity with visible evidence, producing a national dramaturgy of appearances and representations that beckoned toward modernity and brought it into being. Or so it seemed. In what became the magical realism of Nigerian modernity, the signs of development were equated with its substance.

Advertisements of the day capitalized on this equation quite directly. As the new middle class remodeled its parlors and living rooms with the lavish accoutrements of the modern bourgeois family, the television and the camera became loaded icons of achievement, bringing the nuclear and the national into focused alignment. Color television not only entertained family members and guests as they sank into armchairs and couches on carpeted floors, but more important, it brought modernity into the domestic sphere, where watching became a form of witnessing. One popular advertisement for National Colour Television proclaims that "the picture's so real—you're part of the action." The ad continues,

> The advanced electronics of National means you get a picture of startling reality. . . . Feather-touch switches, automatic voltage control and instant picture and sound are just a few of the technological merits of National TV. See all the action with tomorrow's technology—now.

Featuring a "20 inch Colour Super Deluxe Furniture Look Console TV" with "Magic Line Fine Tuning," National Colour Television not only brought the modern world to the new Nigerian at the push of a button and the turn of a dial, but more significantly, it framed the national ontology of the oil boom onscreen, where spectacular images conjured the real. As the National logo, like the Nigerian nation, pointed "all ways ahead" it simultaneously brought tomorrow into the here-and-now of the modern household. It hardly mattered that the company was

Korean. Framed by National Colour Television, like the moon landing shown in the ad and reproduced onscreen, the wonders of "tomorrow's technology" were brought home with a "picture so real" that Nigerians could take part in the action (fig. 1.3).

In a similar visual register, Polaroid offered an "instant picture camera" that produced push-button images of tomorrow's world electronically and automatically, appearing "before your eyes." An appropriate allegory of Nigeria's "instant development" during the oil boom, the Polaroid promised quick and beautiful color photographs that miraculously printed themselves. As if reassuring skeptics, the ad insists, "You don't believe it? Ask your dealer to show you the new Polaroid 2000. Seeing is believing!" In stages, we see the faint outlines of an image becoming clearer, culminating in the finished photograph of two well-dressed children, the boy with a truck and the girl with a doll (fig. 1.4)— a celebration of the new Nigerian family in Western bourgeois form. The magic of Nigeria's oil-fueled modernity, like the self-developing Polaroid picture, was instant, effortless, and above all spectacular. Not all ads featured expensive imported technology, and a host of soaps, cosmetics, blood tonics, and packaged foods flooded a broader economy of bodily images and practices. But the television and camera advertisements vividly exemplified the seeing-is-believing ontology of the oil boom, in which images of development took on a reality of their own. Perhaps the clearest expression of oil's money-generating mysteries is

FIGURE 1.4 Instant development. Nigerian advertisement for Polaroid camera, 1970s.

FIGURE 1.5 Magical money. Nigerian advertisement for Saxon Photocopiers.

an ad for the Saxon Photocopier, equating the art of electronic repro-duction with the production of new wealth (fig. 1.5). Called "The Money Maker," the photocopier "copies absolutely anything," so that "anyone in your office can make money—simply by pressing two buttons." A re-laxed-looking woman operating the machine produces copies effort-lessly with one hand resting at her side and the other balanced on the machine, blending work with repose. Her dress, we notice, is covered with brand-new naira bills, quite literally refashioning her in money. "If that isn't making money," the ad concludes, "what is?" Clearly marketed for the Nigerian business office, the ad touches on the forbidden theme of money magic and medicines, here updated with "Saxon" technology, intimating that the photocopier can copy anything—including money. As a key to success, the photocopier virtually dispenses with the intermediate role of the commodity form, moving directly to the money form, which it copies according to Marx's faithful formula $M - M'$—magical money indeed.

When the state blamed unpatriotic elements for the failures and shortages of its grandiose schemes, citizens of the new Nigeria were not unduly concerned. Refashioning themselves in the dazzling images of the oil boom, they were interpellated into the action. The point to reemphasize, however, is that the circulation of industrial capital in nineteenth-century Britain differed significantly from the circulation of oil capital in 1970s Nigeria, even if similar conversions between money and commodities took place on the surface. We have seen that Nigeria's oil-based commodity boom owed little to social relations of indigenous production and almost everything to the state's control over oil revenues and royalties, which were diverted into private hands and converted into social and political capital. Disassociated from the nation's productive base, the sphere of circulation was driven by oil to resemble industrial development in its "fetishized" forms, such as utopian state projects featuring the latest technology and the conspicuous abundance of money and goods. Underlying the appearance of instant development, however, was a negative dialectic of internal consumption that expanded the state at its own expense by pumping money into the public sector while privatizing public offices and resources—partly along ethnic lines—and by absorbing organized assaults on its position (Berry 1985, 14). To restate the obvious, oil profits were not productively absorbed. They reproduced and expanded the means of distribution rather than the means of production within the national economy. To recast the situation in more Marxian terms, what appeared as a surplus from the standpoint of circulation was a deficit from the standpoint of capital and labor. The magic formula $M - M'$, which in its classic context converted surplus value into exchange value, in Nigeria belied a loss—an illusory wealth that, like a fading photocopy, increasingly lost touch with its material base.

With the contradictions of the oil economy and its phenomenology of value forms thus examined, we can better appreciate why the Nigerian state invested so heavily in FESTAC, and how this event remodeled the nation in the image of the money form. Or, from a slightly different standpoint, how FESTAC converted oil—the lifeblood of the nation—into the general form of culture.

THE PRODUCTION OF CULTURE

Although Nigeria's commitment to the Second World Black and African Festival of Arts and Culture did not go unchallenged in the public sphere, it made political sense to the petro-state as an important mechanism of national development. Criticisms of the "Great Jamboree" represented the wide variety of viewpoints and voices that the new Nigeria could afford to accommodate. Muslims and Christians warned against the revival of paganism, Marxists condemned traditional culture as conservative and reactionary, economists questioned the investment in culture, while nearly everyone noted, with pride or opprobrium, the grandiose preparations for the global event. For the Nigerian leaders involved in its planning, however, FESTAC '77 would serve a patriotic purpose. From 1975 to 1976, when the Constitutional Drafting Committee (CDC) convened to prepare a return to civilian rule, it identified the "Promotion of National Loyalty in a Multi-Ethnic Society" as a political imperative, resolving that "[t]he State shall foster a feeling of belonging and of involvement among the various sections of the country, to the end that loyalty to the nation shall override sectional loyalties" (Joseph 1987, 43). Given the petro-state's limited vision of ethnic patronage and "unpatriotic profiteering," FESTAC would foster national unity and integration by producing a Nigerian national culture that could be exhibited in museums and choreographed onstage. Within the ideological register of what J. Scott (1998) has called "high modernism," the state's production of national culture took its place within a larger scheme of directed development and national renewal.

Prior idioms of Nigerian national culture had been cultivated under colonialism through the founding and dissemination of *Nigeria Magazine,* which published "ethnographic" pieces on indigenous arts and festivals, and the establishment of national museums, monuments, and universities. As early as 1937, E. H. Duckworth, one of the magazine's founding editors, wrote, "Our African contributors by researching into and describing the antiquities, the craft work, the customs of the country, *can help to create in the mass of the people an appreciation of Nigerian art and culture*" (my emphasis; quoted in Fasuyi 1973, 24). In 1952 the Jos Museum opened to display the national heritage of the Northern

Region, rivaled five years later by the Nigerian National Museum, founded in Lagos. As I will demonstrate, this north–south divide would periodically flare up, reflecting regional politics in cultural policy. When the Nigerian Arts Council was founded on the eve of the nation's independence in 1959 to promote the literary, visual, and performing arts of Nigeria, including cultural festivals and exhibitions, the Northern Region responded with its own Nigerian Cultural Society based in Kaduna. Both groups competed to represent the nation, organizing separate cultural programs and annual art festivals, and merging only after 1967 when the regions were broken up into twelve states by the Gowon regime. Thereafter a "federal model" of cultural development took shape, headed by a national organization that supported a variety of cultural centers, museums, artists' societies, and musicians' unions within each state. According to plan, every state government would organize an annual festival featuring the music, dance, and arts of its indigenous groups, selecting winners from local competitions to represent its local government areas and divisions. From each state festival, in turn, the best group would be selected to participate in the National Festival of the Arts, thereby ascending the administrative hierarchy from local and state government to the nation at large. Given the scale and logistics of such stagecraft, the festival cycle was not completed every year; but national festivals in 1970, 1971, and 1974 did take place, according to a rotational plan whereby "Nafest," as it came to be called, was held successively in different state capitals "to encourage the spread of culture and promote national unity" (Fasuyi 1973, 49). I will examine the performance genres and conventions of the state festivals in later chapters, focusing for now on the centralizing tendencies of national renewal.

Beginning in the colonial period, government-sponsored festivals incorporated local cultural identities and ethnicities into the administrative categories of indirect rule, as particular dances and performing groups were officially represented by their local government designations. This basic framework remained after independence. By the early 1970s, during the Mid-Western State festival, for example, performers featured their cultural traditions not as Edo, Isoko, Ika, or Ijaw but as representatives of Benin East Division, Isoko Division, Ika Division, or Western Ijaw Division, assimilating ethnic difference to an overarching logic of bureaucratic rationality. As the ordering and staging of "the local" from above rendered ethnicity equivalent and commensurable within the very "progress" of the festival cycle, the state abstracted general significance from particular groups and performances, thereby converting local traditions into national icons. This abstraction of national identity from local, ethnic, or provincial differences is of course a common feature of national carnivals and festivals the world over, but under the impact of the rising Nigerian petro-state, the production of national culture was "homogenized" to an unprecedented degree. As Nigeria prepared for FESTAC it established a more robust National Council of Arts and Culture and built a monumental National Theatre to provide a fixed rather than a floating venue for promoting national unity. From the commanding heights of the oil-rich regime, national culture, like education and the economy, could be directed and stage-managed with "push-button" control.

Located in Lagos and built for FESTAC within a network of new highways, the National Theatre established the "exemplary centre" (Geertz 1980, 11–18), not only of festival activities, but also of a revitalized Nigeria. Its circular structure, occupying 23,000 square meters and rising 31 meters high, resembled the hub of a cosmographic wheel radiating out through architectural "spokes" and superhighways to embrace the global oil economy. Viewed from outside, the Theatre's facade looked like a giant crown rising out or the earth, as if linking the wealth of the land—its chthonic traditions and subterranean oil—with national territory and sovereignty. A closer look revealed the Nigerian coat of arms perched like a jewel at the center of the architectural diadem. This image evoked a direct association between the National Theatre and the military regime, whose "head of state" wore a military hat that also resembled the Theatre's facade and sported the same coat of arms on its "crown." Members of FESTAC's National Participation Committee jokingly referred to the National Theatre as General Gowon's "cap." By the time it was formally opened two military governments later, the same joke worked with General Obasanjo's disembodied "head." [31]

Viewed from within, the National Theatre offered state-of-the-art facilities. The Theatre Hall was the major showpiece, providing an extravagant venue for cultural performances and "dance dramas," with five thousand seats, a rotating 33-by-44-meter stage, an orchestral stand, a rampart of stage lights, and a set of earphones at every seat which were hooked up to interpreters' booths equipped for simultaneous translation into eight major languages. Stage-directing, like directed development, could be "dictated" by remote control. As the program of the National Theatre's opening ceremony explained,

> Three rows of curtains, a back drop and a double cyclorama for creating silhouette effects are all easily amenable to the dictates of any play director. The resilience of the stage depends not only on press buttons but also the mech-

anism of hydraulic lifts located in the side sections under the stage. . . . The lighting system, intercommunications and the public address are built with remote control equipment and electro-acoustic system.[32]

A high-modernist vision was clearly inscribed on the surfaces and in the spaces of the National Theatre, embracing the latest audiovisual and administrative technology in black Africa's largest and wealthiest country. The theater housed radio and television booths to broadcast FESTAC performances to the outside world, and installed closed-circuit televisions in the hallways and foyers to project performances beyond the stage. A smaller Conference Hall with fifteen hundred seats boasted identical translation facilities for foreign delegates and visitors, for it was here that the much-vaunted FESTAC Colloquium would take place, with scholars from around the black and African world presenting papers on black civilization. These two major venues were to serve the two most basic components of FESTAC '77: the choreographed performances of traditional cultures and dramatic arts, and the more intellectual exchange between participating scholars. Equally important, however, were two large Exhibition Halls for displaying traditional sculpture, musical instruments, and architectural technology as well as modern artworks, mostly by Nigerians. Within this structure and beyond, FESTAC offered equal time and space to its participants, making the rotating main stage available to guest performers and allowing two hours and fifteen minutes for each major dramatic production. In the Exhibition Hall, similar parity was accorded to exemplary visual and plastic arts displayed on walls and in cases.

The point is not that all Nigerian—and, by extension, black and African—cultures were thus exhibited, but that in principle they could be. All "traditional" signs acquired the same national meaning within the master narrative of national culture that shaped official display. Nigerian performances represented the "federal" character of the nation in two ways: as winners of a national festival selected from local and state competitions, and as amalgamations of dancers and actors from Nigeria's different regions and ethnic groups. Nigerian artists featured in the National Theatre's formal opening included a minstrel from Jos, a dance group from Benin City, the Obitun Dancers from Ondo, and a choral group from Enugu, as well as dancers, musicians, puppeteers, and acrobats from Borno State, Cross River State, Kano, and Plateau State.[33] For Nigeria's national drama, *Lambodo,* the actors would later be recruited from the nation's three major regions into one integrated FESTAC performance. Thus through the legislated equivalence of spatial and temporal categories (in Foucault's terms, its "architecture of distribution"), the National Theatre homogenized ethnic differences into distinctive representations of equivalent national and Pan-African value.

In addition to its considerable investment in the National Theatre—officially reported at 144 million naira [34]—the petro-state poured money into Festac Village, accommodating FESTAC's international participants within a modernist grid that captured the logic and spirit of statist development. An unwitting reversal of the "primitive villages" that housed "savages" in the colonial expositions and world's fairs of Europe and North America, Festac Village evoked the very "norms and forms" of modern urban design in the manner of the Parisian *"plan-masse,"* with its "Grille des équipements" and "zones d'habitation" imposing uniform technocratic standards over local conditions (Rabinow 1989, 4–5). Equipped with its own electrical generators, transportation centers, supermarkets, banks, health centers, police posts, public toilets, and fire station, as well as international telephone, telex, and postal services, Festac Village became a model township and master plan of national development. With over 5,000 dwelling units consisting of two- and three-bedroom flats and duplexes, each "equipped with all the modern amenities," including parlors and wardrobes in contemporary styles and bright colors, the village was planned for 45,000 visitors as well as cadres of Nigerian protocol officers.[35] According to a regimented schedule, meals would be served in twelve communal restaurant-canteens for residents using meal-tickets purchased in advance. Transportation needs would be served by professionally trained drivers of luxury FESTAC buses that picked up and dropped off at fixed times and places. Most emblematic of the new Nigeria was the grid design of the residential layout, with the major avenues from 1 to 7 crosscut by the closes A, B, C, D. As one of the social development officers explained,

Festac Village was a masterpiece, a model city, a vision for developing the country as a whole. If you lived at 5112, you knew you were on 5th Avenue. 721 is 7th Avenue. After that, the Closes, like 5th Avenue, A Close, or 2nd Avenue, D Close. You always knew where you were or where you were going.[36]

There was, he added, a model of Festac Village in the National Theatre, as if to commemorate and reconstitute the residential plan on a national scale while linking both sites by the same rational imperatives. Like the assimilation of ethnic difference by equivalent categories of performance and display, homogeneity became one of the watchwords of Festac Village. One journalist proclaimed, "Despite signs posted in front of each building designating the occupant's country or community, and

the abundant banners, pennants and flags draped all over, an uninitiated person might mistake the Festival Village for any homogenous
community in any Black or African nation."[37] Like its theatrical counterpart, Festac Village abstracted identity from difference, projecting
unity of form and purpose from a modernizing prototype of national
renewal.

AS FESTAC expressed the rationality of the petro-state through its
"forms and norms" of cultural production, a related transformation of
national "substance" mirrored the circulation of value in the national
economy. Like the 1889 Paris Exhibition, with its Gallery of Machines
and Eiffel Tower heralding the "triumph of iron" (Buck-Morss 1993,
130) in heavy industry, FESTAC '77 represented the "triumph of oil" in
the postcolonial era of high OPEC prices. In many ways, this national
lifeblood infused the body politic with not only new energy and purchasing power, but the general form of culture itself. Just as oil functioned as the currency of national development in the sphere of resource allocation and commodity exchange, so it became the "invariant
substance" (Balibar 1991, 86) of the Nigerian nation form in the arena
of cultural production.

   At issue in this transposition was nothing less than the conversion of
money into "blood," not through incantation and human sacrifice understood as the basis of illicit wealth, but through the basic transformation of petro-naira into the common "substance" of national culture.
Understood in material terms as the investment of oil money in a grand
cultural festival, the investment itself can be broken down into two key
processes. The first concerns the conversion of oil into the "general
equivalent" (Goux 1990, 3) of the money form, providing the symbolic
means by which oil became the measure of all value. The second involves the conversion of money into culture, or more accurately, of the
"general equivalent" of the money form into the "invariant substance"
of the nation form. As we shall see in subsequent chapters, this secondary conversion of value forms during the oil boom was accomplished by the commodification of cultural difference into exchangeable
icons of a singular national heritage. Such commodification was not,
strictly speaking, an economic enterprise, since the state was not ex-
pecting enormous profits from ticket sales or from the cultural replicas
that it sold as souvenirs to tourists (despite initial attempts), but rather
can be understood as a mode of *objectification* characterized by the spectacle of modernity.

Like the phantasmagoric city described by Walter Benjamin, with its "magic-lantern show of optical illusions" produced by rampant commodity fetishism (Buck-Morss 1993, 81), the city of Lagos was both a booming marketplace and a site to behold. If all manner of imported goods were hustled off the docks and hawked on the streets for the pleasure of the nouveaux riches, visions of excess and access were available to all. As Buck-Morss (1993, 81–82) explains, following Benjamin, "the key to the new urban phantasmagoria was not so much the commodity-in-the-market as the commodity-on-display, where exchange value no less than use value lost practical meaning, and purely representational value came to the fore." Occluded in this spectacle, reflecting "people as consumers rather than producers," were "the class relations of production" which remained behind the scenes (ibid.). Unlike industrial Britain or fin-de-siècle France, I have argued, the productive relations of Nigeria's commodity boom were based on the privatization of public resources rather than the extraction of surplus value through wage labor. Thus within the dialectics of a self-consuming state—a rapidly expanding public sector that was simultaneously privatized by kickbacks and subsidies—Nigeria's commodification of national culture made ideological sense, masking divisive ethnic cleavages and the absence of indigenous production through the production of Indigenous Culture.

CHAPTER TWO

Nigeria at Large

Le rapprochement auquel l'Exposition Universelle a donné le signal devra amener une entente commune pour l'adoption d'un type uniforme des poids et measures, et d'une échelle précise pour la correspondance établie entre les monnaies des divers États.
—Baudrillart (1884)

The commodity law of value is a law of equivalences, a law which functions in every sphere.
—Baudrillard (1988)

ADDRESSING THE multitudes, ministers, and foreign dignitaries assembled at FESTAC's opening ceremony in the National Stadium, Lieutenant General Olusegun Obasanjo inaugurated a new vision of the black and African world amidst the din of a twenty-one-gun salute and the flurry of a thousand pigeons released into the sky. "On this occasion," he announced, "it is appropriate that we consider our place on the world scene. . . . For a long time our place in the world was mapped, analysed and interpreted by others . . . the Black and African peoples of the world, while yet living were, through this process, reduced to inert if not inanimate objects of Western speculation. . . . We invite you to look around you and appraise for yourselves what the future holds for us."[1]

For those who squeezed through the closely monitored gates and into the stadium, representative contingents of the black and African world could be seen in full regalia as they paraded in the official march-past, beginning with Ethiopia as FESTAC's Star Country and ending with Nigeria as befitting the host. Beyond the stadium bleachers and the throngs of spectators barred at the gates stretched the sprawling city of Lagos, with its new bridges and superhighways, decorated venues, congested streets and ports, luxury hotels, and recently completed Festac Village, all reflecting the breathtaking growth of a booming national economy. In the festive atmosphere of economic takeoff, Obasanjo could proclaim, "the star of our peoples is on the ascendancy."

As Africans seized the gaze that had rendered them "inert" in this moment of collective self-apprehension, Nigeria's place on the world scene was indeed changing. The infusion of petrodollars from high-grade oil not only accelerated domestic growth but boosted Nigeria's position among the Western economies as well. If, during the geopolitical realignments of the oil crisis in the early 1970s, Britain, Europe, and the United States were not exactly brought to their knees by rising inflation and energy costs, they could be called to attention by the member states of OPEC, which Nigeria had joined in 1971.[2] As multinationals and business interests from all over the world scrambled for a piece of the action, Nigeria became a land of big contracts and profits, a global marketplace for Asian and Eastern European as well as Western entrepreneurs.

Whereas in the previous chapter we saw how oil reshaped Nigeria, this chapter will examine how the booming economy motivated FESTAC's vision of the black and African world. In concrete terms, this included Australasia and North Africa within its zonal framework, and broke with the more separatist implications of Négritude and African Personality. Although contested among participants and member states, FESTAC's vision of blackness reinscribed the centers and antipodes of the colonial world. In design if not always in execution, "blacks" from India, New Guinea, and the Torres Straits would share the stage with their "cousins" from London, Paris, and New York. As Obasanjo emphasized in his opening speech, "Let me quickly stress that the aim of the festival is not to underrate or debase the cultural values of other races. Rather we seek to exert our values in a world which is highly competitive so that the Black and African cultural heritage can co-exist with the cultural values of other nations . . . based on human respect." In its broadest reaches, the Nigerian vision of universal blackness not only faded into lighter shades at the edges, but ultimately sought to embrace all of humanity.

To show how Nigeria established itself at the center of an expansive black imperium, we begin with FESTAC's administrative organization. Since Nigeria underwrote 99% of FESTAC's expenses, it had a strong voice in controlling the show; but as we shall see, debates over definitions of blackness and Africanity reflected a multiplicity of political issues and interests. At the top of the administrative hierarchy, two military coups, conflicts between co-organizers, and turf wars between top Nigerian ministries destabilized the festival from above, while conflicts within the zonal committees of participating nations created unanticipated turbulence from below. These political dimensions of FESTAC's administration reveal the incipient forms of transnational political community that an ostensibly cultural production could create, as well as the different modalities of racial politics that it unwittingly brought into play.

Moving to performance venues, exhibitions, and events, we will then examine how FESTAC mediated political frictions through forms of cultural commodification. As cultural and national "traditions" were accorded equivalent value in the festival's exhibitions and displays, evacuated of historical specificity to become tokens of a singular black heritage and civilization, Nigeria emerged as the unequivocal leader of the new black world. Spending lavishly on its global citizens, the Nigerian state accrued political capital as master of ceremonies while recasting the nation in indigenous terms as the *fons et origo* of virtually all black cultural traditions. FESTAC was thus a repossession of origins—not just a celebration of indigenous traditions but a return to the very locus of black cultural dissemination. In the strongest expression of Nigeria's centrality within FESTAC's global cultural economy, the modern oil-exporting Nigerian nation was portrayed as the aboriginal exporter of black and African culture. If traditional choreography emerged as the principal genre through which this genealogy was demonstrated, there was no shortage of rhetorical and even scientific devices to bolster the claim. In the final section, we will see how FESTAC's depiction of the origin of humankind reflected Nigeria's Pan-African image of itself.

ANATOMY OF AN EMPIRE

If, as Watts (1992, 35) has argued, Nigeria's oil boom *internationalized* the state by projecting it into global circuits of capital, nowhere is this more tangibly expressed than in FESTAC's administrative organization. Reaching out of Africa from "Papua New Guinea to Watts, California" (as described by one *New York Times* reporter), the festival divided its expansive empire into sixteen zones, each containing several black countries or communities and headed by a vice president who sat on the International Festival Committee (IFC) in Lagos. The African continent proper was "repartitioned" into ten zones along fairly recognizable regional lines. These were Eastern Africa, with Ethiopia, Sudan, Somalia, Malagasy, and Mauritius; Southern Africa, with Zambia, Botswana, Lesotho, and Swaziland; East Africa Community, with Kenya, Uganda, and Tanzania; Central Africa I, with Zaire, Rwanda, Burundi, and Chad; Central Africa II, with Cameroon, Central African Republic, Republic of Congo, Gabon, and Equatorial Guinea; West Africa (Anglophone), with Liberia, Gambia, Sierra Leone, Ghana, and Nigeria; West Africa (Francophone I), with Senegal, Mauritania, Mali, and Guinea-Bissau;[3] West Africa (Francophone II), with Ivory Coast, Upper Volta, Niger, Benin, Togo, and the Republic of Guinea; North Africa, with Egypt, Libya, Tunisia, Algeria, and Morocco; and finally, Liberation Movements recognized by the Organisation of African Unity (OAU). Contained within this continental framework were a number of ideological and regional cleavages reflecting cold-war alignments and geopolitical rivalries that occasionally erupted into conflict during preparations and performances. Guinea and Senegal vented their ideological differences through threatened boycotts, while Mobutu Sese Seko left Nigeria in a huff rather than attend the Kaduna Durbar with Angola's new leader, President Agostino Neto. The most protracted conflict occurred between Senegal and Nigeria over North African Arabs and their participation in the FESTAC Colloquium. For the most part, however, the comity of African nations prevailed throughout the event, based on rhetorical appeals to brotherhood and unity reinforced by collective opposition to South African apartheid.

Beyond Africa proper, six more zones covered the African Diaspora in the widest terms that could be agreed upon. Not all countries within each zone actually attended FESTAC, but here I am concerned with the festival's horizons of blackness before turning to the participating contingents themselves. The South America zone included Brazil, Ecuador, Colombia, Venezuela, Panama, and Peru in a sweep reminiscent of Garvey's Universal Negro Improvement Association, but it would become apparent that most of these countries hardly identified blackness in culturally valorized or even explicit terms. Of this group, only Brazil played a prominent role in FESTAC, boasting its controversial mythology of racial democracy while celebrating the Yoruba legacy of Brazilian Candomblé. Within the Caribbean zone, Cuba, Guyana, Jamaica, Barbados, Trinidad and Tobago, Suriname, and even Saint Kitts achieved cultural visibility at FESTAC, whereas Haiti, the Dominican Republic, the Bahamas, Antigua, Montserrat, Saint Lucia, Saint Vincent, Grenada, Bermuda, and finally Belize were also invited. The remaining four zones bypassed national boundaries to embrace black communities within nonblack states, welcoming the "first" world within FESTAC's fold in ways that imposed a racially inverted form of second-class citizenship on the former colonial powers. Thus the USA/Canada zone, with its historic black communities; the UK/Ireland zone, with its resident blacks; the Europe zone, with the blacks of France and its overseas departments (Guadeloupe, Martinique, French Guiana); as well as of West Germany, the Netherlands, and residual "others" (for example, blacks of Sweden); and finally, the Australasian zone, with its variety of "blacks" from Australia, New Zealand, Papua New Guinea, India, and even black islanders from Oceania, were all incorporated as black communities and not nation-states. Thus those countries with black minorities could only join FESTAC and communicate with the IFC through their zonal representatives, but not directly. For example, whereas black and African nations could communicate with the committee through ambassadors and ministers of culture, countries like the United States and Great Britain had to go through the zonal representatives of their black communities (fig. 2.1).

The political repercussions of such differential incorporation of minority states into the new black order are well represented by the USA/Canada zone, whose vast domain experienced internal schism and obstruction by the State Department. Established as early as 1972, first under the chairmanship of actor and filmmaker Ossie Davis and then over to Jeff R. Donaldson, artist and former chair of Howard University's art department, the North America zone (NAZ) organized an initial delegation of 2,500 participants to represent "both the horizontal and vertical dimensions of the African Culture in the North American diaspora." Drawn from eight administrative regions in the United States that extended FESTAC's zonal system across the country to include Alaska and Hawaii, the North Americans formed a self-defined "nation within a nation" that received private-sector support from Chicago's black publishing magnate, John H. Johnson, and eventually secured limited funding from Howard University, the US Department of State, and the National Endowment for the Arts.[4] Troubles with the State Department began when one of their $50,000 grants came with strings attached, stipulating control over the selection of artists using the funds—an offer that Donaldson flatly refused. On their part, "State Department representatives did not understand why the IFC had not officially invited the U.S. government but rather the Afro-American community," clearly resenting this political slight.[5] In retaliation against State Department interference and obstructionism, the NAZ committee effectively fought

FESTAC '77
Adminstrative Organization of the Black and African World

International Festival Committee's 16 Zones of the black and African world, containing countries or communities* that were formally invited:

Grand Patron
(Obasanjo-Nigerian Head of State)

International Festival Committee
(President-Fingesi-Nigerian Naval Commander)

(Sec. General - Diop/Mbia)

(Zonal Vice -Presidents)

National Participation Committee

National Secretariat

International Secretariat**

1. SOUTH AMERICA: Brazil, Ecuador, Columbia, Venezuela, Panama, Peru
2. CARIBBEAN: Guyana, Haiti, Jamaica, Trinidad and Tobago, Cuba, Surinam, Dominican Republic, Bahamas, Barbados, St. Kitts, Atigua, Montserrat, St. Lucia, St. Vincent, Grenada, Bermuda, Belize British Honduras.
3. USA/CANADA: United States of America*, Canada*
4. UK AND IRELAND: United Kingdom and Northern Ireland
5. EUROPE: France* (Guadeloupe, Martinique, French Guiana), West Germany*, Netherlands*, black communities not covered (e.g. Sweden)
6. AUSTRALASIA: Australia*, New Zealand*, Papua New Guinea*, India, Islands in Oceania inhabited by black people.
7. EASTERN AFRICA: Ethiopia, Sudan, Somalia, Malagasy, Mauritius.
8. SOUTHERN AFRICA: Zambia, Botswana, Lesotho, Swaziland.
9. EAST AFRICA COMMUNITY: Kenya, Uganda, Tanzania.
10. CENTRAL AFRICA I: Zaire, Rwanda, Burundi, Chad.
11. CENTRAL AFRICA II: Cameroun, Central African Republic, Republic of Congo, Gabon, Equatorial Guinea.
12. WEST AFRICA (ANGLOPHONE): Libera, Gambia, Sierra Leone, Ghana, Nigeria.
13. WEST AFRICA (FRANCOPHONE) I: Senegal, Mauritania, Mali, Guinea-Bissau
14. WEST AFRICA (FRANCOPHONE) II: Ivory Coast, Upper Volta, Niger, Benin, Togo, Repubic of Guinea.
15. NORTH AFRICA: Egypt, Libya, Tunisia, Algeria, Morocco
16. LIBERATION MOVEMENTS RECOGNIZED BY OAU (SWAPO, ANC)

**Although claiming to represent its "true status... as an international organization", the secretariat--established by the Nigerian government as the institutional organ of the I.F.C.-- was in fact dominated by Nigerians.

through festivals, urging FESTAC's IFC to boycott the U.S. bicentennial celebrations. In a formal appeal attached to their zonal report, they wrote,

> The NAZ Committee is greatly concerned about the motives of the Smithsonian Institution in extending invitations to African governments to participate in the American Bicentennial and also about the uses which will be made of the African cultural representatives. Our concerns are two-fold: 1) there is a general feeling among Afro-Americans that their past 200 years is not much to celebrate about. We are worried that African cultural representatives will serve to validate racist stereotypes of Africa in the U.S. . . .

2) the Smithsonian in particular refused to help finance America's participation in FESTAC. Thus Africans should boycott African participation in the Bicentennial.[6]

If the skirmish resulted in a much reduced and slightly ragtag U.S. delegation, the conflict itself represents the very real politics involved in FESTAC's construction of a black and African community, one whose "citizens" were entitled to festival badges and identity cards conferring specific rights and privileges in Nigeria. To make matters more complex, the NAZ fracas with the State Department intensified a friction with the National Black Coalition of Canada, which felt alienated from U.S. racial politics and neglected by the NAZ liaison office in New York. They too appealed to the festival committee and president, in this case for independent zonal status in recognition of their bilingual national character and to facilitate direct communications with Lagos.[7]

Not all zonal affairs of black communities were so conflicted, but racialized identities could vary significantly between the center and periphery of the new black imperium. When the IFC broadened the horizons of blackness to include Australasian peoples, the problem of self-identification was raised with some discretion:

It has been suggested that a Zone should be created for Black People in India, New Guinea, Australia, et cetera. So far there is no direct indication as to whether the coloured people of those areas identify themselves with the Black people of the world, although there have been informal tentative inquiries at the diplomatic level from India and Australia. If the Committee decides that a Zone should be created for that area . . . it will be necessary for arrangements to be made for their representation on the Committee after the necessary consultations.[8]

The committee did so decide, within a noted "atmosphere of resistance" from those francophone African members promoting a more circumscribed definition of negritude, which we will explore in due course. For as we shall see, Nigeria would infiltrate and pressure the IFC to promote its own global vision of the black and African world with the noblesse oblige of a civilizing mission. As reported by a Nigerian FESTAC officer who visited the Australasian zone to assess problems and progress,

On the whole, the visit has been quite an eye-opener for me. I see that the Australian Blacks need help in many spheres. They must be made aware as to the achievement of Black people in the world so as to give, especially their youths, an incentive to "walk tall." Education is a vital programme that must be realised quickly and efficiently. It is vital that they impart onto children their "aboriginal identity." We talk about the plight of blacks in South Africa—at least many are educated. There is not a single aborigine doctor. Funds are needed to enable the aborigines, who are scattered all over the country, to meet regularly. I feel many of their brothers in the Black world must now be made conscious of their plight. They need more contact with them and exposure to the world in general. Above all, diplomacy *must* be used as not to antagonize the Australian government too much. The Australian government does not want help for its citizens from Nigeria or any Black country, even though the Black Australians need help desperately.[9]

The passage reveals not only the sense of political mission attending FESTAC's cultural project, but more subtly, an unconscious rhetoric of "indirect rule," in whiffs of paternalism and sympathy for children that could almost have been written by a British district officer describing one of the hill tribes in northern Nigeria. Indeed, with its use of *negroid* and *negritic,* to designate peoples and hence make them eligible for membership in the new black world, the festival reproduced the very racial taxonomies of imperialism.[10] As for the theory of their African origins, John Moriarty, the New Guinea leader of the Australasian zone, was less cooperative. "Nobody knows where we came from," he maintained, "but if you want to use Africa as the cultural test, the answer is no."[11]

In its widest conception, the new black world would have extended into the Soviet Union and the Middle East, but here FESTAC's reach exceeded its grasp. Of the festival dancers and works of art representing the "four black states" of the Soviet Union, nothing ever materialized, while the suggestion to widen the North Africa zone to include the "Black Communities of the Middle East" was blocked by its zonal representative, who maintained that there were enough political problems regarding Afro-Arab participation as things stood.[12] This issue of participation involved a very real power struggle between Senegal and Nigeria for control over the festival itself. Before turning to this important conflict, however, I will consider how FESTAC brought its zonal framework to life, building upon those of world trade fairs and national festivals to establish a transnational ritual field.

In principle, FESTAC was designed as the culmination of a series of preliminary festivals organized at zonal and national levels throughout the black and African world. According to the master plan, recruitment of representative contingents to Lagos would begin within the black countries and communities in "minifestivals" that would serve as publicity for the culminating celebration as well as arenas for talent scouting. Carifesta, hosted by Guyana, actually took place, selecting representatives for the Caribbean zone. Other preliminary festivals were Britain's Commonwealth Festival in London, Kenya's national cultural festival for the East African Community zone, Ghana's national exhibition of arts and crafts, the Republic of Benin's national festival, and Nigeria's own "Nafest," from which its cultural dances were drawn. Although these events were unevenly held, generating only a partially operative ritual field throughout FESTAC's zones, they represent two important aspects of cultural politics set into play: first, they underscore the role of ritual performance and media publicity in constituting FESTAC's black and African world as a visible and viable transnational entity, and second, they reveal a structural tension between the more inclusive zonal units of administration extending out of Lagos, and the black countries and communities which they contained. If according to official plan, FESTAC's preliminary festivals were to be directed at the zonal level, in most cases individual countries took their own initiatives with little if any zonal involvement. In the case of the Republic of Guinea's controversial participation, Head of State Sekou Touré refused to work through the designated zone, insisting upon direct relations with the IFC in Lagos.

In addition to its zonal and national festivals, FESTAC sought publicity in a variety of trade fairs around the world. By May of 1975, the festival was featured in special booths and stands that alerted diplomats and heads of state at the Frankfurt International Books Exhibition; the Frankfurt International Trade Fair; the Plovdiv Trade Fair in Bulgaria; in Zagreb, where General Marshal Josip Tito and his aides came to learn about the "Great Festival"; and at the Dakar International Trade Fair, where President Léopold Senghor met the International Secretariat delegation.[13] By linking up with a variety of world fairs, FESTAC not only promoted its information and image but also entered into a global cultural circuit of commodity exchange spanning both sides of the cold-war divide. To bolster its international visibility, publicity campaigns were mounted to feature electric signboards advertising FESTAC at international airports, together with large festival emblems for display in Nigerian embassies, international airlines offices, travel agencies, and zonal headquarters. In this fashion, FESTAC entered the "modern" global traffic of international travel and media flows, reinforced by news coverage of official visits by heads of state or their representatives to Lagos to pay their $10,000 registration fees or, conversely, covering the reception of Nigerian ministers and festival officers as they jet-setted around the black and African world to convene with zonal planners in five-star hotels. In an ultimately unrealized expression of global encapsulation, plans were developed by the Nigerian Ministry of Communications to broadcast festival events worldwide via radio live relay, television spot relay, and television satellite relay, supplemented by the Nigerian External Telecommunications Company's international telegraph and telephone service. If FESTAC was planned as spectacle to behold, the entire world would be listening and watching.

Like most imperial domains, FESTAC was formally constituted through ritual.[14] On November 8, 1973, a ceremonial hoisting of the festival flag in Ikoyi, Lagos, inaugurated the International Secretariat, which would serve as the institutional home of the IFC for the next four years. In these early days, Nigeria's Head of State, Yakubu Gowon, served as FESTAC's Co-Patron with Senegalese president Léopold Senghor, who in 1966 had hosted the first world festival of "arts nègres" under the direction of Alioune Diop in Dakar. To establish continuity with this first "FESTAC" and to build on prior experience, Diop was appointed Secretary-General of the new initiative, second in command only to Chief Anthony Enahoro, who served as FESTAC's president and principal link with Nigeria's federal military government. As the flag went up, Diop praised the festival Co-Patrons, proclaiming that "the Black people of Africa and of the Diaspora are meeting at government levels to evolve official structures of cultural solidarity." After Diop's "allocution," FESTAC's president Enahoro gave the official toast that would reverberate throughout many festival openings and events: "To our ancestors, our contemporaries and our descendants."[15]

The FESTAC flag—bearing the official festival emblem of the Benin ivory queen-mother mask—would soon become a ubiquitous sign of a developing Pan-African nation. Within the Nigerian capital, it flew alongside the national flag, marking an international dominion of black power and privilege. As promulgated in the formal agreement between the federal military government and the IFC, "The Host Government agrees that the official flag of the festival may be hoisted, flown, or displayed at the International Secretariat, the Festival Village, venues of events, along the streets of cities and towns in Nigeria, and on vehicles used by the Grand Patron, Patron, president, vice presidents, and the Secretary-General of the festival. The emblem of the festival may be similarly displayed and may be used on official festival vehicles."[16] Representing an incipient black United Nations, IFC members had diplomatic immunity in Nigeria, with access to special cars and motorcades and coveted VIP treatment.[17] Their national flags were prominently displayed at the International Secretariat while, in a complementary exchange of political icons, the FESTAC flag was distributed through them to be flown by ministers of culture and vice presidents in their respective countries and communities.

The FESTAC flag represented the emerging black world order as an inclusive, quasi-sovereign transnational entity, establishing its center in Lagos and extending its territory throughout all festival zones and communities, and consolidating a complex spectrum of meanings that pervaded (to quote Barthes in another context) FESTAC's "empire of signs." In overt allegorical terms, the flag carried an explicit message:

> The flag of the Festival is a tricolour flag of three equal perpendicular rectangles. The two outside rectangles are black and the central rectangle is in gold. Over the gold is superimposed centrally the festival emblem. The black colour represents the black people of the world. The gold color represents two ideas. It represents the wealth of the culture of the areas and peoples embraced by the festival. It also stands for the non-black peoples associated with black people in the Festival. (FESTAC '77 [1977], 137)

Within this unambiguous explanation, a less obvious "triple synthesis" took place. First, the black people of the world were being endowed with cultural value by associating a racial notion of a singular culture with that fetish of the money form that resonated with Nigerian oil, also known as "black gold." Blackness was thus implicitly informed by the substance of intrinsic monetary value (fig. 2.2). Second, the same gold rectangle that valorized black culture extended beyond it to "non-black peoples" connected with the festival but not included as "citizens." Interpreted literally as a welcoming gesture to nonblack visitors, as well as a technical reference to those second-class citizens of nonblack nations whose black communities were included in FESTAC, this secondary designation pushed the festival's frontiers beyond conventional limits. No clearer break from more militant forms of black nationalism can be found than in this allegorical blending of black into white. But FESTAC's trademark emblem "superimposed centrally" over the gold rectangle carried the greatest symbolic density and political weight within its horizons.

The choice of the sixteenth-century Benin ivory pectoral mask as FESTAC's official logo and emblem was historically ironic if not over-determined. Crafted with that naturalism that came to signify the precolonial grandeur of classic African kingship, the original ivory was seized by the British during the 1897 punitive expedition against Benin (fig. 2.3). Prized as war booty, the mask remained in the British Museum, where, together with the genre of Benin bronzes commemorat-

FIGURE 2.2 The alchemy
of blackness, 1970s. In Lahey
[1977?], unpaginated. Photograph
by Richard Saunders.

ing Edo kingship and Portuguese contact, it was exhibited in what became a virtual shrine to British imperial power and ingenuity.[18] When
the British refused to lend the mask for FESTAC due to its fragility and
possible loss or theft, unless the federal government provided an indemnity of 2 million naira (worth $3 million US at the time), outraged
Nigerians proposed a resolution at the 1976 UNESCO General Conference in Nairobi to mobilize international support for restitution.[19] As
one Nigerian reporter wrote, "Britain should be condemned for her in-
triguing attempts to undermine the success of the festival."[20] But if Britain's tenacious grip represented the historical realities of colonial theft
and neocolonial power, the proposed insurance bond or "ransom" for
the mask confirmed the extraordinary value of black and African culture
in explicit monetary terms. As Felix Idubor, the Nigerian artist who
carved a replica for FESTAC, stated, "the prestige of art in Nigeria has increased greatly since the British government insisted on the indemnity
for the original mask . . . people have laid more value on art work since
this controversial issue."[21]

There is more to be said about the Benin ivory itself, both in its original form—as an icon of kingship and queen-motherhood, Portuguese
contact, military commemoration, and ritual mimesis (see Kramer
1993, 203–4)—and as a master trope of commodity value in FESTAC's
discourse of modernity.[22] In the more tangible immediacy of the festival's iconography, however, two general axes of signification can be

FIGURE 2.3 FESTAC's trademark Benin ivory mask. Front cover of *FESTAC '77*, a souvenir book (London: Africa Journal Limited, 1977).

specified that placed Nigeria at the apex of the new black world order. First, emblazoned at the golden center of the FESTAC flag, the Benin mask as festival emblem extended what was already a politically charged symbol of Nigerian nationhood throughout the black world and its associated nonblack peoples. Within this expanded semantic field, Nigeria widened its national boundaries to invest the world of black culture with new meaning and value. Second, the festival logo fanned out laterally, as it were, holding a wide array of circulating signifiers within its orbit. These were found in the proliferation of FESTAC souvenirs and broadsheets that bore the imprint of the festival emblem, including buttons, badges, pens, coins, postage stamps, handkerchiefs, identity cards, and certificates of participation that not only were currencies of gift exchange but also connected public ceremonies and launchings to the more practical and quotidian spheres of consumption and exchange.[23] Given their symbolic significance and power, it is no wonder that the choice of the FESTAC emblem and flag initiated a more general controversy between Nigeria and Senegal over the meaning and scope of blackness.

BEYOND NEGRITUDE

"A tiger does not proclaim its tigritude . . . before it strikes." These words, coined by Nigerian playwright and activist Wole Soyinka, became something of a mantra among Nigerian critics of Senghor's distinctively francophone vision of blackness, condemned as romanticist, elitist, and at once separatist and assimiliationist. One indignant journalist wrote in a scathing piece, "The Black Frenchman," that "[n]egritude is the whiteman's trojan horse to African culture; Senghor and his French masters should be ignored."[24] In general terms, Nigerian antipathy toward the concept of negritude reflected different colonial cultures and epistemologies as well as different styles of nationalism. Anglophone African nationalist movements favored greater pragmatism with focused political and economic goals, as embodied by Kwame Nkrumah and his more instrumental notion of "African Personality" revived from Edward Wilmot Blyden. From this perspective, Senghor's negritude was too mystical and quixotic, seeking liberation and deliverance through literature, poetry, and the arts. Admittedly, Senghor's cultural politics should not be so easily dismissed, nor its contrast with realpolitik overdrawn.[25] But whatever its larger dimensions and ideological complexities, negritude was recast by FESTAC '77 according to a number of contemporary concerns, stemming from the First World Festival of Negro Arts hosted by Senghor in April 1966 and extending into regional economic integration and geopolitical competition for continental influence and cultural leadership. Powered by its oil economy, Nigeria would win the battle, imposing its will on the IFC to remake the black world in its national image.

Nigeria's break from Senegal can be framed as a tension between succession and usurpation. FESTAC '77 was initially conceived as a continuation of Senghor's First World Festival, in terms of both organization and personnel. Although more modest in scale, the Dakar festival had built a new national theater and *Musée Dynamique,* as well as new flats and hotels for visitors. It featured music, drama, film, plastic arts, poetry, and prose in addition to traditional and modern dance among its major cultural events, with a *Colloque* of black intellectuals to highlight and refine the philosophy of *négritude.*[26] Nigeria's presence at Dakar was enhanced by its honorific Star Country status, which bestowed a leading role in festival events that not only accorded Nigeria a special exhibition in the Hall of Honor in Dakar's Hotel de Ville, but also conferred responsibility for hosting the second FESTAC in the future. Senegal's choice of Nigeria for this role angered several francophone West African countries, who felt overlooked; and if Senghor defended his decision on strictly cultural grounds, describing Nigeria as a "Black Greece" at the opening of the Star Country exhibition, he would criticize Nigeria's lack of finesse in a way that captured francophone ambivalence and disdain. As Nzekwu (1966, 86) described the mixed response,

> The exhibition, the largest Nigeria has ever mounted abroad, was designed to give the visitor general information on the country's agriculture, arts and crafts, education, forests, government, industry and mineral wealth. Despite the fact that the exhibition was criticized as being a little unimaginative because it had a trade fair flavour; though it fell short of the expectations of President Senghor who intended that the exhibition should feature Nigerian culture, and notwithstanding the fact that the festival office imposed a gate fee of 200 CFA (5s-10d) which drew the exclamation *"escroquerie!"* [swindle!] from French-speaking visitors to the exhibition—much to the embarrassment of Nigerian officials—it was attended by thousands of visitors including Emperor Haile Selassie of Ethiopia and the Gambian Prime Minister, Dr Dauda Jawara.

Not even Wole Soyinka was immune from such *snobisme* when the world premiere of *Kongi's Harvest*—a political satire on African dictatorships—suffered a walkout by "the vast medal-bestrewn members of Dakar's social elite" during intermission.[27] If on a more popular note, the Juju-Ashiko music of I. K. Dairo and his Blue Spots Band drew warm applause, as did the sensuous movements of Ondo's Obitun dancers, in general many Nigerians were offended and demoralized. Adding national insult to artistic injury, the clause in the festival agreement providing that the Nigerian and Senegalese flags fly together was never honored. Nigeria's flag languished between those of Niger and Uganda or Mauritania, lost in the alphabet of African nations.

But if Nigeria felt spurned by Senegal's hauteur at Dakar, FESTAC '77 offered ample opportunity for revenge, although it is difficult to identify the causal pathways between former incidents and more regional trends. Whether Nigeria's past grievances were nursed or forgotten, the Second World Festival would move systematically away from Senegal and beyond *négritude*. Initially conceived as a continuation of the Dakar festival, the second FESTAC retained Senegal's first festival president (and editor of *Présence Africaine*), Alioune Diop, as Secretary-General of the IFC, to gain from his experience and expertise, with Senghor and

Gowon serving as festival Co-Patrons. Troubles began, however, as early as 1973, with dissatisfaction over the festival flag and motif. The francophone zones recommended the Dakar festival symbol for the second festival, to represent the black world as an extension of Senghor's *négritude* project. Objections were raised over the suitability of the symbol in an anglophone challenge to Senegal's cultural politics. As noted in the IFC minutes,

> It will be recalled that the Committee agreed to adopt the Motif of the Dakar Festival and to incorporate it in the Festival Flag. Representations have been received objecting to the nature of the Dakar Motif on the grounds that it is too totem-like and does not present Black culture in an illuminating manner. One of such representations was made by the West Africa (Anglophone) Zonal Meeting recently held in Monrovia, Liberia. Accordingly, vice presidents are invited to bring with them to the next meeting any suggestions they may have regarding a suitable Motif and Flag.[28]

It is difficult to judge how calculated this move may have been to impose Nigeria's Benin ivory emblem on a new FESTAC flag, using the pretext of open debate to push a national symbol into a transnational domain; but as the same minutes note, "the Francophone VP was very angry over the rejection of the Dakar emblem . . . or the possibility of shelving the issue."[29] It seems that the Senegalese bloc could see the writing on the wall, sensing that procedural protocol would be used against them. There was also the sting of the criticism itself, which dismissed negritude's master symbol as "too totem-like," thus eliding the primitive with the aesthetics of primitivism. A glance at the Dakar emblem reveals a modernist if somewhat mystic sensibility, captured by the words of the artist who created it: "The black man, at the same time a receptor and a receptacle of the effluviums and the waves of the universe, assimilates, translates, and returns them to the world, magnified and brightened by his human and spiritual grandeur. This is Negro Art."[30] By rejecting this glyph of negritude for the more sober naturalism of Benin court art, the committee rejected the doctrine itself.

The change of festival motif along with the change of name from "Negro Art" to "Black and African Culture" signaled the broadening horizons of Africanity. It also triggered a temporary Senegalese boycott. At issue was a seemingly technical point that resounded with broader political implications. If the Senegalese-led francophone zones accepted the creation of a North African zone with great reluctance, they firmly opposed such "Arab" participation in the Colloquium, which was to focus on exclusively black cultural and philosophical themes. The question was whether North African Arabs were racially entitled to partake in studies and discussions of "Negro-African" civilization, since, as the Senegalese contended, they belonged to a distinctively Arab-Berber cultural zone. As a compromise gesture, Senghor considered granting North Africans nonparticipating "observer" status, but this suggestion was crushed as discriminatory, raising the specter of black second-class citizenship and undermining the spirit of black unity and brotherhood. On this issue Nigeria stood firm, highlighting its role in spearheading the move to include North Africans in the first place and defending the decision on political and cultural grounds. Politically, the North African states were full-fledged members of the OAU, and were thus entitled to full participation in all festival events. To deny them this privilege could undermine the OAU itself. Culturally, they were linked to Sub-Saharan Africa by Islamic religion and the Arabic language, the latter infusing regional languages such as Hausa and Swahili. And geographically, they belonged to the African continent. In one of many official statements by Commander O. P. Fingesi, commissioner for special duties who took over as president of FESTAC '77, Nigeria's stand became a matter of military policy:

> The Federal Military Government has re-affirmed its stand that participation in the Second World Black and African Festival of Arts and Culture should be open to all member States of the Organisation of African Unity, Black Governments and Communities outside Africa and Liberation Movements recognised by the O.A.U . . . it will be tantamount to sheer prejudice if we prohibit the full and wholehearted participation of the North African Arabs to the Festival.[31]

The battle lines were drawn. Senegal organized a faction of West African states who threatened to withdraw—with Senegal actually announcing its boycott—if North African Arabs were fully involved in the Colloquium.

The Nigerian response, working through the IFC, was swift and brutal. As newspaper editorials denounced Senghor's "unstately outburst" and neocolonial mentality ("Today, I want to hammer down the lid on the dead orphan called Negritude . . . a mummification of the romantic African past, oblivious to contemporary material advances"),[32] Commander Fingesi removed the increasingly isolated Alioune Diop from his post as Secretary-General on the grounds that his loyalties to Senghor and the festival at large would otherwise be divided. Fingesi's official statement is worth quoting at length, because it reveals the unilateral direction of the decision itself—made by Nigeria in the committee's name—and belies, by Fingesi's boastful denial, the importance of oil money in advancing Nigeria's political agenda. Addressing the ninth meeting of the IFC, he announced,

> The Secretary General in the person of Dr. Alioune Diop had to be relieved of his duties following the confirmation that the Senegalese government had taken definite decision to boycott the festival. I am sure that all our Zonal Vice-Presidents were fully briefed on this matter through the number of documents we had sent to them during the past few weeks. You all know that the Senegalese decision to boycott the festival was in consequence of the decision of the International Festival Committee to allow full participation in the Festival to all member States of the Organisation of African Unity. . . . That decision of the Senegalese government to boycott the festival did consequently compromise the position of Dr. Alioune Diop, who is a Senegalese citizen, as well as the Secretary General of the International Festival Committee. It must be emphasized that the move to relieve Dr. Alioune Diop . . . was in no way a direct personal affront to him. It was a decision that had to be made on issues of principle as well as pragmatic realities. What was foremost in our mind in all the processes of our decision was not the issue of personality cultism, nor that of political aggrandizement, but rather the issue of our objective commitment to a functionally positive organisation for the success of the 2nd World Black and African Festival of Arts and Culture. *Nigeria, as the host country does not, has never, and will never, under any circumstances, in matters affecting the Black and African Peoples of this world, utilize her economic fortune to intimidate any member of the Black and African World. . . . It is therefore unthinkable that Nigeria will use her God-given wealth to hoodwink or intimidate any member of the Black and African Communities of the world.*[33] (my emphasis)

The double entendres of this pious pronouncement are quite abrasive, since Senghor's "personality cultism" and political grandstanding were precisely what was highlighted in the popular press, as was the oil bonanza that galvanized Nigeria's muscle.[34] It hardly seems coincidental that the salaries of festival committee members were doubled from the previous OAU scale at this very time, based on the Udoji Commission awards, "in order to retain the services of experienced Officers" for FESTAC.[35]

Eventually, Senegal capitulated to the more open Colloquium in a move that diminished Senghor's influence and prestige while enhancing Nigeria's stature. Senegal lost Alioune Diop to Cameroonian Ambroise Mbia as the new Secretary-General, and relinquished control over the Colloquium through the reorganization of the Cultural Council and the demotion of Father Englebert Mveng.[36] With so much lost and nothing gained, why had Senegal been so adamant about excluding North Africans from what was widely perceived as the "heart" of the festival? As Senghor himself explained, it was not based on any deep-rooted prejudice, for although he was a minority Catholic, did he not incorporate Arabic and Islamic learning into the national education system? Officially, the problem was one of philosophical principle. As zonal vice president Alioune Sene explained, "We do not see how the non-blacks with different culture . . . can contribute effectively to the projection and promotion of black culture."[37] Such a statement reflects what Sartre called the "anti-racist racism" of negritude in no uncertain terms, but more than philosophical principle was at stake in Senegal's stand on the Arab question.

Two underlying issues, I would argue, motivated Senegal's convictions. The first concerns the thrashing that Senghor's ideas of negritude received by Arab nations at the Algiers Pan-African Cultural Festival of 1969, which mobilized a more radical political agenda for the OAU with Senegal's regional rival, Guinea, taking a leading role under the militant Marxist Sekou Touré. For Touré and the Committee for African Revolution, negritude had become a reactionary idea that had outlived its role in anticolonial struggle, serving to divide the postcolonial African continent along racial lines and divert the imperatives of organized revolutionary action. For Senghor, the colloquium of FESTAC '77 would restore negritude to its rightful place as a suitable philosophy and national policy for black Africa, provided the North African voice was repressed. If the OAU was moving away from negritude in favor of more materialist state socialist programs, Senghor could recover and bolster his ideas among the "authentic" citizens of the black and African world.

The second factor contributing to Senghor's belligerence concerns Senegal's more general eclipse by Nigeria in the newly formed Economic Community of West African States (ECOWAS), an effort toward regional economic integration designed to eliminate tariffs and standardize trade procedures, to benefit the fifteen associated francophone and anglophone West African nations dealing with international trading partners. The provisions and protocols of the ECOWAS treaty—approved in May 1975 and signed on November 6, 1976, thus coinciding with the crucial planning period of FESTAC '77—are complex and in some cases obscure, ranging from controls on licensing, import duties, and the re-exportation or "dumping" of goods to the relative contributions of member states into the community's compensation and development fund. But general developments within ECOWAS cast the Senegalese conflict in the broader context of Nigeria's oil economy, grounding the ideological debates over the meaning of blackness in the changing topology of the petro-naira.

From its inception, the major goal of ECOWAS—to break the structures of economic dependency upon Western markets by fostering interregional trade—was linked to issues of monetary cooperation and foreign exchange. Reflecting former colonial jurisdictions and territories, West Africa was regionally divided into the franc zone and the pound-sterling area. In 1962, francophone countries had formed a currency union in which the Colonie Françaises d'Afrique franc (CFA) retained fixed parity with the French franc, with convertibility guaranteed by the French government.[38] This arrangement gave France considerable control over the economies of this zone (then Dahomey, Ivory Coast, Mauritania, Nigeria, Senegal, Togo, and Upper Volta), but also had the reciprocal effect of stabilizing and strengthening them with universal access to foreign exchange. Linked by a common and convertible currency that was underwritten by the French government, the francophone zone had already achieved a heightened sense of regional unity, reflecting to some degree the former integrity of French West Africa as an administrative area, but also the commutative power of a circulating value form that distinguished francophone countries from their anglophone neighbors. The anglophone countries of the Gambia, Sierra Leone, Ghana, and Nigeria were similarly associated with the pound sterling area as a fiscal field, but one that formed a monetary area rather than a currency union. The difference is slim but important, in that unlike a currency union, members of a monetary area may use separate currencies that are rendered equivalent by their relationship to sterling. If official reserves were held in sterling, the sterling area countries pursued independent foreign exchange and reserve holding policies, unlike the franc zone, granting greater autonomy to each national economy. In 1972, when Britain allowed the pound to "float," it relinquished exchange control over its former African economies, allowing them to fend for themselves. By comparison with the franc zone, the anglophone economies were less stable and integrated. Their periods of growth and expansion in export commodities such as cocoa and coffee were offset by fluctuations in world demand and the extractive appetites of state marketing boards.

To promote more even development throughout the West African region, ECOWAS considered various monetary instruments that would facilitate direct remittance of funds between countries (thus bypassing France and London) and create mechanisms for pooling regional

TABLE 2.1 Foreign assets (in millions of Special Drawing Rights)

	1969	1970	1971	1972	1973	1974	1975
Benin	7.68	15.8	23.11	26.71	27.99	28.4	12.23
Gambia	4.88	6.61	8.21	8.55	10.93	18.67	22.06
Ghana	62.26	56.95	73.56	111.86	170.1	95.25	148.71
Ivory Coast	72.81	107.01	84.02	81.89	74.76	53.82	84.38
Liberia	—	—	—	—	—	11.88	12.14
Mali	8.24	6.39	5.73	7.99	7.31	6.59	—
Niger	6.87	19.1	31.56	38.85	42.93	37.28	41.78
Nigeria	133.1	222.9	393.5	347.2	540.8	**4807.2**	**4991.5**
Senegal	6.28	22.41	23.14	36.19	10.18	5.29	25.57
Sierra Leone	23.05	22.44	23.05	27.88	34.83	36.52	21.69
Togo	26.88	36.08	38.07	34.26	32.07	44.6	34.33
Upper Volta	26.34	37.14	40.41	44.6	52.97	68.94	62.89

Source: International Monetary Fund, *International Financial Statistics,* vol. 29, no. 7; adapted from Ijewere 1984, 233.

foreign exchange reserves. In the absence of a uniform currency, the community established a West African Unit of Account linked to Special Drawing Rights on the International Monetary Fund, in terms of which national currencies and foreign exchange would be adjusted and converted.[39] Within this field of commensurable money forms, oil-rich Nigeria gained new power and prestige, emerging as the regional center of gravity in the new community of interest. With foreign assets that dwarfed those of all other nations combined, Nigeria held inordinate economic influence, investing in some developing industries among member states (cement in Benin, iron mining in Guinea) while agreeing to underwrite 30% of the community's entire annual budget (table 2.1).[40] Discussions were even held to establish the CFA and the Nigerian naira as immediately convertible currencies for the community, placing Nigeria's symbol of monetary value on a par with the entire francophone zone, although these plans never materialized.

The francophone countries and their currency union were clearly overshadowed by the rising giant of black Africa. Lagos was picked for the new ECOWAS headquarters against fierce opposition from Senegal, which argued for a smaller country and refused to sign the final treaty on November 6, 1976. Ironically, one of the very first meetings to establish ECOWAS had taken place in Dakar as early as 1967, just one year after the festival there. Resurrected and dominated by Nigeria, ECOWAS

was now ready for FESTAC '77, having traveled a parallel journey from Dakar to Lagos.

In terms of brute economic and political power, Nigeria clearly surpassed Senegal as leader of the new black world order, dismissing the outdated philosophy of negritude while broadening the horizons of cultural citizenship from Lagos to North Africa and beyond. As host country of FESTAC and new ECOWAS headquarters, Nigeria was indeed in a strong position to impose her vision of blackness and Africanity by underwriting festival costs as well as the lion's share of regional development. Nor did Senegal's frustration with Nigeria on both of these fronts go unnoticed at the time. In his discussion (delivered in 1976) of tariff and indigenization policies, Ezeani (1984, 508) observed: "Differences between Nigeria and Senegal are increasingly surfacing. First, it was over the forthcoming Second World Festival of Arts to be hosted by Nigeria. Senegal had accused Nigeria of using the oil wealth to impose her will on the whole of Africa. Again, maybe as a result of this, Senegal refused to ratify the ECOWAS Treaty." While true, I am arguing beyond the instrumentalities of material wealth and power, to grasp the more pervasive phenomenology of value forms generated by oil. If Nigeria's strong currency could buy influence in specific cultural, economic, and political arenas, its robust exchange value (1 naira = $1.60 US in 1976) underwrote the "credibility" and veracity of a broader range of discourses and representations that projected the Nigerian nation throughout the black and African world.

As Nigeria's wealth became the wealth of all black nations—in ECOWAS, the OAU, and through FESTAC itself—its nation form qua money form exceeded its own national boundaries, converting national "cultures," like their currencies, into racialized idioms of equivalent value. When such "conversions" occurred in FESTAC's rhetoric of black mobilization and solidarity, whether voiced on the airwaves or choreographed onstage, Nigeria presided over a field of cultural production in which truth-value and exchange value were mutually reinforced. Like a national trademark, the FESTAC emblem guaranteed Nigerian authority over the expansive black world. Nor were such representations consigned to "mere" discourse and iconography. In the more technical terms of economic indigenization, Nigerian citizenship was legally redefined along African commodity flows rather than national boundaries. Under the Nigerian Enterprises Promotion Decree 1972, officially reenacted on January 13, 1977—just two days before FESTAC opened—a Nigerian citizen included "any person of African descent, not being a citizen of Nigeria, who is a national of any country in Africa which is a member of OAU and who resides and carries on business in Nigeria" (Ezeani 1984, 504), given that the person's country "accords a reciprocal treatment of Nigerian nationals" (ibid., 511).[41]

As new blood and money transformed the meaning of Nigerian citizenship, Nigeria redeemed its somewhat tarnished image within the OAU and emerged as a central mediator and power broker. Gradualist and conservative compared with Kwame Nkrumah's clarion call for a United States of Africa in the first days of independence, Nigeria had split with Ghana over the 1960 Congo crisis, siding with UN support of Moise Tshombe's secessionist government against Patrice Lumumba, and even backing the CIA-directed USA-Belgium "Mercy Peace Mission" in 1963 that presaged Lumumba's assassination and Mobutu Sese Seko's long dictatorship. When the OAU summit convened in Accra in 1965, after protracted struggles with francophone confrères, and condemned Ian Smith's racist government in Rhodesia, Nigeria refused to endorse the severing of diplomatic ties with Britain recommended by Ghana, Guinea, Egypt, Tanzania, and members of the "Casablanca bloc"; instead, it held a Commonwealth Prime Ministers' Conference for Britain in Lagos. Nigeria's perceived neocolonial loyalties undermined OAU unity and extended into the economic sphere as well, where, breaking with the socialist countries that sought to improve the terms of trade with the West by forming a protected African market, Nigeria associated with the European Economic Community to improve her own market share. As one editorial recollected, "Nigeria's role in African international relations from 1960-66 was dysfunctional . . . Nigeria dealt a staggering blow to the OAU."[42]

Nigeria's place and direction within the OAU changed dramatically after the civil war and the oil boom. Taking a more militant stand against colonialism and apartheid, it increased regular contributions to the special fund of the OAU Liberation Committee to the tune of 252,000 naira, supplying trucks and heavy artillery as well as medicine, food, and clothing to leaders of African nationalist movements in Mozambique, Angola, Namibia, and Zimbabwe.[43] Spearheading a new philosophy of pragmatism for the OAU in the 1970s, Nigerian leadership advocated "structural changes" fostering "economic and other inter-African areas of cooperation." These included a continental bloc in negotiating the terms of the Lomé Convention,[44] openly reconciling with the four African states that had accorded diplomatic recognition to Biafra, and calling for harmonization with North African "Arab" member states—an issue that was underscored by their inclusion in the FESTAC Colloquium.[45] As oil and money mixed with culture and politics, FESTAC became a veritable offstage forum for OAU affairs, evidenced by one reporter's observation that "President Kaunda's increasingly militant stand against Rhodesia and South Africa prior to this week's crucial OAU meeting in Lusaka was preceded by personal talks with both the Nigerian and the Ghanaian Governments at FESTAC's inaugural ceremonies."[46] At the same Lusaka meeting, the Nigerian delegation proposed the creation of a Pan-African military high command, receiving unanimous OAU support, although the decision was "deferred" to accommodate American mediation in Rhodesia. Describing the Nigerian reaction, the same reporter recorded in a subsequent dispatch that

> the militant mood in Nigeria is unabated and a prominent member of the ruling Military Council showed his dissatisfaction with the delay by commenting during a FESTAC diplomatic party: "What is Africa waiting for? We can afford to buy rockets from Russia if the West won't help us liberate Southern Africa. We want African independence from Cairo to the Cape."[47]

Inverting the imperial rhetoric of Cecil Rhodes ("from Cape Town to Cairo") in a counterimperial vision of continental liberation, these comments reflect Nigeria's growing influence as an elder statesman of Africa, building new economic frameworks and mediating disputes while flexing its muscle with the West. FESTAC signaled new life for the OAU, new blood for the black and African world, and a turning point for African economic development.

If this latter agenda was openly embraced by the U.S. ambassador to the United Nations, Andrew Young, whose high visibility at FESTAC brought black and African business interests to the work of liberation, it found more systematic expression in Nigeria's aggressive promotion of the New International Economic Order (NIEO) proposed by a series of United Nations conferences on trade and development in 1976–77. Within this discursive and institutional arena, Nigeria's projection into a new global order achieved its widest scope, consolidating ECOWAS, OAU, and OPEC energies to help alter the terms of trade between "the rock-bottom prices paid for the developing countries' raw materials and the ever-rocketing prices of the manufactured products they import from the industrialised nations."[48] With the nonaligned oil-producing states using petroleum as a bargaining chip, proposals for new monetary machinery and the establishment of a Commonwealth Fund would guarantee stable prices and lower costs for developing economies, so the argument went. Nigeria's high profile in these debates focused on the economic imperatives of national and regional self-sufficiency, preferential treatment for developing countries in international trade, the right to nationalize foreign businesses, and the full sovereignty of member nations over their natural resources.[49] In the context of Nigeria's oil economy, the nationalization of foreign capital naturalized not only the wealth of the Nigerian nation, in the idiom of its God-given petroleum, but that of all black and African nations, following FESTAC's transmutations of black gold into black culture. Calling on the United States to rally support for concerted action, Lieutenant General Olusegun Obasanjo used FESTAC's language of racial inclusion: "the imperative now is the creation of a world in which nations will relate to one another on the basis of equality, understanding and mutual respect."[50] Thus the broadest horizon of Nigeria's black world embraced the new international economic order at large.

RETURN OF THE NATIVE

"Ordinarily the term diaspora refers to a movement and dispersion away from a centre," FESTAC Grand Patron Obasanjo explained in his opening address, adding, "I would like to suggest that a movement towards the source is also diasporic." Identifying the complementary flows of FESTAC's global cultural economy—one of centrifugal dispersion, the other of centripetal convergence—the general welcomed the "children of the diaspora . . . back to one of your homelands here on African soil." The ingathering of "tribes" on Nigerian soil from all reaches of the black world was more of a homecoming for some than for others. As representatives convened in Lagos different modes of reckoning common descent came into play, as with any large family reunion. Roots-motivated black Americans inspired by Alex Haley's personal odyssey experienced mixed degrees of cultural identification and alienation, reflecting an ambivalence voiced in the earlier writings of Langston Hughes, James Baldwin, and Richard Wright.[51] For the Cuban contingent, the link was ethnically specific: "We Cubans have realized that our forefathers were from the Yoruba race of Nigeria and coming here is a blessing which we and our children will ever live to cherish."[52] But the logic of FESTAC would convert such differences into equivalent expressions of common heritage and identity. In subsequent chapters, we will examine the mechanisms of this conversion in greater detail. Here I will sketch the broader contours of the diasporic return as the converse of Nigeria's self-projection throughout the black and African world, which mirrored not only the global circuits of Nigerian oil but also the forms of capital for which it was exchanged, and the wealth that accrued to the state.

Several images from FESTAC '77 feature films highlight the global pathways traveled by the representatives of the fifty-six black nations

and communities that eventually participated in the festival. For example, *Black Heritage,* produced by the Federal Ministry of Information,
opens with an aerial view of Lagos and the National Theatre, where, the
voice-over tells us, the upcoming events will have the "whole world"
watching. The camera cuts to the newly built Murtala International Airport, where Nigerian honor guards in military formation roll out red
carpets for visiting heads of state. Long shots of Air Gabon, Air Afrique,
and Nigerian Airways aircraft establish that the national carriers of
black power and culture have landed at the hub of the new black world
system. "The children of the greatest diaspora," we are told, "are returning to their origin." As the montage shifts to the official march-past
in Nigeria's national stadium, ethnic, cultural, and national difference
is assimilated to rank-and-file unison. Never mind that some contingents were more prepared and organized than others. The group from
Guinea, like the Libyans, marched in a perfect Soviet-style goose step,
accenting their militant politics with a placard bearing the words "No
Negritude, No Whititude!" in a left-wing jab against Senghor. By contrast, one observer reported that "the Aborigines and the American
blacks had a lot in common; neither group knew what was expected
of them in the parade," and went on to describe how "the Aborigines
entered the arena in European dress, and all they could do in the circumstances was wave boomerangs."[53] Warren McIntosh, an actor from
Chicago's Kuumba Workshop who marched with the casually clad
American delegation, described a moment of desperate if inspired improvisation: "We wondered what we could do. All the other countries
had their acts together, and we felt that we had to do something. Finally,
some dude said 'let's sing "We Shall Overcome,"' and so we did. The response was a standing ovation."[54] But despite the differences and contrasts between representative contingents—the variations in clothing,
uniforms, choreography, and even phenotype—each group is shown
bearing a placard stamped with the FESTAC emblem next to the name
of the country, objectified and subsumed by Nigeria's symbol of Pan-
African wealth and sovereignty (fig. 2.4).

If the march-past homogenized the new and expanded black and African world beneath the master trope of black "exchange value," the
effect was enhanced within a variety of performative and discursive
arenas, two of which—choreography and archeology—warrant preliminary consideration. In numerous accounts, FESTAC demonstrated the
fundamental unity of black peoples and cultures through dance. Expert
choreographers like Molly Ahy (1980, 27) argued that dance "was that
common meeting ground which made it possible for African peoples
from the Americas, the Caribbean and other far flung areas to be able to

FIGURE 2.4 U.S. contingent in the FESTAC march-past. In Lahey [1977?], unpaginated. Photograph by Richard Saunders.

identify with Africans and Blacks on the continent and as far as Papua New Guinea and Australia." Repeated like a leitmotif, commonality of movement came to represent common cultural and even racial heritage, producing an aesthetics of recognition among participants and observers that transformed all blacks into Africans. This theme underwent a secondary elaboration among Nigerian observers, who condensed Africa into Nigeria as the sanctified ground of dissemination and return. Thus in the words of journalist Bob Ume, "all blacks of the world can be traced to the same stock, taking into consideration their cultural background. Their dances are very much concentrated on the waistline, wriggling, and jumping and sweating it out. Their masquerades are almost identical that one takes a particular country's masquerade for the other." Thus far the statement reads FESTAC's logic of commensurability and equivalence into history, transposing (in the language of structuralist poetics) the paradigmatic axis of substitution onto the syntagmatic axis of contiguity. Similarity of movement as witnessed in the present implied common generic and even genetic origins in Africa, regardless of the actual "content" of the dances. But Ume takes this strategy an important step further, identifying the locus of origins in Nigeria. As he explains, "One fact came off right on the top and this is that of every dance group that came forward from any part of Africa, and the black world, there is an identical group in Nigeria. Could it be that Nigeria was *the actual exporting nation of all these cultural heritage among blacks?*"[55] The passage reads as an allegory of the oil boom on two levels: first, in the parallel it creates between oil and culture, both of which come out of Nigeria as an "exporting nation"; and second, in its chronotopic displacement of the present into the past, whereby Nigerian wealth naturalizes the nation as the historical source of black heritage.

Within this genealogical framework, specific attributions provided documentary "proof" of Nigeria's long-lost extended family. In the appropriately named *Nigerian Observer,* Charles Okpei named actual relatives:

> The first thing that strikes my mind about FESTAC is the similarity of arts and culture of all black men of the world. Most of their dances are quite similar. Think of a Brazilian dance from across the Atlantic Ocean that has exactly the same steps and body movements with the Oloku dance of the Binis. I watched a dance from Uganda with mouth agape because [of] the re-vibrating chest shaking of the female dancers that was in no way different from the "Ole-Igbama" dance of the Orie people of Isoko Local Government Area. The Cubans performed a dance with steps and music that resemble "Udhe" of the Isokos and Urhobos very much.[56]

There is no doubt that Brazilian and Cuban religious dances have numerous Nigerian analogues, although questions of origins and the Ugandan link remain dubious at best. But the ethnohistorical record was never really at issue. More to the point was how FESTAC's ethnohistorical poetics interpreted formal similarities in terms of common descent. This is a methodological problem that plagues all substantive African diaspora research, but in FESTAC's narratives of black unity and heritage, it converted Nigerian oil into black culture and blood, and transformed the nation into a privileged homeland.

Mirroring the complementary flows of Nigerian oil and global capital, the "children" of the diaspora were brought into the present. Just as the oil-rich Nigerian nation receded into a genealogy of ancient origins, so the primitives of the Pacific and the ur-aboriginals of Australia were rendered contemporary and African by their arrival in Lagos. The Aborigines in particular posed a challenge to FESTAC's global genealogy, in that their own sacred traditions and putatively ancient Dreamtime had nothing to do with Africa, as the leader of their delegation insisted. Nonetheless, they were accommodated by the language of space-time compression (to invoke Harvey's phenomenology of flexible accumulation) as ancient representatives of the new black world order—a kind of chronotope in reverse. As a lead FESTAC article in *Africscope* explained, "Today the black world while seeing Africa as a source, sees the continent from different perceptual spaces in time. The blacks of the Pacific area, are millions of years removed from the source but the racial memory is intact in the spirit of their creative expression."[57] In genealogical terms, the depth of black migration was thus pushed back to extend its global span. If Africa was lost to Aboriginal consciousness, racial memory endured in their works, and would be reawakened by the festival itself.

To ratify this mythic return of Aborigines and Pacific Negritos to Africa, together with their collaterals around the globe, a number of archeological discourses established a theory of ancient black migration. The planning minutes of FESTAC's exhibit Africa and the Origin of Man invoked the authority of science to validate the global reach of the new black world order: "It is known that there was a belt of Black people stretching from southern Europe, North Africa and Arabia into India and Southern China and from East Africa across the Pacific Ocean. Archeological evidence, largely ignored, exists to prove this."[58] Various migration routes were posited with supplementary cultural and linguistic "evidence," including worship of the mother goddess, matriarchy, the cult of the serpent, ancestor worship, as well as vowel harmony, phonological correspondences, and cognate lexical items. One Colloquium paper proposed an Afro-Asiatic protofamily that unified what would become "two great races" and established the black basis of civilization:

> Recent discoveries in the field of archeology enable anthropologists to postulate that the Dravidians of India, the Negroes of Africa and the numerous tribes scattered throughout the hilly regions of the Mediterranean and Near East regions are the survivors of those blackish races which once reigned supreme and laid the foundations of civilization much before the advent of Indo-European and Semitic Civilizations.[59]

An impressive array of disciplinary and methodological approaches established the scientific foundations of FESTAC's global claims. X-rays of Egyptian mummies, images of blacks in pre-Columbian Meso-American art, and representative "physical types" from Australia, Indonesia, Melanesia, and Micronesia, supplemented by eyewitness accounts of contemporary travelers, were all proposed for the elaborate Africa and the Origin of Man exhibit that would establish the festival's scientific charter, reaching back to the primatological dawn of humanity and ending with the depredations of colonialism. Because such a powerful exhibit carried great epistemological and political weight, it would belong to no particular nation, but emerged as a collaborative project with strong contributions from Tanzania, Kenya, Ethiopia, and Egypt. In what sense, then, was Nigeria able to take national credit for the origin of humankind?

According to the basic homology between the global circuits of Nigerian oil and the expanded frontiers of the black and African world, Nigeria's expansive vision, which it had successfully imposed on the IFC, was now scientifically grounded. Indeed, since Africa was the birthplace of humanity, it became the precondition of all "races" and civilizations. But in subtle ways, according to the explicitly *subjective* mechanisms of measuring blackness, Nigeria's place in the scientific exhibit was further enhanced, not backward in time to the dawn of human history, but phenomenologically, in the present, through the mechanisms of racial recognition and self-identification that the exhibit originally proposed. According to plan, these included "various participatory techniques such as the use of mirrors, head and body projections, and tracings in clear acrylic to be utilized for personal comparison, identification and individual involvement. Thus those attending the festival can 'find themselves.' Photo silk-screen techniques are used to transfer photographs onto thick ($^3/_4$") acrylic sheets."[60] In an uncanny permutation of commodity fetishism (uncomfortably close to racial anthropometry), subjective identity would here be reflected in the object of (scientific) production and then mechanically reproduced for personal consumption and verification as a memento of FESTAC's mission. Nigeria not only underwrote exhibition costs, housing the display in the National Theatre (where it still stands), but more important, it enabled self-identification within its expansive vision of the black and African world. The Nigerian homeland was thus further sanctified by the Africa and the Origin of Man exhibit, for through it participants *found themselves* by locating their *place* within FESTAC's Pan-African genealogy.

As we have seen, this dialectic of self-reflection and recognition pervaded a variety of images and advertisements that proliferated during Nigeria's commodity boom. Even the mirrors in the National Theatre's lavatories bore the stencil of the FESTAC logo, framing the reflected faces in Nigeria's master symbol of black culture and commodity value. If Nigeria could not interpolate itself as the locus of human origins in the past, it could *interpellate* itself into the subjective gaze of the black participant in the present—through the individual and collective reawakening of racial memory.

The subjective apparatus of the exhibit on human origins was never fully realized. After Gowon was deposed in the 1975 coup, FESTAC was "scaled back" to control excessive spending and corruption. The "origin of man" remained didactic, narrating a grand epic of human-African evolution and migration throughout the globe, but the body projections and acrylic transfers never materialized.[61] Nonetheless, the original design reveals a telling convergence of subjective experience with objective truth that characterized the "seeing is believing" phenomenology of development during Nigeria's oil boom, as well as the compression of the past into the present accomplished by FESTAC's mythic return of the native. As Nigerian oil flowed out and global capital flowed in, the blood of Africa's past was fortified by the tonic of contemporary petrodollars.

THE THREE related themes discussed in this chapter—FESTAC's imperial anatomy, the remapping of blackness, and the Africanization of the Australian Aborigine—represent cultural manifestations of Nigeria's oil economy as it peaked in the 1970s. The correspondence between the global circuits of transnational oil and the new black world order, as we have seen, was hardly one of direct reflection, but developed dialectically as Nigeria gained new presence on the world stage. The sheer size and scale of FESTAC's zonal administration, with Nigerians holding key offices and controls including the IFC's formidable purse strings, were perhaps the most direct cultural expressions of the internationalization of the state by oil. FESTAC politics became an international affair as black nations and communities negotiated the new horizons of blackness at trade fairs and preliminary festivals and through the circulation and exchange of media images and cultural icons. We have also seen how Nigeria broke from Senegal's leadership and philosophy of negritude, changing the meaning and scope of blackness in a manner that complemented Nigeria's growing influence in regional economic integration (ECOWAS), the Organisation of African Unity, and even the New International Economic Order. In legal as well as symbolic terms, Nigerian citizenship exceeded its national boundaries in a new black order financed by oil. Finally, we have explored the various mythic, choreographic, and archeological discourses that Nigeria deployed to establish its apical status in FESTAC's noble genealogy, transforming Nigerian blood and soil into a sacred center and homeland for its "children" in the diaspora. In this latter capacity, FESTAC mirrored not only the outflow of Nigerian oil but also the complementary inflow of money and commodities.

In more abstract terms, however, these themes represent specific modalities of cultural commodification within FESTAC's imaginary. The model that I introduce here schematically, but will elaborate and refine in the following chapters, establishes a basic equivalence between blackness and oil—not as a simple metaphor or parallelism, but as a matrix of value transformations between figures of blood, at one extreme, and money forms at the other. The transformations are generated by processes of commodification fueled by oil capitalism but extending into black cultural production, including plays, dances, exhibits, and events as well as souvenirs, replicas, and icons of commemoration and exchange. It is through such transformations, we have seen, that the Nigerian nation form (qua commodity form) extended its national boundaries; that national and ethnic displays and performances could be "objectified" as equivalent icons of identity and value; and that the colonial subject of the past became the black citizen of the present. We can even argue, from this preliminary sketch, that the exchange value of different commodities, measured by the general equivalent of the money form, corresponds to the commensurability of black nations and communities according to the general equivalent of common blood and racial heritage. As the following chapters will demonstrate, it is through such conversions and transfusions—some quite direct, others highly mediated—that FESTAC endowed blackness with racial meaning, commodity value, and an implicitly Nigerian national character.

THE SPECTACLE OF CULTURE

CHAPTER THREE

Producing the People

ON JANUARY 15, 1977, en route to FESTAC's opening ceremony, Nigerian president and festival Patron Lieutenant General Olusegun Obasanjo brushed protocol aside by boarding a bus to the National Theatre, where he would inaugurate a new era of black culture and civilization. Relinquishing the official state limousine for a putatively public mode of transportation, Obasanjo arrived at the ceremony as a man of the people, joined by ten visiting heads of state and top-ranking chiefs of the Nigerian armed services. Included in Obasanjo's entourage were high-profile African leaders like Kenneth Kaunda of Zambia, Siaka Stevens of Sierra Leone, and Félix Houphuet-Boigny of Ivory Coast; lesser lights such as King Moshoeshoe of Lesotho, Oumar Bongo of Gabon, and Pinto Da Costa of Sao Tomé; and the key political strongmen of the Nigerian military: Chief of Staff, Supreme Headquarters, Brigadier Shehu Musa Yar'Adua; Chief of Army Staff, Lieutenant General T. Y. Danjuma; and the commissioner for external affairs, Brigadier Joseph Garba. At once a potent symbol of Nigerian populism and a concentrated container of powerful personnel, the executive bus cut through the clamoring crowd at the gates to maintain the schedule of scripted arrivals, beginning with general spectators and followed by obas, emirs, judges, and commissioners, up the political hierarchy of military governors and officers to the culminating entry of His Excellency himself.

Safely installed in his state box, Obasanjo was greeted by a momentary hush from the estimated 50,000 to 60,000 spectators in the National Stadium, followed by a state fanfare, the Nigerian national anthem, and the hoisting of the national flag to a twenty-one gun salute. Ceremonially constituted at the center of the black and African world as FESTAC host, Nigeria gave vision and voice to this larger transnational community by presiding over the march-past of its representative contingents, followed by the lighting of the festival torch (by Shango worshippers from Oyo State) and the hoisting of the festival flag. After opening speeches proclaiming a black cultural awakening to be witnessed by the entire world and the release of one thousand pigeons into the evening sky, the expansive horizons of the Pan-African world returned to Nigeria, reestablished by the closing march of the pageant, its concluding state fanfare, and the playing of the national anthem. Departing in reverse order of their arrival, the distinguished leaders, guests, VIPs, and ordinary spectators brought to an end FESTAC's opening ceremony, which celebrated the unity and fraternity of black culture and community within the hierarchical framework of an oil-rich state. Officially, the ceremony was a spectacular success, broadcast to an estimated 90 million Nigerian viewers and by satellite around the globe.

Offstage, however, in the upper bleachers and among the crowds outside the stadium gates, the people were not so easily contained. In sharp contrast with the participating regiments, viewers and would-be spectators collided with the coercive apparatus of the state. Those Nigerians who queued for hours to get in "quietly filed past stern looking security men assisted by mounted troops and police dogs to their seats."[1] Charlie Cobb, an American reporter for National Public Radio, described his horror at the violence attending the opening event:

> I was working the outside of the stadium doing interviews and I watched how the soldiers and police responded to the crowds, and there was a considerable amount of brutality. Estimates of the number of people who died are around sixty. While I was standing in the middle of the stadium doing interviews, an announcement was made in French and English that simply said, "We are asking the police and military to stop beating the people. The infirmaries are now full. We cannot accommodate any more" . . . I saw people pitched over the edge of the stadium. I know that maybe half the foreign diplomatic corps couldn't even get into the stadium.[2]

Cobb's observations, corroborated by similar reports in the local press,[3] point beyond the logistical travesties of the opening ceremonies to an underlying disjunction that emerged from FESTAC's mode of cultural production. Briefly stated, "the people" produced onstage as objects of celebration and veneration were far removed from the very people whose interests and destinies they ostensibly served. The unruly masses, or crowds, as the state perceived them, threatened the very success of FESTAC and were brought to order with whips and billy clubs. Moreover, the state's incapacity to contain the crowd at the stadium gates and bleachers was matched by an ironic absence of viewers at its center, where vast sectors reserved for the VIPs remained vacant throughout the entire day. As an editor of the *Punch* complained, "Although the popular sides were packed chocabloc and thousands were still contesting the right of entry outside the gates, half of the seats in the reserved areas (usually meant for the elite) were inexplicably empty. . . . We would have thought that some of the Nigerians who were left outside in the sun could have been allowed to take those seats."[4] True to form, the class-stratified field of spectatorship prevailed over aspiring spectators struggling to get in.

In this chapter, I will focus primarily on the making of Nigerian national culture within the broader black and African world, because it brings into bold relief the very logic of spectacle as a form of cultural commodification. I approach this important notion not in terms of an open market for tourist souvenirs or even "serious" art, although this developed informally in limited contexts, but as a basic inversion of simulacrum and original—a kind of commodity fetish writ large— whereby an exhibited "people" became more real and authentic than the lands and peoples themselves. That this transformation was in fact quite fundamental to the political ontology of the colonial exhibition has been well demonstrated by Mitchell (1991) and Lebovics (1992) in their studies of British and French imperial culture, but in the postcolonial context of an oil-rich Nigeria, the consequences were very different. As we shall see, the transformation of the public sphere (Habermas 1992) that Nigeria sought to achieve in FESTAC developed into a simulated arena of national participation which was underwritten by oil, projected from "above," and ultimately detached from its popular base. To trace this dislocation of "the people" from the people, we can follow Nigeria's National Participation Committee (NPC) as it demarcated a field of national culture, organized its major events and exhibits, and converted local cultural artifacts and practices into elements and icons of a national tradition.

At a press conference in Lagos on July 20, 1976, Afro-beat king Fela Anikulapo-Kuti announced his resignation from the NPC because of its "character and composition." As reported in the *Daily Times,* "Fela, who disclosed that he resigned after the last meeting of the committee in Kano, described the program put forward as a 'huge joke.' He claimed that rather than take positive steps to draw up a workable program, the committee, at its last meeting, adopted a bureaucratic attitude toward concrete suggestions which would have helped . . . redirect the thinking of the common man."[5] Members of the committee were quietly relieved by Fela's decision, given the impulsive outbreaks and tantrums that they had already endured. Nor was his opposition to committee work surprising, in light of his flamboyant pot smoking, his haremlike shrine in Lagos, his edgy jazz groove, and his recent musical hit "Zombie," which mocked the mindless submission of Nigerian soldiers to their equally mindless superiors. Indeed, Fela's gadfly political provocations were more shocking than principled, as when he once voiced respect for Hitler during a special FESTAC interview.[6] During his brief time with the NPC, however, Fela did see the bureaucratic writing on the wall foretelling the official framework of a Nigerian national culture that would soon come into being, provided the right orders were followed.[7]

The fundamentals of this framework were forged at the Kano Conference of Federal and State Officials of Information, Culture, and Films, a key event and turning point in the making of Nigerian cultural policy when the NPC itself was reorganized and a set of formal dimensions and concrete proposals took shape. Initially, under the Gowon regime, Nigeria's participation in FESTAC was governed by three independent bodies: a Durbar Secretariat in charge of the equestrian displays of the northern emirates to be held in Kaduna; a Regatta Secretariat for riverine races of the southern and eastern states that would be showcased in Lagos; and the National Secretariat overseeing the national exhibitions of plastic and performing arts, as well as associated events such as the gala evening. During these early stages, in the euphoric atmosphere of the oil boom, FESTAC was dubbed the "festival of awards and contracts." Money poured into the three secretariats and virtually disappeared, emblematic of Gowon's cronyism and lack of fiscal control. After the Murtala coup in July of 1975, a tribunal of inquiry into FESTAC finances revealed a frenzy of unofficial consulting fees, irregular charges, untendered bids, inflated contracts, extravagant purchases, and a considerable amount of sheer personal enrichment. Alhaji Umaru Dikko, in charge of the Durbar, was removed as one of the most egregious offenders. The man who would emerge under the Second Republic (1979–83) as an architect of massive fraud and hoarding schemes, and who was drugged and nearly extradited in a crate from England by order of the (then) head of state, Major General Muhammadu Buhari (see Watts 1994, 433–35), was implicated in dozens of shady deals worth millions of naira.[8] Chief Anthony Enahoro, then president of FESTAC, was also sacked for embezzlement, but his purge was more political than economic, since even the alleged amount of his misappropriation was trivial. I mention the spending spree for FESTAC under Gowon as a backdrop to the "radical pruning" effected under the subsequent heads of state, Murtala and Obasanjo.

The Kano Conference opened with a speech by the NPC's new chairman, Major General I. B. M. Haruna, announcing that his Ministry of Information was now in charge of the NPC and had consolidated the Durbar and Regatta Secretariats within its fold. A new attitude of discipline, economy, efficiency, and centralized control was decreed, represented by the committee's new motto, "We dare not fail." Pressures were indeed mounting. FESTAC was scheduled for January 15 to February 12, a mere six months away, and the committee was virtually back to square one. Aside from the millions of naira already poured into the Durbar Hotel, the National Theatre, and Festac Village, Nigeria's exhibits and events were still in the planning stages, and were constrained by a new budget of a mere 5 million naira ($8 million US), a ceiling deemed "as low as possible without prejudice to [FESTAC's] essence."[9] Major projects at the international level that were scrapped by cutbacks included a taxidermy display, an exhibit on traditional chieftaincy, and a grandiose plan to build a planetarium that would have projected FESTAC into the heavens.[10] To gain a sense of the squandermania that had prevailed under Gowon, we can note that the amount he had allocated for color television equipment in the National Theatre (5.2 million naira) exceeded the entire budget for national participation authorized by the new regime.

Under these urgent circumstances, the Kano Conference moved quickly on several fronts. In the spirit of vertical integration, Haruna convened a special session to "map out national strategies for the total mobilization of Federal and State publicity resources for the attainment of national objectives."[11] Nigeria's participation in FESTAC was elevated to the official status of a national campaign, like the national census or Operation Feed the Nation. From the standpoint of concentrated "informational capital" (Bourdieu 1999, 61–62), information services would provide the key to successful political, sociocultural, and economic development. These included the establishment of an official

News Agency of Nigeria (NAN) and associated Press Council, the "take-over and rationalization of television broadcasting stations in the country," and the "harmonisation of the ownership of national newspapers" to facilitate what was called "the adequate flow of information and effective use of communication."[12] To adequately publicize FESTAC throughout the nation, government would enlist "mass communication mobilizers" who would set up Public Enlightenment Units in each of the nineteen states. In a programmatic statement of this totalizing vision, Haruna announced,

> The present administration believes strongly that the continued existence of Nigeria as a virile and progressive nation depends upon meaningful and reliable communication. Unless the remotest villages in this country are in contact with one another and the centre, this nation cannot be truly integrated. Our people, most of them illiterate and living in distant places from Lagos, are too busy minding their own business to be able to find out for themselves what is going on where and why. But they all require and are entitled to know. And it is the sacred duty of Government to inform and enlighten the people. In view of this, the Federal Ministry of Information in conjunction with the States' Ministries of Information, should, through their Public Enlightenment Units . . . ensure that the public is aware and fully understand [sic] Government's intentions and policies. Through these agencies the various Governments and national institutions would have a feed-back.[13]

I have quoted this statement at length because it not only captures the spirit of enlightenment from the commanding heights of the petro-state but also reveals the contours of a giant publicity machine that sought to manufacture a public sphere within the framework of an ideological state apparatus. The "sacred duty" of government to "inform and enlighten," evoking the spirit if not the letter of former colonial imperatives in Nigeria, did not exactly entail reciprocal rights and entitlement on the part of the people. Feedback from local areas and media were of two basic types, "favourable or unobjective." When unobjective and "unsavoury," the report continues, the machinery of government media analysis must identify "the depth of hostility" according to a set of security factors and concerns that involved documenting "unfriendly publications or broadcasts" as well as the identities of the sources.[14] Within the guise of cultural research and documentation, with its expanding cadre of ethnographers and cultural officers, a national security system took shape.

In the explicit terms of legitimate national culture, public enlighten-ment applied to officers and gentlemen as well as the illiterate masses. Cultural officers would undergo disciplinary "training and grooming" in accordance with professional standards of documentation and patri-otism specified by a code of conduct for journalists, government pub-licity agents, and ethnographers. Promoting a "cultured" appreciation of national culture among the masses, the specialists would uplift the nation through an integrated notion of culture itself:

> We are generally aware that when we talk of cultural festivals or culture gen-erally, what comes to the mind of the average Nigerian are girls dancing with bare breasts. To these people, traditional dances is culture. It should be em-phasized that culture is interrelated and manifests itself in such aspects of life as dance, music, literature, folklore, oral tradition, craft, religion or spir-itual contentment, heritages, and even science and technology.[15]

FESTAC thus doubled as a celebration of civilization and a civilizing mission for Nigerians throughout the land. To disseminate awareness of the festival and its national themes, Public Enlightenment Units equipped with textual and audiovisual material were established in four zonal sectors covering the nineteen state capitals and beyond, through fifty subcenters or field offices in the rural areas. In another recom-mendation, the committee advised that "government should ensure that the prices of colour television sets are brought down in view of their importance in the promotion and presentation of culture in the coun-try."[16] Although these latter plans never materialized, they were part of an effort to "establish listening and viewing centres in villages, towns, schools, libraries and various places in each state" to bring FESTAC to the people.[17] This radial distribution of authoritative enlightenment, supported by a nationally integrated network of radio, television, and press agencies, would provide "dynamic persuasion to gain public sup-port for all government efforts at nation-building," and would "enhance acceptance and the genuineness of the postures of the Federal Military government."[18] Postures indeed! Combining federal propaganda with the collection of political intelligence, the development of a legitimate national culture would elevate the masses while guarding against polit-ical and economic saboteurs.[19]

As the ideological state apparatus took control over the communica-tive framework of national culture, the federal Department of Antiqui-ties remained in charge of its more substantive dimensions. Attached to the Ministry of Information, this department oversaw the representation of Nigeria's cultural patrimony through the "preservationist" model of colonial knowledge from which it derived. Organized into three main divisions of archeology, ethnography, and museums and monuments, supplemented by educational and audiovisual units, the department framed the contents of national culture: historically, in terms of its major archeological collections from the Nok Valley, the Benue Valley, Owo, Ife, and sites around Jos; and ethnographically, in research and documentation of traditional artifacts and festivals throughout the nation. Although these conventions and categories of anthropological knowledge and museum display did not exhaust or even dominate the contents of Nigerian culture within FESTAC—which, as we shall see, was enriched by other genres—they did establish a normative baseline of objectivity to which Nigeria's more mass-reproduced and mediated representations of the nation were related, and from which they derived.[20]

To locate the exhibited contents of national culture within the public framework forged by the state, and to identify key processes of cultural commodification, we can examine how the exhibits and events took shape in the rush to meet festival deadlines. In addition to the Lagos Regatta and Kaduna Durbar (discussed in chapters 4 and 5), Nigeria's formal participation in FESTAC followed categories standardized by the International Festival Committee (IFC). These included performances and displays in the areas of books, dance, drama, visual arts, the FESTAC Colloquium, literature, crafts, traditional domestic arts, traditional musical instruments, films, traditional costume, contemporary women's fashions, music, and a special exhibit on Nigerian culture at the National Museum. Not all of these exhibits and events were equally important to members of the NPC or to FESTAC at large, and related to national culture and participation through a prism of class distinctions, regional divisions, gender politics, ethnic idioms, and the ever present frictions between local, state, and federal jurisdictions.[21] To highlight the interplay of these forces within what was an explicit field of cultural production (Bourdieu 1993), I shall treat Nigeria's main exhibitions and events not simply as given but as endpoints of productive processes, or as temporal vectors and trajectories representing the trials and tribulations of planning and execution. From this diachronic perspective we can grasp the significance of unrealized goals due to cancellations, usurpations, interventions, and political clashes that would not be legible—as absences and silences—from the final products. We can also identify the processes of cultural objectification as much as the "stuff" objectified, an insight developed by Handler (1988, 194–95) in his pathbreaking study of national culture in Quebec. And finally, we can begin to compare these vectors in relation to festival activities and broader national trends to discern the investments, conversions, and dispositions of value involved in producing the Nigerian people.

VECTORS OF CULTURAL PRODUCTION

The letter, written on International Secretariat letterhead with its FESTAC Benin ivory logo, was scrawled by hand on July 15, 1976, and addressed to Dr. Garba Ashiwaju, the secretary and leader of the National Participation Committee:

> Hello! Just heard I've been put down on some committee (for Literature?) at the Kano conference. Answer to that is No! No! No!!! I am overstretched already, far too overstretched. In fact I was going to come to Kano only to give one or two opinions on methodology of preparations, then insist that I *not* be part of the National Committee. Impossible! I'm already around the bend with the International Secretariat, now you want to certify me altogether! So please—scrap my name! Wole.[22]

With characteristic verve, Wole Soyinka declined his appointment as Supervisor for Nigeria's literature event in no uncertain terms. Already embroiled in the censorship struggles of the FESTAC Colloquium, where he lambasted "the robots of leadership politics with their narrow schematism" (Soyinka 1977, 45), he was hardly about to take on more *wahala* (trouble, obstructionism). Indeed, working with Professor S. A. Babalola (an expert on Yoruba *ìjálá* chants), whose committee on Nigerian participation in the Colloquium formally resolved that the texts submitted for consideration "be produced for experts to scrutinize and that any paper whose contents are against national interest and security would be withdrawn," Soyinka's energies were fully engaged.[23] The position of Literature Supervisor went to Cyprian Ekwensi, the more conservative and less controversial easterner from Enugu whose masterful novellas and short stories, such as *Jagua Nana* and "Lokotown," had earned him a place in the pantheon of Nigerian writers.

The literature event was one of the less vaunted components of national and Pan-African cultural celebration during FESTAC, relegated to one of the cinema halls in the National Theatre and neglected by the media. Live readings could hardly compete with the dazzle of dance, drama, film, and music, and would appeal more to the literati in any case. But even the micropolitics of this unspectacular event—selecting national texts and literary talents—reveals the regional fissures within a national tradition. We may note that Soyinka's initial recruitment to the NPC, based partly on his early prominence at the Dakar festival in 1966, resonated with a certain Yoruba chauvinism in matters of intellectual and educational attainment, rivaled only by Ibo claims of achievement and acumen so brutally represented by their technical wizardry during the Biafran war.[24] The question of Ibo involvement in FESTAC is tricky, since the obstacles that many encountered were matched by a begrudging reluctance to get too involved. In the literature event, however, Ekwensi was a willing if less dynamic second choice after Soyinka, and he dutifully followed IFC divisions into fiction, drama, essays, and poetry, recommending that five internationally known writers fill the slots and that new and aspiring writers be featured in a special anthology published for the event. As head of Star Printing and Publishing Co. in Enugu, Ekwensi also invited publishers to participate, opening the process of cultural production to marketing forces.

More interesting than the proposed format, however, was the opposition it triggered from a northern committee member. Alhaji El-Yakubu brought northern pride and prejudice into the discussion, advocating Hausa-Fulani writers from Kano, Kaduna, and Sokoto for inclusion, and arguing that languages other than English and French (in other words, Hausa) also be represented. Significantly, the highly political issue of national language planning in postcolonial African states did not arise in this discussion (although it would soon be engaged by Obasanjo and Soyinka), but was quite literally relegated to the sidelines, in that works by "traditional" writers were considered for "side shows."[25]

In the more traditional area of crafts, national selection took on a more "representative" character in transforming local objects into national icons. Headed by Chief Udo Ema of Cross River State, the Crafts Committee forged a touring schedule combining centralized planning and control from the center with limited inputs from the states. With bureaucratic ingenuity, the nineteen states were divided into three zones, each with a corresponding team from the NPC that visited the arts councils of each state within. In principle, each state arts council would be apprised of the visit, and would have made a preliminary selection for the touring team to collect and transport back to Lagos, where a final selection by federal officers would be made for the national exhibit. The teams embarked—with new Volvos and Peugeot 504s—on October 17, and for the most part the operation worked. Officers from the states' arts councils assembled collections of crafts from local villages, towns, and government areas, which were then loaded into government vehicles and brought back to the capital by touring teams.

If the inventories collected from the states varied in quality and quantity, the records reflect the serious commitment and hard work of the cultural officers. Whereas some states, like Plateau, simply listed their contributions as "mat, tul (smoking pipe), spear, or bishak," without any information other than their corresponding costs, others, like Ondo, provided significant cultural information such as functions of the craft, sex of the producers, and area where produced. With the Iyasi Omolore staff, for example, was the note: "Iyasi is used by the Oba on ceremonial occasions. The Oba dances with Iyasi. It signifies a noble birth."[26]

Where obstacles were encountered or communications broke down, fissures in the political field of cultural production can be discerned. In a bristling letter to the NPC, a frustrated permanent secretary from Makurdi complained of failed appointments and general neglect:

> May I draw your attention to the rather nauseating situation and the manner in which your office has handled the affairs involving Benue State participation in FESTAC. Your letter No. NPS.14.1.32 of 23rd September, 1976 was belatedly received in Makurdi on the 1st of November, about three months [?] after it was written. May I also note that Messers [sic] Agbo Folarin and the Principal T. C. Kano never came to Benue State to pursue the programme as scheduled. Just before we received your letter, the Principal T. C. Kano arrived Makurdi on one Saturday in the evening to select the artworks. Since the artworks were not assembled in one place due to lack of previous information, he could not select any and he left for Jos, Plateau State in continuation of his tour of States listed in Zone 3. . . . Your Office has not kept in touch with this State and consequently, we are unaware of the mode of our participation at FESTAC. This is rather unsatisfactory, and I hope that something will be done urgently to ensure full participation by Benue State.[27]

In addition to difficult communications and working conditions, the letter reflects the structural tension between federal and state levels of cultural politics and administration, expressed by complaints from the arts councils that "they were being ordered around by Lagos rather than being involved as equal partners in the participation activities," and at least partially redressed by attaching state coordinators to the NPC Secretariat—with the status of nonvoting observers—in Lagos.[28] Annoyed at being commanded rather than consulted by the center, the state officials nonetheless understood that political capital would be gained by participating in the national show. A similar letter from Niger State complained that the only information it received about its own participation in FESTAC came from the radio and newspapers.[29] A complementary movement from the states to the center thus followed the federal tour throughout the zones, not only in arts and crafts but also in personnel who journeyed to Lagos for further involvement.[30]

In addition to these political tensions, conflicts developed over purchasing and insuring the arts and crafts. Local craftspeople were understandably reluctant to part with their wares without any payment, and issues of fiscal responsibility surfaced repeatedly. In some states, arts councils acquired the crafts on loan with the understanding that they would be insured by NICON (National Insurance Company of Nigeria) for their market value and then returned, or purchased them on "credit" to be redeemed by government remittances to the makers. In other areas, officials had to purchase the objects from their own budgets and hope for direct reimbursement from Lagos. Emerging from these squabbles were lines of investment and conversion that transformed local objects into national icons while exploiting the very people represented by their works. In the Crafts Committee's budget, for example, federal funds were mainly allocated for transportation of personnel and crafts between Lagos and the states, hotel expenses for the committee members, insurance of crafts, per diem allowances, and packaging costs, with only one category for "purchase of some crafts for retention by Federal government."[31] The amount for transporting crafts alone was double the commitments for purchase, echoing the state-directed logic of an oil economy that underwrote distribution costs at the expense of domestic production.

In another example of federal costing, funds allocated for insuring arts and crafts equaled those earmarked for special purchases, equating economic with national value. Framed within the idiom of *national* insurance by NICON, objects selected and distributed for presentation were valorized only as national icons, or to invoke Walter Benjamin, not as commodities-in-the-market but as commodities-on-display (Buck-Morss 1993, 81–82). To control this transformation of local objects into national commodities and essentially protect them from the market, NICON stipulated that "the art works will be exhibited in the exhibition centre in the National Theatre, Lagos and nowhere else . . . the cover provided will not extend to exhibition centres outside the National Theatre, Lagos."[32] By restricting this insurance to specific pathways and places, the federal government not only monopolized control over the means of symbolic production, but also confined this production to nationally enshrined spaces where such value conversions would take place. In terms of profit and payoff, the state recouped national representation and "recognition" from its initial investment of oil money, converting local products into national icons, without significant remuneration to the craftsmen themselves. Indicative of how the image superseded the object of value, the state was more willing to pay photography costs for insurance and cataloging purposes than to pay for the arts and crafts—privileging mechanical reproduction over the original. Not surprisingly, the producers were the last to realize any gain, unless one takes seriously the printed certificates of national merit awarded "to craftsmen whose works have been selected," concluding the conversion of oil money into the magical powers of state consecration (Bourdieu 1991, 171–219).

Similar fault lines within the field of cultural production emerged with even greater clarity and force in the exhibition on Nigeria's traditional costumes, organized and executed by Chief J. A. Ayorinde of the historically distinguished lineage of Ibadan military chiefs (*Balógùn*). Combining a judicious sense of inventory and economy with extraordinary political savvy, Ayorinde transformed the touring model of cultural collection into something of a royal procession, expanding his mission to include courtesy visits to military governors and top-ranking ministers. In some cases his group. the Sub-Committee on Traditional Costume, was accompanied by military convoys and police patrols in their ceremonial visits to those traditional or "natural" rulers whose regalia were requested for sartorial display. Ayorinde's decision to focus almost exclusively on the traditional costumes of "natural" rulers was justified mainly on grounds of expediency, given the short amount of time available to collect representative costumes of the highest quality: "In view of the fact that the Government cannot afford the required materials in terms of money, and the time-limit," he argued, "it is essential and profitable to go to the custodians of the traditional costumes because they have the wardrobes from which they can draw."[33] But beneath the pragmatics of keeping to schedule, a significant political agenda took shape. Masquerading, we might say, in the costume of custom was the restoration of traditional chieftaincy to the elevated stage of FESTAC's cultural spectacle, and as far as Ayorinde was concerned, the promotion of Yoruba kingship and chieftaincy at the center of this "traditional" political cosmology.

We may recall that the IFC had scrapped the category of traditional chieftaincy in the spirit of radical pruning, not only because it was expensive, but because it was politically controversial and therefore expendable, given the hostility of socialist one-party states—such as Guinea, Ethiopia, and even Tanzania—to the traditional forces of conservation and reaction. For Ayorinde, traditional costume provided the "cover" for resurrecting traditional chieftaincy. By invoking the language of traditional custodianship, in that the natural rulers were seen as the repository of precolonial arts and culture, he restored traditional chieftaincy to the very fabric of Nigerian national culture. According to plan, Ayorinde would sweep the nation in a three-phased tour of the nineteen states, appealing to the traditional rulers to provide their regalia on loan, and offering national recognition to them for performing their patriotic duty. Such recognition would be registered by plaques and certificates awarded to the rulers for their indirect participation. But more important, their regalia would be showcased in Lagos and featured in the press as a form of national publicity.

Although directed by the NPC at large "to co-opt more members into the sub-committee in order to reflect the heterogeneous nature of the country," [34] Ayorinde nonetheless clearly favored his own Yoruba region in terms of the number of traditional rulers visited and the proportion of royal regalia represented. In his first collecting tour, for example, his subcommittee visited Kaduna, Kano, Bornu, Sokoto, Oyo, Ondo, and Ogun States in what constituted a politico-cultural alliance between Yoruba southerners and Hausa-Fulani northerners. The visits, however, reveal an important distinction between the politics of courtesy and the politics of tradition. In the four northern states, equal if not greater attention was accorded to permanent secretaries, commissioners, and state governors than to the very emirs whose costumes and emblems would be featured. The only "natural" rulers consulted were the Emir of Kano, the Shehu of Borno, the Sultan of Sokoto, and the Shehu of Argungun, each of whom expressed principled commitments to his national contribution. By contrast, traditional obas from the Yoruba states included the Olubadan of Ibadan, the Alaafin of Oyo, the Oni of Ife, the Ewi of Ado-Ekiti, the Olowo of Owo, the Deji of Akure, the Osemawe of Ondo, the Alake of Abeokuta, the Awujale of Ijebu-Ode, and the Akarigbo of Ijebu-Remo. To some extent this greater number of traditional Yoruba rulers reflects the more centralized organization of the emirate system in the north vis-à-vis Yoruba kingdoms, which remained more autonomous throughout the western states. Thus the historic competition between the Alaafin of Oyo and the Oni of Ife for paramount status among Yoruba obas had no parallel in the north, where the Sultan of Sokoto remained the undisputed commander of the faithful. And if Ayorinde's negotiation of this struggle appeared fair-minded, by including these and other obas to avoid the politically charged issues of fixing their relative statuses and rankings, there is no question that his own lineage and political loyalties promoted the Alaafin above the rest. When Ayorinde's subcommittee called upon him in a highly publicized visit to the palace, the Alaafin, Oba Lamidi Olayiwola Adeyemi, not only expressed his personal commitment to the cause but "assured the delegation of the cooperation and support of traditional rulers within the nation in the efforts to ensure the success of FESTAC," elevating his authority by speaking on their behalf.[35] By contrast, the reported visit to the Oni of Ife made no mention of the Oni himself—who may well have been absent—but referred only to his beaded Are crown and gowns of the Olojo festival; that is, not to the power of the person but only the insignia of the office, a perspective consistent with the Oyo-centric vision of Ife as ritually but not politically significant (Apter 1992, 13–34).

Ayorinde's second tour reveals a similar pattern with respect to the east. His sweep through Lagos, Rivers, Imo, Anambra, Bendel, and Cross River states tended to weaken its contact with traditional rulers the further it extended from Lagos. Thus close to home in Lagos State, all obas and chiefs convened with the commissioner for local government and chieftaincy affairs, including the Oba of Badagary and the Oba Ayangburin of Ikorodu to elicit their contributions.[36] In Rivers State, the Sub-Committee on Traditional Costume paid its courtesy call to the military governor, and met with only two chiefs, the Oba of Ogbaland and the Amayanabo of Abonema, whose costumes were displayed and photographed. In Imo State, historic rulers like the Aro of Arochukwu and others "could not be seen because of the long distance and bad roads," with the relatively insignificant chiefs of Akwete serving in their place.[37] It is not too difficult to distinguish the political fallout of the Biafran war from sheer logistical problems in visiting the Ibo chiefs. In Anambra State, the subcommittee met with the Igwe of Ogidi, Chief Osita Agwuna-Igwe of Enugu Ukwu, and most important, the Obi of Onitsha, all of whom evaded firm commitments to FESTAC. Officials in Anambra "complained bitterly in respect of total neglect of the state by the National Participation Secretariat towards FESTAC." The main grievance among traditional rulers in Imo and Anambra alike "was about the damage done to costumes during the last civil war."[38] Whether literally true or emblematic of federal violence more generally during the war, these complaints register the ambivalent location of Ibo political culture within the mandate of "one Nigeria."[39] But the specificities of Iboland notwithstanding, the topology of touring reveals a consistent correlation between number of chiefs visited and distance from the capital. In Bendel State, closer to Lagos (and part of the former Western Region), a distinguished lineup of visits to the Oba of Benin, the Olu of Warri, the Obi of Agbor, and the Orokpe of Okpe brought the outer limits of Yoruba political cosmography within national view, whereas in Cross River State, at Nigeria's southeastern periphery, the delegation met with two officers and no chiefs. In the third and final mop-up tour, the same pattern prevailed. The visit to Kwara, virtually a

Yoruba state (sharing a long border with Oyo and Ondo), brought out the Emir of Ilorin, the Olafa of Offa (with a lively cultural reception), and the Emir of Borgu, whereas Niger, Plateau, and Bauchi mobilized secretaries and commissioners but only one traditional ruler each. Benue and Gongola were missed altogether, the latter responding in the hurt and politically suspicious tone characteristic of the neglected periphery. In a letter from Gongola to the N P C, a permanent secretary complained,

> Even at this crucial time, your team, under the leadership of Chief Ayorinde, failed to show up here in Yola after instructing us to arrange for them to see our natural rulers and chiefs and to get ready on types of traditional costumes for inspection by them. . . . What are we to do with our costumes etc. which were collected from all over the state? We booked hotel accommodation at various establishments in Yola which remained vacant for days awaiting our guests! You may wish to know that we are now beginning to interpret these various activities by FESTAC officials from Lagos as means and ways, intentionally calculated to frustrate our efforts to fully participate.[40]

Such neglect was not in fact "intentionally calculated," since the scheduled flight to Yola from Jos listed in the subcommittee's itinerary probably fell through for technical reasons or due to poor communications.[41] But the peripheral perception of bad political faith highlights the structural distance of such states from the center, where the nation was more visible and the federal government more accessible.

Neither, however, was the view from Gongola entirely incorrect, for Ayorinde's Yoruba-centered vision of Nigeria, however unconsciously, did derive from local and regional models. Within the detailed inventories he assembled, Yoruba outfits and icons clearly predominated, including specialized paraphernalia of the Olubadan made by ancestors of the Ayorinde lineage, as well as "appurtenances" of associated chiefs and deities (*orishas*) echoing the former Oyo and Ibadan empires. But more revealing than the items amassed was their organization into a sartorial lexicon which illustrated the unity of Nigerian national culture in accordance with the exhibition's theme: "Know Nigeria through Costumes." Seeking commonalties among Nigeria's diverse cultures, the exhibit showcased dominant styles of dress to suggest something of a national uniform, and reflected the underlying unity of the national body. During its three-phase tour, the Sub-Committee on Traditional Costume "discovered" that "the big Yoruba gown known as Agbada is called AGWADA in the Northern parts of the country, while the Yoruba under-wear known as Dansiki is usually called DANCHIKI there," adding that "Dandogo, the Yoruba super-gown is known as Baban-Riga in Hausa and Edgi in Nupe; while the trousers like the horse riding bridges [sic] known as KAMU among the Yorubas and worn by chieftains and other members of the aristocratic classes are called Baban-Wondo in some parts of the North."[42]

Underlying this derivation of a national dress code, we can perceive what in kinship studies is called the extensionist thesis, whereby a set of primary focal types is extended to embrace wider social and political relations. Slipped into Ayorinde's national lexicon is the presumption that Yoruba sartorial styles are found "elsewhere" in Nigeria and form the core of the national pattern, even when the etymological evidence suggests northern provenance. Concluding that "the universality of the usages to which the various costumes are put irrespective of their states of origin makes it important for the compilation of names, etc. for the purpose of enriching the vocabularies of the Nation and using same as a unifying factor," Ayorinde insinuated a Yoruba template at the center of the national dress code, in a mode of positioning and projecting that echoed Yoruba cultural nationalism more generally as it had developed under colonialism.[43]

The colonial roots of the traditional costume exhibition are in fact quite explicit, and illuminate a vector of longer historical duration that informed the production of Nigerian national culture at large. Ayorinde's decision to feature traditional rulers was based not just on expediency but also on an important colonial precedent during the 1956 visit of Queen Elizabeth II and her consort. At that historic moment, when Nigeria was preparing for self-government, what was then the Western Region mounted an exhibition in the queen's honor featuring the royal dress and paraphernalia of the major Yoruba obas, including the Oni of Ife, the Alake of Abeokuta, the Alaafin of Oyo, and the Deji of Akure. In fact, the exhibit was so successful that it traveled to Madame Tussaud's Wax Museum in London for a month of further display. Ayorinde's resurrection of this exhibitionary model can thus be seen, implicitly, as the restoration and projection of the former Western Region into a framework of national costume and culture. As the colonial precedent expanded to include the entire federation of nineteen states (but with two left out), it recast the nation through the political iconography of Yoruba "regional" culture. Such recasting and reframing warrant closer examination, for it is here that the very processes of cultural commodification invested traditional "fetishes" and icons with national meaning and value.

At issue are two basic transformations that belong to different temporal orders, which converged in several national displays. In the short-term rush to production established at the Kano Conference, we saw how strategies and tactics for exhibiting traditional costumes reached out to acquire representative specimens for selective display at the center. Acquisition in this context had a special meaning, since the royal regalia and associated ritual iconography requested were technically inalienable, at least in the local fields of political sovereignty and legitimacy where they remained and devolved.[44] As with arts and crafts, the shipment of local treasure was nationally insured "from the centre of collection to the Exhibition hall and back," and at all times was closely supervised by cultural officers and security guards wearing identity badges.[45] Unlike crafts, however, which at least in principle could be sold, the value of traditional regalia was nonnegotiable, hence the necessity of their return. Indeed, the Emir of Kano expressed just such fears about handing over his political sacra; he was assured that photographs could be taken of the originals, and replicas made thereafter for a permanent national collection.

What emerges from this and other exhibitory arrangements is how the representation detached from the original—in the form of photographs and replicas—as the traditional object was upgraded to the status of national icon. Although scaled down by cutbacks, the first plans for the exhibit called for live models and mannequins, as well as mirrors hung "in suitable places" to reflect local objects in the national gaze. Life-size photographs, depicting "costumes of rare nature that may be difficult to move out and away from their sources,"[46] were also called for when originals could not be had, but were eventually reduced to twenty by twelve inches in size. Special glass cases were ordered for the exhibits to protect them from dirt and dust, serving also to sanctify them as national icons—indeed, "inalienable possessions" (Weiner 1992)—set apart for veneration. This is not to suggest that the local was completely factored out. In principle, the exhibits would be supplemented by tapes and slides of music, wedding ceremonies, and market scenes to provide context. Some states actually provided the supportive material, but it was never exhibited.[47] Similarly, the Exhibition Hall itself was to be draped with locally woven material supplied by all the states, thereby fashioning a national tapestry. The exhibits themselves, conceived by the NPC as a pyramid of political traditions transforming costumes and emblems of the historic kingdoms and local government areas into elevated icons of national culture and identity, had their images at the apex effectively detached from the material base, reproduced, reflected, and refracted through the mirrors and display cases to circulate in crafted reproductions and mechanically reproduced brochures throughout Nigeria and beyond.

Not that this national inversion of original and simulacrum was anything new. As I mentioned earlier, it characterized the very logic of the colonial exposition in Europe, where imperial representations of the colonized became more "authentic" than the "subjects" depicted. Ironically, the 1956 resurrection of the Western Region's chieftaincy exhibit in England's most celebrated wax museum brings this ontological transformation of the real back to the very center of colonial overrule where traditional Yoruba chieftaincy was enhanced by association with the arts of the "lifelike" simulacrum. This recapitulation of the colonial "world-as-exhibition" (Mitchell 1991, 13) belongs to the longer *durée* of Nigerian colonial culture, informing the very framework of traditional costume through representative icons of native administration and indirect rule. As I demonstrate more fully in chapter 5, it was through the very processes of cultural production, in which putatively precolonial traditions were exhibited and objectified, that the formal structures and categories of indirect rule were indigenized and thereby nationalized as authentically Nigerian. The "natural rulers" showcased in FESTAC '77 had actually been naturalized under indirect rule, through their very incorporation into native authorities. That Ayorinde privileged Yoruba models of chieftaincy as they were modified by the British and had framed a distinctive western regional culture in the 1940s and '50s underscores the ethnically defined political competition that intensified under the oil economy in preparation for the Third Republic. But the long-term effect of these shorter-term political strategies was the nationalization of Nigerian colonial culture under the very sign of its erasure in FESTAC.

In the more immediate context of cultural production, the exhibit on traditional costumes developed in gendered contrast with women's fashions. Apart from a few references to women in photographs of Efik fattening ceremonies from Rivers State, traditional costumes were typically male. The king or chief as "natural ruler," even when invented by British warrant, formed the paradigm of "traditional costume" and the prototype of its manifold derivations in the flowing gowns of big men, "nobles and merchants"; the royal staffs and carved walking sticks; and the beaded embellishments of high status. Even the festival cloth was ritually male, as in Yoruba Egungun masquerade outfits and hunters' garb. By implication, the sanctity of tradition itself acquired a masculine idiom that descended from the precolonial past to reassert its noble pedigree. And it was within this context of a masculinized tradition that the exhibit of women's fashions—interchanged with women's *modern* fashions—produced a significant contrast with a feminized modernity. In the publicity write-up, the modern Nigerian woman emerges from the chrysalis of tradition to assume a leading role in national development:

> In this moment of flux in all areas of development in the world in general and in Nigeria in particular, the role of the Nigerian woman has expanded tremendously. Unlike her predecessor, she is no longer restricted to the kitchen or to the role of motherhood. Greater demand is being placed on her in nation building. As a result, her adaptability to the various roles she is called upon to play is richly and artistically displayed in her daily wear which is a melange of both her modern and traditional heritage.[48]

Promoting a progressive political agenda, the all-female subcommittee on women's popular dressing cut the new Nigerian woman from national cloth, which would be selected from each of the nineteen states. According to plan, the clothing fell into four major categories: (1) everyday wear, (2) working wear, (3) casual wear, and (4) formal wear. Each category, in turn, corresponded to the four age groups for all Nigerian women established by the committee; namely, (a) young girl, (b) puberty age, (c) middle age (25–50 years), and (d) old woman (50+). Collections from each state, divided into six national zones, would represent each age group in its four associated wearing categories, thereby lifting locally made and ethnically labeled cloths and fashions onto a unifying framework of national proportions. Mannequins ("dummies") and models would represent the new Nigerian woman in mounted displays and live shows. As if to emphasize the national body beneath its clothes, the Women's Popular Dressing Subcommittee agreed to send the chairperson and one National Participation Secretariat (NPS) officer to New York City "because of its specialty in producing *black* dummies" (original emphasis).[49] Makeup artists and hairdressers were called upon to enhance the beauty of live models, bringing color and style to the national skin. Stressing creative innovation over village tradition, clothes were to be solicited from fashion designers developing trend-setting styles from local patterns. Through this abstraction of a national wardrobe from regional and local styles, the new Nigerian woman would emerge.

If this woman did come into being, she was stripped of her voice and indeed turned into a dummy. In a series of mishaps stemming partly from the failures of subcommittee members and partly from the resistance that they encountered, the fashion exhibit was an unqualified disaster. The Ministry of Information failed to send out invitations to designers, resulting in a last-minute scramble for appropriate clothes. Models from the various zones and states never arrived. Those fashions that made it to the stage were deemed inferior and dull. Hairstyles were lackluster. An anguished reporter described her disappointment in a burning review of the opening fiasco:

> It was a wash-out, a real shameful and slip-shod affair of which every Nigerian should be ashamed. . . . Nigeria just didn't show anything to do us proud or that we had fashion sense in this country. . . . Besides the aso-oke (handwoven cloth) highly prized among the Yoruba speaking people of Nigeria, or the Hausa female dress (which certainly wasn't the best from that part of the country), there was nothing else to talk about Nigerian fashion as far as I am concerned, that night. Think of the worst and dullest george material you can imagine with a buba sewn with narrow sleeves and you get a clear picture of what we were told was a typical Bendel State outfit. As if that was not bad enough, whoever dressed the hair of the model who represented a Benin queen (or princess) certainly has never heard of coral beads and royal headdresses in Benin before, she could take a trip down and ask all about it from people who know.[50]

A less damning if more insipid account is provided in the subcommittee's final report, which provides a more bureaucratic accounting of states' representation in the exhibit, irrespective of content or quality. Here we learn that in the official opening of the Nigerian National Exhibitions, twenty-four costumes represented each of the states "with at least a common wear," and that at the second fashion show—at the international level—Nigeria presented forty costumes, with each state represented by at least two costumes.[51] But we also learn of a more serious charge involving the abuse and molestation of models by their supervisors. The incident may have been isolated, but it reveals how the politics of gender and ethnicity intersected and collided in unexpected ways.

The problem arose when the zonal organizer responsible for the northern states failed to produce Fulani, Kanuri, and Hausa models. With the show about to open, a desperate request was issued through the National Planning Committee to find "suitable ladies" from these ethnic groups living in Lagos to participate in the fashion parade. Scouting the Sabo areas of Obalende, Ajegunle, Idi-Araba, and Agege around the city, two officers produced women of the requisite ethnicities, who were delivered to the venue at City Hall the following morning to rehearse for the opening that very same evening. According to a FESTAC officer, just before the curtain rose, at 9:00 PM the models were suddenly informed that they would be replaced by girls "from other tribes" with more "model qualities." When the women complained of unfair treatment "as they were substituted by girls from other tribes to represent the tribes from which they themselves come," the supervisors allegedly "told them off, tormented them and disgraced them publicly," wherefore "the poor ladies returned . . . weeping and disappointed . . . from where they were molested." [52]

Framed in the idiom of harassment and molestation, the reported offense was elaborated in terms of tribalism and the "crime" of ethnic substitution. Really at issue was not abusive behavior as such but the misrepresentation—in the eyes of this official—of Nigeria's ethnic communities by models from other areas or "tribes," who were deemed more beautiful than the women commandeered from the streets. The report explains:

> My observation is that the organisers did not take to their jobs consciously in the interest of the nation in order to present a proper representatives of Nigeria tribes. . . . The Yorubas would like to be represented by the Yorubas, Ibos by Ibos, Hausa by Hausa, Kanuri by Kanuri and Fulani by Fulani. But the organisers thought that some tribes are more presentable than others . . . It is very unfair to deceive the whole world; let's be proud of what we are and make use of what god bestowed on us. . . . If the ladies brought for the show are ugly, that is what the communities could give but if you impose the most beautiful women on them, she is not their own, her demeanour and posture will not make a true representative of the communities concerned. [53]

The full irony of this charge is only appreciated when we realize that the supervisors accused of contemptuous and inhuman treatment were all women, and their accuser was a man. Invoking the language of sexual harassment, the crime of ethnic substitution was framed as a moral violation of the national order, an unpatriotic act of tribal favoritism and misrepresentation. The very logic of ethnic transcendence promoted by the women's popular dressing exhibit was condemned by male officials as lacking tribal sensitivity. Whatever actually happened that evening—and no doubt tempers were running hot—we can nonetheless perceive how the forces of male "tradition" responded to the new Nigerian woman in the language of high moralism and patriotic duty.

We can also see how the logic of commodification encountered certain limits. Whereas the clothing in the exhibit could be reframed onstage in national terms, uplifted from ethnic and regional contexts to assume a generic place within a national wardrobe, the models themselves remained ethnically anchored. National dress, in the last instance, clothed ethnically female bodies. It was only in the inanimate exhibits and window displays that "black dummies" could fully transcend such ethnic particularism, in a commodified and racialized icon of national womanhood devoid of flesh, blood, and voice. To more fully appreciate how the politics of gender and ethnicity converged in the making of national culture and the negotiation of its public body, we can turn to the more dramatic arts.

CHOREOGRAPHING THE NATION

The secretary of the NPC, Dr. Garba Ashiwaju, described the national importance of dance in the following terms:

> Dance is an important aspect of Nigerian culture. When a baby is born it is through dance that you celebrate its birth. Every major change in an individual is accompanied by dance and song. When he dies eventually it is also through dance that they take him to his grave . . . irrespective of where he comes from, whether he is a Christian or not or whatever, he is in Nigeria.[54]

For Ashiwaju, who dedicated his career as a festival director to the "uplifting" of Nigerian culture, dance forms an implicit category of cultural citizenship linking the individual directly to the nation, regardless of ethnic, regional, or religious affiliation. Trained in history at the University of Leipzig, where—to invoke Goethe and paraphrase Gellner (1998, 22)—he studied the needs of *Gesellschaft* in the language of *Gemeinschaft*, Ashiwaju saw himself as an engineer of national culture, "building the machinery," as he put it, that would transform grassroots traditions into a modernizing mechanism of national development. Well-placed to pursue this mission, he chaired the fourth National Festival of the Arts (Nafest) held in Kaduna in 1974, which was designed to bring local dances from villages and towns up through the states and into the national arena to celebrate Nigeria's "unity in diversity" and establish a representative pool for final selection to FESTAC. To examine this machinery for uplifting culture, I will trace the genealogy of cultural festivals as they led up to Nafest and FESTAC, and, more important, identify the transformations of choreographic structure and practice as dance "ascended" from villages and towns to its final and highest "stage" within the nation. As we shall see, this process of selection and abstraction occurred in the two dominant choreographic modalities of traditional dance and modern dance drama.

Traditional dance received far and above the greatest attention in state and federal cultural festivals. Beginning in the 1960s after Nigeria gained independence, administrative divisions throughout the regions, later reorganized into states, featured cultural dances in gong festivals, competitions for the best performing groups, who received gold, silver, and bronze gongs. The gong was considered an appropriate indigenous symbol of value and of "the promotion of national cultural exchange," not only as a musical instrument but also as "part of the town crier tradition" for mobilizing the national community (Bello 1992, 2). It further symbolized an ideological break from the colonial tradition from which it evolved; namely, the local arts festivals staged at various centers before independence, including the activities organized by Empire Day celebrations (Apter 2002).

Always already mediated, we might say, by the colonial framework of indirect rule, the dances extracted from the villages and kingdoms were seen as precolonial roots of Nigerian culture ratifying the natural rulers and traditional authorities of local administration. In southwest Nigeria, these events became prized outings for the obas, who mounted pressure on cultural officers to have their associated dances chosen for the limelight.[55] Moreover, the extraction involved important modifications. Although in some cases dancers were recruited directly from the villages to perform as elders or initiates (as from Plateau State), for the most part, cultural officers would recruit talented high school students and younger teachers who would come together in camps to be groomed for competitions. After independence, such grooming was seen as an important channel of transmitting Nigerian culture through the schools, putting dance into public pedagogy and exposing students and teachers to translocal traditions. Thus, in the process, two basic choreographic transformations took place. First, dances were stripped of repetition, condensed into stylized segments, and distilled into purer forms. Second, as the dancers changed, the dances moved into new corporate bodies. The priestesses, hunters, maidens, and elders who performed the dances in their "original" settings were replaced on the divisional and state levels by groomed troupes representing wider administrative localities and secularized sodalities.

As a choreographic grooming ground for FESTAC, Nafest 74 represents the most sweeping and systematic effort to view, catalog, and classify traditional Nigerian dances to promote cultural awareness and national unity. In sheer numbers alone, 6,000 dances were initially previewed at the village or divisional level, from which 1,305 were selected by the then-twelve states.[56] These were performed in the stadiums and racecourses of each state capital—such as Port-Harcourt, Sokoto, Ilorin, and Lagos—in three- to four-day festivals attended by federal ministers, state governors, state commissioners, and traditional rulers, and featuring dances from every administrative division. In this way, every minority was represented, if not by ethnicity then by local government area. The official programs published for these events list each division with numbered descriptions of all the dances indicating ceremonial contexts and basic themes. Rivers State, for example, listed 80 dances from its 18 divisions, with notes on warrior dances, masquerades, mermaid dances, and so forth. Western State featured 100 dances, spanning Akoko Division to Oyo North. Celebrated in a sequence from 1973 until November 1974, these festivals documented each state's representative dances not only in official programs but also on film.

The film archive of these festivals, established initially by the Ministry of Information, provides an important record. But it also constitutes an important mediation in the cultural representation and communication of dance itself. In terms of its documentary value, for example, the film of traditional dances from Mid-Western State provides didactic commentary on their broader meanings. Discussing the "evolution" of a royal Bini dance performed by schoolboys, the voice-over proclaims that "what was formerly available to only kings and nobles is now available to the general public." The same dance features a "mock oba" seated at the center of the stage and dressed in full regalia, given taboos against the real oba appearing in such a secular arena. Of a group from Sapele, we learn that the uninitiated performers "should dance, but not ask, not know, the secret of the cult dance." Local war dances, we are told, reveal "of what stuff Nigerians are made." A New Yam ceremonial dance is similarly applauded for showing that "religious homage can be staged in any venue." Sacred dances performed at long intervals, like age-set initiations or royal burials, we are told, "have been appropriately modified for the public"; that is, purged of propitiations and sacrifices.

The state flag flying beneath the national colors represents the state within the federation. In addition to VIPs and ministers seated in special boxes, the arena is flanked by advertisements from corporate sponsors: Aworo and Sons (books), Kola Studio, Cut Keys Enterprises. Clearly the movement of such dances from their local performative contexts to the festivals of the states involved a mode of objectification and even commodification. On such stages, the "original" was severed from its initial relations of production, condensed, drained of local political and religious meaning, endowed with national value, and transposed into a "secondary" iconic register in which, for example, a mock king represented the wider public more adequately than the actual Oba of Benin and his sovereign subjects. As sacred dances were secularized and ritual functions sanitized, choreographic form surpassed local function, the representation its referent. As one of the cultural officers explained, "In modern Nigeria, people are not interested in ritual on stage . . . in translating ritual dance into art, we must take away the sacrifices and spirit-possession."[57] Extending the secondary meaning of this iconic transposition into the public sphere of mass communication, the filming of these events for national archiving and dissemination further elevated dance to one of the highest forms of mechanical projection and reproduction.

Moving onward from the state festivals to their culmination in Nafest, the selection process continued in favor of those specimen dances that featured broader themes and national meanings. Seen as the second phase of "a crucial journey which took officials . . . to all corners of our great country in an attempt to rediscover ourselves through the various forms of our traditional dances" (Ashiwaju 1974, 9), the Fourth National Festival of the Arts, in Kaduna, transposed the final cut of 390 dances into a singular national grid. This was done consciously by seeking the broadest distribution of dances and choreographic styles and assimilating them to a transcendental table of categories that placed the nation before the states.

Dan Awodoye, who was coordinating secretary of Nafest and later served as FESTAC's publicity director, was intimately involved with all levels of choreographic selection, taking cultural officers from the states to remote areas where even they had never ventured. Approaching dance as diagnostic of culture, he described the basic principle of choreographic selection as one of widest possible relevance:

> My job is to promote and develop Nigerian culture. You also observe cultures which are irrelevant. If a culture is not really relevant, if it doesn't relate to other people, then you leave it in the village where it belongs. If the culture transcends the particular local area, you bring it to the national level. So that is the foundation of cultural unity.[58]

Awodoye specified three criteria of choreographic relevance. First, the dance must be congruent with one of the national categories. These consisted of (a) masquerade dances, (b) maidens' dances, (c) war dances, (d) acrobatic dances, (e) puppet theater, (f) vocational dances, (g) ritual dances, (h) elders' dances, (i) creative dances, (j) social entertainment dances, and (k) ceremonial dances. The more closely the dance corresponded to one of these ideal types, the greater its relevance to the nation at large. Second, the dance must communicate easily to the observer. And third, it must be beautifully performed.

During our interview I did not think to ask Awodoye what he and others took to be communicative clarity and aesthetic excellence. Trained in theater arts and criticism at the University of Ibadan, Oxford University, and the University of Iowa in the 1960s and early '70s, he clearly brought to choreographic tradition a modernist appreciation of form and technique, but as he explained, he was not the judge of the selections. Rather, he worked "as a bureaucrat, a technocrat, an expert" to produce the write-ups of the dances and present them to the final selection committee, consisting of Chief Anthony Enahoro, federal commissioner for information and labor at the time, and the commissioners from the states working under his jurisdiction.

Nafest thus fashioned a distinctively Nigerian cultural festival from traditional material generated successively by the states. Organized by genre rather than by provenance, its dances were true to national form. As their frame of reference expanded, their local movements and meanings were abridged and condensed. Detached from the grass roots, filtered through the states, and relocated within a unifying typology, their "traditional" value was ultimately converted into the value of national "tradition." As for the ritual dances that might require appeasements, such as killing a cock, Ashiwaju—who served as Nafest's chairman—explained, "The dancers do that before leaving home. I back them up by insuring them with the National Insurance Corporation in case of accidents."[59] Like local gods, the nation exchanged protection for veneration.

Monumental as it was in scope and execution, the national promotion of traditional dance witnessed a complementary development of dance theater or dance drama, representing the innovative, creative, and dynamic components of a distinctively modern choreographic genre. Pioneers of this genre, such as Fidelma Okwesa, Duro Lapido, Akin Euba, and Peggy Harper, self-consciously adapted traditional dances to the modern stage by incorporating them into dramatic stories based on a concept such as Abiku (the Yoruba born-to-die spirit) or a mythohistorical event such as the deification of Shango. Politically framed as a rejection of Western ballet and "Anglo-theater," the dance drama promoted national cultural awareness by selecting choreographic segments from dances around the country and weaving them into an overarching performance. The self-conscious modification of traditional dance was seen in terms of its incorporation into a larger choreographic narrative, enhanced by set design, blocking, lighting, sound, and, as Awodoye explained, "how to come in, how to go out, how to rearrange things, using new idioms—these are the creative things." In many cases, the same traditional segments selected for Nafest provided material for the FESTAC dance dramas, according to the guiding principle of widest distribution and appeal, but reframed in modern and creative contexts as elements and episodes of the larger drama itself. And unlike the traditional dance festivals, which groomed dancers from local areas and high schools, the dance drama troupe was a multiethnic company with recruits from all over the country to represent the "federal character" of the nation.

The development of this important performance genre in Nigeria was a complex process that I can only crudely sketch. There were, for example, internal variations and debates over how much song or dialogue should be used, if any, or what type of improvisation was appropriate. F. O. Begho, a choreographer from the University of Ibadan who served as one of the dance drama judges for Nafest, complained that none of the four entries were any good because they merely imposed folktales on traditional dances without creating anything new. As he explained,

> We can distinguish between purely traditional dance and the Neo-Traditional Creative Dance Theatre wherein movements of our established traditional dances are freely extracted and put together to create entirely new dances. . . . Of contemporary creative dance theatre is expected that choreographic effort, with the aid of suitable creative music, to discover appropriate movements through total improvisation and then stabilize and arrange these with a view to arriving at a unified dance composition which may depict life, characters, moods or report or take a stand about issues of the moment or indeed may say nothing save exhibit the mere beauty of dance and architectural geometric designs like the ultra-modern painters for whom the beauty of colour and incomprehensible abstractions are enough motivation and grandeur.[60]

This rather long-winded statement identifies important features of the new genre, framed here in neotraditional terms. Foremost is the emergence of a new choreographic language, in which extracted traditional forms are recombined into "entirely new dances." Improvisation is stabilized into unified arrangements that vary in meaning from the political and allegorical to the purely aesthetic and formal. We also see an important tension between the reinterpretation of traditional themes and the modernist celebration of color and form, as if reflecting the modernity of the nation form itself. In more general terms, however, the basic opposition between traditional dance and modern dance drama represented complementary models of national participation, and was already in place when Demas Nwoko joined the NPC as director of the Subcommittee on Dance.

The immediate challenge confronting Nwoko was the final selection of traditional dances and the production of a new dance drama for

FESTAC. Although there was general agreement that Nafest had duplicated dances in the name of state balancing, considerable controversy broke out over what the new criteria and selections should be. Dr. Ola Balogun insisted that dances not be taken out of their cultural contexts, recommending that "the ritual aspect of the dances be included in Nigeria's presentations."[61] Nwoko guaranteed that all nineteen states would be represented, adding that in the case of new states formed since 1974, miniperformances should be held for further selections. He also proposed merging traditional dances for purposes of economy, provoking heated debate over possible damage to state identity.[62] Furious over the politics of state balancing and the sacrifice of talent to bureaucratic myopia, Chief Hubert Ogunde — eminence grise of dance and drama — resigned from the subcommittee, warning that Nigeria's prestige was imperiled.[63] But the two largest conflicts concerned the Obitan dancers of Ondo State, and the bare-breasts debate. If the first reveals how the politics of state balancing played out within one state, the second illustrates how the "elevation" of national culture reformed the female body.

The Ondo conflict arose when the Obitan Dancers were mysteriously dropped from Nigeria's final program. We may recall from chapter 2 that Obitan was performed in Senghor's Dakar festival. Having participated in the preparatory festivals, including a special appearance at the formal opening of the National Theatre, the dance group was en route to FESTAC when they heard a rumor that the Ekitis were pulling a fast one and taking their place. The troupe went directly to the oba, the Osamawe of Ondoland, who lodged a complaint on their behalf, stating in a letter to the permanent secretary of the Ministry of Defense that "we all felt that there had been something trickish from the Ministry responsible in Ondo State and unless something is done to check such a trick, cooperations in Ondo State are at stake."[64] The effort failed, and Ondo State was indeed represented by a group from Ado-Ekiti performing the Ijomole dance, otherwise know as Imole Oloba. The latter name reveals that the dance "belongs" to the Oba of Ado, reinforcing the ethnic conflict between Ondos and Ekitis with political competition between their traditional rulers. Although I never did get to the bottom of the conflict, it appears that an Ado-Ekiti faction used some influence with the state commissioner to replace the Obitan dancers with a group of their own, thereby maneuvering into the national arena. Awodoye recalled that Obitan — a dance displaying "maidens" ready for marriage — was favored precisely because of its wide distribution in many areas of Ondo State and beyond, including Lagos. Although it had no particular association with the Oba of Ondoland, the actual troupe was connected to one of his chiefs.[65] Thus we see how concrete networks linking political levels and ethnic affiliations were mobilized by the selection process, ranging from subordinate chiefs of traditional rulers to the NPC and the Ministry of Defense.

The bare-breast debate developed from the other direction, top-down from the IFC to the dances selected by the NPC. Banning the wearing of wigs and the exposure of breasts by female participants in FESTAC, the IFC was itself divided between two schools of thought. One, proclaiming that bare-breasted dancers were indigenous to African culture, argued that such dancers should perform at the festival "in all their pristine beauty without making any concessions to modernism." The opposing school argued that because culture is dynamic, not static, and survives by adapting to new conditions, the move from a rural setting to an urban stage changes the cultural context in such a way that "attention moves away from aesthetic spirit to the aesthetics of the flesh," running the further danger of confirming to the outside world that Africans are primitive and uncivilized.[66] When the latter position won out, members within the NPC dissented. The sanctimonious chairman, Major General I. B. M. Haruna, enthusiastically endorsed the IFC's recommendation, but Dr. Ashiwaju and his Dance Subcommittee did not. Nafest had featured bare-breasted dancers without controversy, but in FESTAC the stakes were raised. Ashiwaju recalled, "It became so heated an argument that we thought, OK, let them have their way, but you can't stop the artists from the way they want to perform. That was the halfway house I then suggested to them, and that was it. We just had to do that."[67] In the end, some female dance groups covered their breasts, others did not, and nobody seemed to care (fig. 3.1). The discourse of the exposed female body was more important than its actual exposure, reframing the journey from village to nation in the civilizing mission of bodily reform (Comaroff and Comaroff 1992). In the globally framed discourse of the black public sphere, the female breast became a private part.

In the meantime, Demas Nwoko had more immediate problems to contend with. In addition to trimming the traditional dances down to size and finalizing arrangements with the states, he was also producing *The Children of Paradise,* his own dance drama, and holding nationwide auditions in Benin City, Ibadan, Calabar, Kaduna, and Kano to recruit a representative national cast (with at least one member from each state) for grooming and training in Ibadan. An allegory of colonial devastation followed by African revolution and recovery, *The Children of Paradise* is set in "a land flowing with milk and honey, a land of music and of dance; of precious minerals and priceless art works." There the children of paradise are attacked by albinos who prevail by dint of their superior weapons. A "Black Moses" is born in the figure of Ogun, who cuts out the

FIGURE 3.1 Female dance troupe in the National Stadium. In Lahey [1977?], unpaginated. Photograph by Richard Saunders.

white heart of the Albino King, whereupon he is ambushed and killed by albino loyalists. At his funeral, mourning becomes revolution as the people overthrow the albinos and regain their rightful place in paradise. The allegory plays on the very function of FESTAC in an oil-rich Nigeria, restoring precious minerals and priceless artworks to the postcolonial black and African world. Organized in a series of choreographic tableaus, it featured a series of masquerades and dances performed by dancers from around the country. Anticolonial in form as well as content, the program contrasts African with Western dance in terms of heaven-bound versus earth-bound, harmonic and melodic versus rhythmic and percussive.

Under difficult conditions, Nwoko fulfilled his charge. The traditional dances were performed only once, in two batches at two different venues—first at Tafawa Balewa Square, and later at the sports hall of the National Stadium. The final performance of all traditional dances together was cancelled without warning to make way for a special gala night. Planned sideshows of traditional dances around the city never materialized, although some of the dances were used for Nigeria's command performance with Ethiopia. *The Children of Paradise* suffered similar setbacks. Because the production was pressed for time, its opening performance was also its dress rehearsal, and was cut off midway to make room for other unscheduled shows. Moreover, the first full-length performance in the National Theatre was ruined because the amplification system had been removed. Nwoko concluded his final report on a discouraging note: "On the whole the general impression one got about arrangements for our participation was total indifference to downright hostility of programming officials of the festival, to the Nigerian input." With the arrogance of its bureaucrats, the state could exact extraordinary demands and intervene at will. It may seem surprising that dance, the very paradigm of culture itself, was brought with such great effort and expense from the villages and through the states to such an anticlimactic conclusion. But the making of national culture, we have seen, was less the product than the process.

RETURNING TO the main theme of this chapter—the production of "the people" over and above the people—we have seen how the state created a national culture that lost touch with the very public it was supposed to elevate and represent. "Harmonized" within a national framework of information and public enlightenment, the various media for bringing cultural awareness to the masses were constrained by state censorship and surveillance. In the exhibits and events featuring Nigeria's national participation in FESTAC, the producers of culture were divorced from their products, which—insured by NICON—were reinvested with national value. If national literature relegated vernacular languages to the sidelines, arts and crafts assimilated vernacular styles to a national standard, privileging the distribution of objects over their production while reducing consumption to display. In traditional costumes, we saw how Chief J. A. Ayorinde promoted a distinctively Yoruba cultural template to recast the nation in terms of the western region, resurrecting traditional chieftaincy through a set of exhibitionary conventions and categories that transformed "originals" into reflected images. Confronting the traditional male, the modern Nigerian woman emerged in popular dress, pushing gender beyond ethnicity at the risk of silencing and commodifying the body beneath the clothes. And in the exemplary arena of traditional dance and modern dance drama, we saw how even the most systematic efforts to build a national choreography from traditional grass roots transformed dances into formal tokens of a transcendent national type. Similar processes of abstraction and relocation came into play in the areas of art, music, and drama.

I am not suggesting that such reifications could or should have been avoided with better plans and policies. The nation is, after all, "a fiction in politics" (Trouillot 1990, 26) that has no fixed content or stable referent. Rather, I am interested in specifying the various modes of reification involved in the production and commodification of national culture. I have until now avoided the familiar term *fetishism,* and invoke it here with particular characteristics in mind.

Marx's well-known commodity fetish, like any good fetish, remains mysteriously powerful despite the rich critical commentary it has inspired. Returning to its basic meanings, we can note the severing of the commodity from its relations of production, the misrecognition of its value as a "congealed" object of labor with a price, and its formal convertibility into money. Proceeding by analogy, we can say that culture was commodified and fetishized in just these ways. Crafts were quite literally removed from their local productive contexts, despite the reluctance of the artists and artisans, and transported to Lagos, where they were recommodified as objects of national value, insured by NICON at an established price, and removed from the "actual" market to serve as inalienable national icons and possessions. Here they were redeemed by certificates of merit—the currency of recognition—awarded by the state. With traditional costumes, the political fetishes of royal regalia (worth considerable sums on the international African art market) were likewise resacralized as national treasures.[68] In a narrow economic sense, we can say that these crafts and costumes were de-commodified as objects of economic production and recommodified, indeed refetishized, as objects of national culture. So too with women's popular dress, as well as traditional and modern dance. In fact, the dance of money and commodities that Marx (1978, 329–36) describes in the general formula of capital began, in FESTAC, with the conversion of oil money into cultural commodities, not for direct purchase or sale but for symbolic exchange and consumption in display.

Here is where our analogy points toward a material connection. Where Marx's M − C − M' yields an economic gain (in the misrecognized extraction of surplus value), FESTAC converted the cultural commodity into a different form of value, that of national recognition both of and by the state. It is no coincidence that the Nigerian nation emerged in FESTAC as the highest form of cultural value—simultaneously the most spectacular and the most abstract—where it doubled as the general equivalent of ethnic difference and the source of tremendous wealth. National culture was thus produced not just as a symbol of political unity but as a distinctive form of exchange value that derived from oil and reflected its vitality. Its "substance" remained mystical, part money and part blood.

The political economy of cultural production and its national sphere of circulation in Nigeria converted money into political and cultural capital: political in that recognition by the state—through its bureaucratic categories and typologies—was rewarded to those performers, producers, and brokers who could convert ethnic particularities into the general, that is, national, form of culture; cultural in that the "elevation" of national culture itself—fetishized as an exalted object of knowledge and reflection—masked the contradictions of the oil economy in the *name* of the people whom it purported to serve. In the spectacle of FESTAC, national signs were taken for wonders. Whether waiting at the periphery of the nation for instructions from Lagos, or clamoring at the gates of the National Stadium and National Theatre to get in, it didn't really matter that Nigerians were left out.

CHAPTER FOUR

War Canoes and Their Magic

IN HIS discussion of art as enchanted technology, Alfred Gell identifies the quintessence of magic as a kind of conjuring, a bringing into being of an object, valuable, or commodity, without labor or cost. "Magic," he wrote, "is the baseline against which the concept of work as a cost takes shape" (Gell 1999, 181), because, like the goose that lays the golden egg, it produces wealth and riches without apparent effort. It serves, in this capacity, as "the magic-standard of zero work" (ibid., 180), a hallmark of Edenic or utopian paradise from which ordinary mortals have been banished, destined to endless toil by the curse of labor and the institution of private property. Whether overtly represented in its millenarian manifestations or implicitly embedded in all notions of work, Gell's magic formula remains something for nothing, gain without pain.

To illuminate the magical power of work degree zero, Gell invokes Simmel and the Kula canoe. From Simmel (1978, 66) comes a Kantian notion of value (with strong hints of Hegel) based on an object's resistance to our desire:

We desire objects only if they are not immediately given to us for our use and enjoyment, that is, to the extent that they resist our desire. The content of our desire becomes an object as soon as it is opposed to us, not only in the sense of being impervious to us, but also in terms of its distance as something not-yet-enjoyed. . . . As Kant has said: the possibility of experience is the possibility of objects of experience—because to have experiences means that our consciousness creates objects from sense-impressions. In the same way, the possibility of desire is the possibility of objects of desire. The object thus formed, which is characterized by its separation from the subject, who at the same time establishes it and seeks to overcome it by his desire, is for us a value.

Adding that for Simmel, exchange is the primary means for overcoming this resistance of desired objects, and that money is the pure form of the realization of desire through exchange, Gell curiously drops the "economic" line of argument to make a more limited point about art. In his more exclusive focus on aesthetic enchantment, Gell separates artistic production from exchange, and reflects on the magical value of objets d'art as products of the "occult technician." And here is where the Trobriand Kula comes in, or more specifically, the dazzling prow boards of Kula canoes. What makes this object "powerful" as a work of art is—in a word—its magic, its efficacy in influencing Kula trading partners to "disgorge their valuables" and give more than they receive. As a technology of enchantment, in this case directed at the trading partner, the prow board produces value at no cost. Gell emphasizes, however, that the magic derives not from the logic of exchange but from the technical production of the prow board itself, by a carver who applies the right magic to his craft. Moreover, the art of canoe magic is not of innovation but of replication, or more accurately, of mimesis, in that actual Kula canoes are themselves tokens of an ideal type—the mythic, archetypical flying canoe which travels without effort or resistance to appropriate valuables virtually without cost.

I open this chapter about the FESTAC Regatta with Gell's reflections on the value of art not only because they throw the main themes—canoes, magic, money, and exchange—into bold relief, but also because they foreground the problem of value itself. Briefly stated, Gell uses Simmel to establish a basic *contrast* between magic as ideal technology versus money as ideal exchange. Whereas the technology of enchantment produces objects of value without expenditure, exchange assumes a form of commensurability and equivalence established by money, Gell's aesthetic argument is quite subtle and complex, developing a set of homologies or "scheme transfers" between the technical processes and social relations of art production, but these "precede" exchange in any economic sense. And it is this resolutely neoclassical notion of value as "scarcity," somehow prior to exchange, that remains all the more curious in light of the Kula example invoked to explain it, since the Kula system of ceremonial trade is above all about the value *of* exchange. I prefer a more Marxian approach to Gell's very argument, incorporating Simmel into a more complex *equation* of ideal technology with ideal exchange. Focusing on war canoes of the Niger Delta rather than Kula canoes of the Trobriand Islands, I will argue that their magical capacity to produce value without labor derives precisely from exchange, and is an idealized expression of pure exchange value. Rather than contrast magic as ideal technology with money as ideal exchange, the war canoe's magic renders them equivalent. From this formula, the ultimate expression of magic is found not in goods or valuables but in money itself, mysteriously produced as if by a currency-generating machine.

With this equation of magic and money in mind, we can grasp the hidden transformations of value involved in FESTAC's Regatta, an elaborate celebration of Nigerian heritage through its earliest icons and symbols. Featured as one of FESTAC's major highlights, with a full roster of VIPs and heads of state, the Regatta brought the canoe culture of the Delta region to Lagos, where it became a unifying expression of the Nigerian people. Like the National Exhibition discussed in the previous chapter and the northern Durbar explored in the next, it served as one of Nigeria's main events, producing a national culture from regional materials and projecting it throughout the black and African world. The Regatta proved to be a dazzling spectacle and a great success, uniting representative contingents of eight Nigerian states beneath the banner of the nation. Indeed, it was so successful that the head of state, Lieutenant General Olusegun Obasanjo, extended it for a third day. It seemed, in fact, that the riverine canoes brought their own kind of magic, variably associated with the early days of coastal and hinterland trade, the Nigerian Protectorate, the amalgamation of ethnic minorities located throughout the Delta and Cross River areas, even the Union Jack and the British Crown. As we shall see, the historic canoe culture of the Niger Delta region developed from its beginnings as a guarded gateway to the hinterland into a highway of imperialism as British commercial interests gradually penetrated the coast up the Niger River, consolidating control though the Royal Niger Company. In the process, something akin to a hybrid or creole culture developed along the coast and up the inland creeks and estuaries, well before the formal establishment of colonial overrule.

If the commercial beginnings of colonial Nigeria have been well studied (Dike 1956, Jones 1963), the pivotal role of the war canoe in developing the cultural economy of this historic region has been overlooked. Following Gilroy's (1993) observation that slave ships of the Middle Passage played active roles in the making of black Atlantic culture, we can discern a more localized process of cultural mediation by the Delta war canoes—not merely as symbols of wealth and power but as vessels of "transvaluation" through economic exchange.[1] Here is where the canoe magic of the FESTAC Regatta begins, with the accumulation of new forms of money and value. And here, implicitly, is where Simmel returns, specifying the social and semantic properties of money as a medium of exchange.

As we shall see, the revolutionary rise of the palm-oil trade in the nineteenth century produced a creole lexicon of political identities, social values, sartorial styles, and even forms of money and credit that now characterize the Niger Delta region. Historically, with reference to European contact and trade, and the ceremonial protocol of palavers and treaty negotiations, we thus trace the origins of the canoe regatta as a "traditional" cultural institution, further elaborated in later colonial productions and again by the postcolonial state. And in the second "great transformation" which followed, when the political economy of the region shifted from palm oil to petroleum, the war canoe's magic extended throughout the nation at large. Underwritten by oil in FESTAC '77, we will see why the canoe regatta provided such a powerful template for petroleum's mysterious money-generating powers, bringing a historic symbol of pure exchange value—based on palm oil and its regional associations with money and blood—to a nation flooded with petro-naira. But let us return to the spectacle itself.

CANOES, CARS, AND CROWDS

Impeccably attired in white top hat, tie, and flowing *agbada,* Chief H. J. R. Dappa-Biriye, chairman of the National Council for Arts and Culture, poured a libation to the water gods of Five Cowrie Creek for the success of the Regatta, and for the peace and prosperity of the nation. He was joined by Chief Fagbemi Ajanaku-Araba, the Araba of Lagos, whose more "traditional" white robes and kola-nut offering represented the highest authority of Ifa divination. The ground—and water—thus ritually sanctified, Lieutenant General Obasanjo officially opened the event, which featured "a colourful armada" of two hundred war canoes from eight of Nigeria's nineteen states, more than four thousand paddlers and dancers, and a mammoth crowd of spectators graced by visiting dignitaries and key military strongmen like General T. Y. Danjuma and Brigadier Shehu Yar'Adua. Addressing the multitude, Obasanjo introduced the Regatta as a shining example of "rich cultural heritage," inviting the assembled community and the larger black world "to gain inspiration from what was left behind by our ancestors."

The official program introduces the Regatta as "the most picturesque and colourful entertainment among the people inhabiting the delta and riverine areas of Nigeria . . . popular in parts of Bendel, Imo, Rivers, Kwara, Lagos, Ondo, Ogun, and Cross Rivers States." Given such wide distribution, the event was readily converted into a "national" tradition, subsuming local and ethnic meanings and variations within a singular idiom and theme. As the program explains, its original socioreligious and military functions "for offensive or defensive purposes" during the precolonial intertribal wars developed into "a show, a sporting competition, or generally, as an annual event or entertainment for distinguished visitors." Abstracted into an ideal type, the Regatta's former associations with wars and battles were transformed into images of national harmony and order:

> In a typical regatta, a large fleet of canoes colourfully painted and decorated with flags and bunting span the river rather like swans on a fishing spree, the difference being that there is orderliness or artistic formation. The canoes are ingeniously roofed and adorned with symbolic inscriptions. They are segmented and the apartments are occupied by different groups of participants. The leader or Chief and his entourage are seated in the middle of each canoe. Drummers, singers and dancers occupy the bow and stern, flanking the canoe and painted paddlers. The coxswain sits or stands at the stern to give orders.[2]

Thus portrayed, the Regatta embodied the bureaucratic ideals of the petro-state, with its flags, rational organization, political authority, and chain of command as the coxswain, serving his chief, gave orders that were dutifully followed. If its traditional ceremonial functions included the performance of coronations, the celebration of military victories, the performance of funeral rites, the appeasement of water gods (like Mami Wata and Olokun), the reception of important visitors, and the marking of important community events, its meaning for FESTAC was more transcendent, resonating with the new Nigeria.

Located in the historically elite area of the Queen's Drive foreshore in Ikoyi, Lagos, the Regatta showcased the nation-state in microcosm. Employing the Nigerian Navy and Police to direct traffic, maintain security, and coordinate transportation of canoes and participants, the FESTAC task force for the event followed the fanfare and clockwork of a modern naval exercise. Seating arrangements in the Regatta Pavilion reflected state hierarchy, with the head of state and members of the Supreme Military Council taking their places on a central grandstand, flanked by the Chief Justice of the Federation, members of the Federal Executive

Council, traditional rulers, leaders of public institutions and corporations, and finally "any others as directed."[3] Arriving in reverse order and at fifteen-minute intervals, beginning with lesser lights and ending with the inner circle, the audience was brought to order by the national anthem, which was followed by prayer, libation, and the official opening.

After a fanfare by the Police Band, the parade of boats was scheduled to begin rowing past the grandstand in strict alphabetical order, beginning with Bendel State and followed by canoe contingents from Cross River, Imo, Kwara, Lagos, Ogun, Ondo and Rivers states. In what would appear as a textbook case of confirmatory ceremonial, each state contingent was clearly marked by relevant uniforms, flags, and bunting, followed by a "command unit" of one war canoe, two ceremonial canoes, two race gigs, one ambulance boat, and one ordinance boat manned by members drawn from each of the participating states. Bearing Nigeria's national colors in its bunting and flags, the command unit operated as a national body, replete with the firepower of the petro-state. In addition to its cannon, xylophones, and drums, the unit carried a wireless radio set connected by walkie-talkies to each canoe contingent, the pavilion on land, and the police boat, ensuring direct communication in case of accidents or emergencies.

After various salutations and mock battles staged by the war canoes, the convoy would be reorganized, bringing the nation into explicit focus. As the preliminary Regatta program explains, "the return journey to the mooring ground will be done not according to State contingents but by categories of vessels—the sporting canoes in six rows; followed by the racing gigs, the ceremonial gigs and the war-canoes. The command vessel unit brings up the rear."[4] Thus regrouped into a national flotilla, the nation would rise up from the river.

As with the opening ceremonies in the National Stadium and popular performances in the National Theatre, choreographed plans turned into strategies of containment. The sheer energy of the Regatta, according to one reporter, "turned the lulling lagoon into a tidal wave of canoes, cars and crowds," with vip stands spilling over with people.[5] Disrupting the alphabetical order of the boat parade, the Ogun State contingent quite literally jumped the gun in paddling past the grandstand, preempting Bendel State's opening position in the lineup. Dressed in pink and red uniforms, the Ogun State team danced and paddled to drumbeats and singing, staging a mock battle and shooting their Dane guns directly at the shore. By adorning the front of their boat with the national flag, they were clearly claiming Obasanjo as one of their own, an Egba man from Ogun State, thereby claiming special liberties and privileges as well.

Bendel State followed with two contingents of Ijaw warriors and Itsekiri ceremonial boats, which together stole the show. With faces daubed in charcoal war paint originally designed to terrorize their enemies, the Ijaw team waged more elaborate mock battles, invoking the intertribal wars with their war songs, dances, and gunfire. In blue canoes bedecked with raffia fronds and mock carronades, they represented local divisions of the Niger Delta, with flags bearing identification such as Amoun Aro, Ogodobiri Town of Western Ijaw Division, Okrika War Canoe, Ayakaromo War Boat, Agoloma War Canoe, and so forth. Complementing this military group, the Itsekiri contingent emphasized the "grace and grandeur" of its slower rhythms and female paddlers, who leaned back against the water with every stroke.[6] Bendel was followed by Imo, Kwara, Lagos, Ondo (fig. 4.1), and Rivers states, each with its identifying themes, colors, rhythms, flags, and bunting.[7] Imo featured Ibo masqueraders, Kwara brought calabash floats from its Pategi Regatta (founded in 1953), and Lagos displayed the Agemo masquerade, incorporating an Ijebu chieftaincy ritual into its ceremonial canoe.

If local divisional and ethnic identities were sustained by canoe iconography, these were reinforced to some extent by representative leaders and groups on the shore, dressed in the expensive flannel and worsted woolen fabrics so emblematic of authority in the Delta states, and bedecked with heavy coral beads and tiger molars. There were also side performances by Itsekiri masqueraders and dancers. But in order to promote one nation united by oil, local traditions were celebrated and revalued in terms of national heritage. As described by U. N. Abalogu, a career officer in the Ministry of Culture who was closely involved with Nigeria's exhibits and events, national form prevailed over specific content:

> The paddlers, who were sometimes made up of men or women entirely or mixed, flanked the canoes on both sides with their artistically carved and gaily painted paddles. They showed their dexterity as they gleefully rowed rhythmically and in unison with the music. . . . Some canoes carried dancing masqueraders or puppets on the deck. . . . The climax of the first day was the clustering of all the canoes before the Grand Stand, apparently in salute to the Nigerian Head of State and Grand Patron of the FESTAC, Lt. General Olusegun Obasanjo. *It was a pageant of colours and a kaleidoscopic view of Nigerian traditional heritage of different ethnic cultures.* Thereafter they made a "U" turn and returned to their mooring base at Moroko. (Abalogu 1980, 101; my emphasis)

At the end of the day, the command unit was unable to regroup the canoes into a national fleet. Instead, "participants were too enthusiastic in their passionate display to conform easily to the general order," with command vessels and contingents jumbled together in the water (ibid., 102). But if the spirit of the nation exceeded the boundaries of the state, it hardly mattered, since the official discourse of national unity was firmly established.

A more revealing divergence between plans and execution concerns the removal of Obasanjo and the natural rulers from the Regatta canoes themselves. In his preparatory notes, Chief Dappa-Biriye emphasized the important place of political leaders in traditional regattas: "The quintessence of meaningful traditional regatta is the *direct participation on board* of the Head of Government or of the paramount traditional ruler or both," adding that "the regatta resolutions at that level are the metaphysical-communion so vital to a nation's existence and future."[8] I will return to these notions of resolution and "metaphysical communion" in due course, as expressions of exchange value produced by regattas. For now, I simply wish to highlight the original plan to bring Nigeria's head of state on board the command vessel, sail out with its accompanying flotilla across the creek, and return after one hour to deliver him back at the grandstand. Accompanied by an entourage that would include FESTAC's president (Commander O. P. Fingesi), the chairman of the National Participation Committee (Major General I. B. M. Haruna), and the Regatta supervisor (Dappa-Biriye), the festival's Patron, Lieutenant General Obasanjo, was to receive a welcoming address read on board, and would deliver a fitting response. The boarding invitation would also be extended to all interested visiting heads of state wishing to join the entourage. In supporting roles, natural rulers from the riverine states would also board the canoes of their representative contingents.

Although these plans of direct participation never materialized— Obasanjo remained onshore while those natural rulers who actually attended were pushed to the periphery of the VIP bleachers—they evoked an era of coastal politics and canoe diplomacy which established the historical basis of the FESTAC Regatta. As we shall see, such boarding invitations and exchanges were critical to the palavers and trade agreements that established British presence and consular authority on the coast and gradually up the Niger River. But this history was virtually erased from FESTAC's collective memory. Instead, a genealogy of colonial exhibitions and commemorations was listed in the official program and broadcast in running commentary during the event, including one regatta brought from Ijebu in 1896 to perform at the Olympic Games in Paris, another held in Lagos to mark the 1937 coronation of George VI, and a regatta held in 1960 to celebrate the centenary of Lokoja, where the Royal Niger Company had once established an important base. This is not to suggest that noncolonial regattas were completely ignored. Indeed, the FESTAC Regatta was explicitly identified as a composite of ritual practices and fishing festivals linked to local kings and chiefs, coronation ceremonies, and colonial displays. It is precisely the making of FESTAC's national regatta from this historical and cultural material, however, which the following sections pursue, not simply to illustrate the triumphant march of national culture, but to identify the less obvious forms of inversion, conversion, and exchange involved in its production.

MASTERS AND SLAVES

In the late 1400s—the precise date is difficult to confirm—Don Duarte Pacheco-Pereira, Knight of the Household of John II of Portugal, embarked on a secret mission for his country to navigate the Guinea Coast and assess the emerging trade in ivory and slaves. His *Esmeraldo De Situ Orbis,* published circa 1518, records a brief stop at the Rio Real, now identified as the combined estuaries of the New Calabar and Bonny rivers:

> The people of this river are called Jos [Ijaws] . . . and they are all cannibals. At the mouth of this river is a very large village of some 3,000 inhabitants, where much salt is made. The bigger canoes here, made from a single trunk, are the largest in the Ethiopias of Guinea; some of them are large enough to hold eighty men, and they come from a hundred leagues or more up this river bringing yams in large quantities . . . they also bring many slaves, cows, goats and sheep . . . they sell all this [merchandise] to the natives of the village for salt, and our ships buy these things for copper bracelets, which are here greatly prized—more than those of brass; for eight or ten bracelets you can obtain one slave. The negroes of this country are all naked, wearing only copper necklaces an inch thick . . . they are warlike and are rarely at peace. (Pacheco-Pereira 1937, 132)

Several features stand out in this earliest European description of the Ijaw people and the "village" of Bonny.[9] First, the canoes themselves figure as massive craft manned by eighty men, indicating their great size and importance in the early Delta polities. Second, as trading vessels they bring hinterland commodities such as yams, slaves, goats, and sheep to the coast, in exchange for salt in Bonny and copper bracelets from the ships off the coast. These ships belong to Portuguese slavers already at the scene, introducing the famous bronze and copper manillas that became a regional currency for centuries to follow.[10] And third, the natives, adorned in the very metal of their money, are constantly at war. Given colorations of the marvelous through which this scene was undoubtedly observed, it nonetheless establishes an early historical baseline for the "protoregatta" of the Delta canoes, illustrating what Sahlins (1985) has called "the structure of the conjuncture" between African and European contact. The war canoe, serving as a trading vessel, mediated this conjuncture as a vehicle of exchange, converting slaves into manillas and manillas into slaves.

Nearly two centuries later, the Dutch explorer Dapper described the extensive markets and associated commodities and currencies that had developed in the Rio Real. As summarized by Jones (1963, 36–38), Dapper's *Description de l'Afrique* (1686)[11] documents Holland's trade in slaves, and the emergence of small copper rods—"each a cubit and a quarter long and weighing five '*carterons*'"—supplementing manillas as the preferred currency for purchasing human cargo, at the rate of fourteen or fifteen per slave. Like his Portuguese predecessor, Dapper was impressed by the war canoes, which he described as

> fifty to seventy feet long with twenty "rowers" (paddlers) on each side, each with his shield and bundle of throwing spears (*trousseau d'assagayes*), these people always being at war with each other. The canoes can carry sixty to eighty people, are pointed at both ends and six foot wide in the centre, the thwarts are planks "as large as one's open hand." Each canoe has its own hearth for cooking and the master can lie down at full length. There are holes in the thwarts for carrying forked poles which support a mat awning beneath which they can shelter should they have to spend a night on board. (Translated and summarized by Jones [1963, 38])

Again, we can appreciate the elaborate design and structural specialization of such an impressive craft, representing not just a considerable force of arms on the water, equipped as well for cooking and overnight journeys, but also a sociopolitical unit—what will develop into the named residential canoe house on land—with its master at the center. And in economic terms, the war canoes were central to the slave trade, both in capturing prisoners to be sold and in transporting them to the European slavers anchored off the coast; in effect, converting prisoners into commodities by exchanging them for copper manillas and rods.[12]

The role of war canoes in the slave trade of the late seventeenth century is further illustrated by the French brothers John and James Barbot, who bought slaves from Kalabari and Andoni merchants. John Barbot observed of Bonny,

> It is well peopled with *Blacks,* who employ themselves in trade, and some at fishing . . . by means of long and large canoes, some sixty foot long and seven

broad, rowed by sixteen, eighteen or twenty paddlers carrying *European* goods and fish to the upland *Blacks;* and bring down to their respective towns, in exchange, a vast number of slaves, of all sexes and ages, and some large elephant's teeth, to supply the *Europeans* trading in that river. Several of those *Blacks* act therein as factors, or brokers, either for their own country-men, or for the Europeans who are often obliged to trust them with their goods to attend the upper markets, and purchase slaves for them. (Cited in Jones 1963, 39; original emphasis)

What quite literally stands out in his *Description* is the italicized contrast between blacks and Europeans as partners in trans-Atlantic trade, with the emergence of mediating "factors" or brokers and an important form of credit called "trust."[13] It is precisely this class of middlemen or brokers that gave rise to the dynastic ruling houses of the riverine trading states, accumulating fortunes and competing against each other for political power and market share. And it was these houses that owned fleets of canoes that functioned as vessels of mediation and exchange, combining European and African icons and elements into their very fabrics and structures.

The Apotheosis of Richard Lander

Thus far I have identified the earliest descriptions of war canoes, narratives emphasizing their interstitial role in the Atlantic slave trade. For us to appreciate the modalities of value and exchange associated with their "magic," and to trace the development of the canoe regatta out of its earlier protoforms, I turn to the travels and tribulations of the English brothers Richard and John Lander, who discovered the terminus of the River Niger. Their journey is of critical importance because it set off a series of exchanges between British and African traders that shaped the course of riverine Delta history and its regional cultural economy. What concerns us with their account is not the geographical discovery itself, but the fundamentally inverted logic of gift giving which carried them—quite physically—to their final destination.

In 1830, the Landers began overland from Badagary to Bussa, joining the Niger River at the very place where—twenty-five years earlier—Mungo Park's ill-fated expedition had perished to the man. Following Park's lead, their strategy was to begin their canoe travel inland and reach the coast wherever the river might lead, inverting, as it were, the normal orientation of European coastal contact. After many meetings and skirmishes with local natives and rulers, the Landers approached the Delta creeks and tributaries, where they were attacked and taken hostage. Their remaining goods and supplies seized, they found themselves transformed into controversial objects of exchange, implicated in a protracted series of reversals and deferred payments that extended beyond their final destination to successive expeditions. This momentous turning point in European-African relations began with the ominous approach of war canoes that inspired within Richard Lander a certain shock of recognition:

> We . . . saw about fifty canoes before us, coming up the river. They appeared to be very large and full of men, and the appearance of them at a distance was very pleasing. They had each three long bamboo canes, with flags flying from them, one fixed at each end of the canoe, and the other in the middle. As we approached each other I observed the British Union flag in several, while others, which were white, had figures of a man's leg, chairs, tables, decanters, glasses, and all kinds of such devices. The people in them, who were very numerous, were dressed in European clothing, with the exception of trousers. (Lander and Lander [1832] 1965, 232–33)

If Lander saw signs of British sovereignty and civilization adorning the advancing war canoes, his initial happiness soon turned to horror. As the war canoes approached, it was not just British symbols but also arms that confronted the explorers. Each canoe was equipped with swords, boarding pikes, muskets, and, lashed to the bow, a small cannon "that would carry a shot of four to six pounds." Following a brief struggle in which they lost their boats, goods, even jackets and shoes, the Landers had no choice but to obey their new masters (ibid., 233). Taken thereafter to the "Kirree" market (now identified as Asaba), they were again struck by the mixing of European and African symbols and categories, not only on the war canoes but in the arenas of exchange. As Richard's brother John observed,

> Nothing could exceed my surprise, on approaching the market, to observe, as I thought, large European flags, affixed to poles, and waving over almost every canoe that was there. On a closer examination I discovered them to be imitations only, though they were executed with uncommon skill and neatness. British colours apparently were the most prevalent, and among these the Union flag seemed to be the general favourite. Nor did my former surprise diminish in the least . . . on finding that the market-people were clad in European apparel, though . . . none of them were dressed in a complete suit of clothes. One wore a hat only, with a Manchester cotton tied round his waist, another a shirt, another a jacket, etc. . . . . The multitude formed the most motley group we have ever seen; nothing on earth could be more gro-

tesque or ridiculous. Many of the men had a smattering of the English and French tongues. (Ibid., 235)

What amazed the Lander brothers, apart from their sudden misfortune, was the extent to which European cultural forms and commodities—from flags, clothes, and cottons to English and French "tongues"—had already penetrated inland from the coast, not as isolated objects or elements but in hybrid, even creolized, patterns. As the Landers had learned previously in "Katunga" (Old Oyo), Europeans were long preceded by their gifts and commodities in the African hinterland; but at Kirree they found highly developed forms of symbolic appropriation and revaluation that appeared "grotesque" and "ridiculous" because they confounded the fundamental alterity of the African.

The precise mechanisms of such creolization are difficult to determine, but they were clearly associated with coastal trade and riverine markets. If the war canoe itself as a vessel of exchange came to embody the icons and arms of its European trading partners, either directly or through secondary elaborations up the river, so the trading centers like "Kirree" developed patterns of distinction and stratification marked by new forms of value. Thus regarding Lander's puzzled observation of a "native" union jack decorated with glasses and decanters, illuminating evidence comes from Captain Becroft, who navigated up the Niger in 1840 in search of trade routes that would avoid the Delta marshes. In a meeting at Lechee in the river's upper course, Becroft (1841, 186) described a rather typical gift exchange with striking details:

> The chief, who was very eager for rum, brought out a decanter (such as are on the coast called *trade-decanters*) containing some ardent spirits, likewise a wine-glass—all of which he said he had purchased from the town of Raka, in the Yarriba country—from which it would appear that there is communication between Raka and the coast, probably with Whydah or Lagos.

The passage places the decanter and wine glass within conventions of trading etiquette and ceremonial, explaining their efficacy as "potent" icons of coastal trade as it traveled up the river into the interior. If the "Whydah" (Ouida) reference is correct, it further explains other devices on the flags described by Lander, such as the figure of a man's leg and of animals, also found on Dahomean flags. As for the Union Jack, it is possible that leading canoe houses traded with particular nations with whom they enjoyed protection to the point of carrying their flags.[14] Whether or not such direct affiliations developed, evidence that flags formed an important part of the symbolic capital invested in trade relations comes from Becroft's subsequent exchange with the Emir of Nupe:

> After the usual compliments and salutations were over, I thanked him for the ostrich he had sent to me the day before. . . . He then presented me with deer-skins and a tanned hide, blackened on one side, and neatly bound with coloured leather; likewise a metal jug full of Gooroo [kola] nuts. I asked if he would accept of my sword if I sent it on shore to him. He said he would and would be proud to wear it. I told him that I would send it with the flag which I had promised to him, as soon as I went on board. He thanked me—desired me to remember him to the Queen of England, and hoped she would think him worthy of her notice. Here the ceremony ended . . . *I accordingly sent, by the return of the boat, my sword and belt, with an union-jack.* (Becroft 1841, 188; my emphasis)

The prestigious gifts of the sword and Union Jack—carrying the charisma of the captain and his queen—were thus added to the emir's prized possessions, and in like manner could be incorporated into war canoes. It is interesting to note that the Union Jack, with sword and belt, were sent "by the return of the boat," as autonomous emblems detached from the giver's person and body.

It is thus in such contexts of ceremonial exchange that the seizure of the Landers is better understood. For the brothers Richard and John were literally turned into commodities, reversing the relations of European coastal trade in a master-slave dialectic of historic proportions. Moreover, as their journal records, this great transformation entailed their relocation into African canoes, where they remained on the water and under guard, moving from one war vessel to another with value added in each transaction.

Stripped, like King Lear on the heath, to the most primitive condition of "naked, unaccommodated man," deprived of clothes, property, even of head covering under the burning sun, the Landers were "constrained to remain in the canoes" while a major palaver was held in the market to determine their fate. After heated deliberations, they would be taken to "*Obie,* king of the *Eboe* country," who would make a final decision (Lander and Lander [1832] 1965, 241). Thus began a historic association with one Ibo leader, mistaken at the time as a "paramount" king, and successive European expeditions up the Niger in the development of "legitimate commerce" and the palm-oil trade. For now, however, I will focus on the complex reversal of fortunes that followed.

The Landers, naked and miserable, and King Obi, magnificent and "splendidly clothed," inverted the standard opposition between the primitive African and civilized European. This king, bedecked in coral beads and bracelets around his neck, wrists, and ankles, and wearing a conical beaded crown, incorporated into his royal insignia "a short Spanish surtout of red cloth, which fitted close to his person, . . . [and was] ornamented with gold epaullettes . . . and overspread with gold lace" (ibid., 252). The hybrid outlines of this royal outfit and its distinctively Spanish influences point to the Obi Ossai's involvement in the slave trade, from which he accumulated handsome profits. In keeping with this calculus, he offered the trading chiefs of Bonny and Brass to exchange the Landers "for as much English goods as would amount in value to twenty slaves," while restoring to the brothers as much of their goods as could be recovered (ibid., 256). This initial price was itself complex, figured in terms of English commodities that were valued in relation to slaves, establishing an implicit human currency in the form of metal bars (with an ad hoc exchange rate of ten Africans to one European!). But the price was hardly stable. The offer was accepted by one King Boy, a Brass prince of considerable means whose reputation for shrewdness and cunning would grow with successive European expeditions. King Boy took the Landers on credit, as it were, paying the Obi his price but demanding full compensation from the Landers, plus an additional fifteen slaves' or bars' worth of European goods and a cask of rum "as a remuneration for the hazard and trouble" incurred in transporting them to Brass.[15] Thus increased from twenty to thirty-five bars, the price of the Landers' redemption was to be covered by one Captain Lake, a Liverpool palm-oil trader anchored off the coast, who in turn would be reimbursed by the British government. In guarantee of this payment King Boy had the Landers' word.

The plot thickens as the Landers changed masters and canoes. King Boy was something of a young Turk, dealing with Spanish slavers and Liverpool palm-oil merchants while investing his profits in economic and political capital. His fully armed war canoe proclaimed his importance as a major coastal trader, and began to resemble a small frigate:

It is paddled by forty men and boys, in addition to whom there may be about twenty individuals, or more, including a few slaves and ourselves—so that the number of human beings will amount to at least sixty. Like Obie's warcanoes, it is furnished with a cannon, which is lashed to the bow, a vast number of cutlasses, and quantity of grape and other shot, besides powder, flints, etc. It contains a number of large boxes or chests, which are filled with spirituous liquors, cotton, and silk goods, earthenware, and other articles of European and other foreign manufactures; besides abundance of provisions for present consumption, and two thousand yams for the master of a Spanish slaver, which is now lying in Brass river. In this canoe three men might sit with ease abreast of each other . . . the canoe is supplied with two immense speaking-trumpets . . . and is commanded by regularly appointed officers, with sounding titles, in imitations of European vessels, such as captain, mate, botswain, coxswain, etc, besides a cook and his minions. (Lander and Lander [1832] 1965, 259–60)

In addition to its revealing inventory of slaves, firearms, and European commodities, the canoe has begun to replicate titled officers as well, absorbing, as it were, the political structure of its European counterparts, a trend adumbrated by the adoption of European titles (such as king and duke), personal names, and nicknames by the traditional Delta trading houses (Jones 1963, 22 passim) centuries before. The Landers record a parallel process of mimesis and creolization in King Boy's house, a structure that doubled as a residence for his wives and storehouse for his goods, contained four apartments in its oblong "European" design, was furnished with doors and cupboards made from the wood of a salvaged shipwreck, and featured "an old French print representing the Virgin Mary" (Lander and Lander [1832] 1965, 268). For the Landers it would also serve as a prison until they could negotiate their release, but before we reach this deferred denouement, we turn to the "fetish ceremony" performed on their behalf.

Just before their arrival at Brass, King Boy, with his entourage and precious cargo, made a ritual detour to appease the gods. Here we see another important riverine ancestor of the FESTAC Regatta that incorporated the Landers into a local field of ritual categories and relations. The brothers were told that the ceremony was being performed to protect them against any misfortune due to their unprecedented arrival *down* the river; that is, from inland toward the coast. In a sequence echoing Captain Cook's violation of mythic spatiotemporal order in Hawaii (Sahlins 1985), the Landers had arrived at the coast *from the wrong direction,* throwing the conjunctural categories of African-European relations into confusion. In a sense, the brothers' slavelike status at this point can be seen as a function of this categorical violation, and their incorporation into ritual a method for setting it right. More concretely, since gods were thanked after any successful slaving expedition, the ritual can be seen as a thanksgiving for their procurement and protection against European retaliation.[16] Given its many layers of meaning and purpose, the ceremony corresponded with yet another canoe transfer for the Landers, this time into that of King Forday, King Boy's father. This jurisdictional transfer would add another four bars to their redemption, since as Forday explained, "it was customary for every white man who came to the river, to pay him four bars" in "comey," or trading tax.

The fetish ceremony is noteworthy in several respects. First, from the Landers we have a fairly rich description of a war canoe ceremony that —we can assume—followed a conventional pattern. Stripping off his European clothes, the "fetish priests" covered King Boy "from head to foot with chalk," adding only a silk handkerchief around his waist and on his head a tight cap made of grass and decorated with the wing feathers of a black and white buzzard—the "fetish-bird of Brass-town." Two chalked spears were placed in each hand, and thus were adorned all members of his canoe. King Forday's canoe was less elaborately prepared, its members receiving mere chalk marks on their foreheads, while the Lander brothers were exempted from even this formality. Leading the group of assembled canoes, which included King Gun (King Boy's "brother") and the servant Damuggoo, who had been with the Landers when they were captured, King Boy made his final approach to Brass:

> The whole procession formed one of the most extraordinary sights that can be imagined. The canoes were following each other up the river in tolerable order, each of them displaying three flags. In the first was King Boy, standing erect and conspicuous, his headdress of feathers waving with the movements of his body, which had been chalked in various fantastic figures . . . his hands were resting on the barbs of two immense spears, which at intervals he darted violently into the bottom of the canoe, as if he were in the act of killing some formidable wild animal under his feet. Under the bows of all the other canoes fetish priests were dancing . . . their persons, as well as those of the people in them, being chalked over in the same manner as that of King Boy; and to crown the whole, Mr Gun, the little military gentlemen, was most actively employed, his canoe now darting before and now dropping behind the rest, adding not a little to the imposing effect of the whole scene by the repeated discharges of his cannon. (Lander and Lander [1832] 1965, 265)

Before landing at Brass, the canoes stopped at a "fetish island" where an egg was broken into the water with libations, with the canoe men jumping in after. Of the "extraordinary ceremony" thus witnessed, the Landers concluded "it was evident that we were the persons principally concerned" (ibid., 266).

There is of course more than meets the European eye in this impressive account, but even at face value we can recognize basic features of the FESTAC Regatta—the ceremonial adornment of the boats, their orderly procession with flags and spears, the cannon proclaiming chieftaincy over the waters. Even Mr. Gun's boat, darting back and forth against the general advance, anticipates the smaller, playful gigs of the FESTAC Regatta. But what of its function? Following the logic of ritual readjustment and incorporation, it is noteworthy that the canoes, having left the Niger River through the tributary Nun, changed direction in the coastal estuary and turned up the Brass River to Brass-town itself, bringing the two Europeans properly to shore, in accordance with their culturally mandated arrival from the sea.[17] From this perspective, King Boy's "fetish ceremony" neutralized the Landers' problematic appearance by reversing horizons. Support for this reading—inspired by Sahlins (1985)—comes from Talbot (1932), whose discussion of *owu*, or Delta water spirits, resonates with King Boy's triumphant return in telling details. From Talbot's collected testimonies, we learn that "all nations make juju when anything remarkable is seen in the river; for it is thought that the sight may be one or other of the genii become visible to our eyes" (Talbot 1932, 34). The Landers' association with such *owu* is plausible because all water spirits, even those of the inland creeks, come from the sea, and are "pale of face and body, much like white men" (ibid., 33). One such spirit, the Owu Amap, is further described as "white as if cut by chalk" (ibid., 34). They are all, moreover, children of the great water spirit Adumu, who is their father and chief, and has a great shrine with priests and priestesses at Brass. And Adumu, if not the biblical Adam, appears to be Portuguese, or at least incorporates Portuguese power through mimetic appropriation.[18] On his shrine is carved "an old Portuguese 'two-master'" (ibid., 36) approaching from the sea; his carved effigy depicts him "with the pointed moustache and beard, the ruff and feather-trimmed hat of a don of the period when these bold seafarers first penetrated to the lower regions of the Santa Barbara" (ibid., 38).

Whether the Landers, or the Portuguese for that matter, were initially taken for gods as such I am not prepared to argue, since I think the issue is ambiguous, much like the ritual icons themselves. Fundamental to the logic of hybridization through exchange—what I call more generally *transvaluation*—is not the assimilation of objects or perceptions to a rigid set of cultural categories but more of a synthesis through which new icons and identities emerge. In the carved arch at the Shrine of Adumu sketched by Talbot (1932, 18), we see the mythic figure at the very boundary between land and sea, mediating, if not establishing, the European and African conjuncture (fig. 4.2). Neither European nor African, Adumu is both. He exists in the mix, an identity-in-difference.

That Portuguese icons of power and value are thus incorporated into local ritual horizons does not negate their foreign provenance but quite literally fetishizes it. From this more dialectical perspective, the Landers' ambiguous status as slaves, Europeans, and possibly gods poses not a matter of interpretation for us to decide—since theirs was indeed an ambiguous condition—but a practical problem for King Boy and his community to solve.[19] And here lies the corrective logic of the fetish ceremony on the water, signifying a mythic return of the white man from the coast, in the company of priests and canoe men whitened by chalk. It is perhaps significant that the Landers themselves remained unchalked, since culturally they were already white, although "not a little tanned" (Lander and Lander [1832] 1965, 265). As particularly charged objects of a precarious exchange, the brothers were liminal and dangerous, and their arrival at Brass required ritual incorporation. Clearly King Boy, transformed into a vulture spirit, made some kind of sacrifice in his boat and again on the "fetish island." Needless to say, for both parties the final transaction was a disaster, portentously deferred.

Mr. Lake, the captain of the English brig *Thomas,* was in no mood to advance the Landers' ransom. With half his crew dead and the other half dying, he took no interest in the situation of his countrymen, and only grudgingly offered them transport to Fernando Po, where the British had recently established a base for warships. In the tense days that followed, the brothers engaged in "contemptible subterfuges of deceit and falsehood" (Lander and Lander [1832] 1965, 277), misleading King Boy while planning to slip away. The final confrontation between King Boy and the Landers took place on board the *Thomas,* with the former sent away empty-handed by force of arms and the latter escaping with their honor in shreds. The Landers' redemption was morally and economically unfulfilled. According to the terms of exchange, they remained in King Boy's debt, setting the stage for many historic returns.

Thus we see in the Landers' extraordinary journey more than a rich illustration of transvaluation through various forms of symbolic and material exchange. To be sure, it reveals the role of the canoe "regatta" in the mysterious production of exchange value, and illustrates those "creolized" forms so potently condensed in the war canoes themselves. It also exemplifies the Hegelian spirit of this exchange, which for the Landers was a master-slave dialectic when they were kidnapped and converted into objects of increasing value. It is all the more extraordinary that their historic discovery—the terminus of the Niger River— occurred through the momentum of this radical reversal, when they were captured, taken by canoe to the coast, and ritually reoriented toward Brass.[20] But in a very concrete sense, the Landers also opened the floodgates of change. Their discovery of that "highway into central Africa" which beckoned to the adventurous with untold riches inaugurated subsequent expeditions that prepared the way for the Royal Niger Company. And if the Landers opened this door, they also set the pattern of expansion by establishing a set of enduring relations with local leaders and traders that would gradually be fixed by treaties and amalgamated into a protected market. To appreciate the pivotal role of the "regatta" in establishing and expanding this presence and authority, we turn briefly to four expeditions which followed: those of Laird and Oldfield from 1832 to 1834, Trotter and Allen in 1841, Baikie and Crowther in 1854, and MacDonald and Mockler-Ferryman in 1889.[21]

Of Time and the River

Backed by Liverpool investors who formed the African Inland Commercial Company, the Laird and Oldfield expedition was the first organized response to the Landers brothers' discovery, voyaging to the terminus of the Niger to penetrate upcountry and develop hinterland trade. Focusing primarily on the palm-oil trade, of which exports to Britain were already valued at one million pounds per annum, the company aimed to bypass "the caprice and extortion" of the African chiefs serving as middlemen on the coast, and to establish "direct intercourse between the producer and consumer," benefiting both in unrestricted trade while opening markets for British goods (Laird 1837, 2–3). Members included one naval officer, Lieutenant William Allen, who surveyed the river for the government, and whose sketches provide remarkable images of these early encounters; and none other than Richard Lander himself, who brought his knowledge of the river and its people to the team. Following, we might say, the Landers' previous voyage in reverse, Laird and Oldfield piloted the first steam-powered vessels up the Niger, negotiating initial entanglements with King Forday and King Boy before holding an important "palaver" with "King Obie" at Aboh—the man who first ransomed the Landers as slaves and played a pivotal role in facilitating trade with Europeans.

Little is recorded of Richard Lander's return to the Niger and reconciliation with his former "master," King Boy. We know from Hallett (1965, 292) that Lander's debt had been settled by another trader, Captain Townson, and that King Boy received a special reward "in various handsome presents" sent out by the British government, as well as a Highland uniform with kilt and red stockings sent out by Laird's father. We also learn from Oldfield (1837, 314) that Lander personally brought him "fifteen or sixteen guns, two barrels of gunpowder, fifteen soldiers' canteens, knives, spoons, and soldiers' coats, with various other articles," with which he remained unsatisfied. But the real imbalance of debts and counterdebts, mirrored by gifts and countergifts, would not be settled until the meeting with the Obi Assai, restoring the former "slave" of this captor to equal if not superior status. In this historic reunion, a "regatta" of the English launch led by King Boy's war canoes, we can appreciate the pageantry of the moment not merely for the protoimperial theater that it was but as a form of reciprocal *misrecognition* (Bourdieu 1977) in terms of the debits and credits, losses and gains, disguised by the giving of gifts. In Allen's account of this event, illustrated by his majestic engraving (fig. 4.3), the meeting restored faith and face through the moral economy of ceremonial exchange:

> The palaver was soon "set" with Obi's messenger, who agreed that his master, as compensation for the injury his people had done to the brothers Lander, in seizing their goods, and in selling them as slaves, should pay two bullocks, ten goats, and four hundred yams. . . . In order to have a more imposing effect, we made our appearance in our gayest uniform. Lander had on that of a general officer; I wore my own; and some of the gentlemen of the expedition displayed fancy coats of many colours, turbans, sashes, &c. Pasco, the chief of the interpreters, with his subordinates, variously and gaily attired, preceded us in the jolly-boat. We followed in the pinnace, sheltered by a prodigious umbrella, of all the colours of the rainbow; with old Jowdie—a Doma slave, who had been purchased by Lander, and manumitted on his first journey,—seated in the bow, in the character of "Sàliki-n-maïkidi," the chief of the drummers, the proudest of the proud . . . with more noise than music giving ample note of our approach. King Boy, who accompanied us with all his canoes, vainly attempted to marshal the procession . . . by paddling about in all directions with canoes of every dimension; from the large war jilligi, capable of holding thirty or forty *pullaboys*, besides warriors and

passengers of all ages and both sexes, to a little frail thing in which only one person could sit. . . . Yet they paddled boldly, threading the openings between the *larger craft* with great swiftness and dexterity. Some canoes were paddled by eight or ten women. On we went, amidst the shouts and admiration of the natives . . . all striving to catch a glimpse of the procession . . . they were dazzled by a magnificence greater than the most glowing imagination of their poets. (Allen 1840, 9)

Clearly a "hybrid" creation of African and European pomp and circumstance, and a political signal of triumphant return, this "regatta" developed out of prior events and exchanges—not just the capture and sale of the Landers by the Obi, but also their transshipment and ritual reorientation toward Brass by King Boy and his "fetish ceremony." Seen against these earlier reversals, indeed as a continuation of them, Richard Lander returns as master of the situation, even wearing "a feather in his cocked-hat that almost reached the ground" (Laird 1837, 94), a theme doubled by Jowdie—his manumitted slave turned chief of the drummers and "proudest of the proud." As the conclusion of a longer movement of dispossession and repossession, the regatta represents the repayment of a debt with interest, in this case the cooperation of the Obi in promoting British commercial interests and access to the hinterland. For as we shall see, further gifts to the Obi were intended to secure his cooperation with the British cause.

And here is precisely where the ambiguities of exchange reemerge. While Allen's description represents triumphant closure, the journals of Laird and Oldfield present a more complex account of the same situation in which the Obi gained the upper hand. On receiving news of the Obi's imminent gift, Laird (1837, 93) wistfully conceded, "like all the kings who have made us presents, he will, I presume, receive double their value." It appears Laird was right. Counterpresentations included an armchair lined with scarlet cloth, a large "looking-glass," two casks of rum, and decorated scarlet Turkish trousers "trimmed with dozens of bell buttons" which, significantly, *were placed in the king's canoe.* In a reciprocal regatta the following day, the Obi was escorted by seven war canoes and "fifty others" (ibid., 99) as he embarked in his grand state canoe—"containing eighty or ninety persons" and bearing a Union Jack on its lofty pole—to visit Lander, from whom he received "a splendid officer's coat," an additional mirror, and "begged almost everything he saw" (Oldfield 1837, 388).

Although cast in a discourse of African avarice, the observation is telling in that the clothes and commodities, including coveted mirrors, allow the Obi to gaze at his own reflection, "surveying and laughing at himself for a some time . . . no doubt the happiest of monarchs" (ibid., 385). Whatever the deeper meanings of his scrutiny and laughter (cf. Comaroff and Comaroff 1991, 170–97), his mirror reflected no mere mimicry but a more powerful logic of identity and equalization. As the Obi demanded Oldfield's shirt, stockings, shoes, and suspenders, he uttered, "I shall be all the same as white man!" (Oldfield 1837, 389) This moment of radical equalization through exchange, mirroring the emergence of the money form, represents the mystical kernel of the riverine regatta, converting gifts, commodities, even racial differences between givers and receivers, into expressions of equivalent status and value. To understand the profits accumulated through such exchanges and conversions, whether symbolic, political, or purely economic, we turn to the expansion of riverine trade.

The ultimate goal of the Laird and Oldfield expedition was to establish a "factory" at the Niger-Benue confluence.[22] From here the African Inland Commercial Company would collect hinterland commodities directly from producers and transport them downriver to cargo vessels at the coast. The plan was never realized due to a series of disasters, including Lander's demise from a riverine ambush; but even if it failed in concrete terms, it established a purpose and pattern that gradually emerged in the expeditions and enterprises that followed. One of the significant discoveries of the ill-fated explorers was the extent to which palm oil was indeed available and "underproduced," emerging as the dominant export commodity over indigo, ivory, and other hinterland valuables. And even if the economic returns from hinterland penetration would take years to realize, a cartography of conquest and protection took hold that would shape the very contours of modern Nigeria. As we shall see, the Niger-Benue confluence became the inland locus of increased European presence and authority, establishing a Delta region of rivers and waterways stretching from Benin to Calabar.

The next major expedition to follow in the wake of Laird and Oldfield was that of Captain H. D. Trotter and Captain William Allen, the latter for his second ascent up the Niger. Unlike the previous, privately funded venture, this one was planned and promoted by the Society for the Extinction of the Slave Trade and for the Civilization of Africa, headed by His Royal Highness Prince Albert with Lord John Russell, the Secretary of State for the Colonies. Noting the rapid expansion of the external slave trade despite British efforts to police the coast, the society aimed at the problem's source—the inland slave markets serving overseas demand—designing an expedition "which should ascend the River Niger and its great tributary streams, by means of steam-boats, with the view of entering into 'commercial relations with the Chiefs and Powers on its banks, within whose dominions the internal Slave Trade of Africa is carried on, and the external Slave Trade supplied with its victims'" (Allen and Thomson 1848, 1:26). Thus emerged, in the name of abolition, the ideological basis of British authority in Africa, with treaties and contracts to eliminate slavery and promote commerce and civilization. Deploying economic means to serve higher, moral ends, the expedition enlisted further support for teaching agriculture together with religious instruction. In addition to providing economic incentives for chiefs to abandon the lucrative trade in slaves, the expedition would establish a Model Farm for cultivating African soil and souls.

Like its more explicitly commercial predecessor, the expedition was ultimately decimated by hardship, treachery, and death from "tropical fevers." The treaties that were signed carried no teeth, and the Model Farm, which was to serve as a beacon of civilization and the nucleus of a growing British colony, fell into ruin. But again, it is not the concrete achievements and failures of the expedition which here concern us, but the form and purpose of those projects that eventually prevailed. In this respect, King Obi yet again played important roles, signing one of the first trade "treaties" to forsake slavery in favor of palm oil, and recognizing consular authority. And here too, the regatta played a pivotal role. In a virtual rerun of the meeting with Lander and the Obi nearly ten years before, Obi's "cortege" of canoes turned out in full glory, with an improvised Union Jack, crimson umbrella, and a galley of slaves paddling in stylized unison to a "royal Ibu air" played on a native flute and accompanied by drums. Dressed in the officer's jacket and scarlet trousers he had received from Richard Lander in the previous exchange of gifts and affections, the Obi boarded the *Albert*—so named after the expedition's princely patron—and found himself among commissioners of Her Majesty the Queen. In this official arena of British authority, the regatta took a new political turn, incorporating the Obi into a sovereign code expressed in the language of contract.

In the extended dialogue and negotiation that followed, officers of the queen established the terms for outlawing slave trading, promoting native produce, providing the Obi with trading revenues, and—from the missionary Schön—explaining the Christian faith. Although the Obi appeared to understand and agree, requesting less talk and more action with respect to the arrival of British goods, his general response reinforced a more formal contrast that was emerging in the imperial imagination.[23] On two occasions, the Obi subjected the "rational" code of the treaty to the ritual obligations of fetishism. First, as witnessed by his English guests, he made ritual preparations to secure the success of the treaty:

> Guided by the occasional sound of a tom-tom and an opé, they looked into a house, where they found Obi "making Ju-ju" and calling upon his deity for success and advice, previously to proclaiming to his people the Treaty he was making with the white men. He had in his hand a naked sword, with which he touched the end of a large baton, surrounded with iron rings, which he reversed after every touch—something like the operation of magnetizing. At the same time, two of his attendants performed certain mystical motions in the air with large fans, made of palm-leaves, in order probably to keep away the Evil One. (Allen and Thomson 1848, 1:232–33)

In this eyewitness account of a private ritual, the fetish appears to effect a reversal that, as the metaphor of magnetizing suggests, manipulates the flow of mystical power or energy to attract value, wealth, and profit. The second intrusion of fetishism into the negotiation occurred on board the *Albert*. Just after all parties had signed the official document, the Europeans performed a ceremony asking "the blessing of Almighty God" for the success of their larger mission, whereupon the Obi, kneeling with the assembled body, suffered a crisis of confidence:

> In that solemn moment, when the stillness was unbroken, save by the reverential voice of the clergyman, and all were devoutly engaged, Obi became violently agitated. On the conclusion of the ceremony he started up, and ut-

tering a sudden fearful exclamation, called aloud for his Ju-ju man to bring his protecting "Arrisi," or idol, being evidently under the impression that we had performed some incantation to his prejudice, the adverse tendencies of which, it would be necessary to counteract by a sacrifice on his part. He stood trembling with fear and agitation; the perspiration streamed down his face and neck, showing how great was the agony of mind endured. The priest had heard the cry of his sovereign, and rushing into the cabin with the idol—a piece of blackened wood, enveloped in cloth—which the King placed between his feet, was about to offer the customary libation of palm-wine, etc, when Captain Trotter, also much disconcerted at the idea of a heathen ceremony being performed in our presence, and in opposition to the rites of our holy religion, interrupted him. (Ibid., 1:258–61)

Whatever theological dimensions of transvaluation were here involved —and the question of whose god we trust in any economic exchange is never fully absent—the incident represents a general confrontation between European and African commercial understandings that would develop through the hybrid idiom of fetishism itself. From the European perspective, the proponents of natural commerce in the Niger Delta would wage a protracted campaign against the fetishism of commodities.

With this spirit of natural commerce in mind, the expedition continued to Iddah, where the Attah of Egharra (Igara) more or less agreed to the terms of the treaty outlawing slavery and human sacrifices while promoting legitimate trade. He also agreed to cede a portion of land at the Niger-Chadda (Benue) confluence for the expedition's Model Farm, a territory that extended sixteen miles along the river and four miles "from its margin," and which effectively became a Crown possession for forty-five pounds' worth of cowries. Thus started the inland colonization of Nigeria, a dismal failure in execution but an enduring locus of British presence. As it turned out, the appointed leader of the little colony, Mr. Alfred Carr—"a West Indian gentleman of colour"—would disappear under mysterious circumstances never fully brought to light; the corn and cotton would fail; and the political organization of the pioneer community (thirty-two strong) collapsed under "mutiny" and "insubordination" (Allen and Thomson 1848, 2:358–64) because the settlers preferred to exploit the natives with whips than to uplift them with industry. Although officially abandoned, the settlement reemerged under the guiding spirit of William Balfour Baikie.

In contrast with its predecessors, Baikie's 1854 expedition up the Niger was a resounding success, largely due to the discovery of quinine in protecting Europeans against malaria. During its sixteen-week journey, the group—composed of twelve Europeans and fifty-four Africans, including the Rev. Samuel Ajayi Crowther as missionary and interpreter—traveled 250 miles beyond the previous exploration of the Benue (Tsadda) River, and returned without a single loss of life. In addition to its more scientific side, collecting "natural history specimens" (Marwick 1965, 8) and filling notebooks with linguistic, "ethnological," and geographical data, Baikie's team reestablished commercial relations with local chiefs and kings—including Prince Tshukuma, one of the sons of the deceased King Obi—and began to differentiate the ethnic segmentation of the palm-oil trade in terms of control over internal markets. The "Ebo" of previous accounts begin to separate into Ijaw, Itsekiri, Okrika, Ibibio, Andoni, and other ethnic designations variously defined as producers, middlemen, bulkers, and retailers of the new "staple commodity" (Baikie 1856, 21) en route to the sea. Again, the canoe played a pivotal role, not only in the pro forma regattas of trade negotiation and gift exchange, but also in the increased trade on the "Oil Rivers." In one casual description of trade upriver near the Bassa Creek tributary, Baikie recounts, "We passed some trading canoes laden with palm-oil, each of which carried a corronade in their bows. . . . Some large canoes were there, flying showy flags, on some of which were the letters K.B., probably for King Burrow, one of the lower Delta potentates" (ibid., 38–39).

If the image of the war canoes outfitted for palm oil was already emerging in Trotter and Allen's narrative (Allen and Thomson 1848, 1:236–37), there is no question that the scale of such activity had increased exponentially by the mid-1850s, with evidence that King Boy, if not King Burrow, was fully involved with the inland markets. Indeed, the abominable trade in human cargo destined for the plantations was finally in decline, giving way to the rising demand for palm oil to lubricate the machinery of the Industrial Revolution. Baikie's expedition promised new access to inland territories, with greater documentation of its peoples, routes, and waterways. The narrative of his first expedition concludes, "We have discovered a navigable river, an available highway, conducting us into the very heart of a large continent. . . . We have met on friendly terms with numerous tribes, all endowed by nature with what I might term the 'commercial faculty,' ready and anxious to trade with us" (Baikie 1856, 385–86).

It was during his second extended visit, from 1857 to 1864, that Baikie tried to bring his vision down to earth by establishing a base for a series of inland trading posts at the very Niger-Benue confluence where the Model Farm had briefly struggled in the sun. In the new town of Lokoja, he became something of a Christ-like Kurz, sacrificing personal comfort and gain for the benefit of native trade and industry, and was so respected as a mediator of local disputes between the Nupe emirate and its surrounding "tribes" that the entire district was placed under his protection. The new Christian-styled community became a model of farming, trade, wage labor, and austerity, as well as a haven for freed and escaped slaves while Baikie remained in charge, eventually winning the support of the Foreign Office (Mockler-Ferryman 1892, 283).[24] And although he died in 1864 from exhaustion and self-neglect, Baikie had achieved his ambition of "securing for England a commanding position in Central Africa."[25]

And it was here that the Royal Niger Company would establish a base for its hegemonic monopoly over riverine trade, prefiguring in its company flag the shape of the Nigerian nation. In Sir George Goldie's explication of the tripartite device—a coat of arms in the most literal sense of the term—"the three arms symbolize the three main waterways in the territory on which the Company is established . . . the triple form symbolises stability. *Ars* and *Jus* are finger posts which, supported by *Pax,* are leading Europeans into the heart of Africa" (quoted in Baker 1996, 301). The three pillars of commercial monopoly—ingenuity, equity, and peace or justice—were indeed the hallmark of the Royal Niger Company, whose ingenuity took an aggressive lead in the imposition of peace with a swift and Machiavellian sense of justice. While he was consolidating European trading factories along the waterways, Goldie's pursuit of company interests was expedited by the Royal Niger Constabulary, a "miniature army" of imported Africans and European officers "called upon frequently to undergo some very rough bush-fighting" (Mockler-Ferryman 1892, 30).[26] The company charter was eventually revoked due to his excessive zeal in violating his powers, and it was during investigations into such abuses by a government commission that the exchange relations embedded in the regatta became increasingly one-sided.

Captain A. F. Mockler-Ferryman's *Up The River* is in many ways a transitional document, representing the last of the great Niger narratives and the beginning of formal colonial overrule. True to the genre, with scenes of flora, fauna, native superstition, and traditional life, the tone is scornful and mocking, betraying a deeper sense of superiority than the optimism and enthusiasm of previous travelers allowed. Strangely absent from the text are any but the most cursory references to the expedition's raison d'être, which, we are told, is "of little real interest to the ordinary reader" (Mockler-Ferryman 1892, vii), being to investigate charges brought against the Royal Niger Company of "exceeding" its charter. Led by Major Claude MacDonald, the Consul-General of the Oil Rivers Protectorate, the commission was instructed "to make formal inquiries on the spot" and "to hold personal interviews with all the emirs, kings, and chiefs of the rivers Niger and Benue, over whom the Royal Niger Company claimed jurisdiction" (ibid.). Although the fact-finding mission was supposed to be impartial, Mockler-Ferryman's account is totally one-sided, painting company progress and virtue against native cannibalism and vice. Three paradigmatic passages capture the spirit of this contrast, wherein the canoe regatta reappears as a mediating mechanism.

In the first, describing a "palaver for peace" between the oil-trading chiefs of Opobo, Bonny, and New Calabar, the central role of fetishism in regulating market competition illustrates the misguided foundations of the African economy:

> These three tribes had constant feuds for some time amongst themselves, and had been disarmed as far as possible by the English men-o'-war on the station; but to satisfy themselves that they now possessed no arms and intended to remain at peace, the chiefs assembled to swear together, or, as they term it, "swap juju." All the forenoon a multitude of large canoes, covered with gaudy bunting and propelled by numbers of almost naked slaves, shouting in time to the dip of their paddles, entered the Bonny river from the Opobo Creek and the New Calabar River, and drew up on shore above the factories. Early in the afternoon the chiefs, dressed in their best, proceeded to the palaver house where the ceremony took place. It was of short duration, and merely consisted of an address from the head chiefs and the offering up of juju to their gods, each party vying with the other to offer the strongest juju, or that which they considered would have most weight with their fetishes. The men of New Calabar poured out libations of trade gin as their peace-offering, while the chiefs of Opobo had provided themselves with a human leg sewn up on cloth, which was no doubt considered by all present as the stronger juju of the two, for, on the conclusion of the palaver, the New Calabar men hurried home, to all appearances thoroughly scared, and the fear of bringing down the anger of their gods upon their heads will probably prevent them in the future from picking a quarrel with the men of Opobo. (Mockler-Ferryman 1892, 6–7).

Opposing this immoral economy of fear, superstition, and even human dismemberment is the rational order of European contract, promoted and protected by the Royal Niger Company. What appears to be a purely African regatta maintaining peace between the most powerful and volatile canoe houses of the Delta states (Jones 1963, 114–55) nonetheless includes English men-o'-war as interested and coercive parties in absentia. The rise of Opobo and the eclipse of Bonny as a major center of palm-oil trade was indeed an important development in the history of the region, illustrating the impact of European trade on the political dynamics of canoe houses. In this condensed allusion to a profound historical process, however, a familiar trope of African fetishism—detached from European contact and associated with indigenous heathenism—foregrounds inverted economic reasoning. As a result, the fetish associations are seen to control trade with secret pacts and "fetish vetoes," and cults such as the Idion Society of the Ibibio, the Ekpe Society of the Efik, and the dreaded Long Juju of the Arochuku would be attacked as repugnant obstacles to civilization and its natural markets (see also Pietz 1988, 121).

It is thus no surprise that the progress of the Royal Niger Company was associated with "pulling down the idols," waging a punitive expedition in 1888 against alleged human sacrifice in Asaba until "every temple, juju-house, and idol was destroyed, and the chiefs, thoroughly cowed, gave up their arms and sued for peace on any terms" (Mockler-Ferryman 1892, 29).[27] Framed within the idiom of a humanitarian crusade against the depredations of savagery was the assertion of a new economic order, pursued in the language of fair trade and rational contract. The new masters of the river were the Niger Company factors with their guns and their law. And it is to a final call for justice that our final regattas on the Niger River can be traced, more a ceremony of conquest than an exchange of gifts and goods.

Arriving at Lokoja, MacDonald's mission held a major "palaver" to interview chiefs about their dealings with the Niger Company. Like most of the palavers recorded in his account, Mockler-Ferryman said nothing of the allegations at issue, but described the scene in customary terms:

> The arrival of each chief caused considerable stir in the town, and was a most interesting and picturesque site. The first warning of a chief's approach would be a distant drumming sound, mingled with the hum of the paddlers, and then, far away down the river, are seen half-a-dozen specks on the water, which gradually grow larger and larger until they shape themselves into long dug-out canoes, each flying a certain amount of bunting. Under a small awning in the foremost canoe sits the chief, arrayed in his durbar garments, and generally very much over-hatted; the drummer, seated in the centre of the little craft, beats steadily with his wooden drumstick on a powder-keg or box, thus giving the time to the twenty or thirty half-naked slaves, who dig their little paddles into the water with an energy that brings the perspiration in streams from their massive backs. With each stroke the canoe-men give forth a strange, loud, hissing sound, changed occasionally to a shout in chorus; and, on the flat stern of the canoe, stands the helmsman, motionless as

a statue, directing the course of his vessel with a long-bladed oar, and guiding her into port a little below our moorings. At the landing-place, the professional drummers of Lokoja meet the chief and play him and his attendants up to the town. (Mockler-Ferryman 1892, 146–47)

Converging at the riverine crossways of the Company territory, the chiefs were interviewed to no account. Whatever grievances they bore were silenced by the picturesque image of customary respect, for they had been reduced to "peace on any terms." If the 1896 commission of inquiry into the "Disturbances at Brass" is any indication of what the chiefs were up against, including the killing of prisoners, raping of women, seizing of canoes and cargo, diverting of trade, and imposing of price controls and unfair terms of trade, then the last regatta on the Niger River was no mere ceremony; it marked a new era of subjugation.[28]

As the expedition continued into the deeper hinterland reaches of the Territory, the natives became more "savage-looking and hideous" (ibid., 237), with images of pestilence and depravity offset by ludicrous caricatures of their European clothes. In a major palaver at Oguta Lake, on the northern limit of Company Territory, the chiefs arrived at the station in state canoes "decorated with the gaudy flags of their owners" while accompanied by the "din of the chief's drums and the shouting of the paddlers":

> The head chief . . . was dressed in a loin-cloth and the long red coat of a Chelsea pensioner, with a lady's tiny straw hat set coquettishly on one side of his head. The other chiefs were equally oddly attired. Some wore black frock-coats of broadcloth of undoubted London build, others, tunics of the Line; and one old gentleman was disguised as a commander of the Royal Navy, though the trousers had been forgotten. Their choice of hats was also varied. The Church, the Army, the Navy, the Piccadilly "swell," and the little girl at the seaside, all were represented here. (Ibid., 238)

In this scornful rhetoric of colonial mimicry, the African chief is reduced to a diminutive half-wit, feminized and further compromised by his pathetic attempts at dignified dressing. The powerful icons of Church, Army, and State are seen not as signs of European power and prestige but as articles woefully out of place on savage bodies in a savage land. According to Mockler-Ferryman, the palaver focused on the "barbarous customs" (ibid., 239) of the natives. Requesting permission to sacrifice slaves for the burial of the recently deceased Oguta king, the chiefs were quite literally dressed to kill.[29]

If I have focused extensively on the early regattas of the Niger River and the area consolidated by the Royal Niger Company, it is because their descriptions are so rich and reveal the larger cycles of successive reciprocation that they entailed.[30] The ceremonial exchanges of the Niger expeditions were not the only canoe regattas taking place in the territories, but it is here that their critical role as mechanisms of economic exchange, political protocol, and cultural transvaluation becomes apparent, not simply reflecting British penetration into the hinterland but establishing the conjunctural framework through which it occurred. In the Oil Rivers Protectorate to the east, beyond the jurisdiction of the Royal Niger Company, an older pattern of palm-oil trade was already established, with in many respects a more developed body of what Curtin et al. (1978, 224) have called "Afro-European commercial custom." The urbane sophistication of Old Calabar and Creek Town on the Calabar River, each with its European residents and warehousing "factories," signified a more highly "creolized" eastern Delta already in place as the Niger River opened up.[31] Describing the political elite of Old Calabar in 1888, H. H. Johnston (1888, 754) observed "a number of native kings and chiefs, some of them of long descent and proud lineage, who live in handsome well-built European residences, and on Sundays and feast days dress elaborately in European clothes, at other times and seasons preferring to walk about in scarlet chimney-pot hats or the peaked caps of the mercantile marine, and little else."

And here too the canoe regatta was a mediating mechanism of consular authority in the Protectorate. Although less well documented than its counterpart on the Niger, its elements derived from the earlier ceremonies of "breaking of trade" between European captains and African kings (Jones 1963, 108–9), condensing the history of coastal exchange into the icons and bunting of war canoes. During his duties as Vice-Consul for the Oil Rivers, Johnston ascended the Cross River in a convoy of three native canoes to make treaties with local leaders and settle disputes, proceeding within the framework of the regatta:

> My first object in going up the Cross river was to settle an outstanding quarrel between the people of a district called Umon and the natives of Old Calabar. . . . As I appeared in the light of a mediator, I was most warmly welcomed. An imposing fleet of eighty large Calabar canoes reached Umon soon after I arrived, and formed a really pretty sight, as they were all painted in brilliant but tasteful combinations of colour, like aesthetic "Noah's arks;" their little houses hung with bright carpets of leopard skins, each canoe being decorated with gaudy banners, and hoisting a Union Jack—for the people of the Oil Rivers are aggressively British in their display of bunting. The crews were most fantastically dressed in gorgeous clothes, with Life-

guardsmen's or policemen's helmets, or native head-dresses of Colobus mon-
key skin, or of black-dyed filaments of palm-fronds. The beating of drums,
the blowing of horns, and the firing of guns made a clamour most disturbing to my comfort, which I promptly stopped. (Johnston 1888, 756)

Clearly outclassed by Calabar's show of force, Johnston soon found himself loaded with gifts and provisions, and quickly turned back. But his
mission of establishing treaties and expanding trade would continue,
together with plans for extending the Niger Company's royal charter
throughout the Oil Rivers Protectorate. Fortunately for the Delta chiefs
and communities within the territory, the Company's royal charter was
revoked, and in 1900—as we shall see in the next chapter—General
Frederick Lugard inaugurated a new imperial order at Lokoja. Thus
marked the end of the Nigerian regatta as a historically formative ceremonial exchange. In the changing framework of administrative reorganization, a new regatta would emerge in the image of the old.

COLONIAL CONVERSIONS

When colonial officers arrived in southern Nigeria, they knew not what
they saw. Neither the bureaucratic emirates of the north nor the centralized kingdoms of the west were in evidence, and given the relative absence of hereditary chiefs and even clearly demarcated lineages and
clans, confusion was the order of the day. To be sure, the tapestry of ethnic minorities, languages, and dialect clusters in the Delta and Cross
River areas is of legendary complexity compared with the more homo-
geneous western and northern regions, even if the contrast is often
overdrawn, but in the eyes of the early colonial administrators—trained
in politics and public service—traditional institutions were hard to
find. Mistaking the creolized urbanity of the trading city-states and
associated hinterland for cultural disintegration through European
contact, these officers took the absence of "natural groupings" (Perham
1937, 234) as signs of racial inferiority and degeneration. As expressed
in one officer's intelligence report on Aba Division in 1920:

> Unlike the Mahometan (sic), the pagan negro has no institutions of which
> he is proud and jealous; he is being moulded like wax by his European teach-
> ers; he is as imitative of them as a simian and will retain little of his pre-
> twentieth century self but the vices which are inherent in the negro charac-
> ter to which are being added those of his conquerors. . . . Chiefs who a few
> years ago could hardly boast of the possession of a decent garment to cover

their nakedness now dress in the latest European style complete with sun helmet to patent leather boots and drive about in their own motors.[32]

Not all officers expressed such strong opinions, but the passage reflects a general reaction to the creole character of the region and its significant wealth. Mistaken for weakness and degeneration was a range of flexible polities and social systems based more on the accumulation of wealth from trade than fixed ascription of status or title.

The key to this confusion was the transformation of the canoe house in the nineteenth century and the political economy of the palm-oil trade. As Jones (1963) has rigorously demonstrated, if the slave trade gave rise to dynastic canoe houses in the eighteenth century, the palm-oil trade of the nineteenth century broke these royal corporations apart through the proliferation of middlemen making separate fortunes and establishing canoe houses of their own. The problem for colonial administration was that these houses did not fit prevailing models of native authority, since strangers, kinsmen, fictive kin, affines, and clients of all shades and grades were incorporated together with little regard for the lineage or clan. Internally stratified according to "kings," "princes," "chiefs," "gentlemen" (including "Parliament Gentlemen"), "niggers," "boys," and "pulla boys," or canoe paddlers, the nineteenth-century canoe house was framed by European status categories (Jones 1963, 58–62). And what was worse, it had slaves. Not human chattel, of course, but pawns and bondsmen who worked for their freedom, often rising up to replace their former masters as in the celebrated career of King Jaja of Opobo (fig. 4.4).[33]

It may be argued that the administrative problem posed by the canoe house was never really solved. Briefly recognized by the House Ordinance as a viable local unit, it lost out when the ordinance was revoked in favor of a court area system that revived the language of the clan.[34] But if the historic canoe houses of the nineteenth century represent the sociopolitical framework of the war canoe, it is not their structural dynamics as such (Jones 1963, 159–76) that concern us but the economic conditions of their proliferation. Put another way, we might say that the cultural economy of the palm-oil trade, *based almost exclusively on profits from exchange,* converted economic surplus into new forms of social and political capital characterized by the canoe house. In addition to its status as a central economic asset, the war canoe condensed a spectrum of social, political, and even ritual value forms into its symbolism and structure, operating not only as a potent icon of value but as a critical mechanism of its conversion. Creating creolized sodalities before the

formal advent of colonial rule, the war canoe and its associated magic subverted the very meaning of *native* administration.

For this reason, I would suggest, the regattas of the nineteenth cen- tury mediating European coastal penetration and trade were not recon- stituted as central mechanisms of administrative reorganization in the 1920s and '30s. Unlike the durbar, as we shall see in chapter 5, the regatta has no corresponding "traditional" unit that could be selectively rationalized into native administration. Not that they were entirely excluded from the dominant spectacles of colonial culture. District officers introduced regattas to honor the British Crown, as in Minna Province, during the 1937 coronation celebrations for George VI:

> Particular mention should be made of the Celebrations at Wushishi organised locally by the Government School Teachers assisted by the ladies of the Sudan Interior Mission and by Mission Teachers from Zungeru. Here in addition to sports a small regatta—the first of its kind in the Province—was held on the 7th May and the greatest keenness was displayed both by polers on the water and their friends on the "tow path." [35]

Cast in the context of competitive sport established by the conventions of Empire Day, the term *regatta* is used here with its Oxbridge meaning more or less in mind, to denote a boat race on the river with animated spectators. Even where the colonial regatta resonated more directly with its riverine antecedents, it was incorporated into sports and entertainment. Thus in 1944, when the Resident A. F. B. Bridges took the Chief Commissioner and Secretary of the Eastern Provinces on a tour of the creek areas, war canoes appeared in friendly welcomes, faintly echoing their earlier place in the history of riverine politics and trade:

> All the places we visited had been prominent in the earliest history of this part of West Africa. The *Valiant* was not exactly a speedboat, and it took us a day and a half to reach Bonny, where we were met by the A.D.O. Brass and a number of war canoes which escorted us ashore to see some school sports, followed by a school concert in the Chief Commissioner's honour . . . Our return . . . was signalised by an escort of seven war canoes, with bands, flags and school children. (Bridges 1990, 156–58)

Canoe races also figure in Bridges' account of fundraising festivities for the war, taking place together with "tribal dances, school sports, a display of the Boy Scouts, a netball match . . . the whole finishing with a fun fair and bazaar in the Residency garden" (ibid., 159). Organized by a "mixed committee" of Europeans and Africans, the regatta as canoe race echoed its former mediating functions within the wider fanfare of colonial festival.

In many ways, the colonial regatta was severed from its historic contexts and relocated within a broader tapestry of imperial ceremony. Evoking its past, it was simultaneously diminished and exalted—reduced to the festivities of schoolchildren and their sports, it remained

intimately associated with the greater glory of the Crown. In this respect, its connection with coronation ceremonies was central to its emergent national significance. Thus, to celebrate the coronation of Elizabeth II in 1953, a "canoe carnival" was staged in Lagos which prefigured
many features of the FESTAC Regatta. According to plan,

> eight canoes will take part in the Carnival. They will be decorated for the oc-
> casion, and the paddlers will wear special dress. The canoes will start from
> near Carter Bridge and should arrive opposite Government House jetty at
> about 4.0 P.M. There will be a small panel of judges who will award prizes in
> order of merit to the four best turned-out canoes. Each canoe has been spon-
> sored by one of the Lagos White Cap Chiefs.[36]

Although cast within the framework of Lagos chiefs and their local jurisdictions, the "canoe carnival" or regatta could be expanded or con-
tracted to fit local, regional, or national horizons. In this coronation regatta, if each canoe represented a Lagos chief, by 1977 each would stand
for a specific state within the federal republic. Moreover, it is worth noting that the 1953 regatta took place within a larger context of cultural
production which also foreshadowed much of FESTAC '77. Complementing the canoes were set pieces of African dancing performed at the
Racecourse, representing not the national tapestry that would emerge
during FESTAC but an assortment of communities and immigrants in
Lagos.[37]

During the same year, the Pategi Regatta (of what was then Ilorin
Province) was introduced among the Nupe to become an annual festival
supported by Kwara State. Designed by the district officer to promote
unity among Nupe along both sides of the River Niger, the festival appears to have played an integrative role among factions of the Tsoede
ruling dynasty in the relatively young Pategi emirate. Given that the first
Emir, Idrisu Gana, was installed in 1898 by the Agent-General of the
Royal Niger Company as a reward for his support in their campaign
against Bida, the regatta would seem to resonate with the region's early
colonial history (Hogben and Kirk-Greene 1993, 520). But its 1953 inception suggests a more immediate trajectory from Lagos, either following the coronation ceremonies or participating in them from afar.
This particular trajectory of cultural production is interesting because it
confutes the more linear and even evolutionary logic of a national tradition arising from local festivals. Rather, the Pategi Regatta appears to
have been inspired by the center and thereafter localized in an upstart
Nupe emirate (Idrees 1988). In form, it combined the canoe races of
Empire Day—all awarded cash prizes, except for the European canoe

race—with the more stately procession of war canoes "decorated with flags and canopies . . . of every colour and texture of cloth, from velvets and tapestries to locally-dyed baft," and carrying Angale drummers and singers in their low, squared sterns (Vernon-Jackson 1957, 291–92). In keeping with its colonial prescriptions, the new tradition mandated that the district officer must jump into the river if nobody else fell in! (ibid.)

The Pategi Regatta held an important place in FESTAC '77 as a mini-regatta (held in 1974) seeding finalists for Lagos, and as an authentic re-gatta in its own right. By 1977 it was an indigenous local tradition worthy of national recuperation. Variably descended from the Royal Niger Company, the coronation of Queen Elizabeth II, and the ruling charters of the Etsu Pategi dynasty, which identify the succession of Tsoede with a royal bronze canoe (MacRow 1956), its colonial heritage would be downplayed in favor of more traditional meanings and royal pedigrees. And yet, as with kingship and chieftaincy throughout the former colony, the regatta remained intimately associated with the central symbol of British sovereignty—the Crown. Nowhere is this connection more clearly revealed than in the Port Harcourt Regatta of 1956, honoring the arrival of the queen and the Duke of Edinburgh.

Despite the militant nationalism of the Eastern Region led by its vigilant premier, Dr. Nnamdi Azikiwe, perhaps as a farewell courtesy salute to the great colonial power on its way out, the "Pageant at Port Harcourt" reveled in the glory of imperial symbolism and ceremony. Three features stand out in the last of the great colonial regattas performed while Nigeria was preparing for independence. First, from press photographs of the event we can note the extent to which the most potent icons of colonial authority figured on land and water. Together with ritual cloth and feathered effigies of river gods and ruling chiefs, the traditional war canoes and state gigs featured larger-than-life portraits of the royal pair in full regalia, as if incorporating the charisma of the king's "two bodies" into their architecture (fig. 4.5). We can also see dancers in traditional cloth sporting white pith helmets—already out of date among the last generation of British district officers[38]—and waving miniature Union Jacks. The flag and bunting of the historic riverine regattas are thus in full evidence at this salute and farewell to colonial arms, witnessed by the queen and duke from their royal stand onshore. Second, the boats themselves represented the historic trading states of the Niger Delta, including Bonny, Okrika, Kalabari, Degema, Opobo, and Brass Divisions of the then Rivers Province, invoking the great war canoes of King Boy, King Jaja, and other palm-oil magnates mediating coastal trade through their legendary houses. The long *durée* of coastal trade and transvaluation was thus condensed in this final performance, bringing the op-

posed terms of exchange between the sovereign couple and their loyal subjects into bold relief and temporary equivalence. As an exchange in its own right, the Port Harcourt Regatta transposed money into purely political capital, pooling divisional funds for a collective gift to the queen in return, we might say, for her recognition when each chief was presented before the royal stand. And here is where the third significant feature emerges, as a work of reenactment and reproduction. For the chiefs' gift to their queen was a replica, "a perfect carved miniature of a war canoe" encased in glass as a collective representation, an object of condensed historical meaning and value (fig. 4.6). Even the war canoes used in the event were imitations:

> To keep in contact with each other during battle, each canoe had a big drum and drummers, and seven hollowed wooden pieces played by two other drummers. The canoes used in the display, however, were not the real ones. These have long since rotted away, the last river battle having been fought in the late 19th century. So special canoes were constructed and rigorous rehearsals carried out to ensure that the show was a perfect reconstruction of the old time battles. (*West African Review* 1956b, 283)

FIGURE 4.6 Modern canoe fetish: Queen Elizabeth receives a replica of a war canoe as a gift from the chiefs, Port Harcourt regatta, 1956. *West African Review* 27, no. 343, p. 285. Photograph by official photographer for HRH Elizabeth II.

Firing salvos "in simulated battle," the Port Harcourt Regatta became a second-order representation of its historic "original," a simulacrum of the real regatta, objectified and fetishized by the gift encased in glass. What is so remarkable in this work of cultural abstraction and reproduction is not only how it recapitulates the ontology of colonial representation—in which, following Mitchell (1991), the simulacrum surpasses the original—but how in the process, the very logic of the historic regatta is condensed, inverted, and erased. In my discussion of the role of the regatta in developing coastal and riverine trade, we saw how the ceremonies of diplomacy and exchange—the gun salutes, the gift-giving, the transposition of hybrid identities—mediated conflict and gave rise to creole cultural forms. These aspects of the regatta, however, were lost at Port Harcourt, where the war canoe was stripped from its ceremonial moorings to commemorate actual battles instead. It is precisely this elision which warrants special attention, for it is through such processes of historical repression and erasure that the "exchange value" of the modern FESTAC Regatta emerges.

What I am suggesting is that by 1956, when commercial quantities of petroleum were just being discovered in the Delta regions, a model of first and final contact with the British came together, transforming the "creole" culture of the southern coast and waterways into a distinctive region of the new Nigerian nation. The war canoes of Bonny not only commemorated the historic houses of the Delta trading states, but developed into tokens of a regional type, an exalted, ideal war canoe abstracted from history and offered as a parting gift. As object of congealed history—its historical origins misrecognized and even inverted by the very regatta it purported to represent—the model canoe emerged as the modern canoe fetish, marking a new regime of national value over and above its constituent groups. Fit for the queen, the simulacrum represented the abstraction of value from ceremonial exchange, the war canoe's magic in concrete form. By 1977, the British Crown had withdrawn from Nigeria's shores, and the FESTAC canoes assembled in Lagos represented regional variations of a national type. But if the bunting and flags changed colors, and Nigerians occupied the royal VIP stands, the British Crown remained offshore, an uninvited but ever present participant in the congealed history of the Nigerian regatta and its spectacle of culture.

WHAT, THEN, is the war canoe's magic? Let us return to Gell's Kula canoe and his discussion of aesthetic value. We may recall that his "something for nothing" magical formula informed both the making of the Kula canoe prow and its strategic function in dazzling trading partners "to disgorge their best valuables, without holding any back" (Gell 1999, 176). We may also note that his approach to aesthetic production involved a series of "scheme transfers" adopted from Bourdieu (1977) to identify practical homologies between technical and social processes. In the Kula example, a master carver deploys technical activities modeled on images of flowing water and fluttering butterflies which are transposed into the social sphere of exchange to ensure the unimpeded flow of valuables. The efficacious canoe prow, moreover, is a token of the archetypical flying canoe that travels swiftly without effort or resistance. Its sympathetic magic derives from a perfect model via resemblance and mimetic appropriation. And as we may finally recall, the entire theory rests on Simmel's idea that an object's value lies in its resistance to our desire. For Gell, just as the technical production of the canoe board precedes its social deployment in actual Kula exchange, so does its magic—and the value which it so effortlessly acquires—as an a priori condition.

Let us return to the Delta war canoe and its magical history in the Nigerian regatta. Although lacking the detailed ethnography of its Trobriand counterpart, we know from Talbot (1932, 270) that the Kalabari canoe had mystical powers associated with its prow. As he explained,

> Perhaps it is not wonderful when one considers how large a part canoes play in the lives of water-side peoples that all such craft are thought to have souls living in the bow. Kalabari chiefs used to consult with the canoe spirit before setting forth on any venture. For an ordinary dug-out, on such occasions, a chicken was sufficient sacrifice, but for a war canoe nothing less than a bottle of rum must be poured over the bow before starting. Should a new boat, by some misfortune such as failure to offer the proper sacrifices, or carry out the necessary protective rites during building, be inhabited by a mischievous or malignant spirit, this will never rest until it has overturned and drowned those aboard.

Several parallels with Kula canoes are established by this passage. Like its Kula counterpart, the Kalabari canoe had its magic in the prow, not an insignificant similarity given the dyadic argument I am about to develop *contra* Gell. Magic was also involved in its technical production, in the form of "protective rites." We further see how fetishism figured in the ordinary business of riverine trade, developing into a highly contentious zone of mediation between European and African traders. And finally, by implication, the canoe spirit is associated with the sudden and radical reversal of fortune due to its capricious capacity to capsize the boat. If proper sacrifices safeguarded against such a travesty, it remained—as it were—structurally immanent. The canoe fetish thus served two ritual functions: to produce handsome profits through successful ventures, and to safeguard against accidents and reversals on the waters.

We have also seen from historical sources that, at least from the middle of the nineteenth century, the Delta war and trading canoes had cannon and "carronades" lashed to their prows. Combining ritual power with firepower, their magic was in no way diminished by powder and cannon shot. But what of their aesthetic design? Flags and bunting aside, the only information about Delta canoe prows is negative. For according to Jones (1984, 114), "Canoes were not painted or embellished with carving either on the hull itself or on boards attached to it." However, an interesting effigy at the Manchester Museum suggests otherwise. There on display is a carving from Brass, dated from the mid-nineteenth century, which is identified as a figure from the prow of a war canoe. As the caption further explains, the sculpture, representing a woman or sea goddess, is an imitation of figureheads adorning the bows of European sailing ships. In this instance at least, the carved prow of the canoe from Brass derives, in part, from its European trading partners. I say in part, because the carving appears to be somewhat hybrid, blending European with African aesthetic features—perhaps those of the "human Delta head" (ibid., 169) or the Brass Ijo figures with attached arms representing the founder of a canoe house (ibid., 167).[39] I would like to think that the figurehead came from King Boy's canoe, since he was the dominant Brass trader of that time, but whether or not it was actually his, the carving serves as an appropriate icon of the war canoe's magic as a generative scheme. Following Gell, we can identify a logic of "scheme transfers"—not "prior" to exchange, however, but at its dialectical center.

Returning to the canoe prow from a phenomenological perspective, I begin with the practical a priori that it is fundamentally other-oriented. The war canoe begins with the other in view as an enemy to vanquish or a trading partner with whom to exchange. Lacking conventional prow boards, the Delta canoe—as the hybrid figurehead from Brass suggests—incorporated the other into its bow to generate profit and minimize loss. The initial scheme transfer for a successful transaction was one of sacrifice to the canoe spirit and appropriate deities, establishing a homology between ritual exchange and the economic business to follow. Sacrifice, we recall, was made from the bow of the boat into the water, and in associated "juju houses." The other is *always already present* in the preliminary acts of ritual investment, logically if not chronologically prior to the pursuit of profit and the fulfillment of desire. Lacking detailed descriptions of these ritual preliminaries, the travel narratives and early ethnographies provide enough glimpses to suggest two key processes at work—the conversion of blood into surplus value and the reversal of dyadic exchange relations. In addition to its blood offering, the sacrifice transformed the giver into the receiver, and thus the receiver into the giver. Prefigured by propitiation to a deity, the scheme extended into the social spheres of political diplomacy and economic negotiation. As Laird ruefully perceived, King Obi would receive double the value of his gifts in return, besting his betters at their own game! The war canoe's magic *was* this surplus from exchange.

Placing this scheme in historical context, I have traced the roots of the Nigerian regatta to the arrival of Europeans. I began with examples of the slave trade in which canoes functioned as vessels of exchange, providing slaves in return for European commodities and emerging forms of money and credit. If the profits accruing to coastal rulers were considerable, the value thus generated was variably invested in different forms of social, political, and symbolic capital. Through such transvaluation, I have argued, a hybrid or incipient creole culture developed along

the coast and inland estuaries of the Niger Delta, establishing a conjunctural framework of European and African relations which was regulated and sustained by the early regatta. The exploration of the River
Niger was central to this historical process, revealing not only the concrete mechanisms of gift-giving and treaty formation as British authority penetrated the hinterland, but the dialectics of hybridization itself as
gifts and commodities, givers and receivers, found equivalent forms of
valuation. In terms of its magic, or generative scheme, the war canoe
converted both the blood of fetish sacrifice and that of living slaves into
surplus value, realizing profits measured in bars, manillas, and cowries.
Even where barter appeared to prevail, commodities were exchanged in
relation to established monetary values.

When palm oil surpassed slaves as the dominant regional commodity, the dynastic trading monopolies gave way to a proliferation of middlemen, with canoe houses doubling as political units and trading
corporations. As profits rose, the canoe houses incorporated European
idioms and emblems into their architecture and social organization.
War canoes routinely adopted flags and bunting in the mid-nineteenth
century, appropriating the emblems and devices of their trading partners in gifts and local copies followed by commissioned imports.[40]
When the palm-oil economy developed and expanded, the networks of
middlemen linking inland producers to the coast gave rise to a distinctive regional culture and identity, naturalized by the very designation
"Oil Rivers" and characterized by the circulation of value. The regatta
developed into the central mechanism of mediation at this time, establishing commercial treaties and trading partnerships while pitting the
language of fetishism against that of contract. Whereas Europeans saw
fetish customs as barriers to open markets, Africans bristled under pro-
tectionist contracts that promoted monopoly in the language of free
trade.

With the rise of formal colonial rule, the era of the historic regatta
came to an end. When southern Nigeria was amalgamated into a Protectorate, the regatta dropped out of sight as a mechanism of European
and African mediation, gradually reappearing for Empire Day and coronation ceremonies. Reemerging in the context of British colonial culture, the regatta remained intimately allied with the Union Jack and the
British Crown, but within a political rather than economic sphere of
capital, exchanging loyalty for recognition by the colonial administration. If in economic terms the native canoe remained salient as the paramount vessel of riverine commerce—served in fact by "snag busting"
marines who exploded sunken trees and barriers to maintain free
trade—its ceremonial functions shifted registers, mediating political

relations with the colonial state and condensing its history into an idealized past.[41]

It is precisely this process of condensation which the FESTAC Regatta extended and refined, transforming a regional riverine tradition into a national flotilla in Five Cowrie Creek. Financed by oil revenues allocated to each of the participating states, the Regatta effectively decolonized its past, converting the European legacy of its history into a singularly African spectacle. In this process of cultural commodification, the regatta was detached from its traditional base to emerge as an object of national value. Despite initial plans to include them, the riverine chiefs were not required to participate and had no clear place in the boats or on shore. No longer recognized, the historic canoe houses were subsumed by states and local government areas, each with its representative flags and bunting. More important, the "creole" cultural forms that developed through the historic regatta were nationalized and Africanized. In his top hat, tie, and *agbada,* the chairman of the National Council for Arts and Culture and Regatta supervisor, Chief H. J. R. Dappa-Biriye, was indeed well dressed for the occasion.

CHAPTER FIVE

A Genealogy of the Durbar

The processes of cultural objectification are as much a part of national cul-
ture as the cultural "stuff" that is objectified.
—Richard Handler (1988)

I<small>T</small> H<small>AS</small> become a commonplace, if not a *banality,* to acknowledge that
traditions are invented. Since the publication of Hobsbawm and Rang-
er's important collection of essays, "the invention of tradition" has come
to mean more than the domain of staged rituals and symbolic practices
originally specified (Hobsbawm 1983, 1) and to encompass a general
critical perspective, shared by many anthropologists and historians, toward all cultural representations of the past. Hobsbawm's initial distinction between invented traditions on the one hand, and "old," "genuine," or "evolved" traditions on the other, has been lost, overshadowed
by a new episteme in which, for example, if all traditions are invented,
so too all communities are imagined, and all ethnicities constructed.
Benedict Anderson's (1983) critique of the primordial foundations of nationalism is perhaps the best-known turning point in this direction. Another is Corrigan and Sayer's *The Great Arch* (1985), which identifies the
cultural foundations of the English state, and examines state formation
as cultural revolution. In this and similar approaches, cultural forms

and practices move from a secondary explanatory status—as mere symbols or window dressing for the political and material relations that they represent—to the more fundamental position of necessary conditions. Cohn (1983) makes a similar argument for Victorian India, as do Ranger (1980) for Northern Rhodesia and Callaway (1987) for colonial Nigeria. The "thin white line" of imperial power in the colonies rested not on British force and fortitude alone but on the foundations of colonial culture.

This groundwork is useful, especially for the historical anthropologist whose domain of expertise can fruitfully extend to the very cultural conditions within which traditions are invented, communities imagined, ethnicities constructed, states formed, and empires built. But within this constructivist episteme, new developments are pulling the cultural rug from beneath our feet. This latest shift is signaled by Pemberton's (1994) critical ethnography of "traditional" Javanese culture, which, he argues, developed as a "culture effect" first under Dutch colonialism, then under Soeharto's New Order regime. Javanese culture, much like the anthropologist's, emerges under specific historical conditions not only as an object of knowledge and reflection but of production and reification as well. Thus culture too is invented.[1]

How can culture serve as both a condition of state formation and as its consequence? How do we distinguish the prior "cultural foundation" from the consequent "culture effect"? Clearly such questions invite a closer look at the complex relations between culture and power, and the ways they are dialectically and historically informed. Hence the more general goal of this chapter, which *returns* to Hobsbawm's initial if relative distinction between older and more "genuine" versus invented traditions in order to sketch a genealogy of the Nigerian durbar as it developed under British colonialism and came to represent the Nigerian nation in FESTAC '77.

In a sense, the durbar is an invented tradition par excellence. It was devised by the British with specific political objectives in mind, first in Victorian India and then in West Africa. In the latter it initially signaled the Royal Niger Company's transition to Imperial Protectorate— a portentous event held on January 1, 1900, quite literally at the dawn of the new century—whereafter it naturalized the policy of indirect rule in choreographed public spectacles honoring emirs, governors, district officers, and even such distinguished guests as the Prince of Wales (1925) and Queen Elizabeth II (1956). By 1977, however, the durbar's colonial content was mysteriously phased out. Staged in FESTAC to recuperate indigenous culture, the state memorialized a "precolonial" durbar—explicitly associated with Islamic Sallah celebrations—with which the new Nigeria, enriched by oil, could celebrate its national development. Like the oil industry that financed FESTAC, the durbar was seen as a natural resource in the fertile fields of cultural production and was nationalized. This process of objectification and indigenization was in fact a *subvention* of tradition, an underwriting by the oil-rich state that, in the context of Nigeria's political history, reconsolidated Hausa-Fulani hegemony by projecting a northern regional identity over the nation at large. Thus the genealogy of the durbar reveals how the cultural foundations of colonial authority were transformed into the culture effect of a postcolonial state.

In terms of the broader themes addressed by this study, the case of the Nigerian durbar carries the arguments and perspectives of Mitchell and Bourdieu into the postcolonial situations of third world nation-states. Following Mitchell's discussions (1988, 1999) of the emergence of "the state" and "the economy" not as functional domains of institutional differentiation but as representational "effects" of modern political practices, we consider the domain of "culture" in a similar light. The point here is not merely synthetic, adding a new domain variable to Mitchell's analysis of the state, but instead follows his radical shift in perspective on the very processes of institutional differentiation and objectification. In brief, this refers historically to the practical and technical demarcation of internal distinctions—"methods of organization, arrangement and representation"—that come to be seen as external boundaries between the state and civil society, the state and a "free" market, or in the case of the Nigerian durbar, the state and its national "culture." As we have seen, it was through Nigeria's cultural events and national festivals that the domain of "Culture" was rendered visible and autonomous, distinguished from, if financed by, the state with its booming oil economy. From this perspective, Nigeria's postcolonial "culture effect" should not be seen in isolation but as concomitant with the distinctive political and economic spheres that emerged under oil capitalism.

The historical development of an autonomous sphere of culture in Nigeria addresses central issues in Bourdieu's critical sociology of the state as well; most specifically, what he has called "the field of cultural production" (1993) in modern Europe and its specific economies of symbolic and cultural capital. Like Mitchell, Bourdieu (1999) shows how internal distinctions generated by the state become universalized and objectified into rational forms and functions—of administration, adjudication, even thinking and knowing—that extend into the organization of the natural world according to the model of the imprimatur. Unlike Mitchell, however, Bourdieu relates the genesis of these structuring domains to positional fields of interest within which agents compete for different forms of capital. Bourdieu thereby introduces issues of agency and value into the cultural constitution of modern political orders, specifying the hidden strategies as well as technical mechanisms of the bureaucratic field and its distinctive domains. As we shall see, such strategic concerns and forms of "capital" accumulation and exchange were central to the various agents and actors who participated in durbars and operated behind the scenes.

DUBIOUS ORIGINS

Featured as "the greatest and biggest event to be staged by Nigeria," the Grand Durbar was the grand finale of FESTAC '77, and as such acquired regional, national, and international dimensions.[2] As a regional festival, it brought together emirs, chiefs, and district heads from Nigeria's ten northern states under the traditional jurisdiction of the Sultan of Sokoto, still recognized as "Commander of the Faithful."[3] As a national event, organized by the National Participation Committee through various ministries and secretariats, it epitomized the grandeur of Nigeria's cultural heritage. But it was in its global dimensions that the durbar best captured the spirit of FESTAC, connecting the black world to the world system by flying in dignitaries and heads of state as guests of the multimillion-naira Durbar Hotel built specifically for distinguished visitors, and by broadcasting the durbar via satellite to worldwide television audiences. And at least temporarily, the durbar shifted the exemplary center of FESTAC's black and African world from Lagos, Nigeria's congested and bustling port city on the Atlantic coast, to the northern city of Kaduna, the administrative headquarters of the former Northern Region, where spacious vistas and savanna winds offered temporary relief from the steamy south. In a concerted logistical initiative, the federal military government commandeered buses, trains, and the national airline to transport many of the estimated 200,000 spectators from Lagos to Kaduna and back again.[4]

On February 8, 1977, in Kaduna's Murtala Muhammed Square, Lieutenant General Olusegun Obasanjo once again addressed the black and African world. He spoke from a dais that included U.N. ambassador Andrew Young of the United States, Prime Minister R. C. Bradshaw of Saint Kitts, and seven African heads of state, together with Kaduna's state governor and other top brass from the Supreme Military Council.[5] Praising the horsemanship, drumming, dancing, and acrobatics of the participating emirs and their colorful retinues, Obasanjo also discussed the durbar's broader significance as a genealogical charter for FESTAC itself, explaining how "the FESTAC was in a sense, one Grand Durbar in which African people with their kith and kin were in one event trying to recapture their common identity and pride which was a beginning of a new independent and collective future."[6]

It was in terms of this ideological project—building a postcolonial black and African world on precolonial cultural foundations—that the durbar's historical pedigree was defined. It was portrayed as a precolonial tradition of a great indigenous civilization, with horsemen, warriors, standard bearers, musicians, camels, dancers, bodyguards, and jesters representing their leaders and expressing their loyalty in the climactic charge of the *juhi* (or *jinjina*) salute. As Obasanjo made abundantly clear, "In witnessing the Durbar and savouring its splendid spectacle we are symbolically paying our respect to a civilization that existed here in this country, as well as in many other parts of Africa, at various times in our continental history before the advent of imperialists from Europe." As a specific institution, he maintained, it derived from the emirate system of the north, where it served as a mechanism to unite different African peoples within an overarching state. In this respect, the durbar was portrayed as a constitutional expression of good governance and political accountability, in which "the opinions of the governed counted greatly in influencing the conduct of policies and popularity of Emirs." Obasanjo continued, "to my mind the Durbar is a device whereby the Emir can judge the popularity of his rule as well as an indication of loyalty of those governed to his rule."[7] Thus the durbar provided a fitting parable for a general who would soon return his country to civilian rule, with the northerners in power.

On a more militant note, the federal commissioner for information, Major General I. B. M. Haruna (who also served as chairman of Nigeria's National Participation Committee for FESTAC), warned against the imperialist propaganda surrounding the durbar. In his opening speech, he disassociated the Grand Durbar from its colonial history in India and Nigeria, where durbars had been staged to incorporate local rulers into British administrative structures:

> Those of you who have read and absorbed the imperialist literature would have concluded that the word "Durbar" is used in English to describe the receptions which used to be held for "Native Princes" at the courts of the British viceroys of India. You might also have read that first British Viceroy of Nigeria (as Lord Frederick Lugard pictured himself), aping the practices of his more distinguished colleagues held the first durbar for the chiefs of Northern Nigeria in Zaria in 1911, and that thereafter this became a regular practice of the imperialist rulers of this country, designed to remind the people

whom they had conquered of their enforced allegiance to the British king. (Haruna 1977, 18)

Instead, the major general assured his audience, the Grand Durbar of FESTAC '77 boasted an older, nobler lineage from precolonial times: "This great gathering of emirs and their officers and horsemen that you are going to see bears only some very superficial resemblance to the assembly of chiefs that were ordered by the British in 1911. In fact, this is something quite different. It is perhaps something akin to those great gatherings of nawabs and rajas which were held at the court of the great Moghul sultans of India which were called 'Durbar' long before the British stole the Urdu tongue of the rulers of that country" (ibid.).

The Nigerian durbar is thus "akin" to its Indian counterpart in that both belonged to civilizations that predated British conquest, upheld indigenous empires and states, and were appropriated, transformed, and disfigured by the British. The Nigerian durbar, moreover, is older than its Indian cousin, hence its pedigree even more distinguished. Haruna explained,

> I can also assure you further that what you are about to see is still not an old Moghul custom that by some strange act of cultural subservience we have adopted here, for we had been practising this custom long before the rise of the Moghul Empire. . . . What you are about to see in ceremonial form is variably called Wa'rigo Pucci, or Kawuske, or Hawan Dawaki, [which] means "the mounting of the horses." This is something which has been done year after year for more than half a millennium on one part or the other of this country; and the memory of it and of what it has stood for over the centuries, are basic elements of our cultural heritage: something which has not been wiped out by the impact of foreign imperial rule, but which remains strong and active in the hearts and minds of our people to this day. (Haruna 1977, 18)

In the spirit of FESTAC's recuperation of cultural origins, and translated into Fulani, Kanuri, and Hausa terms, the Grand Durbar would purge its colonial accretions and resurrect its traditional political and spiritual values to rebuild the black and African world.

In genealogical terms, two lines of "descent" were thus articulated. One, the imperial-colonial tradition that Britain imposed on Nigeria via India, represented the exogenous lineage of a cunning stepfather, an alien monarch whose superficial imprint could be erased and finally transcended. The other, an equestrian tradition of well-staged statecraft reflecting the glorious histories of the Sokoto Caliphate and the Borno empire, represented the indigenous lineage of the African motherland, something of a submerged matriline under colonialism that FESTAC would restore. According to Haruna, this latter line extended "as far back as the 12th century . . . when the Mai Dunama Humaimi [the forerunner of the Shehu of Borno] could put 100,000 horsemen and 20,000 infantry and an impressive personnel guard into the field" (ibid.). According to this history, then, the "original" durbar existed among the Habe ruling dynasties and their surrounding kingdoms—such as Jukun, Gwari, and Nupe—before the nineteenth-century Islamic *jihad* of the Fulani invaders and the rise of the Muslim emirates.

It is easy to dismiss this indigenous lineage as speculative history motivated by politics, as indeed it was. The pre-Islamic durbar grounds an original ancestry for all Africans of whatever religion or denomination, whereas once Islamicized, it glorifies northern Nigeria and Muslim Africa at large. Haruna was quick to point out the Islamic virtues of Hawan Dawaki, as he preferred to call the durbar. It mobilized society for defense of the community, it fostered loyalty to leaders and fulfillment of political obligations, and it embodied the Islamic spirit of a nation in arms. Quoting a passage of the Holy Qur'an from which, he claimed, "the principles and practice of the hawan dawaki derive" (ibid.), Haruna recast the black and African world in an Islamic idiom, a world that should keep a vigilant watch for enemies from within and neocolonial racists from without, as both are enemies of God.[8]

The three official sources of the durbar are thus unstable. If the British source, via India, is "false," appropriating a prior Mughal tradition, the African source, which is "true," is pre-Islamic (older even than the Moghul empire) and yet derives from the Qur'an. These inconsistencies are hardly surprising, since we know (from the celebrated Tiv case) that all genealogical charters are manipulated according to whose interests and claims are at stake.[9] Rather than dismiss this genealogical charter, however, as yet another invented history of the present, I would like to take its claims seriously, not to authenticate a particular pedigree, but to better understand the historical conditions within which such pedigrees are constructed. With due respect for the sins of anachronism, I briefly review some available evidence of the Nigerian durbar's mysterious ancestry.

The pre-Islamic evidence of an indigenous "durbar" is perhaps the most difficult to establish with any certainty, given the impact of Islam in the region and the predation the so-called pagan tribes suffered at the hands of the slave-raiding emirs. Generally associated with equestrian cultures, it was presumably connected with local kingship, performed during funerals, installation rites, and agricultural festivals. Kirk-Greene (1959, 18) has quoted the earliest written account (circa

1829) from the explorer Denham, who encountered the people of Bornu and described how "three separate small bodies kept charging rapidly towards us, to within a few feet of our horses heads, without checking the speed of their own until the very moment of their halt." A partial glimpse of such practices is provided by Meek's (1931) classic monograph on the Jukun-speaking peoples of Nigeria, whose kingdom was heralded as "the only remaining example of the type of state which was characteristic of the Western Sudan before the advent of the Muhammadan religion and culture."[10] Discussing the Jukun institution of divine kingship, Meek described a festival of Puje (literally, "booths of menstruation" [ibid., 144]) associated with the harvesting of corn, beans, and millet, during which the king proceeded on horseback, was attended by a royal drummer and fiddler, and was surrounded by Ba-tovi grooms in rank and file who "support him in the saddle when necessary, shout his praises, and draw attention to any impediments on the road" (ibid., 149). Behind these grooms followed senior officials from vassal communities, each "surrounded by his own courtiers and attendants" (ibid., 150). After performing sacrifices and ablutions within the Puje booths or pavilions, the Jukun king returned in state, this time following rather than leading the procession back to the palace. Each group of attendants was preceded by "Akie," men with peeled sticks who drove away spectators to clear the king's path. At this point, Meek (152) described what may well the precursor of the Islamic durbar's "jahi" salute:

> Then follows the Abô Achuwo who rides in at a gallop with the other senior officials. All turn their horses swiftly and gallop back again to meet the king as he enters the eastern gate amidst loud shouts of welcome from his people. . . . The procession then moves forward in a swaying mass, and at intervals the king pulls up his horse in order to survey the people and receive their acclamations. It is noteworthy that whereas during the day the king and his officials are all dressed in the typical Jukun fashion, i.e. with a cloth rolled at the waist and extending to the feet, the upper part of the body being left bare, these garments are changed for the triumphal return to the capital. All the officials wear gowns, and the king dons the coat known as *nyikpo*, which is decorated with red and white representations of birds and scorpions. He also wears a decorated fez. . . . After visiting the north and south gates the king returns to the palace and there dismisses the people, saying: "I thank you all. I have performed the custom of our forefathers."

Now if this custom of the forefathers represents a pre-Islamic practice, one that—like the Jukun kingdom—may have been characteristic

of the western Sudanic states more generally, can we assume, genealogically, that it preceded the Islamic "durbar" which came to be associated with Sallah, the high holidays of Id el Fitr and Id el Kebir in the
emirates? The answer is complicated by the fact that some of the subordinate chiefdoms ruled by the Jukun king were already Islamicized in
the nineteenth century, and may have influenced Jukun rituals in the reciprocal exchange of gifts and tributes built into their political relationship. For example, the decorated fez mentioned by Meek may well be an
Islamic innovation, incorporated into the iconography of Jukun kingship. Or perhaps it was adopted from the uniforms of Africans serving
in the colonial administration, as illustrated by the fezes worn by soldiers and policemen in northern Nigeria. I mention this not to confirm
or deny the historical priority of a pre-Islamic "durbar," but to indicate
that the "pagan," Islamic, and even colonial traditions had most likely
been mixing for some time.[11]

Three ethnographic snapshots from colonial Nigeria illustrate this
composite character of the Islamic durbar, or Sallah.[12] Analyzing Hausa
praise-singing (roko), M. G. Smith (1957, 29) described the political relationship between a district head and his king in Zaria as dramatized
by salutations and the distribution of gifts:

> At Sallah, when the District head has to attend the king at his capital, the
> band of maroka accompanies him on horseback, and plays him into the city
> with bugle and drum. After the Sallah rite on the prayer ground outside
> the city (masallacin Idi), the District head, together with his subordinate vil-
> lage chiefs and administrative staff, declares allegiance to the king by a cav-
> alry charge with drawn swords outside the palace, while the maroka [praise-
> singers] who take part in this gallop, drum, pipe, and blow their master's
> title-praise (kirari) on horseback. During the distribution of largesse which
> marks Sallah, the maroka are rewarded by their lord with meat, kola nuts,
> clothes, money, occasionally a horse, and titular promotions.

Here we glimpse the administrative relations between king, district
head, and the district head's subordinate village chiefs mobilized by
the performance of Sallah, legitimated by the district head's "cavalry
charge," and negotiated by gift-giving. Already the critical components
of the Muslim durbar can be distinguished: the state, the salute, and the
circulation of symbolic capital. The state structure of the emirate is
clearly made manifest, even if it is already mediated by the administrative framework of indirect rule, while the cavalry salute—in this case
with drawn swords—appears to be a potentially rebellious act, ritually
framing the latent possibilities of armed resurrection against the king.

Finally, the "distribution of largesse" sets up the "durbar" as a political arena in which hierarchical relations are ritually sanctified and, in cases of promotion, reorganized.

Nadel (1942, 144) provides a more elaborate description of a Sallah festival in the Nupe kingdom, ruled by an emir bearing the title of *Etsu* from the capital city of Bida. The basic components of the "durbar" can be discerned within a more complex description of sociopolitical relations:

> The *Sallah* feast is like a Friday celebration on an immensely enlarged scale. On the first day the king on horseback under the state umbrella and surrounded by his noblemen and state officials, leads the vast procession to the praying-ground outside the town, where the *Liman* holds the service. After the service the procession returns to the royal residence. Here a great display of horsemanship takes place, at which the bodyguard of the king, his police, and officers of state parade before him and his guests of honour—the foremost among whom are the District Officer and all the Europeans living in Bida Emirate. On the second day of the *Sallah* the *Etsu* holds the great *nko* of the year, a reception at which everyone who holds rank and title and every person of consequence comes to salute his sovereign, to offer gifts of loyalty and to receive counter-gifts expressing the king's favour. For two days tens of thousands of people crowd the streets of Bida and assemble in front of the royal residence—Bida people as well as peasants from the villages who flock to the capital to see the *Sallah*. There they watch their rulers ride past in all their splendour, equipped with their paraphernalia of rank; they listen to music, drum signals, and songs of praise; they join in the general rejoicing, made more joyful by the largesse and gifts of food and kola-nuts which a gracious sovereign causes to be distributed among his loyal subjects.

Like the Puje ceremony among the Jukun, the Nupe king rode with his bodyguard and retinue to a sacred place outside the town, and returned to the palace for a great display of horsemanship.[13] And like the Sallah at Zaria, the Nupe state turned out in its hierarchical glory, with all social groups and categories in their proper place, from exalted nobles—including the district officer and resident Europeans—to lowly peasants and strangers. We can also discern additional reciprocities within the ritual economy of distributed largesse, in that the Etsu's loyal clients and chiefs brought him gifts and received countergifts, thereby exchanging fealty for protection while representing, and in some cases negotiating, status distinctions and political relations. Presents from the king ranged from a small bowl of kola nuts (on which the king held a royal monopoly) to a silk gown or a horse. As Nadel explained, not only was rank indicated by the type of gift received from the king, but it could also be stripped or restored: "At the great Mohammedan festival of the year, the *Sallah* as it is called in Nigeria, every one of the hundreds of people who by the right of birth or status are entitled to the king's attention are honoured with a smaller or larger gift. To be left out means disgrace; and the sending of a present to a man with whom the *Etsu* was known to be on bad terms expresses conspicuously reconciliation and new favour" (ibid., 91). Indeed, the emir's gift economy exchanged personal power and religious authority. If personal loyalty to the sovereign could be demonstrated with gifts, it could be rewarded with a title, which was conferred by the presentation of a turban and a sword—insignia of office (ibid., 143) and conversion or submission to Islam.[14]

If the Nupe Sallah described by Nadel reveals a growing British presence, this was not limited to administration and personnel. The presence of the district officer and other Europeans as guests of honor raises interesting questions about who was ultimately in charge and control and whose loyalty was tested and expressed. Clearly the agents and representatives of the colonial government legitimized the emir's authority in the Sallah, even as they were drawn into its orbit of obligations and its economy of signs. But here is precisely where the currencies of symbolic capital—the mutual investments of gifts and countergifts—become blurred. For if the Sallah operated at the intersection of the colonial state "above" and the native emirate "below," expressing in its cavalry charge a potential rebellion against the colonial order, it also harnessed colonial forms of power and value. This can be understood abstractly as an appropriation of colonial charisma and seen concretely in the adoption of European commodities and in the reversal of ritual roles.

Two final examples illustrate the point. The first involves a subsequent Sallah that Nadel observed, noting the "corrosive" influence of market forces on traditional craft guilds:

The Great *Sallah,* once the occasion for numerous orders from the court, which kept the workshops of Bida busy for weeks, is now an occasion for making purchases at the stores that trade in European goods. At the *Sallah* of 1935, the first *Sallah* of the newly installed *Etsu,* the traditional royal gifts of kola-nuts were sent out, not in ornamental brass bowls of native make, but in newly bought enamelled teapots; the king's bodyguard, newly equipped, wore, not Bida gowns and turbans or native-made straw hats, but red blankets and Trilby hats; and many notables who would have appeared formerly on horses with costly trappings and gorgeous saddle-cloths, rode in on new, shining bicycles. (Nadel 1942, 292)

Here we see how major shifts in the political economy of colonial rule, such as breaking the king's monopoly on certain commodities and liberalizing the market for labor and goods, involved the ritual substitution of prestige symbols and wares. The new Sallah introduced imported commodities into its ritual economy of icons and gifts, commodities that carried with them changing relations of production and consumption. To a significant if limited extent, blankets replaced gowns, Trilby hats replaced turbans, and bicycles replaced horses. Clearly key symbols of Nigerian Islam were making way for British industry. In the language of genealogy, foreign blood was thereby introduced into the Islamic Sallah and its body politic.

A second example, from the Yoruba emirate of Ilorin, illustrates another colonial variation on the Sallah theme. Describing the festival in 1960, just months before Nigeria's formal independence, P. C. Lloyd distinguished pre-Islamic ingredients of Yoruba sacred kingship absorbed by the Sallah from more recent adaptations to the colonial situation. Of special note in his account is how the Islamic "church" and British "state" were ritually separated and combined. As the emir with his retinue left the palace for the prayer ground, where his war chiefs (*Balógun*) were waiting, the Resident of the province, with his senior administrative officers and their wives, assembled on the tower of the palace gateway to watch a different set of ceremonies. Here the police band marched back and forth, "playing everything from highlifes to Scottish laments" (Lloyd 1961, 278). As the colonials gazed from on high, the emir returned, following an attendant bearing his official staff of office, which was "presented to him on his accession by the Governor or his agent," and flanked by bodyguards, sword bearers, war chiefs, musicians, even the Native Authority police—all in a spectacle of color and a "cacophony of sound" (ibid., 268). In this manner, with the customary cavalry charge, the emir was reintegrated with the secular state and greeted by the Resident and his subordinates at the palace. And in what amounted to a reversal of ritual roles the following day, the emir and his chiefs rode in procession to the Residency, where they were entertained, "just as the Emir had earlier entertained his Baloguns" (ibid.). The Ilorin Sallah was thus ritually encapsulated within the political framework of indirect rule, with the British controlling the distribution of largesse.

These ethnographic vignettes of the precolonial and Islamic "durbar" pose the usual problems of inferring earlier ritual practices from contemporary performances. From the available evidence, my examples are already mediated by the colonial situation, and reflect this mediation in interesting ways. My intent in sketching the "matriline" of the durbar's genealogy is not to demonstrate its ideological impurity, which would be easy, but, despite the methodological challenges(to affirm that it exists,) which is much more difficult. What these vignettes illustrate is not a pure ritual bloodline polluted by foreigners—FESTAC's vision, more or less—but that the indigenous ceremonies associated with "durbars" were active sites of political negotiation and mediation during which local and regional identities and authority relations were reshaped and remade. To a greater or lesser degree, Habe, Nupe, and Yoruba practices were surely incorporated into Fulani Sallahs, and these in turn were reconditioned by the changing colonial order. But in the meantime, at the dawn of a new century, a different kind of durbar had made its royal entry, giving birth to the Protectorate of Northern Nigeria. And it is here that we turn to the imperial durbar in the making of colonial authority.)

COLONIAL AUTHORITY

The first colonial durbar performed in Nigeria was an imperial rite of passage, marking critical transitions for a number of key actors and conjunctural relations. For Sir George Goldie, it marked the surrender of the Royal Niger Company, Chartered and Limited, to the administration of the British Crown. If the Royal Niger Company had consolidated a trading monopoly on the River Niger, it suffered, as F. D. Lugard ([1922] 1965, 19) had put it, "the inherent defect of all chartered government, where dividends to shareholders must inevitably compete with administrative expenditure." General Lugard (soon to become Sir Frederick and later, Lord) took charge of the takeover, staging it rather dramatically at the Niger-Benue confluence on January 1, 1900. Through this first official durbar, the Protectorate of Northern Nigeria came into being at Lokoja, bringing with the new century a new government and High Commissioner. As reported by Perham (1960, 24–25) and described by Callaway (1987, 58),

> At 7 am General Lugard . . . walked on to the parade ground to read the Queen's Proclamation to the assembled units of the Royal Niger Constabulary and the West African Frontier Force. The flag of the now defunct Royal Niger Company was drawn down, and the Union Jack raised as the visible sign of British authority. Guns fired in noisy salute and then the military band struck up the chords of the national anthem. Next, the Nigerian troops gave three hearty cheers for their new sovereign, Queen Victoria. After Lugard had been sworn in as High Commissioner, the troops executed a march past and were praised for their excellent appearance. Both during this event

and the two days of sports which followed, the Nigerian troops and the watching crowds showed intense enthusiasm. This impressive celebration served at once to display mystical authority and to incorporate the Nigerian military units and local populace into British Empire.

No clearer statement of symbolism and purpose could identify this durbar with colonial authority. Later elaborations, as Callaway (ibid.) notes, would incorporate the galloping *jafi* and *jinjina* cavalry salutes of Fulani horse and camel divisions, but the durbar's exogenous, colonial line came directly from British India, where it had fulfilled a number of ceremonial functions.

One such function was the proclamation of Queen Victoria's accession to the imperial title of Kaiser-i-Hind, a neologism designating Empress of India (Cohn 1983, 201), during viceroy Lord Lytton's extravagant imperial assemblage. As Cohn (1983) has illuminated so clearly, the elaborate planning, staging, and choreography of this event, with its feudal pageantry and *feux-de-joie*, brought the art of the imperial durbar to new heights. On a scale rivaling Hollywood stagecraft, with elephants, coaches, and trumpeters "attired in medieval costume" (ibid., 204), Lytton mounted his "throne" before thousands of spectators, including princes and troops in precise formations, declaring that it was to "unite the British Crown and its feudatories and allies that Her Majesty had been graciously pleased to assume the Imperial Title" (ibid., 206). Calculated "to satisfy native sentiment" (Trevithick 1990, 563), one wonders whether British sensibilities were equally at stake. Certainly the organization of ceremonial space placed the Crown at the center of a grand imperial cosmology, but historical timing was equally significant.[15] The Imperial Assemblage took place on January 1, 1877, not only marking the dawn of new majesty but also commemorating the anniversary date of Queen Victoria's original 1858 proclamation extending royal authority to India (Nuckolls 1990, 535). It was this inaugural moment—when the Crown took over from the East India Company—that Lord Lytton recalled in Delhi and which Lugard clearly recuperated on the banks of the Niger at Lakoja.

More generally, the colonial durbars of British India were held when the viceroy went on tour or were staged by governors or lieutenant governors representing their regional princes and chiefs. In a process which Nuckolls (1990, 531) calls "feudalization," loyal Indian princes were incorporated into a rigid administrative order established by Indian titles that were ultimately granted and confirmed by the viceroy. Durbars served as the ceremonial contexts in which these titles were conferred, thereby adapting and transforming a Mughul ritual of kingship to serve Britain's civilizing mission. Cohn (1983, 174–80) describes how in the early days, the governor-general would hold durbars for one Indian ruler at a time to bring him under Crown command, but by 1876, these rulers convened at larger durbars where they were ritually, indeed *ordinally,* ranked by clothes, weapons, gun salutes, retainers, and their proximity to the viceroy receiving them. Through this organization of traditional titles, and by establishing an order of Indian knights to reward loyal service, India's political present came to embody Britain's feudal past. This fundamental precept of the British Empire— that lower races could be helped along their evolutionary path—rationalized both the colonial presence and the population which they governed. As Cohn (1983, 184) summarizes the imperial imperative, "India was diversity—it had no coherent communality except that given by the British rule under the integrating system of the imperial crown."

The colonial and imperial durbars of India did not exist in ceremonial isolation but belonged to an elaborate cosmology and culture of rule expressed as much by the rational techniques of governmentality—mapping populations, codifying laws, collecting taxes, or training troops—as by political ritual and everyday routines. If the colonial order was visible, even spectacular, its habitus was hidden in the details and disciplines of new forms of etiquette and knowledge. The durbar does stand out, however, in this total ideological context as a powerful mechanism of its production, whereby indigenous ceremonial and social orders were both underwritten and reorganized by the colonial administration and naturalized by the colonial sciences of native races and their evolutionary paths. I am in no position to examine this dense historiography, but I would suggest that the colonial cosmology and administrative logic exemplified by the imperial durbar in India were brought by Lugard to Nigeria, where they took root and developed in similar ways.

As in India, for example, the first colonial durbars in Nigeria served as rituals of virtual enfoeffment.[16] From 1900 to 1903, Lugard undertook a series of military operations that forced the northern emirs and the Sultan of Sokoto to recognize the higher sovereignty of the British Crown. In 1900 he deposed the ruling *Etsu* of Nupe, replacing him with a new emir over a more limited jurisdiction, who "having accepted British conditions, was formally installed at Bida, before a full parade of British troops and a great assemblage of his own people, in February of 1901" (F. S. Lugard [1906] 1964, 428). Lugard then pacified the Kontagora, Yola, and Bauchi emirates, installing new rulers under ceremonial oath before taking over Kano and finally Sokoto. With this latter victory, the former Sokoto Caliphate and its theocratic domain were incorporated into the colonial administration, a framework that preserved the form of the emirate system while transforming its political and procedural content (M. G. Smith 1960). In more symbolic and ideological terms, the locus of politico-theocratic authority shifted profoundly. Although the emirates could remain Islamic, the sultan was subject to the sanctity of the British Crown, and it is with respect to this new political cosmology that we can reexamine the colonial durbar.

On March 22, 1903, the installation of the new Sultan of Sokoto transformed the terms of ceremonial exchange. The symbolic idiom was to some extent "traditional," following customary patterns of Fulani investiture, but the logic was in key ways reversed. As described by Lady Lugard ([1906] 1964, 453), "The details of the ceremony were determined in consultation with the proper Mohammedan authorities, and it was arranged that, in sign of the acceptance of the sovereignty of Great Britain by Sokoto, the sultan, who had never hitherto received a gift of investiture, should, like the lesser emirs, receive a gown and turban from the hands of the representative of the king of England. These were to represent the insignia of office, which up to the present day it had been the custom for Sokoto alone to present on installation to his subordinate emirs." An Islamic ceremony was thus reinscribed within a British imperial cosmology, wherein the symbols of theocratic rule—the turban and the gown—traced back metonymically to the English monarch. As the giver of gifts became the recipient, the investor became the invested (fig. 5.1). Moreover, the Sultan of Sokoto was politically displaced from the center of the Fulani empire to the periphery of British Empire, receiving his insignia of office from the hands of an infidel. And if such arrangements were deemed unacceptable to the locals, new stage props brought the firepower of the foreigners into full view:

> The installation ceremony was performed with some pomp. The troops, with guns and Maxims mounted, were drawn up on three sides of a hollow square. An immense crowd of natives were assembled. On the arrival of the High Commissioner on the spot he was received with a royal salute. A carpet was spread for the emir and for his principal officers of state. The High Commissioner then made a speech. . . . On the conclusion of the speech the High Commissioner called upon the Sultan to say if he fully understood the conditions of his installation. The Sultan replied that he understood and that he accepted. The High Commissioner then proclaimed him Sarikin Muslimin and Sultan of Sokoto, and the gown and turban were presented to him as the insignia of office. The High Commissioner shook hands publically with the Sultan, and gave permission for the royal trumpets, which can only be sounded for a duly appointed and accepted emir, to be blown. A prayer

was recited aloud by the criers, and the crowd dispersed amid discordant sounds of rejoicing and expressions of mutual goodwill. (Ibid., 453–54)

Similar if less momentous installations at Kano, Katsina, and Zaria followed. The Protectorate of Northern Nigeria was thus formalized, with gowns, turbans, staves of office, and letters of appointment accorded to every recognized emir and district head.

It was through such installation durbars that the Nigerian Protectorate was both ritualized and rationalized. Emirs and chiefs who had been loosely federated under the Sultan of Sokoto by ties of ceremonial tribute were now clearly ranked and ordered into four grades, represented by the appropriate staves and certificates of office. Staves of the first order, reserved for the Shehu and the great Fulani emirs, were surmounted by silver headpieces; those of the second order were decorated with brass, whereas the third and fourth graded staves were "short and of plainer design" (F. S. Lugard [1906] 1964, 437). And as F. D. Lugard ([1922] 1965, 212) pointed out, they signified not only differences of rank, but also British overlordship and protection: "These staves of office, which are greatly prized, symbolise to the peasantry the fact that the Emir derives his power from the Government, and will be supported by its exercise." In addition to their staves, chiefs of each grade were received by political officers according to elaborate protocols that marked privileges and status differentials down to the smallest details. In his *Instructions to Political and Other Officers on Subjects Chiefly Political and Administrative,* Lugard (1906, 193) laid down the following rules:

> When a Resident interviews a Chief of the first grade, he should shake hands with him, and offer him a chair to sit upon. He will never be summoned to an officer's quarters. . . . Chiefs of the second grade should not be given a chair, but should be provided with a raised seat (such as a box covered by a carpet). . . . Chiefs of the third . . . [and fourth] grades should be seated on a mat. . . . A Government official should in no circumstances sit on the ground in the presence of a Native Chief. While himself taking off hat in the house of a Chief, he should insist on a corresponding observation in the case of Chiefs visiting him. A Mohammedan should remove his shoes, and cover his head in the house of a European.

As in British India, such formalized structures of political authority and protocol were part and parcel of a developing colonial regime as well as of a general ideology that naturalized indirect rule. The Fulani emirs were seen as "natural" rulers over the less advanced and racially darker "pagans" whom they had conquered.[17] Closer to the British in racial and evolutionary terms, deemed "Hamito-Semitic" in their heritage, they served as appropriate mediators of the civilizing mission. In the early days of this colonial encounter, the Fulani were likened to Indian castes that could be similarly domesticated. Speaking of the Fulani warriors, Mockler-Ferryman (1902, 170) opined that "eventually, when they get a better understanding of our methods, their greed for gain will induce them to follow in the footsteps of some of the old 'fighting castes' of India, and become peaceful citizens and loyal subjects of the Great White King." The colonial durbar and its associated protocols provided an appropriate mechanism for colonizing Nigeria, bringing many of the ideas and methods of British India to the African territories.[18] As in India, Nigerian durbars moved from dyadic salutations between more independent emirs and political officers to collective events, in which the emirs, entourages, and native troops of an entire province turned out. As early as 1908, Martin Kisch, an Assistant Resident in Sokoto, witnessed and photographed a durbar held for Lugard, who was touring on inspection. The Emirs of Argungu and Gando and the Sarikin Mussulmi (Sultan) of Sokoto turned out for the event, fully robed and turbaned, with contingents of horsemen and camels totaling fifteen thousand. In what he described as "a very grand sight," with twenty-five thousand mounted infantry and "natives" assembled to

watch, the emirs and Sarikis were received "in turn," providing sixteen ponies for Lugard as "dash," and prostrating before him on the ground (fig. 5.2).[19] What is so remarkable about this illustrated description is first, that Lugard actually accepted the rather substantial tribute, as would befit the former sultan, and second, that even the Sarikin Mussulmi prostrated in an expression of fealty and respect. Cohn (1989, 329) describes how in colonial India it was not until the imperial durbar of 1911 that the leading princes were told to prostrate in what was dubbed "the homage pavilion." In Kisch's account we find an African precedent for this innovation, in which the colonizer reworked the ritual of the colonized, and appropriated its center of command.

As Callaway (1987, 58–59) points out, the durbar was employed "as a regular feature for imperial celebrations," including one marking Lugard's appointment as Governor-General of Nigeria in 1913.[20] As such, it belonged to the more general theater of empire that punctuated daily life in the colonies, where social distinctions of the metropole were refined and elaborated, differing only to the degree that Africans were explicitly included *in their place.* But if durbars formalized local authority relations, they did so within a general imperial cosmology of truly global proportions.

Much has been written both for and about the Coronation Durbar of George V, held in Delhi in December 1911. *The Coronation Durbar, Delhi, 1911: Official Directory with Maps* lays out the entire schedule of events with an inventory of camps and important personages; there is also a special Souvenir edition of *The King Emperor and His Dominions* (1911), replete with scientific appendices, not to mention recent historical and anthropological analyses. But precious little has been written about the Coronation Durbar held in Zaria, admittedly less elaborate than its Indian counterpart and lacking the dramatic person of the king himself (represented instead by His Excellency) but for that very reason particularly significant, because its very performance brought northern Nigeria into the global imperial order. In the Coronation Durbar at Zaria, the political structure of the Northern Protectorate was sanctified by the ultimate investiture of George V, echoing the providential plan of Britain's national destiny throughout the world.

A contemporary description (*Blackwood's* 1912b) of the durbar at Zaria dwells on grand themes in purple prose, interpreting the ceremony as a local expression of a higher moral purpose. Of interest is not the imperial ideology writ large, but the way the "chaos" of Africa was reduced and informed by colonial spectacle. First, there is the organization of the African forces, a "seething mass of colour presented by the brightly caparisoned throng—reds and blues and greens and masses of dazzling white," which forms into a line and "comes tearing down the avenue of soldiery, gathers way momentarily, and comes to a halt in front of his Excellency" (ibid., 356). Line after line of horsemen follow, "all jingle and glitter and flashing colour . . . like wave following wave," charging their "wild eyed" horses in the "Jafi" salute before halting a few yards in front of the Acting Governor.[21]

Much can be read into this ritual confrontation between the master and his subjects, incorporated from the Islamic Sallah into the colonial durbar proper. There is the threat of armed rebellion against the colonial order, as well as the reciprocal demonstration of imperial authority and domination.[22] Clearly portrayed by the organization of riders and the sequence of their salutes to the "King," however, is the hierarchy of races in northern Nigeria, ranked according to their natural abilities and propensities to rule and be ruled. First, among the native races come the Fulani aristocrats, born to ride and rule; beneath them the Nupe and Yoruba traders, followed by diminutive swarms of pagans:

> Men of Kano, followers of the Emir of Katsina, gallant in red and white robes; Zaria men in Cossack-like caps of black goat-skin; Bornu riders with white shields and curious Crusader helmets. . . . There are Filanis [sic] from Muri and from Yola too. Warriors all these—well mounted—the aristocracy of the many races that go to make up the people of the Protectorate. After the warrior, the man of trade. And now we see, lolloping gently up the ground,

portly, panting envoys of Ilorin and Bida, Yorubas and Nupes, excellent worthy fellows all, moneyed men, fathers of the coming race of trousered Negro
lawyers, but they don't sit a horse well, these trader men, not as do the Kano
and Muri and Yola and Bornu people. (*Blackwood's* 1912b, 356)

Thus the durbar choreographed the native races of Nigeria, "feudalized"
into a caste-like order that was clarified by colonial administration. We
see how the Fulani aristocrats were identified by place as well as position, the different emirs serving as sole native authorities within their
respective administrations, and how these in turn were stratified into
lower racial orders with associated occupations. If the Fulani represented landed aristocrats, the Yoruba and Nupe possessed the virtues
and limitations of a nascent bourgeoisie, "moneyed men" destined for
business and the professions, perhaps more educated than the Fulani
but less refined. But it is the third category, the brutish pagans, occupying the lowest position in the colonial pecking order, that best capture
the moral imagination of the coronation durbar:

> Last of all comes a very wondrous sight indeed. You are to imagine, if you
> please, a swarm of bees represented by men: smallish, black men, *very* scant-
> ily clothed, armed all of them, some with spears, others with knives, or clubs,
> or swords, or axes; others again with nothing more deadly than a drum, or a
> horn. . . . Arrived in the presence, the swarm breaks, and the swarmers en-
> gage in a dance, abating in no wise their musical (!) activities, and there is a
> halt in the morning's proceedings what time the Political responsible for
> these pagans walks amongst them, trying to reduce them to some sort of or-
> der and consciousness. . . . His excellency is an old hand in Northern Nige-
> ria, and knows the pagan, none better, so receives them in a fashion that
> delights their primitive souls, and sends them off perfectly, not to say franti-
> cally, happy. (Ibid., 356–57)

Naked, black, swarming like stinging insects, the pagans are "reduced
to some sort of order and consciousness" by the civilizing mission and
its rational administration. They are, moreover, *included* in the durbar,
protected by the British from Fulani slave raids and encouraged to come
out of their caves and down from their hilltops in order to engage in
peaceful agriculture (F. D. Lugard [1922] 1965, 581). The hill pagan, as
he was called, represented primitive savagery and arrested evolutionary
development. Hunted and persecuted by his superiors until the British
Pax, he could now assume his natural place *within* the imperial order of
things.[23]
    The administrative order of the Northern Protectorate was ceremo-

nially mobilized through such durbars, as moral in inspiration as they were rational in plan. A regional coherence was ritually sanctified, drawing together emirs, chiefs, and pagans and putting them in their proper place. It served, I would argue, as one of the key expressions of indirect rule, designed by Lugard in the north and eventually extending throughout Nigeria after the Northern and Southern Protectorates were amalgamated in 1914. But my argument is less about causality, because durbars were part of a general political transformation of the colony, and more about a form of cultural production that was implicated in the process—an inventing of traditions that, as Ranger (1983) has sketched out for colonial Africa more generally, involved the codification of customs and tribes into administrative schedules and categories. Nonetheless, drawing on indigenous durbars and Sallahs in what has been called— in another context—"the central institution of ceremonial interaction" (E. Haynes 1990, 461), the colonial administration forged a northern regional unity that acquired a distinctive political culture vis-à-vis the south. As Coleman (1958, 353–68) pointed out, the Northern Region was the last to develop a nationalist movement in Nigeria, and when it did, it remained cautious and parochial. Its dominant political party, the Northern People's Congress, was controlled by the traditional ruling class of emirs, mallams, and hereditary officials whose privileged position and sense of natural entitlement had been upheld by colonial authority.[24] I mention this here to illustrate the extent to which the formal hierarchies of native administration in the north, partly racialized in the coronation durbar, were *naturalized* within an emergent regional culture which, later on by the 1950s, had become explicitly antinationalist and hostile toward the south. In the normative terms of colonial distinction, the northern emirs held more common cause with the nobility of Britain than with the invasive southern barbarians.[25] And what better occasions to affirm such common cause than the imperial durbars of 1925, held in Kano for the Prince of Wales, and of 1956, staged in Kaduna for none other than the queen herself?

The durbar for Edward, then Prince of Wales, was part of his general tour of West Africa—in the battle cruiser *Repulse*—which included stops in the Gambia, Sierra Leone, and the Gold Coast before reaching Nigeria. In each of these colonies the heir apparent received the appropriate traditional authorities, some bearing gifts, others kissing his hand (Adock [1925?]). In the Gold Coast, a Grand Palaver was held in the polo ground, where the prince met chiefs of the Ashanti Confederacy as well as representatives of the northern territories, seated under umbrellas and arranged into fifty-four groups. But it was the durbar in Kano— the commercial capital of the Northern Region—which the royal souvenir book describes as "the most gorgeous and impressive that had yet been staged for the Prince in Africa" (ibid.). Surely great prestige accrued to the Emir of Kano, who played host not only to the future king-emperor, but also to the Sultan of Sokoto, the Emir of Bauchi, and the Sheik of Dikwa from the Cameroons. In addition to the Nigerian durbar's signature "salute of the desert," in which "fierce-looking warriors in helmets and chain armor or cloaks and turbans . . . gallop[ed] furiously almost up to the Royal stand before they abruptly reined in their flying steeds and wheeled aside," the "Emirs and Chiefs were conducted to the dais and presented in order of precedence by the Resident . . . [where] the Prince addressed them and the assembly at large."[26] An official photograph of the emirs "making their obeisance to the Prince at the Durbar" reveals the vertical dimensions of colonial authority. The prince, leaning down from his throne on the dais, shakes the hand of the sultan, which stretches up as he prostrates with two emirs behind him on the ground—fealty with a personal touch (fig. 5.3). This helping hand of colonial overrule had growing horizontal implications too, because it was through the durbar itself that greater regional integration and awareness was achieved. As Nigeria's *Colonial Reports—Annual* for 1925 recorded, "A Durbar was held in Kano which was attended by practically all the chiefs of the Northern Provinces. Not only were the chiefs impressed by the magnificence of the spectacle, but they met people and tribes many of whom were but names to them or in some cases traditional enemies, and found they were all at one in their allegiance to the king, whose son's personality so . . . impressed their imagination."

Thirty-one years later, Nigeria was preparing for independence. The Richards Constitution of 1945 had sought to reconcile the native authority system as the primary unit of self-government with more representative parliamentary institutions advocated by the nationalists. The resulting compromise was intensified regionalism, with three new regional Houses of Assembly to be established at Kaduna, Ibadan, and Enugu, each with its own budget. Although regionalism was criticized by many southern nationalists as separatist and divisive, "to all northerners it was the single most attractive feature of the constitution" (Coleman 1958, 277), which gained the overwhelming support of the traditional emirs who formed the Northern House of Chiefs. In the developing political climate, the native authority system became increasingly antiprogressive, allied with the forces of conservation rather than the tides of change. The National Council of Nigeria and the Cameroons protest campaign (1945–47) notwithstanding, regionalism emerged as the primary focus of Nigerian nationalist development (ibid., 319), articulated in increasingly politicocultural terms. The dominant northern

FIGURE 5.3 Emirs paying homage to the Prince of Wales, Kano Durbar, 1925. In Adock [1925?], unpaginated.

party, the Northern People's Congress, was led by the Alhaji Ahmadu Bello, the Sardauna of Sokoto, who became Premier of the Northern Region, while his kinsman, the Sultan of Sokoto, became official patron of the party.

Within this political tug-of-war between conservatives favoring regional autonomy and more militant nationalists pushing for enlightened self-government, the royal tour of Nigeria in 1956 and its "crowning" event, the Kaduna Durbar, took place. And it was in this context, in the administrative capital, that the last imperial durbar in Nigeria expressed a cultural unity for the Northern Region, representing its distinctive position vis-à-vis its southern and eastern counterparts within the emerging nation-state. The selection of participating representatives from all twelve provinces extended down to the lowest administrative levels through a series of associated grassroots competitions. David Williams, then editor of *West Africa,* described his impressions of this extensive preparation to the Royal African Society: "I remember, for example, being present last December at an agricultural show in far off Adamawa where a dancing competition was held to choose a team to go to Kaduna. This competition was itself the result of organisation in remote villages, and was typical of what was happening all over" (Williams 1956, 113).

In the end, contingents from the region's twelve provinces arrived "by canoe, road, horse and rail" (ibid.) from as far as seven hundred miles, spending up to five weeks in the saddle, to settle in the durbar camp in preparation for the spectacle. For the provincial emirs, the event boosted their senior status and perhaps their political clout. As Letchworth (1956, 29–30), the Senior Resident of Bornu Province reported, "At Kaduna the Shehu of Bornu, now over eighty-two, insisted on taking his place on horseback at the head of his contingent in spite of the fact that he had not ridden since 1948 and the Emir of Fika, aged sixty, accompanied by the Emir of Biu, took a leading part in the traditional gallop to the foot of the Royal stand. As one Fika trader said with great satisfaction on hearing of his Emir's part in the proceedings, 'Ah ha, that will lengthen Mai Fika's beard.'" Similarly, Cooke (1956, 11), the Acting Resident of Bauchi Province, quoted the leading emir's annual report, that "The memory of the Royal Visit, which has put the Northern Region on the map, will never be forgotten in the history of the Region." Of more immediate interest to Cooke, however, were the durbar's political consequences for Bauchi Province, since it was through their cooperative efforts at the regional celebration that the five native authorities of Kaltungo, West Tangale, Waja, Dadiya, and Cham saw that they could get along, and agreed to federate (ibid., 11). For the most part, however, local voices and perspectives are difficult to discern from available sources. Internecine political struggles were surely simmering beneath the surface, as indicated by the politically motivated Kano riots of 1953.[27] The media tended to focus on the bigger picture, and there was plenty to see.

The queen and the Duke of Edinburgh arrived in an open Rolls, circling the racecourse twice before taking their seats on the dais of the durbar pavilion, where they were joined by the governor of the region, Sir Bryan E. Sharwood-Smith, and his wife, Lady Sharwood-Smith; by the premier, the Sardauna of Sokoto; and by the Sultan of Sokoto and the Shehu of Borno, who left their seats only to lead their contingents on horseback. The region's twelve provincial contingents were grouped into blocs within the durbar arena, with a Jahi group composed of representatives from each contingent in front. During the inspection, the marching bands reflected the regional government, with the military band of the Nigeria Regiment followed by separate police bands of the native authorities.[28] After the orderly march-past of the provincial contingents, including horsewomen from Bauchi, jesters from Jos, and pagan dancers from Numan wielding agricultural tools, the culminating *jahi* charge took place. As featured by the *West African Review* (1956a, 274), "A solid phalanx of screaming warriors, on horseback and clad in chain mail, thundered across the ground in an awe-inspiring gallop. With a great shout, they halted, seemingly inches from Her Majesty, dipped their standards and lances and wheeled proudly away—an unforgettable sight." Here is one of the finest if final expressions of colonial ambivalence in Nigeria, a charge that carried all of the contradictions of indirect rule to the sacred center of colonial authority.[29] The northern emirs no longer prostrated before the Crown, but they still acknowledged fealty. Later in the evening, the queen invested the Sultan of Sokoto with the Knight Grand Cross of the Order of the British Empire and bestowed other honors on local chieftains and notables.[30]

In sketching the imperial paternity of the durbar as a tradition of colonial incorporation, I have highlighted the descent line that FESTAC suppressed. What began as the cultural foundation of indirect rule under Lugard, and what Haruna called "imperialist propaganda" in his FESTAC speech, developed into something else. If in 1925 the imperial durbar upheld expanding colonial interests in Nigeria, promoted by the Prince of Wales's visit to the commercial capital of the northern provinces, by 1956 it consolidated the Northern Region's political identity and autonomy vis-à-vis the imminent nation-state. In this latter capacity, the official durbar was no longer a regular feature of state ceremonials, since colonial authority was on the wane. The naturalization of authority relations that the earlier durbars expressed gave way to a different if related project—*the making of a regional culture*. This was not to deny ethnic difference, as the Kaduna Durbar testified, but to redefine it in the more lateral terms of regional unity, contra the south and east. As Kirk-Greene (1959, 16) proclaimed on the eve of independence, "[the Durbar] is something we in the North should be proud of—both the splendour of the event and the national characteristics so clearly discernible in that representation of the long history and colour of the Northern Region. . . . The thesis developed in this article is that of the durbar as the 'Heart of the North'; as a ceremony symbolizing not only the quintessential North but also springing from the very inspiration of the Northern peoples."

In the twilight of British colonialism, we can thus grasp the beginnings of a fundamental shift in the cultural politics of the Nigerian state, whereby the invented traditions of the colonial order were indigenized by Nigerian political elites. It was a process, which FESTAC later clarified, whereby the cultural foundations of the colonial order became "quintessential" expressions of the new nation-state.

NATIONAL CULTURE

By February 5, 1977, when FESTAC's Grand Durbar took the nation's center stage, the Nigerian state had changed dramatically. After achieving independence in 1960, six years of federalism under the First Republic broke down in the first of a series of military coups. Immediately, a tendency away from regionalism and toward unification accentuated the role of the state in national affairs.[31] In 1967, Nigeria's federated regions were reorganized into twelve states, and again into nineteen by 1969. The bloody secessionist Biafran war (1967–70), in which an estimated two million people were killed or starved to death, brought home the need for a strong national center. But the greatest single factor in fueling the growth and centralization of the state was the oil boom of the 1970s, combining military rule and economic statism (Joseph 1987, 69–90) in "the bureaucratic petrostate" (Watts 1992, 36).

It was through the state's subvention of FESTAC '77 that the invented traditions of colonial authority were nationalized, erasing the very colonial history in which they developed and took shape. If the Grand Durbar was lauded as a representation of indigenous tradition, its scale, organization, and execution resembled the imperial durbars that it explicitly disavowed. To be sure, basic allegiances had shifted. Ties with Britain were strained over the British Museum's refusal to return the original Benin ivory that served as FESTAC's trademark. The absence of any high-ranking British representatives at the Kaduna Durbar was offset by the presence of Andrew Young, U.S. president Jimmy Carter's ambassador to the United Nations, who saw Nigeria as America's strongest African ally in promoting business on the continent and fighting apartheid in South Africa.[32] More to the delight of the Nigerian media, however, was Young's deference to the Sultan of Sokoto, for whom the ambassador knelt in showing his respect. Here was the incarnation of historical justice, as a black representative of the world's leading super-power paid homage to traditional African authority. Young was amused—and slightly annoyed—by the excessive attention that his gesture received.[33] In terms of the politics of the imperial durbar, it made perfect sense, revoking the helping hand of Britain's Prince of Wales that had extended to the kneeling sultan half a century earlier. But if Andrew Young and the Sultan of Sokoto were prominently seated in the first row of the reviewing stand, they were joined by a select group of very important persons who watched the horsemen and dancers from the northern states, followed by the collective *jahi* salute.[34]

Bearing the national flag, Nigerian police mounted on horseback stood by as contingents from the states and their emirates marched past, each with its own banner and retinue, including hunters, warriors, dancers, acrobats, and mounted guards. The Wasan Burtu dancers from Borno State, dressed in animal skins with bird heads to lure game, were joined by the Shehu's standard bearers, Kanuri "Kazagama" dispatch riders, and Waziri Dumas dancers. Tambari mounted musicians her-alded the Emir of Kano, flanked by his Dogorai bodyguards and Yan La-fida heavy cavalry unit riding horses protected by quilted armors. Camels from Katsina and Bori dancers from Zaria added local variation to Kaduna State. If subordinate leaders and district heads commingled in the festive confusion of music, dance, and dust, seniority was sorted out by the seats allocated to emirs and chiefs in the State Box, where the paramount traditional rulers from each state retired from the saddle.[35] Thus was the traditional culture of the northern emirates displayed, cel-ebrating precolonial ceremonies and values through the very adminis-trative forms and categories that the colonial durbars innovated, but that somehow got lost in the spectacular fanfare. For example, the Borno State contingent, comprised of the Borno, Dikwa, Fika, Biu, and Bade emirates, represented a heterogeneous population whose unity was im-parted by what had been Borno Province under the British, now reor-ganized as a state (fig. 5.4). To indicate this political unity, the Borno contingent invented an appropriate uniform. The minutes of Borno State's Durbar planning committee reported, "For purposes of distinc-tion, uniformity and some kind of identity for the Borno contingent in costume was discussed. It was finally agreed that this identity should be in the 'Aji' cap and the turban Akkal which all Borno horsemen should be wearing."[36] Thus was the colonial order displaced into the past, by the very innovations that commemorated an earlier tradition. Even the venue at Kaduna Racecourse, now remodeled into Murtala Mohammed Square, preserved the same location where the Queen of England and

the Duke of Edinburgh surveyed equivalent contingents from the Northern Provinces in 1956.

The new players at FESTAC's Durbar were not on the field, but on the viewing stand (fig. 5.5). In addition to Andrew Young, Sir Abubakar (the Sultan of Sokoto), and Nigeria's Head of State, General Obasanjo, they included members of the younger and more educated northern military elite, whose alliance with the old aristocratic order would ensure northern control over the country and its petroleum resources. Seated next to Young was Joseph Garba, Nigerian commissioner for external affairs, and Brigadier Shehu Yar'Adua, chief of staff, Supreme Headquarters; both had engineered the coup against General Yakubu Gowon to place Murtala Mohammed—"scion of the traditional establishment of Kano" (Joseph 1987, 130)—in power, and represented the real military muscle of the Obasanjo regime. Yar'Adua in fact belonged to the Fulani establishment in Katsina, in northern Kaduna State. Among other prominent northerners were Kaduna State Governor, Group Captain Usman Jibrin, and the Chief of Army Staff, General Theophilus Yakubu Danjuma, also rumored to be an architect of the previous coup. Present also was Muhammadu Buhari, who would soon become oil minister in the Second Republic before bringing back the military in his 1983–84 New Year's coup d'état. At the time, however, with elections for the Second Republic in the planning stages, this consolidation of northern hegemony would prove to be portentous. But even before the 1979 elections,

FIGURE 5.5 Brigadier Shehu Yar'Adua and the Sultan of Sokoto on the VIP Dais of the FESTAC Durbar, 1977. In Augi 1978, 22. Photograph courtesy of G. O. Nwaobi, M. O. Omole, and A. Francis.

Obasanjo knew how to play his cards. As Joseph explains, "General Obasanjo, the second non-northern leader of Nigeria since the brief rule of General Ironsi in 1966, knew that the stability of his regime depended on his retention of support from the traditional and modern elites of the North and he was assiduous in ensuring that this support never wavered" (ibid., 130).

I suggest that FESTAC's Grand Durbar in Kaduna was a cultural concession to such northern hegemony. Not only were large sums allocated to its northern planners, with finances for the expensive Durbar Hotel included, but cultural capital was invested as well.[37] Framed in the idiom of precolonial northern culture, a regional culture that—we have seen—came into focus under colonialism, the durbar was nationalized as an allegory of Nigerian culture and as a template for African civilization and governance, further consolidating the political hegemony of the north. Planned and produced by Nigeria's National Participation Secretariat, the durbar represented a time-honored tradition that disguised not only the historical conditions of its colonial development, but also the political agenda behind its successful execution. After witnessing the Grand Durbar, a *New York Times* correspondent reported, "it seemed that the North was trying to outdo its Southern rival in a single spectacular afternoon" (Darnton 1977). He could not have summarized the situation more concisely.

IN TRACING the genealogy of the Nigerian durbar, I have "excavated" its history as a composite tradition stemming from two sources: one indigenous, with its own complex layers of sacred kingship and equestrian culture (in some sense represented by the Jukun ethnography) assimilated to the Islamic religious calendar, and the other exogenous, as an imperial ceremony imported from Victorian India. This model of "double descent" is not unproblematic, since the exogenous "patriline" and the indigenous "matriline" can never be established as historically "pure." We have seen, for example, how the pre-Islamic Jukun "durbar" showed signs of Islamic and colonial influence and perhaps is better historicized in parallel rather than prior terms. We also saw how the Nupe Sallah incorporated relations of colonial authority and commodity value into its ritual economy. But these influences in no way undermine the lineage model; rather, they illuminate the changing political fields in which the indigenous durbar developed.

Like all genealogies, the pedigree that I have sketched for the Nigerian durbar is structurally selective and inevitably incomplete. I have overlooked some of the durbars recorded in colonial memoranda and early press reports, as well as the Northern Region's independence durbar of 1959 and the Haile Selassie Durbar of 1972.[38] These latter durbars undoubtedly prepared important ground for the Grand Durbar of FESTAC '77. My more analytical aim, however, was to explore the distinction between the historicity of the durbar, which, as professed by FESTAC's genealogy, recuperated a precolonial African purity, and the durbar's "actual" history as an important colonial tradition. I am not suggesting that because the durbar was colonial, with roots in British India, it was therefore not African. The organizers of FESTAC may have rejected the colonial patriline on ideological grounds, but my goal has not been to deconstruct, in turn, the precolonial matriline. Rather, I am interested in the process whereby the colonial durbar in northern Nigeria became regionalized, nationalized, and Africanized as its imperial pedigree was erased. This process divides into three general phases.

The first phase, spanning 1900–1925, involves the constitution of colonial authority through imperial rituals like the durbar itself. Here the colonial durbar was directly associated with indirect rule, ranking native races in administrative categories and transforming "tradition" through its codification and preservation. As the central institution of ceremonial interaction between colonial and native authorities in the north, the durbar served as the cultural foundation of an administrative system that was extended throughout Nigeria. The colonial durbar made no claims of cultural authenticity. If it respected native emirs and their bureaucratic institutions while rearranging them into the colonial order, its officers innovated without customary constraint. In this capacity, the durbar belonged to the political machinery of the colonial state. The past that it recuperated and projected onto Africa was not an African past; rather, it came from feudal England and the feudatories of Victorian India.[39]

The second phase of the Nigerian durbar belongs to the liberalization and decline of colonial power, from after the war until 1956, culminating in Queen Elizabeth's ceremonial farewell. During this time the durbar came to represent a conservative northern regional culture in the context of growing militant nationalisms in the south and east. In the imperial durbar of 1956, the Northern Region distinguished itself in two ways. First, unlike its regional counterparts, its ruling aristocracy allied with the British Crown, postponing the transition to self-rule while requesting continued colonial custodianship. Second, it defined itself in explicitly cultural terms invoked and made visible through ceremonial display. In this capacity, the durbar provided the ritual idiom and cultural framework for consolidating northern political hegemony over an imminently self-governing Nigeria. The significant development to emphasize here is one of separation and objectification, in that a regional culture forged under colonialism emerged as an explicit and autonomous domain—a natural feature, as it were, of Nigeria's national landscape rather than a political instrument of the state. Thus the very administrative hierarchies and categories that the first colonial durbars naturalized in racial terms became *nationalized* in the language of regional culture. As culture emerged in the spotlight of spectacle, taking on an independent life of its own, the postcolonial state took shape behind the scenes. And in the political context of Nigerian federalism, the north remained "on top."

After independence, the durbar entered its final phase as a national charter for an oil-rich Nigeria promoting a new Pan-Africanism. If the state was centralized and internationalized by its access to global capital, it was controlled by an inner circle of established emirs and new elites, represented by younger military officers and the so-called Kaduna Mafia.[40] In this context of state expansion and rapid national development, traditional culture was not just objectified but commodified and fetishized by state-sponsored festivals.[41] Further disassociated from its relations of production, the durbar was universalized as Nigerian national culture and globalized as black and African culture (Apter 1996). FESTAC's official genealogy of the Nigerian durbar could thus explicitly disavow its colonial heritage while maintaining it in political terms as continuous northern domination. In this capacity, the durbar emerged as a culture effect of the bureaucratic petro-state. Produced and financed by the state, the durbar came to stand outside of it, as historically prior to Nigeria's colonial past and indicative of its future.

If the genealogy of the Nigerian durbar illustrates how the cultural foundations of colonial authority became the culture effect of an oil-rich state, it stands as a variation on the more general dialectics of national culture in the postcolony. In crude terms, the problem is how to naturalize a sovereign territory based on arbitrary boundaries, like those drawn up for Africa at the Berlin Conference. Politically, it concerns the transition from colonialism to self-government, involving, whether consciously or not, a negation of the former metropole and a recuperation of indigenous tradition. Intellectually, it produces varieties of ambivalence ranging from *négritude* in French and consciencism in English to a principled return to indigenous languages as a way of decolonizing the mind.[42] The predicament of national culture in the postcolony is thus one of national identity politics, growing out of anticolonial struggle, to some extent sustained by neocolonial struggle, but leading in no clear direction. Forged by the colonial categories that are negated and transcended at independence, the postcolony remains caught in apparent ideological contradiction. And the contradiction will remain as long as the terms of struggle remain categorically opposed: African versus European, indigenous versus colonial, traditional versus modern, even black versus white. What the genealogy of the Nigerian durbar really reveals is not, as FESTAC proclaimed, a decolonization of cultural tradition based on the rejection of imperialism, but rather the nationalization of colonial tradition by the postcolonial state. Explicitly erased, such traditions were indigenized through the very festivals and ministries that objectified culture for citizens and tourists.

Similar trends have been noted before.[43] Following the colonial durbar in India up to the eve of independence, Douglas Haynes (1990, 527) concludes that the adoption of imperial ritual idioms by the Indian National Congress shows only too clearly that "liberating a society from the mental models of authority provided by imperialism can be an even more difficult task than bringing about the formal end of colonial power." I would argue from the Nigerian case that it is time to abandon this binary logic, and its political rejection of colonialism's culture. The imprint of imperial pasts can be transformed into national tradition, but never fully erased. In FESTAC '77, the conversion of the colonial durbar into an exalted expression of Nigeria's national heritage was not the intention of the regime's cultural renaissance but its effect.

CHAPTER SIX

The Mirror of Cultural Production

*If there was one thing Marx did not think about it was discharge, waste,
sacrifice, prodigality, play, and symbolism. Marx thought about production
(not a bad thing), and he thought of it in terms of value.*
—Baudrillard (1975)

[E]nergy finally can only be wasted.
—Bataille (1991)

"ONE EVENT of utmost joy to me is the fact that at last the colossal
waste of resources that is FESTAC has come to an end."[1] Thus wrote
Dr. C. O. Ezeani of the Lagos Teaching Hospital, voicing a common
criticism shared by many Nigerians that FESTAC was nothing more than
an extravagant potlatch. Heralded as a great cultural awakening and return to origins, maligned as a deplorable spectacle of primitive self-
glorification, FESTAC's value as a national priority was contested from
the start. Political luminary and Yoruba cultural nationalist Chief Obafemi Awolowo had condemned the festival as "a wasteful venture" during its planning stages, calling for science, agriculture, and education
rather than atavistic "primitive exhibitions."[2] Christian and Muslim fun-
damentalists saw FESTAC as a pernicious pagan revival that would derail
the nation's moral and economic development. Leftists saw FESTAC as a

diversionary tactic for a rent-guzzling comprador bourgeoisie. Others saw it as symptomatic of conspicuous spending during the oil boom, a time of "sports festivals, cultural festivals, cock fighting festivals, I-have-married festivals, tenth-burial of my father festivals," when celebration and showing off were ever escalating to greater heights.[3] But whatever the sectarian differences within the anti-FESTAC camp, concerns with extravagance, expenditure, excess, and waste were noisily proclaimed in the popular media. Focused primarily on FESTAC itself, the debates mirrored wider anxieties about the quasi-mystical character of petro-naira.

Of immediate concern was the money spent on the event—how much, how wisely, toward what ends, and with what effects. To be sure, the festival had its share of kickbacks and corruption revealed by a Tribunal of Inquiry and several subsequent probes, reflecting the culture of contracting in the oil economy more generally. As we shall see, the Leyland Bus scandal and food shortages in Festac Village, not to mention vanishing funds and even fleets of cars, confirmed that FESTAC was an exalted "festival of awards and contracts" (Osofisan 1981, 36) covering "dirty and secret deals."[4] But even where it succeeded, its critics saw a deeper failure to invest Nigeria's oil money in national development. What did FESTAC actually produce? How was it financed and what did it really cost? Who were the beneficiaries of FESTAC, and how was the festival consumed? And finally, what was the value of cultural production?

I begin with such questions not to settle the debate but to identify and further explore the underlying problem that it represents. It is the problem put forth crudely in chapter 1 as deficit production, stemming from the state's dispersal of oil revenues into public projects and private hands. It concerns the paradoxes of prosperity generated by oil and its associated forms of commodity fetishism, including, as we saw in subsequent chapters, the conversion of money into national culture. In this chapter we move from conversion to inversion, seeing in FESTAC neither rationality nor prodigality, but the mirror image of production under oil capitalism. If I selectively deploy Baudrillard (1975, 1981, 1988) and Bataille (1985, 1991) toward this end, it is not to endorse their reduction of surplus value to expenditure, excess, and symbolic exchange, but just the opposite—to clarify the inverted relationship between production and exchange that characterized oil capitalism. Both theorists help make sense of the Nigerian petro-state because there, in the 1970s, oil replaced labor as the basis of national development, producing a deficit of value and an excess of wealth, or a paradoxical profit as loss. To resolve this apparent contradiction, we return to the mysteries of money

in FESTAC, as well as the metaphysical subtleties and theological niceties of the culture it produced.

THE PROBLEM OF EXPENDITURE

To the question of how much FESTAC cost, the *FESTAC '77 Report and
Summary of Accounts* provided an official answer. Published under the
direction of Dr. G. B. Leton, Federal Commissioner for Information, the
report (111 pages) appeared in June 1978, generating an aftershock of
critical reactions to government spending and accountability. The report's grand total of 141 million naira—between $213–225 million US,
depending on the given rate of exchange—was generally perceived as
a whitewash job, disguising millions of stolen funds and misused assets. Whatever the actual amount might have been, with serious estimates reaching 2 billion naira, a precise accounting was virtually impossible, given the mercurial qualities of money itself during the
"throes of the fantasy that was oil-wealth euphoria."[5] Like the booming
bonanza that underwrote its costs, money for FESTAC was elusive and
unstable, manifest only in the traces of its discharge and expenditure.
Issued by the federal military government through five primary "spending points," FESTAC funds flowed quickly through mysterious channels
to meet growing operational and infrastructural demands. Illuminated,
if briefly, by vouchers, letters of credit, payment certificates, and pay-
roll ledgers, but often difficult to redeem in cash, such money was in a
sense always in motion, already departed in multiple directions including overseas accounts where it could hide in obscurity. To appreciate the
complexities of federal costing in FESTAC, and its economic forms of inflation, waste, and loss, we can begin with its notable scandals and in-
efficiencies before moving to official mechanisms of subvention.

A Tribunal of Inquiry established the overt squandermania of FESTAC
under General Yakubu Gowon, mainly in the form of inflated contracts,
excessive consultancy fees, illegal kickbacks, and the infamous mobilization fees. Probing dozens of businesses and contractors, it revealed
a culture of contracting out of control, with the grossest violations clus-
tering around the National Theatre, Festac Village, and the Durbar Committee in Kaduna. As a monument to mismanagement, the National
Theatre faced escalating costs due to a contract awarded to the Bulgar-
ian firm Technoexportsroy without competitive tendering. In addition
to inflated figures for materials, "Gold" clauses to offset the devaluation
of the U.S. dollar, and an 8% additional consultancy fee paid to the company to supervise its own work, the Bulgarians received nine months'
worth of "arrears" of the Ugoji salary increases reserved for public ser-

vants. If FESTAC contractors Alhaji Tatari Ali and Mr. G. A. Dada were rebuked for these unauthorized payments—including 403,000 naira for redundant surveying and 450,000 naira for artistic embellishments—it can be assumed that they received healthy kickbacks from these and other favors they dispensed. The calculated loss to the federal military government from excess profits above the Bulgarians' contract alone was recorded at 12.6 million naira, and we can assume this was a conservative calculation.[6] Nor does it include the amount lost in the construction of special access roads that sank before the land was properly drained, estimated at half the cost of the Theatre itself![7]

If the National Theatre involved collusive deals between Nigerian officials and foreign firms, Festac Village became a feeding frenzy among Nigerian and joint-venture companies that entered the game. Before the land for the development was drained and cleared, millions of naira had already disappeared in mobilization fees that had provided 20% of the total contract up front. Designed to cover starting costs, these fees often vanished with no means of recovery if the contractor defaulted. As one editorial advised, "The tribunal should visit the village site and discover for itself how many of the contractors have anything to show for the mobilization advance they collected. It is no longer a secret that some contractors who collected as much as seven million naira or more have not even cleared the bush of the area assigned to them."[8] The tribunal did just this, exposing flagrant violations among seven major Nigerian companies, and demanding the return of over 16.8 million naira in misused funds that, needless to say, were never recovered. The panel also cancelled an extravagant 45-million-naira contract for luxury furnishings, recommending less expensive alternatives and noting with alarm that the contract for draining Festac Village had not yet been awarded, and that the blocks of flats "made no provisions for chimneys and cooking-platforms."[9]

Meanwhile up in Kaduna, Durbar supervisor Alhaji Umaru Dikko was making a killing in dubious deals, including projects that never materialized. In one such project, the tribunal noted, "this contract should be terminated in view of the fact that the contractor has never been to the site since collecting mobilisation advance."[10] In addition to receiving kickbacks from shady partners, Dikko was charged with inflating prices, awarding unauthorized consultancy fees—possibly to himself—and building boys' quarters on his private property with funds diverted from FESTAC operations. Dikko of course was a Kaduna Mafioso, and, as North-Central State Commissioner for Education at the time, was protected by his bosses. Although never officially established, he may have had a hand in the Kaduna Language Centre scandal as well, in which plans to train Nigerians as French interpreters for FESTAC were hopelessly derailed. Of the students initially sent to France for intensive training, forty-five were abandoned and forgotten, living on feeding allowances from the French government in lieu of Nigerian funds that simply dried up.[11] Chief Anthony Enahoro, who cut off their support, was later charged with using funds from the Kaduna Language Centre Units to build a house on Victoria Island, although the amount was small and his persecution politically motivated. Moreover, when FESTAC ended, the remaining trainees were left high and dry. As one later complained when forcefully evicted from the Language Centre, "No certificate has been awarded after our 18 month course and we do not know where to go now," adding that no gratuity had been received.[12] But by then, the money was gone. An internal audit revealed that 244,625 naira ($363,290 US) in advance payments and bank drafts could not be accounted for.[13]

Beyond the pervasive opportunism that FESTAC afforded, these cases of graft and unchecked profiteering reveal a scale and magnitude of financial movement that was inefficient, excessive, and self-perpetuating. In addition to the "special" salary scales of the bloated International Secretariat, many of the more than six hundred employees at senior and intermediate levels were housed in expensive hotels totaling 24,000 naira per day. If many of these officers felt ignored or underutilized,[14] others spent more than 4 million naira flying first class to FESTAC liaison offices in Paris, London, and Washington, where they went shopping and attended committee meetings at five-star hotels. Indeed, Dom Perignon champagne flowed in Lagos and abroad as officials toasted to FESTAC's success. According to an internal audit, the biggest abuses of budgetary overspending occurred in the areas of personal emoluments, overseas transport allowances, and office furniture. But perhaps most emblematic of pure waste was the money spent and lost on automobiles—in the form of car loans to FESTAC officers that turned into gifts,[15] fleets of underutilized vehicles attached to the various secretariats, and finally, cars and drivers that vanished into the hinterland. In one report featuring 120 FESTAC cars stolen, "the Peugot and Volvo brands disappeared mysteriously after they were assigned to drivers."[16] Neither cars nor drivers had adequate documentation, and thus could not be traced. Such incidents—and there were several—reveal not only the limit of oil spending as pure discharge or outright theft but also something of the instabilities of value in the unbalanced exchanges of oil money more generally. Drivers without passport photos, cars without registration numbers, payments with vouchers, and vouchers without receipts— all represented a phenomenology of exchange that infused the carnival of oil prosperity with an underlying anxiety of a world turned upside down.

How was such anxiety manifested? Beyond a general sense that oil prosperity was somehow illusory, given its magical mode of accumulation, we can characterize the unease it produced symbolically as a slippage between representation and representatum, or an instability of *sign-value* giving rise to what Baudrillard (1981, 150–57) calls the "mirage of the referent." If seeing was believing during the Nigerian oil boom, appearances in turn could be deceptive, and it is in this light that another FESTAC affair took on special meaning. When it broke in the press, the Leyland Bus scandal offered further evidence of "you chop, I chop" profiteering, implicating the new regime in the same dirty business that had flourished under Gowon. In a story that initially appeared in London's *Daily Mail,* two Nigerian officials allegedly received bribes of 285,000 naira from British Leyland to help secure an 18-million-naira contract for a fleet of luxury FESTAC buses.[17] Masquerading as commissions and gifts, the money ended up in two Swiss bank accounts and was never recovered.[18] Although the government probe resulted in no significant action, popular rumors further maintained that the FESTAC buses were themselves a mirage: old rusty vehicles disguised by fresh coats of paint. The rumors, which transpose the official cover-up into literal elements of material signification, play on the proliferation of forms without value, and of value without substance or stable reference. Not only were funds misdirected and stolen in this popular account, but more to the point, the buses were not genuine articles. Like the oil boom and its signs of development, their shiny exteriors hid corruption within.

Perhaps this undercurrent of Nigerian nervousness during the heyday of oil illuminates what has long remained a nagging puzzle in my memory.[19] During my first visit to Nigeria in July 1977—when the echoes of FESTAC were still in the air—I was invited to a law professor's house in a newly constructed block of campus flats at the University of Lagos. Starting with his three brand-new Mercedes-Benzes parked below in the garage, he gave me a tour of the premises, guiding me through each of the rooms to illustrate the progress of his country. The housing was indeed impressive, but what clashed with my modernist sense of propriety were the small plaques attached to each door, labeling the rooms within—"living room," "dining room," "master bedroom," "kitchen," with precise functional specificity. Given that the domicile of a university professor might represent bourgeois European domesticity, why label the fact in so forthright a manner? My host, trained in London, was no mere nouveau riche, thus I didn't feel the answer lay in simple pretensions of social achievement. The image of those room signs has lingered with an enigmatic significance that I would now attribute to the phenomenology of oil and the forms of wealth and value that it generated. Like a Hollywood set, the rooms of the flat were labeled to fix their existence, as if to prevent them from dissolving into a mirage of false appearances. That such dissolution finally did occur when the oil boom went bust is discussed in the following two chapters. Here we will turn to the incipient forms of slippage and instability during the bonanza itself, tracking the transformations and displacements of money behind the scenes.

From the standpoint of money, the mirage of the referent has a two-fold character: one "internal" to the code, invoking the substance of value that it represents, the other "external," expressed by the commodities—including services and labor—for which it is exchanged. In somewhat provisional terms we can say that during the boom, oil served as the substance of value in Nigeria, whereas the commodities purchased and projects funded represented its external referential domain. Implied by the very term *petro-naira*, oil not only backed Nigeria's currency but also served as currency and underwrote the costs of national development. In what sense was its referential value illusory, like the oil-fueled "mirages of El Dorado" (Coronil 1997, 286–320) in Venezuela? Why were the signs of development unstable, and its substantial foundations called into question?

A glimpse into the recesses of FESTAC's funding provides insights into the larger phenomenology of value that the festival celebrated with such extravagant excess. In July 1975, during the time of the Tribunal of Inquiry's probe, an independent internal audit of the International Festival Committee (IFC) was conducted to account for federal monies thus far dispensed. The International Secretariat, it should be noted, was only one of five major channels of distribution, which included the National Secretariat, the Ministry of Information, the Cabinet Office, and the Federal Housing Authority. Many of the huge costs incurred by the latter office, moreover, remained off the festival's books, since hundreds of millions allocated to Festac Village were reclassified under national infrastructure. But as the administrative arm of the IFC, the International Secretariat held a privileged position as the Pan-African body of cultural production (even if nearly all its members were Nigerians), reflecting, like the commodity that underwrote its costs, the transnational value of the black and African world. Receiving funds directly from the federal military government, it maintained accounts in seven major banks, including the Banque Nationale de Paris, Bank of America (New York), Barclay's Bank International (London), and the Central Bank of

Nigeria (Lagos). But more significant than the amounts it received and controlled were its modes and forms of expenditure, through which the mirage of the referent was endlessly displaced.

Consider the following accounting problems duly identified in the official audit.[20] Regarding missing funds: "In the course of vouching payments shown in the cash books, we could not locate some payment vouchers aggregating in value to N 55,860.77 (US$ 84,349.76). These are in addition to those payments made through bank drafts and transfers for which no payment vouchers are prepared." Regarding travel expenses: "We have noted that payment of per diem allowances is usually effected in advance based on estimate of the numbers of nights the official will spend abroad. While vouching these allowances we were not able to determine whether the number of days traveled was the same as the original estimates, for which the allowance was paid. Staff are not required to submit expense vouchers upon their return from trips." Regarding dubious contracts: "N100,000 (US$ 151,000) was paid to the Kaduna Language Centre in connection with the running of the Center. A further amount of N50,000 (US$ 75,500) was advanced to meet payments in connection with a contract stated as entered for the construction of servants' [quarters] at Kaduna for houses ordered from Canada. Documents showing how these advances were expended have not been shown to us," adding that for a related expense, "it has not been possible to verify whether the payment was made in accordance with a signed agreement but it is understood that the equipment has not been installed." As for furnishings, "There is no proper register of office furniture and equipment maintained to enable us to trace particular purchases of furniture and equipment, as shown on payment vouchers, to their actual existence. Therefore it has not been possible for us to . . . ascertain whether all the items that should be on hand are actually on hand."

Underlying these and other examples of poor documentation and outright fraud are the unstable conditions of the expenditures themselves, represented by dubious trails of receipts and vouchers that in many cases had no final referent. As for the vouchers, their instability as a derivative money form resulted from an extraordinary absence of fiscal controls that encouraged double payments and vanishing acts. The auditors complained,

> Payment vouchers are not given numbers after payment has been effected. Because of the absence of a numbering system we had difficulty in locating vouchers. Moreover we could not be satisfied that all vouchers were submitted for audit. It has also been observed that vouchers are prepared and signed

in duplicate. The necessity for this is not clear and in view of the possible dangers of double payment it is suggested that this procedure be discontinued. Also receipts issued by payees are not attached with the vouchers. . . . We have noted that in many instances supporting vouchers are not cancelled as a precaution against subsequent submission. . . . In cases where payments were effected by bank drafts or transfers, payment vouchers duly certified and containing requisite explanations of the transactions and evidence that the service paid for was given, are not prepared.

The audit continues its long list of related abuses, with millions of unaccounted naira associated with missing certificates of receipt. As the above examples amply illustrate, the money flowed through questionable channels and variable forms, creating a convoluted paper trail with no clear material reference. If the substance of value remained hidden and mysterious, so its objects of purchase were hard to pin down, lacking receipts, inventories, even concrete existence.

One of the more glaring abuses concerned the importation of prefabricated houses for various FESTAC venues and events. Charged to the Exhibitions account were "payments made mostly through bank transfers totaling N 608,218.96 (US$ 918,410.52) said to have been paid to a Canadian firm for the purpose of supplying prefabricated houses in connection with the Festival. We understand that this project was undertaken without any tenders being placed and no written contract was made. The prefabricated houses are said to have been imported but they have not yet been erected." Here we have an accountant's nightmare within an inverted model of national underdevelopment—huge sums wired overseas, no written contract, no competitive bidding, and zero domestic production, as prefabricated houses were allegedly imported but not yet visible on FESTAC's horizon. If these examples illustrate the "mirage of the referent" and the unstable quality of oil money, they also explain the negative returns accruing to the federal government's mammoth investments—and thus problems with the substance of value itself.

From a revenue-generating perspective, FESTAC was an unqualified disaster. Not that the festival's primary goal was to generate a profit, but returns to offset expenses fell well below initial projections. The main source of outside funds was the $10,000 registration fee, which fifty-four participating countries and black communities paid up, in some cases supplemented by donations that together totaled just over $600,000. Beyond that, anticipated revenues from franchise fees for use of the festival emblem by manufacturers resulted in a mere 88,550 naira, with very little interest in the emblem expressed by the private sector. Ticket yields from events and performances totaled 193,000 naira, which was "just a little more than the cost of printing," resulting from the last-minute reduction of ticket prices to encourage greater attendance, the issuing of 5,000 complimentary tickets, and a drop from 22,000 anticipated visitors to an actual 10,000. The greatest shortfall occurred in Festac Village, where an anticipated 3.74 million naira from the sale of meal tickets and accommodation charges was never realized; the returns came to only $50,000. Poor organization as well as fewer guests than anticipated were the official reasons given for the 98.7% fall from projected returns, with food shortages and surpluses caused by the miscalculations and faulty supply. Indeed, "hundreds went hungry in the midst of plenty" in Festac Village, where angry crowds waited in restaurants without food while others, fully stocked, had no customers.[21] As for problem solving, scores of protocol officers abounded but didn't seem to know what was available or where things were.[22] From an economic perspective, FESTAC was bad business. Investments generated virtually no returns, imported commodities bypassed local producers, and oil money disappeared. But FESTAC's main business was culture, not profit, and to grasp the forms of valuation and production in this sphere, we turn to the commodification of culture as such.

CONTRACTING CULTURE

As we saw in chapter 3 with the production of Nigerian national culture, the global culture of the black and African world was basically removed from the market, so to speak of it as commodification makes only limited economic sense. That such culture reflected, indeed objectified, oil money follows directly from the government funds that the IFC received to produce FESTAC in its extravagant glory. But if black culture was animated by the value of oil, it remained economically inalienable. Even when measured in U.S. dollars or British pounds, the great works of African art and culture could not be sold. We can recall in chapter 2 that during its attempt to repatriate the Benin ivory that served as FESTAC's emblem and trademark, the British Museum demanded an insurance premium of 2 million naira before backing off. Similarly, in chapter 3 we saw how NICON insured each state's cultural contributions along limited routes that circumscribed markets. On the other hand, international visitors were invited to purchase works of art: not original antiques, but replicas and contemporary sculptures and paintings that would be sold exclusively through the IFC. As the promotional FESTAC book announced, "The acquisition of any works of art exhibited shall be made through the International Festival Committee. The price of each work shall be shown in (US) dollars. The price of each work shall exclude local taxes."[23] Thus in a sense the "pure" value of an exhibited culture, unperturbed by local taxes, was measured in the international currency of oil. But this invocation of money as the measure of cultural value was ultimately rhetorical, established in principle but never carried out. No machinery for such transactions was set up, nor were sales and commissions reported or recorded, apart from posters, brochures, and special publications. Rather, the opposite occurred, in that the IFC took sole possession of its cultural productions by transforming them into moveable property and limiting their circulation.

FESTAC was turned into cultural property through copyright. All participating countries and communities signed a contract with the IFC, ceding to it authority, authorship, and rights of mechanical reproduction over literary works (published or unpublished), musical and dramatic performances, artistic works, films, records, broadcasts, and even architecture. Literally *branded* by the FESTAC trademark of the royal Benin ivory mask, the entire inventory of exhibits and events was initially appropriated by the festival committee. In its original formulation, the contract specified a long list of definitions and conditions that in the end proved too unwieldy to negotiate. The meaning of copyright was spelled out for each category of work, covering material objects, words and texts, models, performances, originals, and copies, including their production, reproduction, and distribution. Thus for a literary, musical, or artistic work, copyright meant "the exclusive right to control the doing of the following acts, namely, right to produce or reproduce work, of distribution of copies, of public performance for payment and of broadcasting of the whole or a substantial part of the work whether in its original or any form recognizably derived from the original." And as the contract further specified, "the 'Author' of the work is the first owner of the copyright therein," explaining that "the 'author' of a broadcast is the broadcasting authority which first transmits the broadcast, whatever its origin."[24]

This latter clause was especially significant because FESTAC was mass mediated. If the actual attendance of events was limited, the Broadcasting Organisation of Nigeria (BON) handled national film, radio, and television coverage "to spread the joy of the festival all over the country."[25] Within this umbrella organization, the national television service acquired state-of-the-art equipment to live up to the task, including three Marconi Mark VIII automatic color cameras. To maintain control over foreign reportage and film coverage by NBC, BBC, and others, the committee issued a color-coded system of green and yellow accreditation cards that controlled press access and movement.[26] Navigating the National Theatre, Femi Osofisan, then an artistic consultant, described the mayhem that this caused: "we discovered that the building had been divided into various zones, each jealous of the other, and you needed different passes to pass from one to the other . . . an attempt to explain to the fierce-looking soldiers at the gates nearly earned me a flogging" (Osofisan 1981, 39).

But whatever its operational problems, a logic of state ownership emerged that controlled access to the media and its overseas markets. Moreover, since the media coverage was protected by copyright, it belonged to the cultural property that it documented and reproduced, developing it into an even "higher" form. Just as mass communications ("mass com") was emerging as the new modernizing profession on university campuses, keeping step with statist visions of top-down national integration, so it produced a higher form of culture for the black and African world while assuming a central role in its dissemination and transmission.

The final FESTAC contract covered rights of reproduction rather than the original "works" as such. Each participating country or black community ceded not full ownership and authorship of its cultural contributions but full authority—"free of all legal and other encumbrances"—to include them "in a cinematograph film relating to the festival and to be made by or on behalf of the International Festival Committee." This shift from "culture" to its mechanical reproduction represents a mode of commodification that signals—following Benjamin's seminal essay—a shift from use-value to exchange value, or from cult value to exhibition value in the realm of art, further severing the work from its original context and sending it into circulation (Benjamin 1976). Ironically, or perhaps predictably, Nigeria's own fledgling film industry did not benefit from this cultural transmutation, given the state's preference for bureaucrats over artists. Annoyed with the official myopia, Nigeria's star filmmaker, Chief Hubert Ogunde, withdrew from FESTAC, resulting in a lack of professional oversight as well as a poor national showing in the area of film itself. So limited were Nigeria's cinematic contributions that it featured official documentaries and propaganda films like *2000 Years of Nigerian Arts* and *T.B. Can Be Cured*. Here again, FESTAC's films were removed from the market, following vertical channels of national distribution rather than popular interest and demand. But my point concerns less the content than the form of FESTAC's cultural property, which inverted the relationship between reproduction and original and became increasingly abstract. Operating through the

IFC, Nigeria couldn't own the culture of the black and African world, but did take possession of its cinematic reproduction. In the process, the cultural patrimony of participating black nations gave way to the primary value of its mass mediation.[27]

The reversal of sign-value sketched above, in which the medium of cinematic reproduction surpassed the original, represents a scheme or template of inverted value production more generally in FESTAC and for Nigeria beyond. As a form of cultural property, FESTAC's value derived not from commercial exchange as such but from its sign-value, in the form of the FESTAC emblem that doubled as a trademark for generating franchise fees. If the IFC owned the emblem and its incorporated cultural property—or more accurately, the *property* of the FESTAC sign—this body alone was authorized to *represent* the festival in its manifold material and symbolic forms.[28] That these forms included souvenirs and other objects for sale does not imply a sphere of commercial exchange, for such items were sold at a financial loss, not even appearing in the *Report and Summary of Accounts,* and served more as gifts than commodities. In fact after the festival, the remaining souvenirs were officially distributed as gifts. A letter from Supreme Headquarters written by F. Bola Giwa of Dodan Barracks explained,

> It is the wish of the Chief of Staff that, the 200 round neck cotton singlet[s] with sleeves having Festac symbol in front, 100 walking sticks cane-woven with inscription "Afro Festac Lagos 1975," 4,050 cuff-links as well as 4,250 cardboard trays should be made available to the Armed forces and the Police for distribution to their junior officials in acknowledgement of their contributions during Festac. It is also thought that medals and badges are really for school children and that these should be distributed to schools for handicapped kids or other charity managed institutions.[29]

Thus the signs and souvenirs of cultural property sold exclusively through the IFC became gifts signifying social and political recognition. Even when sold directly, these FESTAC mementoes were virtually given away. For commercial exchange lay beyond FESTAC's arena of exhibition and display, in a secondary sphere of franchised businesses that paid fees for the use of the trademark logo. FESTAC's emblem was thereby detached from the "original" arts that it signified and was reassigned to the products of private enterprise, for a fee, in order to generate economic returns. In its "emblematic" moneymaking magic, FESTAC's cultural property remained inalienable, protected from the market by military decree. In this way, culture produced value without being sold.

In the end, as we saw in the previous section, the franchise revenues generated paltry returns in relation to the festival's gargantuan costs. It is telling that one niche market rapidly developed in street photography, combining "instamatic" reproduction with iconic images of cultural value. Thus Sam Ogun recalled "one of the pictures we took in front of the Festival symbol at the National Theatre by the newly popular wait-and-get colour photographers found all over the place with their Polaroid cameras."[30] Another private citizen designed FESTAC handkerchiefs to modest profit and public acclaim.[31] There was even FESTAC toilet tissue that briefly appeared in Lagos markets, combining commercial initiative with critical wit! Apart from their limited economic scale, these examples underscore the secondary relationship of commercial exchange to FESTAC's cultural property, emphasizing metonymic relations between black visitors and the Pan-African dream world through visual juxtaposition and bodily contact. Even King Sunny Ade's popular FESTAC theme song assimilated listener and singer to the expansive black world, with his refrain "FESTAC for you, FESTAC for me, FESTAC for black people" dominating the airwaves. If FESTAC's culture was inclusive and inalienable, its images and effects would produce money and progress. In this larger sense, FESTAC was seen as a model and instrument of national development, building a cultural foundation for economic takeoff. As Grand Patron Olusegun Obasanjo explained, "culture remains one of the most important resources for sanity and meaningful national development."[32]

Beyond FESTAC's higher moral and economic purpose, and reflected in its images, was the spectacle of development itself as oil money transformed the Nigerian landscape into images of national renewal.[33] Through the magic of contracting, as we have seen, the new highways, centers, buildings, processing plants—including the business of FESTAC itself—generated money instantaneously in the form of mobilization fees and less official financial sweeteners for cultivating and concluding successful deals. But if money flowed quickly from contracting development, often in advance and up front, it frequently shifted pathways, disappeared, or dried up, bringing construction and production to a sudden halt. Thus the signs of rapid development in Nigeria often turned into traces of original intent, deconstructing, we might say, into material signifiers of waste, consumption, dissolution, and incompletion. In this pervasive spectacle of national renewal we see an inverted form of production writ large, and it is to this broader theater of development—in which wealth and value were curiously at odds—that we now return.

In May 1976, when the Tribunal of Inquiry released its report on FESTAC's Finances, a second report from another probe was leading to headlines on the notorious "cement armada." The case was paradigmatic of oil-boom contracting, involving huge sums of money up front and under the table, countless tons of imported cement, and a cabal of officials who enriched themselves with public funds. Responding to the probe, the Supreme Military Council explained,

> There was no proper system of accounts, no close scrutiny into the contracts signed so as to ensure the public interest. The quantity ordered bore no relationship to the needs of the Ministry of Defence and the country, or the port's handling capacity. The Tribunal highlighted the failure to follow established procedure and the extensive and unnecessary use of middlemen, or commission agents or touts. These and other lapses resulted in the Ministry of Defence ordering, within a period of only 7 months, over 16 million metric tonnes of cement at a cost of over N557,000,000.00. This amount does not include the millions of Naira lost as demurrage payments.[35]

In addition to its huge initial outlay, the cement armada clogged the harbor, adding further to Lagos port congestion and the huge daily costs of demurrage payments. Moreover, it symbolized the scandal of imported development at large. Iconic of the construction boom, cement—the very material of public building and housing—was ordered in excessive quantities, with "cuts" siphoned off through a skein of officials and middlemen, only to sit in the harbor, incurring further costs as ships queued for months and even years before unloading. Representing the supreme bottleneck of imported development, the Lagos Port, with its semi-operational Customs Quay, was a monument to unproductive expenditure. Importing more commodities than it could possibly handle, and paying daily for their lack of movement, Nigeria was throwing its money away, providing opportunities for a secondary sector of parasitic appropriation as well. This included ships that simply came to take advantage of the demurrage, lying offshore with inferior goods, and bands of local pirates who preyed upon them, stripping them of fittings and equipment if their cargoes were worthless. In one bold raid, a gang of pirates sang war songs as they stole a cargo of beer, prompting the Navy to retaliate with guns.[36]

The cement armada stood out not only for its massive waste and port congestion, but also for the general condition of material accumulation that it came to represent. Offshore congestion was matched by notorious traffic jams and "go-slows" in Lagos, where cars, buses, and trucks would converge for hours without moving, pressing forward into greater gridlock under torrents of rain or the broiling sun. To prevent this congestion from sabotaging FESTAC, the government decreed that only cars with even- or odd-numbered license plate numbers could drive in Lagos on alternating days of the week. Although designed to cut the traffic by half, many Nigerians simply bought second cars. A tour of Nigerian inflation, we might say, would reveal rising highways and heaps of rubble, new banks and corrugated huts, open sewage and crowded streets full of hawkers and vendors selling stereos and soft drinks.[37] Another paradigmatic sign of the times was the car wrecks littering the streets and highways—new Peugots, Volvos, Datsuns, and Benzes smashed in all manner of reckless accidents, with their license plates characteristically removed or covered to disguise the shame and identities of the owners. If Nkem Nwankwo's *My Mercedes Is Bigger than Yours* (1975) captured the drama of such destruction as it extended from Lagos into the rural areas, the destruction reached its highest form in the burned carcasses of tankers. In some cases these burnt offerings to the god of oil resulted from gaping holes or debris on the highways, or from winding roads that simply stopped, unfinished, leading into walls, ravines, or hillsides. In other cases, it was common knowledge that drivers crashed their vehicles to collect insurance.

The incompletion of public-sector projects such as roads, buildings, dams, and factories corresponded to a rise in conspicuous material consumption. Pocketed mobilization fees might result in new cars for project managers and their associates while broken contracts were rarely pursued. Since nearly everybody was in on the game, open secrets were kept secret. But not all extravagant gains were procured directly in these ways. Fortunes were made in legitimate deals, with international corporations like I.T.T. tapping into Nigeria's vast communications markets, and the signs of success were seen in private jets, mansions, expensive lace, and displays of extravagant largesse, as in the "spraying" of guests with new naira notes and even with coveted foreign exchange. It is not my aim to lampoon this Nigerian spending spree, for as I have indicated earlier, it followed a logic of political patronage and social distribution that had developed under the colonial economy, when access to markets was controlled by the state. Rather, in characterizing a mode of accumulation and consumption that intensified under oil capitalism, we can better grasp its associated forms of labor and production.

During the oil boom, Nigeria remained interested in self-reliance through sustained growth and production. Describing the oil economy as a "trading post economy" that remained dependent on overseas markets and capital, Obasanjo called for nothing less than "the qualitative transformation of our economy" to promote indigenous capital and sustainable development.[38] How, then, to foster efficient production?

From the commanding heights of the Nigerian petro-state, the government would transform the economy from above, returning to agriculture, reorganizing labor, and investing in heavy industry. The nation's increasing dependence on oil and the flow of imports fueled by petro-naira caused domestic deficits in food supply that approached crisis proportions in the mid-1970s. In 1977, imported food accounted for more than 10% of all imports into the country, representing an increase of 1100% from 1970 (Falusi 1981, 56). The corresponding drop in local production created staggering food deficits for such staples as yams, cocoyams, sorghum, cassava, and plaintains—the very substance of local cuisine. As the public sector expanded and the agricultural sector declined, with food prices rising in an inflationary spiral, Obasanjo launched Operation Feed the Nation to end these shortages in the land of plenty. The goal, beyond self-sufficiency in food production, was to generate a surplus for export, thereby reversing the trend of "Uncle Bens." Import substitution plans were invoked on a massive scale, with training programs, publicity campaigns, councils, and committees throughout the nation offering fertilizer subsidies, irrigation, tractors, processing plants. These programs and subsidies, however, generally overlooked small farmers in favor of large, capital-intensive schemes. In the end, heightened awareness did not lead to increased production, but rather a landscape littered with decaying equipment, and the "agrics," as they were called, operating at a loss.

Heavy-handed approaches to labor and manufacturing produced similarly negative results and returns. Seeing like a state (J. Scott 1998), the federal government blamed poor industrial output on workers, who needed further discipline and training to promote industrial peace. In a series of national labor acts and decrees, the trade unions were "amalgamated" under a federally funded and controlled central labor organization that imposed a rigid code of conduct on its workers and took the teeth out of collective bargaining by withdrawing the right to strike. Acts calculated to disrupt the economy were seen as unpatriotic if not subversive, warranting fines and imprisonment imposed by a National Industrial Court. That government was a major employer of the workers whose unions it effectively controlled appeared not as a conflict of interest but a rational plan, designed to promote an economic harmony that would increase national production and attract foreign capital. Nonetheless, no amount of worker training and discipline changed the global situation of the oil-financed commodity boom. If total manufacturing output increased at 13% per annum from 1972 to 1980, the industrial sector's contribution to the GDP decreased while imported consumer goods increased over 700% (Watts 1992, 27n4).

In a complementary effort to reverse this trend and produce the nation's steel, the state financed the enormous Ajaokuta Steel at an initial cost of 396,880 naira. The site has become an infamous white elephant, swallowing endless extra costs and suffering long delays well into the 1990s, but its visionary design represented an ambitious plan to convert the waste product of oil—its natural gas—into producing steel through "direct reduction." As we shall see in chapter 8, no image of the excess and waste of oil outdid that of flared natural gas, perpetually burning from the oil rigs of the Niger Delta and consequently squandering a marketable resource while polluting the environment. But if the goal of the Ajaokuta Steel Complex was laudable, its results only added to the downward spiral of real economic growth.[39] Oil, the ultimate wasting asset, was not easily absorbed into local capital. The money it generated was curiously unproductive, with investments yielding negative returns. As Nigeria's wealth continued to increase, the productive value of its land, labor, and capital diminished. Nigeria's commodities, like FESTAC's culture, were produced at a loss.

In this brief chapter on the economics of cultural production, I approached FESTAC as a mirror reflecting the broader forms of waste and expenditure under oil capitalism at large. In crude economic terms, the festival was bad business. Untendered bids, inflated contracts, diverted funds, and poor accounting were only the most blatant symptoms of a feeding frenzy in which consumption typically outstripped production. In the squandermania of government spending, costs kept escalating and projects often failed. In light of its poor communications, hidden fiscal pathways, and mercurial money forms, that FESTAC took place at all was a remarkable achievement. That the festival failed to generate expected returns through ticket sales, room and board, and franchise fees was not a major problem, since FESTAC's business was culture, not profit, relegating souvenirs, images, and replicas to a secondary sphere of commercial exchange. In this sense, culture itself was inalienable, serving as the underlying "substance" of its commodified reproductions.

It is here, in the secondary sphere of commercial exchange, that the "mirror" of cultural production acquires greater focus, reflecting not just the spending spree fueled by oil but also its characteristic phenomenology of value. As we have seen, the rapid influx of oil money generated an unstable field of signification, a form of Nigerian nervousness responding to the pervasive dissociation of signs from their referents. In crude terms, oil prosperity was illusory, producing signs and images of national development that somehow fell short of the mark. If wealth was often ephemeral, wasted in unfinished roads, unsteady cars, and private overseas bank accounts, its value was uncertain, shifting between potent signifiers and hidden referents or substances. The Leyland Bus scandal is illustrative in this respect not merely because of the graft and corruption it revealed, but for the anxiety it generated over the representational value of the vehicles themselves. Popular rumors that the new FESTAC buses concealed corroded bodies under fresh coats of paint placed the signs of development—and of the festival itself—under collective suspicion, highlighting the unstable connection between image and reality through the inversion of signifier and signified.

This inversion, I have argued, provided a model of value production under oil capitalism that was sanctified by FESTAC's conversion of culture into the very "property" of a sign. If the FESTAC trademark illustrates this power concretely—by "conjuring" money through a purely symbolic association with an authentic source—it also characterizes the general form of cultural property as a symbolic relation between copy and original. As a foundation for developing Nigeria, and by extension the black and African world, culture itself was sacred and inalienable but could produce value through a collateral market of mimetic icons and representations. Reflecting oil prosperity and its images of industrial production, cultural property would generate economic value through symbolic association and exchange.

FESTAC thereby established the grammar of a cultural code that was governed by a law of symbolic exchange, giving rise to images of production and development that were taken for economic wonders. In the euphoria of the oil boom, this symbolic economy of value production approximated Baudrillard's realm of the "hyperreal," where referential value is "disarticulated" from the code, receding—like FESTAC's slippery accounts—into a mirage of material alibis. Unlike Baudrillard's self-referential code, however, which predominates "in the era of high-tech capitalism" (Poster 1988, 6), FESTAC's forms of cultural production reflect an industrial era of oil capitalism, a historically specific modality of accumulation and expenditure in a postcolonial enclave economy. In other words, Nigeria's symbolic economy was hardly driven by high-tech financial markets. Rather, it was powered and financed by oil, creating an overvalued exchange rate that inhibited local production and lowered the cost of imported commodities. Nigeria's "structural revolution of value" occurred because real production was undermined by oil.

Ultimately, the problem of Nigeria's wasted expenditures was not one of corrupt leaders and undisciplined workers. It was one of material relations.

And here is where FESTAC's magical mirror captured the material conditions of its symbolic forms, reflecting a negative dialectic of money and value based on primary infusions of oil rents and revenues. *In Nigeria, the historic relation between the sphere of circulation and the underlying, value-generating sphere of production was not merely transformed by oil capitalism but inverted.* The real domestic economy was inert (Schatz 1984). The illusion of growth that Nigeria produced was only sustained by petrodollars—at a loss. In the final two chapters we will see what happened when the oil economy began to run down, giving way to the growth of illusion and the erosion of civil society.

LA MISE EN ABÎME

CHAPTER SEVEN

The Politics of Illusion

On June 23, 1993, the day of the annulment of the national presidential election, the military committed the most treasonable act of larceny of all time: it violently robbed the Nigerian people of their nationhood.
—Wole Soyinka, *New York Times* op ed, August 22, 1994

The government has by its own actions legitimized a culture of fraud and corruption.
—Chief Gani Fawehinmi

[T]he postcolonial state stems to a great extent from its own representation.
—Bayart (1993)

ON AUGUST 26, 1993, Nigeria's self-appointed military "president," General Ibrahim Badamosi Babangida (popularly known as IBB), broke down in tears. At least that is how the story goes. It was during his televised farewell address, when the tired general finally announced that he would "step aside" from office, that he allegedly cried like a baby. Of course the tears were never shown. The momentary breakdown—if it actually occurred—was edited from the final broadcast, in which IBB attempted a graceful exit from the eight years of kleptocracy that brought Nigeria down from a middle-income nation to among the poorest in Africa. IBB had indeed exhausted his country and his options. Democratic return to civilian rule was repeatedly postponed from 1990 until the ill-fated elections of June 12, 1993, which he annulled for reasons that were never formally established. In the following weeks, IBB tried to buy support, disbursing *billions* of naira to governors, senators, even traditional rulers flown to Abuja each week as his guests. But no alliance or coalition formed, and finally, even the military turned against him. By August 26, the game was up. Were IBB's invisible tears those of a leader betrayed by his nation or of a nation betrayed by its leader? Were they a hidden sign of his personal failure or a collective representation of relief and despair? Did they flow from the dictator's body or from the popular imagination? Or were they a smokescreen, part of a well-crafted vanishing act giving IBB the last laugh?

These questions are not merely rhetorical, but reflect a more general crisis of representation pervading Nigeria's postboom society. For most external observers, the failure of "June 12" represented the latest breakdown of Nigerian democracy, undermined by the familiar syndrome of state patronage and rampant corruption unchecked by ineffective courts. As the 1983 elections of Shehu Shagari's Second Republic revealed, in a system where wealth and power depend upon political access to state petroleum revenues, no party can afford to lose the vote. Rather, it will engage in widespread intimidation and electoral fraud before conceding victory to the opposition (Apter 1987; Hart 1993; Joseph 1987). However, the aborted elections of June 12, 1993, represented not just the return of electoral tragedy as democratic farce but a new type of crisis; one that is of a different order of magnitude from mere vote rigging and competition for the national cake. For unlike the 1983 elections of the Second Republic, which were held, even if rules were broken to produce questionable results, the elections of June 12 never really took place—at least not in any politically meaningful sense. As subsequent events and information have revealed, IBB's long-awaited elections were a ruse, a confidence trick, an elaborate simulation of the democratic process. Many believe that IBB had no intention of giving up power. However, my argument extends beyond the ambitions of an individual dictator, beyond personifications of corruption and greed, to grasp the *logic* of his dictatorship—a regime of arbitrary truth and pervasive illusion that developed as the oil economy collapsed.

At issue is the correlation of different forms of value, particularly exchange value and truth-value, as the oil economy boomed and then went bust. As we have seen in the previous chapters, when the nation was flush with buying power, Nigeria's problem was the proverbial fate of all oil economies, which is not how to make money but how to spend it.

The national currency may have been fixed at an artificially high rate of exchange, but it was backed by oil, which was globally distributed through OPEC. Under these conditions, Nigeria enjoyed a high degree of international visibility and credibility, reflected by FESTAC's spectacle of culture. As the quality of everyday life improved for increasing proportions of the population, a new fetishism of commodities animated the nation, based less on the objectification of productive relations than on those of consumption and exchange. In the new object world of imported commodities and rapid growth, I have argued, seeing was believing. The visible signs of national development were in the last instance backed by petrodollars, represented by letters of credit, contracts, trademarks, bridges, monuments, museums, highways, traffic jams, and a rising nouveau bourgeoisie. Whatever practical obstacles to finalizing a contract might occur—be they revised estimates, kickbacks, or successive mobilization fees—Nigerian social, political, and economic life was ultimately redeemable in foreign exchange. If the oil-rich state was not exactly democratic, at least it was accountable in dollars and cents.

All of this created an image of modernity that was backed by hard evidence. Or so it appeared. The infusion of oil money into the economy did not generate the alienated, impersonal, rational calculus of the modern industrial economy as variously portrayed by Marx, Simmel, and Weber. After all, oil capitalism is not industrial capitalism, wherever petroleum's final destination may be. Rather, the monetization of an oil-rich Nigeria gave rise to a celebration of visible "naira power," a national measure of value that could hold its own in international markets while attracting considerable foreign investment.[1] If money remained "magical"—powerful in its capacity to buy influence, erotic in its ability to buy love, its hidden source beneath the ground a state-owned secret—its consequences were tangible. They signified "objective" growth in the universal language of the dollar. The naira was a credible currency not because of its internal semantic properties, such as denominational units or engraved designs, but due to its favorable relation to the dollar and the pound.[2] In the object world of imports and exports, it bolstered the authority of the state by presiding, with its imprimatur, over a regime of national renewal. For whatever Nigeria's boasts or demands, the buck stopped with the Nigerian National Petroleum Corporation (NNPC). Oil thus underwrote the veracity of a range of discourses, from the technical and scientific to the national and even racial, as the redeemable and redemptive wealth of the black and African world. The state emerged as the locus of truth, not because it wielded arbitrary power but because it organized distribution. It pumped oil revenues into the expanding public sector while diverting dividends—such as import licenses, contracts, and jobs—to political clients and even potential opponents of the regime.

By 1983, however, the oil economy had entered its downward spiral. Things began to fall apart. The credibility of the nation and the naira began to wane as the civilian chaos of the Second Republic gave way to a succession of military takeovers. After Babangida toppled the Buhari-Idiagbon regime in the bloodless coup of August 27, 1985, one of his explicit goals was to restore Nigeria's credibility by floating the naira to establish its "free" market value. The new regime sought to attract foreign investment and eliminate illegal traffic in foreign exchange. The result, coupled with a stringent Structural Adjustment Program designed to stimulate domestic production, was massive inflation, devaluation, and extensive deterioration of public institutions and infrastructures (Anyanwu 1992). As the world price in oil dropped, Nigeria's dependence on petroleum increased, creating a political economy of dwindling resources and intensified competition to appropriate them. By the late 1980s, in an atmosphere of frustrated expectations, broken contracts, and unfulfilled national development plans, a new kind of crime began gaining momentum   less violent than the roving gangs of armed robbers who took over at night, but more pervasive within the dramaturgy of Nigerian business culture and everyday life. Referred to colloquially as the "419," after the relevant section of the Nigerian criminal code, it covered a range of confidence tricks involving impersonation and forgery for fraudulent gain. The "419" continued to grow as a major industry in Nigeria, second only to oil (or in some accounts, third, after narcotics) as the nation's major export earner of foreign currency in the 1990s.[3] In what follows, I will explore the failure of the 1993 elections within the crisis that developed after the dollar dropped out of the naira—when the mysterious "substance" of the money form literally disappeared.

THE ART OF THE DEAL

On September 4, 1991, the Singapore International Chamber of Commerce issued a warning against fraudulent deals with Nigerians. In an article titled "Singapore Weary of Nigerian Businessmen," the *Daily Times* reported that according to the executive secretary, at least thirty of its members received letters from Nigerians promising to pay several million dollars in return for help in transferring large sums of money from Nigeria into Singapore bank accounts.[4]

In a related incident, one Singapore computer company lost $23,000 US worth of computers over a shipping deal made on a false bank draft.

By the time the forgery was discovered, the computers were on their way to Nigeria.

These stories are a ripple on a tidal wave of financial fraud that is sweeping across the globe, "from South Dakota to Ulan Bator," according to one exposé.[5] They belong to a hybrid narrative genre—combining low tragicomedy with high moral parable—about greed, corruption, and ruinous deception perpetrated by crafty Nigerians on their credulous marks. The *Economist* called the situation "The Great Nigerian Scam," otherwise known as "advanced fee-fraud" or, more simply, "419" after the Nigerian criminal code enacted to prosecute such cases. Its basic features involve all the trappings of advanced parastatal oil capitalism, replete with faxes, forms, stamps, insignia, letters of credit, invoices, corporate logos, and bank accounts, which figure as props in a well-staged illusion. The *Economist* explained,

> A typical "419" letter is written—supposedly—on the headed writing paper of the NNPC or some other state enterprise. A supposed official cheerfully admits to some scheme to rip off his employers, and offers the foreign recipient a 30% share of the $40m–60m or so which, he says, he needs to send urgently overseas. The recipient, normally a company, simply has to send details of its bank account, invoices for its fictitious services rendered to the state corporation—and some sheets of its own headed writing paper, blank but signed. Absolute secrecy is requested for a "highly classified" transaction.[6]

To set the proposed money-laundering operation in motion, the mark typically greases a few palms with $5,000 in "fees" and few more thousand in "taxes," with some Rolex watches and airplane tickets thrown in to soften senior gatekeepers and bank managers—not unlike ordinary kickbacks of business as usual. In the meantime, the signed letterhead, purportedly used to make the transaction look legitimate, is sent to the victim's bank manager with instructions to transfer thousands or even millions into a dummy account held by the scamster.

In most cases, the credibility of the scam rests on references to excess funds accumulated through inflated contracts negotiated during the oil boom. Many foreigners, including businesspeople from the heartland of America, have some sense of Nigeria's prominence as a major oil-producing nation, even if they cannot locate the country on a map. This awareness, coupled with the misguided sense that the "third world" plays by flexible rules, generates considerable gullibility. An editorial in Nigeria's *Daily Times*, appropriately titled "Much Ado about 419" to play upon the "nothingness" behind the elaborate decoys (and more obliquely, upon the foreigner's shared responsibility for the crimes), elaborates on the techniques of *faire croire:*

> The foreign victims are taken in by fake circular letters or unauthenticated fax or telex messages relating to purported approved transfer of funds running into millions of US dollars arising from excess claims on some alleged foreign contracts awarded between 1979 and 1983. These purportedly authorized letters lend support to enable the transfer of funds from Nigeria to off-shore bank accounts with a promise to share in the illegal proceeds. To make the deals look authentic, the fraudsters infiltrate public places like the Nigerian National Petroleum Corporation (NNPC), the Central Bank of Nigeria, Merchant Banks and strategic government departments. The crooks use government facilities and impersonate public functionaries and in the end leave large sums of unpaid telephone and postal bills. In many of the "successful" cases, the tricksters disappear after receiving substantial deposits as advance payments which are supposedly meant to "soften the ground" and bribe "officials" who might be sitting in on the "deal."[7]

Here we can see how the oil boom, specifically during the last contracting heyday of Shagari's Second Republic from 1979 to 1983, established the backdrop of such financial dissimulation. It provided a historical context of considerable fiscal accumulation and gave rise to the corporate forms and monetary instruments that marked Nigeria's participation in global market transactions. Two remarkable dimensions of the "419" deserve special consideration: the range and scale of operations, and the performance art of the con games themselves, which involve stagecraft, impersonation, and those collusive fabrications which Goffman (1974, 83–123) unpacks with such acute sensitivity in his phenomenology of social interaction.

The global scale of the "419" erupted rather suddenly in 1990, when Babangida deregulated the banking system and foreign-exchange market, sending the naira into its downward spiral. As the naira dropped against international currencies, the "419" took shape, following the circuits of global capital that developed in the era of flexible accumulation (Harvey 1989, 141–200) throughout Europe, Asia, and the Americas. Financial scams reported in Thailand, Canada, Scandinavia, Austria, the United Kingdom, and the United States have engaged the energies of Scotland Yard, the FBI, Interpol, the Royal Canadian Mounted Police, and a variety of private and subsidiary agencies, such as the Better Business Bureau and the Financial Crimes Enforcement Network of the U.S. Treasury Department. According to the managing director of Kroll Associates, a large financial-investigation company based in New York,

"You almost never see a net spread this wide in white-collar fraud."[8] The State Department's Office of Public Affairs even published a pamphlet, "Tips for Business Travelers to Nigeria." Its list of "scam indicators" includes large transfers of funds in exchange for a substantial percentage with discretion, letters claiming the soliciting party has personal ties to high government officials, and "any deal that seems too good to be true."[9] Estimates of the annual income earned by this "well-oiled" Nigerian industry range from Scotland Yard's $250 million to over $1 billion, according to Terry Sorgi, former commercial attaché for the U.S. Embassy in Lagos who handled 474 Nigerian fraud cases in 1992 alone.[10]

Sorgi claims that the average money-laundering sting nets $150,000, although amounts exceeding $1 million have been received from forged real estate purchases and merchandise orders. Among newsworthy Canadian victims, Corrine Baker lost $470,000 (which her sales and promotion company had raised for charities) when she diverted it to Nigerian bank accounts in Germany and England in anticipation of a 30% share of $20 million promised to her by her Nigerian correspondents. They had convinced her to forward them a percentage of the total to get the money released and to pay for legal fees; as a result, she was charged with defrauding her Canadian clients. In another case, a Toronto investment broker lost $690,000 after traveling to Nigeria several times in one month to seal a deal. In a related incident, two Calgary oil and gas companies lost a combined total of $625,000 to Nigerians who said they planned on laundering millions by issuing fake invoices to the government for orders of the firms' oilfield equipment.[11]

Lured by the prospect of windfall profits, overseas businesses have paid dearly for their mistakes. Among the counterfeit purchase order victims, a New Zealand businessman lost $200,000 worth of computers and supplies when he shipped the equipment against a forged letter of credit. In the United States, George Davis, a retired Texas oil engineer, also received a fake purchase order from a Nigerian company for $15 million in industrial hardware from his business, International Equipment. After sending over $70,000 in processing "fees," Davis had to file for bankruptcy. On a more sanctified register, Houston evangelist Jerry Smith (pastor of Woodland Trails Baptist Church and author of religious books distributed in Nigeria) and the Rev. Don Kettler (of St. Joseph's Cathedral, Sioux Falls, South Dakota) lost $32,000 and $90,000 respectively in their efforts to release bogus legacies bequeathed to them in Nigeria. In both cases, the beneficiaries were convinced to pay inheritance taxes and legal fees up front, only to discover that the anticipated bequest did not exist.

In one of the most spectacular cons, EER Systems, a private aerospace engineering firm that has worked for NASA and the U.S. Department of Defense, lost $4.4 million in a simulated deal with the Nigerian Ministry of Aviation. After the firm's president met with his "partners" in Nigeria, they convinced him to use wire transfers to deposit $4.4 million into Nigerian accounts to expedite a $28.5 million deal which, of course, never materialized. Instead, the three Nigerian associates were charged with wire fraud by a federal grand jury, but the Nigerian government never extradited the confidence men. For despite official disclaimers, and the establishment of a Nigerian Task Force on Trade Malpractices in 1992, there is considerable evidence that the Nigerian government's complicity went all the way to the top. Although the Justice Ministry published a wanted list of 1,200 suspects, and investigators have made a few arrests, no convictions to date have been carried by the courts.

Perhaps the most delightful "419," and one that directly implicated the Babangida regime, was the fleecing of South Africa's foreign minister, Pik Botha, in a deal that combined political tactics with financial injury. According to a feature story in the *Guardian*, Arthur Nzeribe, one of Nigeria's most controversial politicians, approached Botha to underwrite a new African magazine that would provide sympathetic coverage for Pretoria, on condition that the South African connection would be kept secret. According to the deal that was struck, Nzeribe's and Botha's foreign ministries were each to put 320,000 pounds sterling into a British bank account from which either could withdraw. When Botha deposited his money, Nzeribe took it out. Whereas the South African foreign minister never recovered a penny, "the Nigerian politician has since gained further notoriety as the military's front-man in using the courts to cancel Nigeria's presidential election." [12]

To be sure, there is a certain degree of righteous third-world banditry to the Nigerian "419." In a country that has been a dumping ground for surplus (and often defective) commodities, operating under unfavorable terms of trade dating to a colonial economy that diverted producer profits into British securities (Helleiner 1966, 161–62), the "419" might appear as just deserts. Some Nigerians see it as reparations for colonialism and the slave trade. Fred Ajuda, a "419" hero who traveled with a police escort in Lagos, called himself "a black man's Robin Hood." [13] Nigerians are quick to point out that the scams could not work without unscrupulous Western dupes seeking illicit profits. Indeed, their techniques—raiding bank accounts, using dummy corporations, banking on trust, building confidence—echo the language of high finance with its corporate raids, hostile takeovers, and most especially its fictitious financing and capital formation (Harvey 1989, 194–95). Of course, the dividing line between legitimate and illegitimate business is permeable, increasingly so as the instruments of financial speculation retreat into virtual reality. Instead of criticizing the perpetrators or the victims of the "419," however, I focus on the underlying conditions of its efflorescence in Nigeria, not only as a phenomenon to be measured in dollars, but also as a phenomenology of *transacting* value.

As we have seen, the spending spree of the oil boom produced nouveaux riches of studiously bourgeois businessmen and contractors. The old elite of first- and second-generation colonial civil servants and lawyers, with school ties to London and Oxbridge, was not so much displaced as swallowed up by this burgeoning bourgeoisie, inflated by new money and the plethora of degrees and certificates afforded by the oil bonanza.[14] Many students from the boom era studied in second- and third-tier schools overseas—in the United States, India, and the Soviet Union—retaining the prestige of "been to" status while relying less on the cachet of school name. Others entered elite ranks by passing through Nigeria's university system, which built new campuses, expanded postgraduate programs, hired more faculty, and graduated more students. Universal primary education—and, in some states, secondary as well—widened the net of middle-class recruitment by providing schooling opportunities in the cities and in the bush. And the military emerged as a popular career pathway to important friends and powerful patrons.

By 1976, however, economic growth produced a new social anxiety, a credibility crisis within the status system as the old hierarchy was overwhelmed. The margins of the elite became vulnerable to invasion by a nouveau riche that grew up as quickly as the new houses and hotels it built. At this moment, a flurry of certificate racketeering scandals emerged as fraudulent examination results were discovered among high school graduates seeking jobs or admission to training colleges and universities. Whatever its scale might have been—and there is no doubt that documents were forged, examinations leaked, and results bought—the discourse to which it gave rise indicated a nation, as Chinua Achebe put it (in his novel of the same title), "no longer at ease." Thus an editorial in the *Nigerian Observer* warned the public to beware of false graduates; maintaining that the few cases of certificate racketeering actually probed were but "the tip of the iceberg," it declared the whole country at risk. The problem was said to have developed in the remote "townships and rural areas" where, "amongst the teeming teenagers will be found pushers and hawkers doing their dirty trade, hustling the young, easily gullible idle student to find a criminal way out of the difficulties of exams." In language reminiscent of nineteenth-century American advice manuals that "protected" country youth from city "seducers" (Halttunen 1982, 1–32), but rerouting the flow of evil from city to country, the editorial remonstrated against false representations—not only of credentials, but of the social identities that they purportedly reflected. In almost prophetic anticipation of the "419," it focused on the social conditions of all official documentation: the "receipts, licenses, currency, cheques," which, like certificates, must be "security printing jobs," that is, "distinctive enough for all to see and identify, yet defy easy reproduction and so improper mass circulation."[15] Read as social allegory, the "improper mass circulation" of bourgeois credentials and identities, propelled by a booming economy, threatened the social basis of a more genuine distinction, which was visible but *not* mechanically reproducible. If seeing was believing during the oil boom, being seen could also mean passing and deceiving.

The social dislocations precipitated by the influx of petrodollars differed from those resulting from the oil bust, but they shared connections beyond money. The anxiety generated by an expanding middle class in Nigeria was not confined to the isolated acts of technical forgery that it may have encouraged. Instead, it grew out of the processes of bourgeois self-fashioning, bordering on the impersonation of social standing, that were produced by the sudden circulation of cash and commodities. Fortunes *were* made during the boom, and the art of the business deal was negotiated with tremendous style and lavish celebration. "You got the contract? Great! Join me for a Gulder!" exclaims the sophisticated executive to his associate on the telephone in one contemporary television beer commercial. Magazine advertisements reveal modern Nigerians dressed for success, with chic couples using Western deodorants and proud mothers cooking with vegetable (not palm) oil for their nuclear families. As the petroleum economy internationalized the state (Watts 1992, 35), the nation followed suit, embellishing cosmopolitan modernity with Nigerian hospitality. Obviously the fruits of the boom were not evenly distributed: most Nigerians could only aspire to the lofty heights of the new elite, even if money flowed into the informal economy through patronage networks and the parasitic service sector. Nonetheless, the hotels, nightclubs, business offices, and banks of Lagos and Ibadan were bustling with deals, and it is from the culture of contracting that developed at this time that the elaborate cons of the Babangida era derived.

To appreciate the more dramaturgical arts of the "419," let us focus on two cases profiled at some length in the press: the first involves a Canadian real estate broker, Ben Vanderburg; the second, Charlie Pascale, an American businessman who tried to outsmart those who duped him.

One of the remarkable aspects of the Vanderburg con is that, despite losing $60,000, the victim was so taken in by his Nigerian associates that he still believed they were sincere in their efforts to protect $32 million against government theft. Vanderburg received a call from a man identifying himself as Dr. Shoga Elias from the Ministry of Finance, with a request for help on behalf of a group of Nigerians who wanted to get their money out of the country and invest in real estate. Included in the proposal was a $10 million cut to Vanderburg for his role in keeping the money "out of the hands of corrupt rulers." All he had to do was fly to Lagos with three Rolex watches for the Nigerian bankers they would be meeting and $15,000 for "processing fees." When he arrived, Vanderburg was met at the airport and driven to the home of another high-ranking official in the Ministry of Finance, where he saw a parked red Porsche. That evening, he was introduced to the "group" trying to get its money out. According to Vanderburg, "I felt very, very comfortable, very much at home. . . . They were cultured, well-to-do people, educated, fluent in English."

The following day, more meetings took place to work out the transfer of funds to Canada. Vanderburg was puzzled that the Canadian-educated, Nigerian lawyer working for the group was named Mike Anderson. But he explained that he had changed his name in Canada. More disturbing was his statement that, according to a new government decree, the group would have to come up with an $800,000 cash fee. At another staged meeting with bankers, government bureaucrats, and the investment group—"many of them wearing Nigerian ceremonial dress and 'looking like a million dollars'"—Vanderburg was praised for the wonderful job he was doing for patriotic Nigerians. He was then asked to raise $170,000 as his part of the processing fee, whereupon the Canadian Embassy in Lagos contacted him and informed him of the scam. Two weeks after his return home, the principals were still contacting him, as if the deal were going through. Even after losing $60,000 in fees, plane tickets, and gifts of watches and cellular phones, Vanderburg maintained, "I would be happy to meet them and give them a hug; that's the kind of people they are. . . . They're so convincing, it's beyond belief."[16]

Like any well-planned con, Vanderburg's story illustrates the "collusive fabrications" whereby one party is "contained" by the activities of a "net" or team (Goffman 1974, 84). Exploiting the difference between social appearances and realities, the con artists simulate a business opportunity in which the mark invests, getting in deeper and deeper until the illusion pops and the game is up. The primary frameworks deployed in the "419" include the instruments of international finance, offices and venues such as the NNPC and the Central Bank of Nigeria, and, most important, the staged habitus of a privileged elite that saturates the mark with subtle cues of shared affinities. The Porsche in the compound convinced Vanderburg that his Nigerian associates were serious, that they were for real. The business meetings and parties constructed a credible social reality of "cultured, well-to-do people," a representation from which material consequences would follow as long as the mark's credulity was sustained. And unlike the constructions of "primary" social reality (Goffman's "keyings"), the truth-value of the appearances is not shared—what is true for the mark is false for the fabricators. Such unequal terms of social interaction create unequal terms of financial exchange: money changes hands in one direction only, despite the expectations of a return. Vanderburg's case was really quite simple, illustrating how deeply he invested in the "reality principle" of his associates.

The case of Charlie Pascale is more complex, because it adds an extra level of framing to the interaction, rather like the logic of counterespionage that his story resembles. Pascale's invitation came directly from Mr. Dodo Oto of the NNPC's accounting department, offering a 25% cut on $35 million in excess revenues that needed to be spent before a year-end audit. In exchange for the use of his Alpha Electronics company account, Pascale would keep $8 million for himself. Recognizing the deal as a money-laundering scheme, he played along, putatively planning an exposé if the deal fell through or proved illegal. Employing his own cloak and dagger tactics, including code words, mail drops, and hidden cameras, Pascale traveled to Nigeria to meet a man named Alhaji from the Central Bank:

> The meeting took place in a parlor filled with tasteful bamboo furniture. Alhaji seemed someone of substance. He was "impressive," Charlie later faxed to [his business associate] Johnson. Things were looking up! The missus served cold drinks and hot tea on a silver tray. Then a man named Julius, who identified himself as a representative of the bank, asked Pascale for . . . $750,000. The money, he explained, was needed to cover the "transfer tax" levied on the $35 million before it left the country.[17]

The stage thus set in a convincing bourgeois interior, the plot thickened. Alhaji appeared taken aback by Julius's sudden demand, and turned on Mr. Oto from the NNPC accounting office, threatening to kill him for apparently bungling the negotiations. According to Pascale, "Oto essentially crawled over on his hands and knees and squatted." Pascale pulled out in time, although he continued to fax his partners from the United States, losing another $5,500 in airplane tickets that he sent to Julius.

What makes this particular case so interesting, beyond the dramatic stagecraft, is the secondary playing of the fool against the fool. The con combined elements of bourgeois respectability with bungling slapstick, playing ever so delicately upon third world "mimicry" (Bhabha 1994, 85–92) and mimesis (Taussig 1993) of the West to reinforce the mark's sense of confidence and superiority. Pascale was taken in by his superiors in the game because they allowed him to feel that he was their superior. A history of colonial stereotypes and paternalistic conceits was thus brought into play—of the evolué who tries too hard, and of the enterprising liberal who thinks he knows better. In some scams, the advance fee is called an economic recovery tax, playing on the possible meanings of economic recovery as "getting better" and "getting back."

As the dialectical laminations of the "419" deals increase in complexity, the foundations of social interaction begin to crumble. Unstable identities are represented by shifting names like that of the Nigerian lawyer Mike Anderson, said to have changed his name in Canada; by general names like Alhaji, which refers widely to any Muslim who has been to Mecca, and can be used even more liberally to denote bigmanship; by first names like Julius, which are untraceable, and by false ones like that of Dan Musa, who, according to one "419" report, did not exist, yet managed to transfer 13,000 pounds sterling through the Central Bank and into a fake company account.[18] As Scotland Yard's fraud investigator explained, "the victim is left facing bogus people with bogus documents. . . . Identifying the people behind one of these . . . is a big problem."[19] In many stories involving elaborate venues (for example, "There was a plaque and a doorman in a hat, and the office had lots of NNPC documents"), the dupe returns to find an empty office, a dead telephone line, and no trace of his or her business associates. One Houston businessman who was offered 4 million barrels of crude oil at $2.50 below the market price was convinced that the deal was straight "because he was taken to meetings at the state-owned oil company, shown paperwork at the Central Bank, introduced to military officers in government offices and shown the tanker said to be loaded with oil."[20]

These examples illustrate how the seeing-is-believing of the oil boom gave way to the visual deceptions of the oil bust, a social world not of objects and things but of smoke and mirrors, a business culture of worthless currency, false facades, and empty value forms. Oil, the "underlying" substance of economic value, might lend credibility to Nigerian business ventures and to the "glib and oily art" (*King Lear*, act 1, scene 1) of the deal. But its pathways—from public institutions into private coffers—have become uncertain. Many "419s" simulate its direct purchase and sale, while others invoke the revenues that it has generated. If its presence or absence makes a real difference in transacting value, its decreasing availability as a national resource has undermined Nigeria's credibility, both at home and abroad. The instabilities of social identity produced at the margins of the rising middle class when the state expanded the public sector with oil revenues during the 1970s have subsequently reached into the center. In the words of Alhaji Aliyu Atta, Nigeria's inspector general of police, "Con men are threatening to submerge the nation's economic well-being into one despicable abyss of fraud and corruption."[21] To understand how democracy was thrown into this abyss when the "419" entered into politics, we can turn to the Big Con of June 12, 1993.

THE 1993 ELECTIONS

Addressing the nation during his 1992 budget speech, General Babangida proclaimed, "We must hold ourselves collectively responsible for the negative image which our nation projects."[22] Speaking for himself and his inner circle of syndicate bosses, he knew what he was talking about. Babangida's personal fortune, estimated between $5 billion and $7 billion (Useh 1993, 13), placed him among world-class kleptocrats like the late Ferdinand Marcos of the Philippines and the late Mobutu Sese Seko of Zaire. Using the military regime to make deals and issue decrees, IBB constructed a labyrinthine business empire that he controlled directly, through the NNPC and the Central Bank (which he moved from the Ministry of Finance to the presidency), and indirectly, through front companies such as Foundation Mira, white elephant projects such as the Ajaokuta steel mill, and military-industrial contracts that provided a constant stream of kickbacks. Dubbed "Babangida Unlimited" by the popular press, this financial imperium emerged from the infamous Bank of Credit and Commerce International (BCCI), with which Babangida became involved just months after coming to power. The BCCI link pinpoints with almost topological precision how international finance and fraud, on the one hand, and national banking and petroleum revenues, on the other, were coordinated by the northern-based bloc of old power and new wealth known as the Kaduna Mafia.[23] The chairman of BCCI's Nigerian affiliate, BCCI (Nigeria) Ltd., was none other than Babangida's godfather, Alhaji Ibrahim Dasuki, whom Babangida appointed as Sultan of Sokoto in 1991. That same year, he installed his finance minister, Alhaji Abubakar, as the

Sardauna of Sokoto, thereby clinching northern dynastic control over Nigeria's political and financial affairs.

In the early days of the Babangida era, after the bloodless palace coup, the regime appeared less venal. Return to civilian rule, not northern politico-economic hegemony, was the order of the day. Turning over a new political leaf, Babangida banned all former senior ranking politicians—going back to the First Republic—from seeking elected office; this in order to produce a "new breed" of honest politicians and to break old party alliances and patronage networks. In the upshot, it was said, would be a new "political class" with a more contemporary and sophisticated political culture.[24] Thus started the official "transition programme" referred to as "directed democracy": a return to civilian rule, stage-managed by the military, which would organize grassroots participation, mass mobilization, and a new constitution, and arrange a series of elections beginning at the local level and ascending to the presidency by 1992. A bottom-up democratic process was imposed from the top down, defining the rules of engagement and dictating the institutional blueprint "represented" by the new republic. The military government formed a new Directorate of Social Mobilisation (MAMSER) to inculcate democratic values and produce an enlightened citizenry, a Constitutional Review Committee to help write a new constitution, and a National Electoral Commission (NEC) to oversee the political process. As we shall see, the Armed Forces Ruling Council, the NEC, high courts, and two political parties that ultimately emerged became the leading actors in an electoral charade that was fabricated, screened, revised, postponed, and choreographed by the regime's inner circle, only to be canceled at the final curtain.

To understand the false starts and stops of democracy under IBB, we might follow two orders of political action: the first, strategic and tactical, illuminates the tricks deployed by the dictator to sabotage the ballot and remain in power; the second, less conscious and more profound, concerns the epistemology of political representation that developed as the democratic process degenerated into shifting claims and truth conditions.[25] From this latter perspective, the question of what went on in IBB's mind—his secret agenda and vested interests—becomes less important than the conditions of structural adjustment and the categories of accountability that established the official fictions of a new politics of illusion, a "liberal" variant of what Mbembe (1992, 11–18) calls a simulacral regime.

The first elections of the Babangida era took place as early as December 12, 1987, in what were then the 301 local government areas of Nigeria's twenty-one states. IBB had already created two new states from

Kaduna State and Cross River State; this was justified as a reform to bring government closer to the people, but actually sought to a spread the national cake (in this case, into his wife Maryam's home area) to increase federal penetration at the grass roots. This strategy was repeated on August 27, 1991, when IBB purportedly yielded to popular demand by establishing nine additional states—which entailed new local government areas and thus new elections. The 1987 nonparty ballot for councilors in the 301 constituencies was annulled by the NEC due to a shortage of ballot boxes and alleged electoral malpractice. Angry protestors rioted in Lagos, burning vehicles and beating two policemen among those stationed to stop people from moving between local government areas to cast multiple votes. In Ondo State, a candidate was arrested with 2,415 voting cards hidden under his bed.[26] While the shortage of ballot boxes and even polling booths prevented many people from voting at all, the net figure of 72 million registered voters was clearly inflated, implying a total population of 150 million–200 million! IBB's transition program was not off to a good start, with grassroots elections at the local government area repeated on March 26, 1988, and again on December 8, 1990, when Nigeria's two political parties finally emerged.

The lifting of the ban on party politics and the creation of the Social Democratic Party (SDP) and the National Republican Convention (NRC) marked a turning point in the reality principle of Nigerian democracy: a shift from the populist mechanism of a general will represented from below to that of a military general or leviathan establishing the conditions of representation from above. Not only did the rules of the game change, so did the game itself—away from the participatory model that IBB avowed and toward the carefully staged con of a political "419" in which elections were more simulated than real. Called "democracy by fiat" by one Nigerian journalist (Ofeimun 1989), Nigeria's "two-partyism" (Oyediran and Agbaje 1991) was promulgated in the new draft constitution of May 1989, a document that voiced the recommendations of the civilian Political Bureau and Constituent Assembly but gave the last word to the Armed Forces Ruling Council (AFRC). The idea of stipulating two parties, given Nigeria's troubled electoral history, was to break the formation of ethnic blocs that characterized the First (1960–66) and Second (1979–83) Republics by limited alternatives that would cut across ethnic affiliations, and by wiping the slate clear of all past parties and politicians. To prevent religious (Muslim versus Christian) and regional (north versus south) divisions from forming, the constitution required that both parties have their headquarters in Abuja, the new federal capital, and that their names, emblems, and mottos contain no ethnic, religious, or geographical connotations (ibid., 222).

Thus the stage was set on May 3, 1989, when the six-year ban on party politics was lifted, and all eligible citizens were allowed to form political associations that might qualify as one of the two recognized political parties, subject to the NEC's approval. In a two-month flurry of political activity to meet the July 15 submission deadline set by the NEC, forty-nine associations emerged around powerful patrons of the Babangida administration, factions within the Constituent Assembly, "geo-ethnic and religious caucuses" (ibid., 224), and former politicians hiding behind clients. Given the short amount of time provided for such associations to organize, raise funds, and develop constituencies, many fell by the wayside, and only thirteen presented themselves to the NEC for registration.[27] According to the NEC, the new generation of "transparent" politicians failed to meet the standards of transparency. In its report to the government, the commission endorsed none of the aspiring associations, charging that

> [a]ll the associations made deliberate false claims . . . from the inclusion of false, including ghost names and addresses on membership lists, to the affixture of somebody else's picture on the membership card belonging to another person; to the padding of names from voters' register; and to the offering of various forms of corrupt inducements to people so that they can pose as members of associations for verification purposes.[28]

Here we can see how the distinctive features of the "419"—unstable identities, misleading images, false numbers, and official registration forms—entered into politics, attributed at this stage to grassroots politicians but playing into the hands of the dictator. Whatever truth there was to the accusations, the incipient system of political representation was nipped in the bud. IBB disbanded all thirteen associations, claiming that "none of the groups had broken decisively with a history marked by tribal politics, religious bigotry, electoral fraud and violence."[29] In their place (and outside the options outlined in the NEC report), he established two entirely new political parties ex nihilo: the SDP, which he called "a little to the left," and the NRC, "a little to the right of center."[30]

At this stage, the big con of the "transition programme" began in earnest. The federal government, operating through the Directorate for Social Mobilisation, wrote and published the manifestos of both parties, each of which mirrored the regime's basic social and economic policies, including its commitment to structural adjustment. If the SDP had a progressive, populist tinge, sometimes characterized as welfarist and even socialist by the opposition, the NRC saw itself as conservative, even ruggedly free market. Echoing the most general qualities of the American Democratic and Republican Parties in the USA, Nigeria's new parties were short on content, long on rhetoric, and considered essentially the same. According to Pini Johnson, a Nigerian journalist and editor, "These new parties have no message. They're just parroting what they've been told to say. . . . The problem is that the military is constantly looking over their shoulders, so they can't say or do anything out of line."[31] Political rallies for the rescheduled local government elections were notoriously vacuous. The parties lacked ideology and social base. But IBB called them "expressive symbols of the new political order"; even if their platforms were drafted by a committee of the AFRC, had they not been "debated" in party conventions at state and national levels to refine the final manifestos?

The imputation of populist involvement was common with IBB. He employed it in the national constitutional conference, in the International Monetary Fund and structural adjustment debates, with the national census, and in changing of election dates; it allowed him to rule unilaterally while pretending to follow the advice of civilians. Like a liberal version of democratic centralism, IBB's new democratic order empowered the military to represent "the people" to themselves. In the name of "directed democracy," a "grassroots democratic" two-party solution permitted the state to design and stage-manage the entire political process, forestalling any real mass participation. This was accomplished by funding both organizations; by building party offices in all local government headquarters, state capitals, and in Abuja, at tremendous expense; by appointing party secretaries at all of these levels (later supervising their replacement by elected officials); and by holding training programs for party officials at the regime's Centre for Democratic Studies while issuing a number of draconian decrees that detained critics, banned professional associations, passed retroactive legislation, and prohibited judicial review (Oyediran and Agbaje 1991, 228–29). With such an overarching political infrastructure administered from above, IBB could recommence the long electoral march to Nigeria's Third Republic.

In the last three years of his misrule, Babangida lived up to his nickname "Maradona," after the Argentine soccer player known for his deft dribbling and zigzagging on the playing field. Nigeria's electoral experience from 1991 to 1993 was marked by sudden election annulments, disqualifications, and rescheduling, and by reversals of bans and balloting procedures dictated from Abuja. In December 1991, the NRC won a small majority in the gubernatorial elections, which had been postponed to accommodate the nine newly created states, while the SDP gained a majority in the thirty state assemblies. To prevent ballot stuffing and stealing, the government developed an "open queue" voting system, whereby registered voters would line up and be counted behind the poster image of their candidate. The method was controversial, subjecting people to intimidation and influence from patrons and employers — and drawing criticism from middle-class professionals who complained of lining up for hours under the hot sun or in drenching rain. In the meantime, IBB lifted his earlier ban against all former politicians and public officials entering the race, announcing that "the time has come for the old and new to mix, to cooperate and compete."[32] A floodgate of power brokerage and influence peddling was suddenly opened, releasing not only the old political guard but also leading members of the military government into the political fray, adding to the collective sense of uncertainty and doubt. But despite the growing cynicism and apathy among the populace, many of whom suspected IBB of a secret agenda to stay in power, elections to the National Assembly on July 4, 1992, were successfully held, with the SDP winning a majority of seats in both the Senate and the House of Representatives.[33] At this point, Babangida's house of political cards began to look real, with a bid for the national presidency a significant challenge. The duties of the National Assembly were not yet specified, and IBB would later dictate that its members could officiate on matters cultural but not political! But with a substantial amount of political machinery in place, the keystone of an elected presidency would establish the reality of the Third Republic. And it was this reality that IBB simulated, projected, and hijacked in the final stages of his political "419."

The presidential party primaries had already been postponed several times: August 4, 1991, to September 7; then to October 19, after the creation of new states and local government areas; and finally to August 1, 1992, upon which the AFRC stopped the fledgling vote, citing vote rigging and widespread malpractice, and commanded the NEC to repudiate the results. One notorious figure to emerge at this time was SDP multimillionaire and presidential aspirant Arthur Nzeribe, who boasted of 25 million pounds sterling (some said 32 million) in his campaign "war chest." Former head of state General Olusegun Obasanjo warned of an emergent "moneytocracy . . . a government of moneymen for more money for themselves and for those who paid their initial bill for the elections."[34] Bills indeed ran high, as both parties imposed levies of 10,000 to 13,000 pounds on each candidate, ostensibly to reduce their number. By the second round of voting on September 19, 1992, the SDP frontrunners were Major General Shehu Yar'Adua and Olu Falae, while Adamu Ciroma (of the Leyland Bus scandal; see chapter 6), Bamanga Tukur, and Umaru Shinkafi led the NRC. All important officials in previous military and civilian regimes, these candidates and their campaign finances were investigated by the dreaded State Security Service in a Catch-22 arrangement whereby the NEC announced its right to ban candidates without explanation after the primaries.

For many, the writing was already on the wall. In October, the military government suspended the primaries and banned the frontrunners from further participation because of their money politics. Another round of primaries was scheduled, and the handover date to civilian rule was pushed back to August 27, 1993. By this time, few illusions remained for Nigeria's enervated electorate. If any enthusiasm could be mustered, it was less for a valid democratic process and more for a way of removing the dictator. In another surprise twist, the NEC announced that the secret ballot would be reintroduced to avoid influence peddling—this time in a modified form called an "open secret ballot," since it was openly displayed but gave voters some measure of privacy.[35] An appropriate name indeed for the open secret, publicly voiced, that Babangida had no real intention of leaving office. With a low voter turnout, the southern business tycoon Chief Moshood Abiola emerged as leader of the SDP, and his northern opponent, a wealthy but relatively unknown Bashir Tofa, captured the NRC. The potential for a north-south split presented by the candidates was softened by the fact that both were Muslim, with Abiola's influence extending well into the north, given that he was the vice-president of the Organisation of Islamic Conference, second only to the Sultan of Sokoto, who was its president.

The final act that followed is now known as "June 12," the date of the long-awaited presidential elections that the AFRC and the NEC kept promising and postponing. Days before the ballot, in a televised debate between the candidates, Abiola's popularity soared when he proposed specific plans for overhauling the national economy and for initiating a rational petroleum policy; Tofa presented no vision or leadership qualities, announcing that he would work out solutions after assuming the presidency. In the meantime, the federal government decreed that no court order could stop the elections from proceeding, thereby according the NEC exclusive regulative powers. This made the regime appear sincere. It seemed even more so when the Association for a Better Nigeria, a conservative organization of former politicians and wealthy merchants representing northern oligarchic interests, won an order from the Abuja high court to ban the polls on June 10, arguing that IBB should remain in power for four more years due to religious tensions in the country; in response, NEC president Humphrey Nwosu invoked his constitutional powers to overrule the order so that the elections could proceed.[36] Again, voter turnout was low (30%–40%), given the frustrations and disappointments of the past. But an international team of observers invited by the military government and led by the British High Commissioner, Sir Christopher MacRae, judged the elections to be the most free and fair in Nigeria's postcolonial history.

Despite a ban on the release of early results—which included a presidential decree to imprison any journalist or editor who published returns prematurely—votes tallied from fourteen states at the NEC headquarters in Abuja (and publicly displayed on an electric billboard) showed Abiola leading Tofa, 4.3 million votes to 2.3 million; estimates had it that he was winning nineteen states to eleven.[37] With a presidential victory so close at hand, the northern-based Association for a Better Nigeria struck again, together with the NRC, declaring the election results "unofficial and unauthentic." This time it won, and sustained a court injunction (from the same Abuja high court) against the release of the final results. Despite the military decree barring judicial intervention, and two counterrulings against the nullification from high courts in Lagos and Benin City, on June 23 the federal military government sealed the returns. It also suspended the NEC, ordered yet another round of primaries, and invented new rules that disqualified Abiola and Tofa from the race. According to popular testimony, the NEC president Nwosu was visited by the State Security Service, which coerced him into accepting the ruling and forced him to confess that he had taken bribes. Civil unrest in Lagos and Ibadan erupted as protestors took to the streets (fig. 7.1), shouting "IBB must Go!" and declaring, at least on one demonstrator's placard, that "IBB=419." [38]

IBB had lost all credibility by wasting the nation's money and trying its patience in an electoral charade of "pro-forma democracy" (Ibrahim 1993, 137) that he himself directed and choreographed. He invented the parties and set the stage; he changed the rules, the dates, the ballots, and the candidates by pulling the strings of his puppet court at Abuja; he reversed his own decrees and subjected the populace to a prolonged series of false initiatives and empty motions in order to maintain power. Ballot fraud there was, but it was stage-managed from Abuja. The equivalence between IBB and the art of the con was not just metaphorical. It was literal. One of the principal actors in the electoral illusion was Arthur Nzeribe, a model mercenary who not only had made a killing by selling arms to both sides during the Biafran war and sought

FIGURE 7.1 Protestors on Ikorodu Road, June 23, 1993. The central placard reads, "Gen. I Bad Bad 8 years of fool and fake of this nation is enough. Go. Go. I Bad Bad Gooo. M.K.O Abiola is our elected president." Photograph by Andrew Apter.

the SDP presidency for himself; also, as we have seen, he had distinguished himself as an international con artist in the propaganda scam pulled on Pik Botha. Abimbola Davis, the ABN's number-two official, confessed—at a news conference held in hiding forty minutes before he fled the country—that the annulment of June 12 was engineered through "an organized confusion by just a few of us to prolong the lifespan of the present military administration."[39] From this account, Nigeria's politics of illusion emerges as the deliberate work of a professional team of confidence men, whose expertise was matched by the enthusiasm of security forces in jailing union leaders and civilian groups like the Campaign for Democracy.

But a more pervasive condition of verisimilitude and dissimulation was also sabotaging the nation. Epitomized by the "open secret" ballot that produced "unauthentic" electoral results, this condition eroded the distinction between truth and falsehood—and with it, the very existence of truth-value. For example, when Abimbola Davis's confession was first published, government newspapers like the *Nigerian Times* proclaimed it a fabrication by enemies to discredit the ABN. But who was the ABN? And who was the government? With senior generals defecting from the military in protest against the annulment of June 12, with courts overturned, with governors and incumbents of the national and state assemblies lost in a legal-rational twilight zone, the state itself began to dissolve.

Not that the battle was over. IBB remained the enemy, and his eventual resignation on August 26 was a brilliant victory for his political opponents, who blocked his every move to buy support. But the very instruments of opposition, the largely symbolic warfare on the streets and in the press, reflect the epistemological uncertainties and unrealities of the time. In addition to general strikes and "stay at homes," which brought public life to a standstill (and in which over a hundred lost their lives), the techniques of "419" were turned against IBB to discredit him further. Plans and secret photographs of his hideout mansions in Minna and around the world were published, with drawings to provide "evidence" of his embezzlements. One photocopied letter that circulated throughout Lagos "documented," in near-perfect officialese, a British banker's inability to transfer 66.5 million pounds of First Lady Maryam Babangida's ill-gotten gains into a Swiss account. The only blatant error was the positioning of his letterhead on the bottom of the page. That these tools of resistance were forged had little to do with their ultimate truth-value, since IBB and Maryam *did* build mansions and embezzle millions (fig. 7.2). This simulacral quality of political protest,

FIGURE 7.2 Draining the nation: cartoon of IBB and First Lady Maryam siphoning Nigeria's oil money into private Swiss accounts (compare with the "circulatory system" of figure 1.2). From the popular magazine *Tell*, no. 41, October 18, 1993, p. 12.

no less true for its falsity, or *real* for its *unreality,* reflected a general quality of the Nigerian state and its phantasms of governmentality.

Take the census, for example, that administrative instrument of bureaucratic rationality which once documented, quantified, and categorized the citizenry—and which, under IBB, proved to be worth its weight in words. "We attach great importance to the 1991 census," he proclaimed, "as a way of laying a solid foundation for a stable third republic." What the 1991 census did provide, in addition to evidence that the population was 25 million less than supposed (down to 85 million), was an opportunity for the state to harass its population, to close all borders, to prohibit all movement, and to command people to stay home from work while officers counted heads. Or consider Nigerian maps, no longer adequate to the nation's shifting territories, local government areas, and dilapidated roads; or its national museums and monuments, once proud harbingers of a new Nigeria and now bankrupt, plundered, and poorly maintained, devoid even of visitors. The forms of govern-mentality that flourished under colonialism were gradually emptied during the Babangida era, deployed not as means of rational adminis-tration and taxation to impose order and control but as tools of obstruc-tion and interference.

Nowhere is the breakdown of governance more clearly manifest than in the civil service reforms associated with structural adjustment. Like the twisted logic of "directed democracy," I B B's version of administra-tive perestroika was designed to streamline the service and protect its leaders from those "mischievous civil servants" who "deliberately mis-led their ministers" into making decisions "inimical to government in-terest" (Imoko 1991, 7). To shelter his loyal ministers from undisci-plined and unpatriotic subordinates, I B B decided to make the minister of each ministry its chief executive and its accounting officer as well. Somehow the "reform" was supposed to emphasize "professionalism" in the service. But, in practical terms, it allowed each minister to au-thorize his own embezzlements without cutting the Accounting Office in on the deal. Unilateral powers of plunder and patronage were thus ac-corded to a restricted inner circle, less expensive to maintain than mul-tiple lines of misappropriation and more loyal to the center. The old 50% rule still applied; it obliged a subordinate to send half of his loot "upstairs" or face the sack. For those at the top, however, there were no longer any strings attached, no potential exposés or incriminating doc-uments that could not be contained.[40] When Ernest Shonekan—head of the ephemeral interim government—probed the N N P C after I B B "stepped aside," the petroleum ministers were unable to account for nearly $12.4 *billion* of missing revenues that had accrued from Nigeria's Gulf War windfall (Ukim 1994, 9).

In an era of planned privatization, a new line of directorates and pro-grams, designed to mobilize the grass roots into sustainable develop-ment, provided unchecked access to the national cake in the name of the interests they were supposed to serve. In 1987, Babangida launched M A M S E R (the Mass Mobilisation for Economic Recovery, Self-Reliance and Social Justice program) to raise political consciousness and lift the masses out of poverty. He then set up the Directorate of Foods, Roads and Rural Infrastructures, with its associated Community Development Associations, Direct Participation Scheme, and Integrated Rural Devel-opment Scheme. Some funds *did* trickle down into fertilizer subsidies and irrigation projects in selected showcase projects. Usually in remote corners of Bauchi and Borno States, these projects had their "launchings" broadcast by the National Television Authority. And in several southern states, local rice cultivation resumed after the price of imported Uncle Ben's skyrocketed. But in general, the regime's directed development, like directed democracy, was an illusion, providing loot for the powerful in the name of the masses. As one market woman replied repeatedly when I asked her to comment on Babangida's regime, "Aiye ti baje!" [Our life is spoiled!].[41] What about conditions for women? It appeared that Maryam Babangida's Better Life for Rural Women program, designed to organize and empower women in the countryside, lived up to its more popular appellation, Better Life for Rich Wives. The first lady, together with the wives of governors, launched their projects in state capitals while sporting the finest lace and fanciest head ties, forever out of reach and out of touch.[42]

But, to appreciate more fully the conditions of simulated governance that dominated and infiltrated everyday life in Nigeria, creating an entire world-as-misrepresentation, let us return to oil, the mysterious and elusive substance of value itself.

THE CRISIS OF VALUE

In 1991, after finishing a degree at the London School of Design, Bisi returned to Lagos, where she set up a small interior design business. Among her first clients was a young woman like herself who was seeking advice on how to design the office space of her own new business. Bisi visited her client's unfurnished workplace to discuss preliminary ideas and plans. While she was there, a man named Alhaji suddenly rushed through the door in an extreme state of agitation. "The deal is off!" he exclaimed to the woman. "The chemicals and paper arrived safely, but the Òòni [of Ife] is pulling out." He then proceeded to unpack his load and demonstrate the efficacy of the paper and chemicals by taking blank sheets of paper from a roll, dipping them in a tray of black liquid, and pulling out crisp new fifty-naira notes. He had barrels of the liquid chemical, but the problem was finding another partner to take the Òòni's place. Only then did he notice Bisi, off to the side, a witness to the demonstration. He was furious. "Who is this woman? She has seen everything! How can we trust her?" At this point, Bisi felt mesmerized and dull, the effect, she later concluded, of the juju medicine that Alhaji was using to make her gullible. Combining threats with propositions, Alhaji and the woman reluctantly agreed to cut Bisi in on the deal at a bargain price. All she needed to do was return quickly with 20,000 naira, and they would "release" her with a share of the money-making supplies. Bisi recalls returning to her office, getting the cash, and calling her sister at the last minute for advice. Her sister brought her back to her senses, and Bisi went home. Days later, she ventured past her "client's" office, and it was vacant.[43]

Bisi's story represents a species of "419" known as the "neon money" scam, perpetrated mainly against fellow Nigerians, although Western-ers have fallen for it as well. In this case, the con artist invoked the cele-brated traditional ruler and business millionaire, the Òòni of Ife, to pro-vide "recognition" and hence credibility to the ruse. In other versions of this con, the "neon" money supplies are said to have been put up as "col-lateral" by the CIA during their covert operations.[44] In both examples, secret sources of wealth and power arc associated with mysterious, if not illicit, forms of procurement and profit. In cultural terms, the roots of this belief in money magic go back to traditional idioms of money fetishism and illegitimate wealth in southern Nigeria. One story I col-lected in Ayede-Ekiti during fieldwork in 1984 related how a rich man kidnapped children by stunning them with juju medicines and leading them to his house, where he had a large calabash that he would fill with human blood and bring to a room with no windows. After he uttered in-cantations, the blood would turn into money, which the man spent whenever he needed it.[45]

This notion of effortless gain at the expense or even "consumption" of others is echoed in various witchcraft beliefs as well, but the un-derlying template motivating it is the conversion of blood into money —bad money, to be sure, sometimes referred to as "hot" or "soaked," curiously "infertile" in its capacity to be spent without reciprocal advan-tage or gain. What is so interesting about Bisi's story, and the genre of neon money in general, is how it transposes this template into the oil economy: a black chemical which, like oil, comes in barrels, possesses the money-producing valences of human blood.[46] As Barber (1982) and Watts (1994) have so vividly demonstrated, Nigerian oil money has al-ways generated a certain malaise, a negative moral tinge if not connota-tions of evil.

It is this negative valence, the unreal quality of the nation's effortless oil wealth, that is reflected in ideas of neon money, the ethereal precipi-tate of the money form that took over after the monetary value of oil de-clined and detached itself from the national currency. This is not to sug-gest that oil became worthless in Nigeria; rather, that the decline in world prices and mismanagement by the state radically diminished its contribution to the national economy. The downward trend, exacerbated by the deregulative measures of structural adjustment, produced a gen-eral crisis of value: of runaway inflation, distressing depreciation, de-faulting banks, and above all the impoverishment of everyday life. As

Anyanwu (1992, 7) has argued, "Unless it is brought under control inflation will destroy the very fabric of Nigerian society." As I have suggested, IBB's regime of fraud and deception gave rise to a national culture of "419," in which illusion became the very basis of survival.

Macroeconomic indicators reveal a precipitous drop in real wealth under General Babangida, with increased proportions of foreign exchange being committed to debt servicing. Just as significant as a net decline in real income and GDP are the sociocultural indicators of privatization and deregulation, particularly in the banking system and foreign exchange market. In an effort to stimulate domestic investment, the Central Bank of Nigeria floated interest rates and authorized merchant banks and investment houses to engage in high-risk speculation.[47] The result was a flurry of uninsured investment companies offering outrageous returns on substantial deposits, such as 30% interest on "Midas Gold Notes" for a minimum deposit of 50,000 naira.[48] Like the legendary Midas touch, these deals seemed to work like magic, with fast profits and turnovers whetting the appetites of the young professionals. The new managers sported fancy cars and even patronized the arts, but their wealth was insecure and ephemeral, invested in nothing more than the future returns on high-risk Ponzi schemes. Soon, the commercial banks and finance houses began to fall like dominos with no government treasury to bail them out, and reports of more generalized bank fraud and counterfeit currency trafficking began to circulate in the press, together with advertisements for "fraudcheck" machines (fig. 7.3).

At the same time, government raised the domestic price of petrol, increasing transportation costs of food commodities that were passed on to consumers, adding to inflation. With characteristically inverted logic, the government then blamed market women for greedy and unpatriotic pricing—as if they were responsible for the rising costs—and periodically mowed down their stalls with armored vehicles. As staples like cassava, beans, rice, and yams soared in price, even middle-class Nigerians began to go hungry, leading to popular expressions of hardship such as "1-0-0," "0-1-0," "0-0-1," and even "0-0-0," where "1" refers to a meal consumed during the day and "0" to meals skipped for lack of funds.

As costs rose and quantities diminished, basic quality seemed to decline, in that people would describe the same foods as less "filling" than before.[49] A new "style" of clothing called "aircondition wear" flourished in markets like Aswani in Lagos that specialize in secondhand clothes, making a jest of penury and necessity. The austerity of the 1980s gave way to desperation in the 1990s. In another manifestation of the "419," a rash of born-again Christian prophets swept the country, promising

profit through prayer while extracting from their followers what little surplus they were able to muster. On a more professional register, business centers with photocopying machines, computers, faxes, and international telephone lines proliferated into bustling sites of activity as job seekers constructed professional resumes, printed up authentic-looking contracts, and purveyed the instruments of finance capital with the tools of the international "419."

As the cost of living rose, real incomes fell, and the professional middle class gradually withered away, oil was transformed from the lifeblood of the nation into the bad blood of corrupt government; or as Watts (1994) has so elegantly put it, from black gold into the devil's excrement. In the process, the rich have become criminalized, their wealth associated with expensive cars and the mansions of "Cocaine Alley" in Ikeja, Lagos; with theft of government revenues from the NNPC and its subsidiaries; with oil bunkering, black marketeering, and the moral bankruptcy of the daily "419." As medical supplies ran out in state hospitals Nigeria became the number-one exporter of Asian heroin to the United States. In the popular imagination, oil money and drug money began to converge at the top, with Babangida's family and inner circle directly implicated in trafficking; so much so, it is said, that he arranged the parcel bomb murder of journalist Dele Giwa in 1986 to prevent him from breaking the story (Olorunyomi 1993). In gendered terms, the inverse qualities of the new Nigerian woman, so conspicuously championed by Maryam Babangida, emerged in the witchlike counterpart of the female courier who used her "womanhood" to smuggle drugs (fig. 7.4). And oil, as I discuss in the following chapter, came to represent a scourge against the natural and social environment as the Ogoni fought for survival against the pollution that ruined their fishing waters, and against a regime that waged a near-genocidal campaign in response to their demands for compensation (Saro-Wiwa 1990, 1992; Welch 1995). Fighting for their civil rights, and for all Nigerians who have experienced the erosion of civil society, the Ogoni—led by the late Ken Saro-Wiwa—were portrayed as subversives and saboteurs, as unpatriotic vermin on the national body, and as a backward and subhuman minority "tribe." In his *Similia: Essays on Anomic Nigeria,* Saro-Wiwa (1991) wrote with brutal wit about "Babangidance," referring to government-by-cheating, a national culture of fraud, and the resultant devaluation of life for all Nigerians as both individual and collective loss.

Significant here in Saro-Wiwa's political diagnoses are the cultural corollaries of inflation and devaluation, less anomic than *anemic.* When oil, the substance or fetish of original value, mutated from lifeblood to bad blood, Nigeria's nation form, once proudly modeled on the money form, grew weak and lost its shine. As the state privatized the oil industry—first by diverting revenues into private accounts and then by auctioning block allocations to private concessions that in many cases simply lifted and hawked the oil, without any new investment or exploration—the public sector virtually collapsed into mimetic representations of itself. Bureaucrats and civil servants still went to work dressed in threadbare suits dutifully starched and pressed; but, by the end of the Babangida era, they were earning about $20 per month, and spending up to a third of their salaries on transportation. Unlike the oil boom, when social distinctions were redrawn to accommodate a growing middle class, the bust set off a great leveling wave of rampant inflation

FIGURE 7.4 Federal Ministry of Information poster denouncing a female drug courier as a figure of illicit wealth. From the *Nigeria Interpreter* 5, no. 4 (July-August 1991).

which, as one contemporary report put it, "is better imagined today than quantified" (Ogbonna and Udo 1993, 6). What sort of instabilities has such hyperinflation created? Reflecting on Weimar Germany, Elias Canetti (1984, 186) has argued the following:

> An inflation can be called a witches' Sabbath of devaluation where men and the units of their money have the strongest effects on each other. The one stands for the other, men feeling themselves as "bad" as their money; and this becomes worse and worse. . . . It is a double devaluation originating in a double identification. The *individual* feels depreciated because the unit on which he relied, and with which he had equated himself, starts sliding; and the *crowd* feels depreciated because the *million* is. As the millions mount up, a whole people, numbered in millions, becomes nothing.

Witches' Sabbath indeed. For all the historical and cultural differences between Weimar Germany and Babangida's Nigeria—and the different magnitude of the inflation rates involved—this passage illuminates a fundamental transformation that occurred during the Babangida regime; namely, the unhinging of individual and collective identities from fixed social coordinates into the everyday arts of the "419."

Canetti continued to argue that the devaluation of the German mark was displaced onto the progressive devaluation of the enemy within, the

Jew, whose destruction would restore the nation's vitality. Following this line, the persecution of the Ogoni people intensified as the economy continued to collapse, given how they agitated against oil and state terror, and were racially "othered" in distinctive ways. The decline of the oil economy under IBB, and the politics of illusion that he fostered, set the stage for Sani Abacha's final coup de grace—the hanging of Ogoni activist Ken Saro-Wiwa. But as we shall see in the following chapter, the Ogoni came to represent the plight of all Nigerians, mobilizing popular resistance against the regime.

CONCLUSION

In expanding the equation "IBB=419," I have suggested that there is more to the relationship between cash and politics than mere influence peddling or vote buying; more, also, than the truism that money is power. Inasmuch as "IBB=419" ties electoral fraud to economic fraud, as indicated on the placard of the outraged protestor, the equivalence flows from an underlying cultural logic that developed under specific historical conditions; these range from the colonial antecedents of the postcolonial state and its inherited forms of governmentality, to the political economy of the 1970s oil boom that went bust in the decade that followed. "419," in short, was not just a "culture of fraud and corruption." It was embedded, from the first, in wider webs of meaning and historical consciousness. I have tried here to penetrate the tissue of illusion that characterizes the everyday practice of "419," in order to grasp a more fundamental transformation of value that occurred during IBB's dictatorship, a transformation that produced a national crisis of representation with thoroughgoing political and theoretical implications.

In this connection, I have argued that the lessons to be learned from the international "419" are not about fraud and dissimulation as such. They are about a symbolic transformation whereby the value forms that emerged during the boom years detached from the value of oil itself to become forms of value and sources of illicit profit unto themselves. The letters of credit, bank drafts, official signatures, and corporate logos that previously legitimated and authorized the international instruments of purchase and sale began to circulate like "floating signifiers," devoid of any real monetary or institutional referent—until, quite literally, they hit their mark, a credulous dupe who went for the bait, losing his or her shirt by giving something for nothing. This truly dialectical transformation from value form to form of value, conflating the economic signifier (monetary instruments, purchase orders, bills of exchange, and so on) with the economic signified (money, commodities) has not, moreover, been limited to the pure realm of economics. It has extended into politics via such authoritative institutions as the NNPC and the Central Bank of Nigeria, which, as we have seen, participated in many ways. Some "bad eggs" working on the inside furnished their partners with the information, forms, letterheads, and even offices needed to work the scams. Others played key roles in siphoning off foreign exchange or petroleum into private, "dedicated" accounts, both for themselves and for others. The inability of the NNPC and the CBN to account for their expenditures and foreign exchange under IBB and Abacha was itself endemic to the international "419," since fictitious forms and ghost accounts undermined the very principle of accountability itself. By breaking its promise to back up its currency (Watts 1994, 441), the state further inflated and devalued the naira, passing the cost of its fraudulent practices onto its citizens while undermining its own credibility and violating the public trust.

Within this nation of masquerading value forms, I have also argued, democracy could not effectively take root. If President Babangida remained unaccountable, making a mockery of the civil courts and even overruling his own decrees, the citizens themselves could not be counted, and did not count. Like the counterfeit value form of the business "419," IBB directed his "pro-forma" democracy, producing manifestos, building hundreds of local government party headquarters, and printing registration forms and ballots—none of which bore any substantive relationship to collective concerns or preferences. The 1993 elections took place in a political vacuum, as if projected on a screen, and were thereby detached from a much abused electorate that had no way of registering its final judgment. There was, in effect, no political representation, since the ballot never really took place. True, the actual presidential vote was judged free and fair by international observers. But, because it was nullified, there was no need to take the trouble of rigging it! Throughout the prolonged succession of aborted elections, banking on the cultivated expectation of a return to civilian rule, IBB was able to neutralize his opponents: first, within the army, since a counter-coup could hardly gain popular support with the Third Republic so near at hand; and second, within the political class, many of whom revealed themselves during the primaries and ruined themselves by spending lavishly for ineffectual support. In this respect, it was almost overdetermined that Arthur Nzeribe, infamous perpetrator of the international "419," would play a critical role with the Association for a Better Nigeria in derailing the June 12 elections. This last point warrants further consideration, since it is precisely in the middle ground between structural determination and individual agency that the culture of "419" writ large assumes theoretical significance for our understanding of the state and civil society in this part of Africa.

Two familiar analytical extremes frame current debate about post-colonial Africa. One, consistent with historical materialism, explains contemporary economic problems, and the so-called crisis of the state, in terms of colonialism and underdevelopment: it is a perspective some-times too easily dismissed as blaming the West for everything that has gone wrong. The other, more consistent with methodological individu-alism, identifies the root causes as corrupt leadership, nepotism, and the siphoning off of public spoils by a privileged few. The politics of il-lusion in contemporary Nigeria, and the culture of "419" to which it be-longs, however, are themselves a product of *both:* a history of global eco-nomic articulation, radically transformed by an oil boom gone bust; and a pernicious cycle of "feeding at the trough" (Bayart 1993) which, with a few exceptional regimes, has gone from bad to worse. Following the utilitarian principle of rational choice, we have seen how the fraudulent deal, as a conscious dissimulation by individuals and teams, was refined almost to an art form in Nigeria. But, underlying and motivating the "419," we have discerned a structural transformation of value forms whereby the public sector (the state) and the public sphere (civil society) have dissolved, leaving only traces of their former existence. The naira is still the naira, but it is now worthless. The same holds for the state, the civil service, and most important of all, even oil. The lifeblood of the nation has become anemic, undermining its credibility at home and abroad.

In more cultural terms, the anemia of the oil economy, and of the body politic through which it circulates, is expressed by a number of idioms that contrast significantly with those that predominated during the oil boom. When oil was king, it informed the nation with the fetish of intrinsic value and the luster of gold—expressed racially, in terms of blackness; culturally, in terms of a glorified national heritage celebrated extravagantly during FESTAC '77 and explicitly represented by the gold rectangle of the festival flag; and economically, in a strong exchange re-lation to the U.S. dollar. Today, oil scarcely circulates. The Warri and Kaduna refineries operate at fractional capacities, chronic fuel shortages lead to endless gasoline queues, and frequently the petrol itself is *diluted with water,* causing engine failure. But if Nigeria today is no longer on the move, its devalued and inflated economy suffers from more than just anemia. We have seen how the Ogoni minority recast oil as pollu-tion, how wealth itself lost its legitimacy, now associated with cocaine and theft, and how the degradation of the money form destabilized so-cial identities and diminished the quality of everyday life. It is not surprising that the civil rights lawyer and activist, Chief Gani Fawehinmi, inveighed against IBB's debilitating pseudopolitics: "This government is infested with socio-economic AIDS and it cannot deliver a socio-economic AIDS-free civilian regime" (quoted in Ibrahim 1993, 134).

In this damning indictment, the transformation from black gold to the fatality of AIDS prefigured the rise of Abacha and the collapse of civil society.

CHAPTER EIGHT

Death and the King's Henchmen

For Ken Saro-Wiwa, 1941–1995. In memoriam.

ON NOVEMBER 10, 1995, Nigeria's military strongman, General Sani Abacha, shocked the world by ordering the hanging of Ken Saro-Wiwa and eight fellow Ogoni activists on trumped-up charges of inciting violence and murder. The activists' trial was a sham, having taken place in a military tribunal that played by its own rules, denying legal counsel, visits from family members, and, after the fact, any kind of public burial for the defendants. Their corpses were purportedly disfigured with acid, literally defaced to prevent their resurrection into martyrdom as fearless critics of the venal military regime. The United Nations condemned the act, countless ambassadors were called home, Nigeria was suspended from the Association of Commonwealth Nations, the United States denied visas to Nigerian military officers—but the only truly effective response, a U.S.-led embargo against Nigeria oil, was never pursued. Oil, Nigeria's black gold turned toxic waste, against which Ken Saro-Wiwa struggled in defense of his land and his people, won the day. After the harsh talk and half-measures taken against Abacha's disreputable regime, the ambassadors trickled back to Lagos, and Royal Dutch Shell brazenly signed on to a $4-billion natural gas liquefaction project.

Saro-Wiwa's fight against Shell was largely environmental, highlighting the ecological devastation of riverine ecosystems in the Niger Delta area, where Nigeria's oil is pumped from the ground. In the global media, the struggle came to represent the rapacious appetite of oil capitalism and the ruthless abandon of military dictatorship as oil spills, burn-offs, and blowouts destroyed the creeks and farms of the Ogoni people with no compensation provided. From the outside, Saro-Wiwa's death was a heroic tragedy of one man against a Leviathan, a hybrid beast of corporate profiteering and military domination violating human rights and destroying nature. Within Nigeria, however, Saro-Wiwa's struggle was tied to ethnic politics, championing the cause of the Ogoni minority against the Hausa-Fulani, Yoruba, and Ibo power blocs that stole from the state and gave only to their own. If Ken Saro-Wiwa was a respected writer, producer, and critic in his own country, many others saw him as a troublesome gadfly who resented his people's lack of patronage opportunities. In the vast Nigerian nation of nearly 100 million people, few really cared about the Ogoni, whom the popular press sometimes likened to pygmies of a lower evolutionary order. What most outsiders forget, or never realized, is that although Saro-Wiwa's demand for oil revenues and reparations began in the 1960s and gained momentum during the oil boom of the seventies and early eighties, his cry was hardly heard. The majority of Nigerians did not really care about the tiny, relatively isolated "tribe" of folk who were considered scarcely human, happy to be fishing their mangrove creeks and planting their gardens, cut off from the modern world. Given this general contempt for the Ogoni people, why did Ken Saro-Wiwa's struggle erupt into a Nigerian cause célèbre?

To answer this question, I will examine how the plight of the Ogoni people came to represent the contradictions of oil capitalism in Nigeria at large. We will see how the pollution of natural ecosystems and environments provided the language for opposing historically specific forms of economic alienation and political dispossession throughout the nation as rentier capitalism and prebendal politics privatized the state and undermined the public sphere; and how the pattern of class involution, discussed in chapter 1, eventually imploded. Only then can we appreciate how Ken Saro-Wiwa's demand for Ogoni autonomy escalated into a struggle for universal citizenship in Nigeria, and why, as the world waited to see what would happen, he was hanged.[1]

THE STATE OF NATURE

Of the many novels, poems, short stories, plays, critical studies, and essays that Ken Saro-Wiwa published in his lifetime, his last two books, *Genocide in Nigeria: The Ogoni Tragedy* (1992) and *A Month and a Day: A Detention Diary* (published posthumously in 1995), chronicle his cause most fully. Reviewing this struggle as he presented it serves two initial purposes: first, it illustrates the main actors and events in the history of Ogoni persecution, leading to the founding of the Movement for the Survival of the Ogoni People (MOSOP); and second, it illuminates the "organic" idiom in which this struggle was framed, and that developed into a *political ecology* of citizenship for all Nigerians.

The main actors in the Ogoni tragedy are the multinational Shell Petroleum Development Corporation, along with its British and Dutch subsidiaries; the Ethnic Majority, referring directly to the Hausa-Fulani in the north who have dominated Nigerian politics since the days of the British Protectorate, but also including the Yoruba and Ibo, who also reign as majorities over the Ogoni and other ethnic minorities; the Military Dictatorship, which—through seven different regimes that assumed power through coups—has ruled by decree and plundered the country; the Ogoni, the paradigmatic ethnic minority who live on the oilfields, and whose society and habitat have been destroyed by pollution; and finally, the American, European, and Japanese markets for Nigerian oil, those impersonal consumers who drive the global oil economy but remain largely in the background. If I recount the Ogoni tragedy as a drama or morality play, it is to highlight some of its mythic themes and to prefigure those allegorical dimensions linking Ogoniland to the Nigerian nation. For Saro-Wiwa, however, *Genocide in Nigeria* was a work of empirical documentation.

The book opens with an account of precolonial Ogoniland as an Edenic paradise or primitive commune (not unlike Nwoko's *Children of Paradise* discussed in chapter 3), where production was for use, and where social, economic, ecological, and religious orders were integrated into "natural" rhythms and routines:

> To the Ogoni, the land on which they lived and the rivers which surrounded them were very important. They not only provided sustenance in abundance, they were also a spiritual inheritance. The land is a god and is worshipped as such. The fruit of the land, particularly yams, are honoured in festivals and, indeed, the Annual Festival of the Ogoni is held at the yam harvest. The planting season is not a mere period of agricultural activity: it is a spiritual, religious and social occasion. "Tradition" in Ogoni means in the local tongue (*doonu kuneke*) the honoring of the land (earth, soil, water). . . . To the Ogoni, rivers and streams do not only provide water for life—for bathing, drinking, etc; they do not only provide fish for food, they are also sacred and are bound up intricately with the life of the community, of the entire Ogoni nation. (Saro-Wiwa 1992, 12–13)

In political terms, this foundational account of an "original affluent society" (Sahlins 1972, 1–39) serves as a charter for Ogoni ownership of the land, a resource framed as a cultural and spiritual heritage that would be spoiled by oil and stolen by the state. According to the correspondences established in this vision, the devastation of land and water is tantamount to the destruction of tradition itself, one that sustained a harmonious balance between ecology, economy, and community. The predations of the military-petroleum complex upon this pristine "state" of nature—organized into the six ancient kingdoms of Babbe, Eleme, Gokana, Nyo-Khana, Ken-Khana, and Tai (what anthropologists would call clans)—are thereby framed as crimes against culture and humanity, violating the sacred foundation of human community. Hence Saro-Wiwa's use of the term *genocide* to describe the destruction of Ogoniland, although military "scorch and burn" campaigns against Ogoni protestors would follow.

As we shall see, the mythic model of Ogoniland served a specific agenda that Saro-Wiwa pursued with total conviction. Although he demanded reparations from Shell and the Nigerian government for the ravages of oil pollution, he also sought a much greater share of reallocated revenues for the Ogoni people, arguing that the oil from their land belonged to them. Small wonder that most Nigerians were uninvolved with this cause. Saro-Wiwa was pleading special circumstances for his people, with that persecution complex that came to be associated with Ogoni "cannibal rage" and ethnic chauvinism.

For Saro-Wiwa, trouble was always associated with outside intervention. In 1914, the British subjugated the Ogoni by force, denying their autonomy by incorporating them into Opobo Division within Calabar Province, thereby subjecting them to a remote administrative center that demanded taxes and ruled through courts. Saro-Wiwa recounts with pride how the Ogoni participated in the 1929 Women's Tax Riots, otherwise known as the Igbo Women's War, in which several Ogoni women were killed. Their deaths attest to the Ogoni tradition of mobilization and resistance against external domination. Under the British, it was not until 1947 that the Ogoni Native Authority was established, framing Ogoni ethnic identity in the administrative terms of indirect rule, and securing representation in the Eastern House of Assembly in 1952. Politically, however, the Ogoni were overwhelmed, swallowed by the dominating Ibo interests of the Eastern Region, to which they were unwillingly consigned by the 1951 constitution. In an attempt to join with other Delta minorities to found an autonomous Rivers State, the Ogoni broke from Nnamdi Azikiwe's National Council of Nigeria and the Cameroons party and voted for Obafemi Awolowo's Yoruba Action Group Party. Zik's party won, and the Igbos took reprisals against the Ogoni, denying them scholarships and social amenities (Saro-Wiwa 1992, 23) and splitting the Ogoni Native Authority into three local government units. In a move echoing the divide-and-conquer tactics of the British, the Ogoni were thus subjected to a form of internal colonialism by the Ibo majority of the Eastern Region, who were to prove even more brutal as overlords during the dark days of the Biafran war.

The federal structure of the Nigerian state in the early years of independence was fragile at best, composed of three semi-autonomous regions competing with each other for power at the center. The three dominant parties of the First Republic had in fact developed largely from cultural organizations and platforms that capitalized on ethnic affiliation—such as the Yoruba Omo Egbe Oduduwa, the Ibo State Union, and the Hausa Jammiyyar Mutanen Arewa in the north—consolidating regional identities in terms of ethnicity and political party, and through regional marketing boards.[2] The balance broke down in 1966 with the first coup after independence, led by Major General Thomas Ironsi, in which, Saro-Wiwa (1992, 26) reminds us, "the Federal Prime Minister, Sir Abubakar Tafewa Balewa was killed along with two other Regional Premiers of the Yoruba and Hausa-Fulani ethnic majorities." Ironsi's regime attempted to replace Nigeria's weak federalism with a stronger unitary state, but the effort was cut short. The Hausa-Fulani retaliated in the north, massacring thousands of Igbos, killing General Ironsi in General Yakubu Gowon's countercoup, and unleashing the tide of violence that swept into the Western Region, where Igbos had to close down their shops, leave their government jobs, and flee for their lives.

Saro-Wiwa's *On A Darkling Plain: An Account of the Nigerian Civil War* (1989) reveals another side of the bloody struggle for secession led by Colonel C. Odumegwu Ojukwu and his aspiring Biafran nation. The Ibo's valiant struggle for Biafra, and their remarkable military and technological ingenuity, earned them the respect even of their critics. Less appreciated and understood, however, was their treatment of the Ogoni and other Delta minorities who were corralled into Biafra against their will. When federal troops swept through Ogoni Division and onward to take Port Harcourt, the Ogoni were scapegoated as saboteurs, and were evacuated to concentration camps and refugee centers where many starved to death. Others were sent to the Training Depots en route to the front, where they were used as cannon fodder. From May to August of 1968, four thousand Ogonis died from forced relocation and Ibo "reprisals." Bombed and shelled by federal troops, the Ogoni were then persecuted by Biafrans. According to Saro-Wiwa's calculations, an estimated thirty thousand Ogonis, over 10% of the ethnic population, died in the war. Whether the figures are biased or exact hardly matters, for it is clear that in the ethnic politics of Nigerian federalism, the Ogoni were universally despised and had nowhere to turn.

After the Biafran defeat in 1970, Nigeria's three regions were replaced by twelve states in a plan to stabilize the federal government, and the Ogoni joined the newly formed Rivers State with other Delta minorities. By this time, however, the Ogoni were fighting another battle for survival—this time against oil. Although Shell-BP first struck Ogoniland oil in 1958, in the village of Dere, production was curtailed by the Biafran war and only began in earnest toward the close of the violence. By the war's end, the Ogoni had come to realize that the oil company's promises of development and economic prosperity were empty lies, as the new industry brought no benefits and only hardships to the area. Virtually no new jobs were created for the Ogoni, and profits were siphoned away without any returns to the villagers. Company undertakings such as the Ogoni Rural Community Project existed in name only, with diverted funds counting as tax deductions. What Shell brought to Ogoniland was not profit but pollution, contaminating the mangrove swamps and farmland with seepage and spills while fouling the air with black smoke and lethal gases from flare-offs that burned day and night. Growing discontent erupted in July 1970, when a blowout in one of Shell's oilfields wreaked havoc on the surrounding villages. An entire village ecosystem was destroyed, prompting petitions to the military governor and protests against Shell-BP's unwillingness to help. One such letter from an Ogoni schoolteacher likens the horrors of the blowout to the violence of the Biafran war:

> We in Dere today are facing a situation which can only be compared with our experiences during the civil war . . . an ocean of crude oil has emerged, moving swiftly like a great river in flood, successfully swallowing up anything that comes on its way. These include cassava farms, yams, palms, streams, animals etc etc for miles on end. There is no pipeborne water and yet the streams, the only source of drinking water is coated with oil. You cannot collect a bucket of rain water for the roofs, trees and grass are all covered with oil. Anything spread outside in the neighbourhood is soaked with oil as the wind carries the oil miles away from the scene of the incident. . . . Thrice during the Civil war the flow station was bombed setting the whole place on fire. . . . Now a worse fire is blazing not quite a quarter of a mile from the village . . . men and women forced by hunger "steal" occasionally into the "ocean" [of oil], some have to dive deep in oil to uproot already rotten yams and cassava. I am not a scientist to analyze what effects the breathing of dan-

gerous gases the crude oil contains would have on the people, but suffice it to say that the air is polluted and smells only of crude oil. We are thus faced with a situation where we have no food to eat, no water to drink, no homes to live and worst of it all, no air to breathe. We now live in what Hobbes may describe as a STATE OF NATURE—a state where peace or security does not exist " . . . and the life of man is solitary, poor, nasty, brutish and short." (Reprinted in Saro-Wiwa 1992, 58–59)

Oil, fast becoming the lifeblood of the new Nigeria as the oil boom took off, was for the Ogoni the scourge of development, transforming the precolonial "natural" economy—considered the food basket of the Eastern Niger Delta—into a postcolonial state of Hobbesian "warre." Prefiguring the hidden costs of an "unnatural" enclave economy that would burn hot and then out, the plight of the Ogoni came to stand for the plight of all Nigerians subjected to the losing combination of oil capitalism and political kleptocracy. In the 1970s, however, Saro-Wiwa's struggle still seemed ethnically motivated in that from his perspective, the ethnic majorities and the nation at large gained at the Ogoni's expense.

At issue was the method of revenue allocation by an increasingly unitary and autonomous state. As Watts (1992, 35–36) has observed, the oil economy transformed the regional structure of the First Republic into a "centralized, bureaucratic petrostate" that consolidated control over oil rents and revenues and embarked on a program of states creation— twelve states out of four regions in 1966, nineteen states in 1969, up to thirty states in the early 1990s—which increased direct fiscal dependency on the center. We have seen how, during the 1970s, Nigeria joined OPEC and became extremely wealthy, with a robust currency backed by petrodollars that financed an expanding public sector fueled by national development schemes. We have also seen how the state became the broker of virtually all productive ventures financed by oil, establishing a pattern of patronage in business and politics that allocated licenses and revenues in exchange for kickbacks and loyalty. As administrative units, each state depended upon federal disbursements, with ethnic blocks consolidating around economic as well as political resources and opportunities.

I will review the rather complex structural consequences of this incorporative and distributive modality in the next section. For now, we can focus on the view from Ogoniland, which was quite simple. For as far as the Ogoni were concerned, the federal government and its expanding circle of "lootocrats" were stealing from the poor and giving to the rich. Denied the black gold that was mined from their land and appropriated by the center, the Ogoni were screwed over twice. First, the federal government successively swindled the local areas out of any share in their oil by revising the revenue allocation formula to benefit the ethnic majorities. Thus the share of mineral rents for the minorities in the oil-producing areas fell from 20% down to 2% and again to 1.5%, which in any case was never paid. By 1979, the constitution of the imminent Second Republic vested all mineral rights in the federal government, adding a land-use decree that appropriated all lands as well. Second, the Ogoni were further oppressed within Rivers State, which diverted federal revenues to its own Ijaw majority at the expense of the most basic amenities and utilities in Ogoniland. Although sitting on the nation's wealth, the Ogoni lacked adequate funds for water, roads, and even primary education. As the nation's program for universal health care and primary education built more hospitals and schools in the arid north and populous west, the local government areas of Ogoniland could not even pay their doctors and teachers.

The situation intensified as the number of states in Nigeria increased, giving the ethnic majorities more states and hence a greater proportion of reallocated revenues while consigning the Ogoni and other oil-producing minorities to virtual if not literal extinction. With characteristic clarity, Saro-Wiwa sums up the systemic obliteration of his people in the language of ethnic domination. At the federal level: "Under the military dictatorships which have ruled the country from 1967 to the present (1992), the determination has been to subvert the federal culture of the country, establish a unitary state, corner the oil resources of the nation at the centre and then have these resources transferred by the Big Man who has come to power either by electoral fraud or military coup to the ethnic majority areas" (Saro-Wiwa 1992, 89). And within Rivers State, the same siphoning underwent a secondary elaboration:

In Rivers State, the majority Ijaws are more interested in their own welfare than in establishing a fair and just state. The constituent ethnic groups spend more time fighting for crumbs which fall from Nigeria's Federal table at which the ethnic majorities preside, than in creating social and economic progress. In short, Rivers State is but a microcosm of Nigeria in which the majority ethnic groups triumph while the minorities gnash their teeth in agony. But it is even worse because the multi-ethnic Rivers State is run as a unitary state without the nod which is made at the centre towards federalism. In such a situation, such ethnic minorities as the Ogoni are condemned to slavery and extinction. Thus, political structuring and revenue allocation have been used to completely marginalize the Ogoni, grossly abusing their rights and veritably consigning them to extinction. (Ibid.)

The Ogoni thus suffered a double indemnity under state-sector oil capitalism, and a double alienation from their resources and rights.[3] Added to such formal dispossession was the prebendalism of public office and the privatization of the state, in the form of kickbacks and embezzlement that again could follow ethnic lines.[4] As we shall see, Saro-Wiwa's nearly exclusive focus on ethnic politics and clientism was one-sided, overlooking the development of class factions and what Bayart (1993, 150–79) calls "the reciprocal assimilation of elites" on transethnic grounds. But the ethnic factor was obvious and striking enough to provoke an ethnically framed reaction.

Called the Autonomy Option by MOSOP, the Ogoni response to oil pollution, government kleptocracy, ethnic cronyism, and the resultant cultural "genocide" was a demand for political recognition that fell short of a full-fledged secessionist movement but invoked the language of independence in its Ogoni Bill of Rights. Presented to President Ibrahim Badamosi Babangida (who turned a deaf ear) and the military governor of Rivers State in October 1990, the manifesto called for greater political autonomy for the Ogoni as a distinct "ethnic nationality," with greater participation in the affairs of the federal republic. The pamphlet highlights seven specific guarantees that define the unit of autonomy and its sphere of operations. These are (1) political control of Ogoni affairs by Ogoni people, (2) the right to the control and use of a fair proportion of Ogoni economic resources for Ogoni development, (3) adequate and direct representation as of right in all Nigerian institutions, (4) the use and development of Ogoni languages in Ogoni territory, (5) the full development of Ogoni culture, (6) the right to religious freedom, and (7) the right to protect the Ogoni environment and ecology from further degradation (Leton 1990, 4). These steps toward a political ecology of citizenship formulated for a specific ethnic nation would become paradigmatic of Nigeria at large as the meaning of political autonomy widened to embrace an embattled public sphere. But in 1990, Saro-Wiwa's Ogoni platform was defiantly parochial, and the benefits that would accrue to Ogoniland were both tangible and enormous.

Although never explicitly defined, the distinct and separate unit of autonomy would presumably be a state, just like the many other new states carved from selected ethnic communities in Nigeria under Babangida's administration.[5] The economic implications of such an arrangement within the national federation involved huge sums of money, based on the assumption that Ogoniland would receive "a fair proportion" of oil revenues—in Saro-Wiwa's judgment a whopping 50%, following the *regional* allocation formula established before independence, although presumably this proportion was negotiable. Depending on calculated exchange rates, net oil revenues, and estimated damages to the land and people, government reparations to the Ogoni totaled about $20 billion. The figure was not exactly realistic, and it is not clear whether Saro-Wiwa sought these damages in literal monetary terms or more figuratively, as a monetary value placed on environment, cultural heritage, and minority rights. Added to the economic guarantees would be instant appointments to "quota" positions in education and the civil service, based on minority representation within the federation. The remaining demands in the Ogoni Bill of Rights identify language (Gokana and Khana), territory, Ogoni culture, religious freedom, and the environment and ecology as guaranteed parameters of an autonomous entity, one which, located between the state and civil society, would become the kernel of a national public sphere. For Saro-Wiwa, however, the Ogoni struggle would remain that of persecuted minorities against the so-called ethnic majority, the lootocratic regime, and the profiteering oil companies. Oil capitalism destroyed the Ogoni state of nature by devastating the environment and draining, through its oil pipes, "the very life-blood of the Ogoni people" (Saro-Wiwa 1992, 82). Saro-Wiwa concludes his *Genocide in Nigeria* with an image of a "vampire-like" Nigeria, sitting over the Ogoni and expropriating their oil to finance a corrupt and wasteful regime. He may not have appreciated how well this model applied to the nation as a whole.

THE VAMPIRE STATE

How did the most robust national economy in black Africa, fueled by an oil bonanza that inaugurated an era of unprecedented prosperity, give rise to the cannibalistic vampire state described so vividly by Ken Saro-Wiwa? How did the engine of development and progress that burned so brightly in the seventies and early eighties—bringing contracts, commodities, and new opportunities to virtually all sectors of the Nigerian economy—degenerate so thoroughly into a self-consuming, predatory regime by the 1990s? To understand how and why things fell apart in Nigeria so soon after they appeared to be taking off, we need to look past the limits of ethnic politics and poor leadership per se and return to the underlying contradictions of oil capitalism in Nigeria's enclave economy. From this more inclusive perspective, Saro-Wiwa's struggle against the majority ethnic oil barons and power brokers took place within more general transformations of the oil economy.

As Coronil (1987, 5) argues from the political economy of oil in Venezuela, the economic autonomy of the oil-based rentier state vis-à-vis society's productive capacity has an enhancing effect, whereby "the state appears to stand above society, and is represented as the locus of extraordinary power." Or as recapitulated by Watts (1994, 418), "the state appears suspended above society—it is represented as *the* source of power since oil is power." This historically specific variation of what Mitchell (1988) has called the "state-effect"—referring to the reification of the state standing apart from civil society—can be understood in Nigeria as a type of state fetishism, in the double sense of the commodity fetish and, following Taussig's "maleficium" model, the state's "aura of might" (Taussig 1992, 112). Unlike Mitchell's discussion of colonial Egypt, however, this separation was effected not by disciplinary practices of learning, policing, and military training—which had already occurred in colonial Nigeria—but by the accumulation and redistribution of oil revenues, in the form of taxes and rents. The distinction is significant because, as I have illustrated in previous chapters, oil capitalism in a rentier state entails a specific phenomenology of power and value, one in which Saro-Wiwa's political ecology must be located to understand his vision of the vampire state.

To appreciate how state vampirism made sense in the popular imaginations of a vast and variegated Nigeria, we must return to the magical qualities of royalties and ground rents in relation to transethnic idioms of moneymaking medicine. As mentioned in chapter 6, the magic of oil money emanating from the ground produced a national anxiety based on pervasive notions of "bad" wealth and "hot" money gained not through hard work but by nefarious means. We saw how such anxieties have been documented in the popular theater of the oil boom era (Barber 1982), drawing on popular accounts of moneymaking medicines of kidnappers who sacrifice humans for money. At the local level, these stories had serious consequences. During my first fieldwork in Ayede-Ekiti, Oroyeye priestesses sang vindictive songs against one Oladiran, who had allegedly kidnapped and killed his paternal half-brother for *lukudi* moneymaking medicine.[6] He was effectively isolated and thereafter died. The crime of effortless gain at the expense or even "consumption" of others is echoed in various witchcraft beliefs as well, but the underlying template motivating this genre is the transmutation of human blood into money—bad money, to be sure, curiously lacking value, without reciprocal advantage or gain. As Watts (1994, 427) explains in his insightful review of money-magic idioms during the oil boom, "money magic, whatever the empirical status of its liturgy of body parts and juju narratives, captured perfectly in this respect the magical and fetishistic (and violent) qualities of the petro-naira," further representing what Barber (1995, 219) identifies as "the convertibility of people into money . . . in the petro-naira narratives of money-magic."

Thus if rooted in local socioeconomic fields and cultural forms, money magic, like the money it invoked, was iconic of the nation and symptomatic of its unproductive wealth. Whether articulated through Hausa distinctions between fertile (*uwa mai anfi*) versus ominous (*jarin tsaya*) money (Watts 1994, 425), Ibo stories of body parts in suitcases (Bastian 1991), Yoruba notions of blood-draining profit, or the many minority perspectives—including those of the Ogoni—between and beyond, the symbolism of evil surrounding the negative values of money fetishism acquired national focus and circulation. Writing from a Yoruba perspective, Matory (1994, 124) contrasts local reports of money magic with its larger relevance to the nation-state: "*Lukudi* and the similar *eda* moneymaking magic occupy a nightmarish space in the national imagination far out of proportion to their actual incidence. They not only tap an extant and widespread symbolism but vividly symbolize the sense that acquisitive strategies in the mercantile capitalist state cannibalize normal forms of collective and personal life."

Following this development of money magic into an allegory of the national economy, we can map its blood-draining logic more precisely onto the accumulation and distribution of oil royalties and rents, not only in terms of the enormous wealth that was mysteriously conjured and publicly invested, but more specifically in terms of the hidden costs exacted by the concurrent privatization of the public sphere—the kickbacks, prebends, and wholesale diversion of public funds into private accounts and personal fiefdoms. If, as we have seen, oil represented the lifeblood of the nation, the petro-state paradoxically expanded by consuming this life blood of the people—sucking back the money that it pumped into circulation while absorbing the process of sectorial competition and even class formation within its hypertrophic belly. The oil economy may have energized domestic markets through the intensified circulation of money and commodities, but it enervated and undermined the real productive base of Nigeria, those agricultural resources that not even a state-sponsored green revolution could revive.

But during the halcyon days of the oil boom and its spectacle of national development, these contradictions were nowhere to be seen. Not even Ken Saro-Wiwa identified the generalized condition of state vampirism gestating within. Perched from 1968 to 1973 as federal administrator for the oil port of Bonny in Rivers State, where he witnessed the beginning of the boom, Saro-Wiwa well understood the siphoning off of oil from Ogoniland to the so-called ethnic majorities, but he remained less concerned about the involution of *étatization* writ large. If his struggle, like his vision, appeared parochial on this issue, it would not remain so, for after the demise of the Second Republic in the 1980s and the failure of the farcical 1993 elections, the vampire state boldly emerged during Abacha's destructive misrule. Thus consumed, oil as black gold turned to "devil's excrement" (Coronil 1997, 321 passim; Watts 1994) and toxic waste. In the next section, we will see how the anemic anatomy of a dying nation took an ecological turn, invoking the state of nature and the sanctity of the land to restore the "natural" conditions of civil society and effective citizenship from the ravages of oil.

THE UNCIVIL SOCIETY

"Why are you people doing this to me? What sort of a nation is this?" (Soyinka 1996, 149). Ken Saro-Wiwa's last words were uttered during the fifth and final attempt to operate the gallows that left him hanging and dead. Softly uttered, his words echoed throughout Nigeria and the international press as the global community waited in disbelief. With respect and dismay, Nigerians shook their heads over the tragic irony maintained by Saro-Wiwa's trenchant wit to the end. His final double entendre implicated not only his killers, from Abacha's ruling band of thugs and the excuse of a nation that they pretended to represent, but the tattered country that could do nothing right—not even kill a man on the gallows. Imported and previously unused, not even this dreaded instrument of execution was correctly operated by the state.

But Ken Saro-Wiwa did die. His death represents not just a dramaturgy of arbitrary power, following Mbembe's model of the postcolonial *commandement* and its farcical mimesis of judicial process and authority (Mbembe 1992), but the ultimate collapse of that elusive distinction between the Nigerian state and civil society, and thus the demise of effective citizenship. We can follow this drama in a linear narrative of linked events, as a convergence of local and national struggles in the global context of oil capitalism, to achieve an instrumental understanding of Saro-Wiwa's death and transfiguration into a spokesperson for all Nigeria. From this perspective, two series of events converged on the annulled national elections of June 12, 1993, and the aborted delivery of Nigeria's Third Republic. From below, Saro-Wiwa's leadership of MOSOP to defend the Ogoni against the military-petroleum complex developed greatest momentum as an ecological struggle for the natural environment, not surprisingly related to Greenpeace's estimates that "between 1982 and 1992, 37 percent of Shell's spills worldwide—amounting to 1.6 million gallons—took place in the Delta" where the Ogoni (and other minorities) reside (Hammer 1996, 62). Organizing an Ogoni youth wing that sabotaged oil pipes and installations, Saro-Wiwa's activism caused Shell to pull out of the region by January of 1993, costing the company and the government 28,000 barrels of crude oil a day (ibid.).

The struggle had been violent since 1990, when paramilitary police called "Kill and Go" massacred about fifty neighboring Umuechem residents demanding reparations from Shell, and fomented machine gun and grenade attacks—thinly disguised as "tribal" animosity—between Ogoni and Andoni peoples. The "slow genocide" of Ogoni by oil pollution was now supplemented by the "scorched earth" campaigns of military death squads, amounting to over two thousand Ogoni deaths and lending eerie credence to Saro-Wiwa's prophetic accusations. Thus when members of MOSOP's radicalized youth wing attacked the conservative chiefs and Ogoni "turncoats," resulting in the death of four elders, the government seized Saro-Wiwa and eight Ogoni associates on charges of incitement to murder, although Saro-Wiwa had been far away from the scene.[7] From the military's perspective, Saro-Wiwa and his Ogoni activists were the saboteurs of the economy. Eliminate the Ogoni problem, and oil could flow freely again. On a more tactical level, Abacha's rush to the gallows followed the colonial logic of divide and rule. If the Ogoni were not alone in opposing the alliance of Shell and the military junta, they could hardly mobilize a Delta revolt when government violence masqueraded as interethnic conflict. According to Soyinka, the immediate execution of Saro-Wiwa was to remove the pivotal figure of opposition around which a united Delta front could emerge. The "trial" was thus a sham:

> Ken Saro-Wiwa's fate had long been sealed. The decision to execute him and his eight companions was reached before the special tribunal was ordered to reconvene and pronounce a verdict that had been decided outside the charade of judicial proceeding. The meeting of the Provisional Ruling Council to consider the verdict was a macabre pretence, a prolongation of the cynicism that marked the trial proceedings from the outset. (Soyinka 1996, 152)

But Saro-Wiwa's struggle also transcended riverine politics to capture the frustrations of a nation that was withering away. The identification was not of course uniform, resonating more immediately with the south's resistance to Hausa-Fulani hegemony and political repression than among northern constituencies.[8]

When Abacha replaced the transitional Ernest Shonekan in a pro forma coup just weeks after Ibrahim Badamosi Babangida ("IBB") had "stepped aside," the final nail was driven into the national coffin. "Now we are finished!" headlined the feature story of *Razor,* a soon-to-be banned magazine. For unlike IBB, who bought off his enemies, Abacha was known as a ruthless hatchet man who—as events would soon prove—incarcerated and killed them. The absolute crackdown on Nigeria's formerly open press; the life prison terms given to such political luminaries as Shehu Yarad'ua and former (and once again) Head of State Olusegun Obasanjo, together with other alleged coup plotters whose death sentences were so benevolently commuted to life terms for crimes cooked up by Abacha's paranoid imagination; the interminable incarceration and eventual death of president-elect Moshood Abiola, whose wife was gunned down by unknown assailants whom everyone knew were government thugs; and of course the cold-blooded execution of Ken Saro-Wiwa and his eight Ogoni associates—these were only among the more blatant symptoms of the death of a nation and the demise of its citizenry, reduced not only to subjects of the northern political oligarchy but to veritable inmates as the government seized the passports of critics and intellectuals. There was no sphere of *res publica* in Abacha's Nigeria; no effective system of interest articulation, legal process, public education, press coverage, or publicity, nor was the most basic protection of life and liberty even recognized by the state. In one of his later editorials, Saro-Wiwa (1991, 131) maintained faith in the nation as he appealed to Babangida to convene a national conference and initiate real dialogue with the people:

> [T]he down turn (to put it politely) in the economy of the nation is exacerbating every possible source of tension and creating new ones . . . it takes a lot to maintain a belief in Nigeria. In these moments of doubt, there is need for self-examination and re-examination, a need to dip into reserves of energy at individual level to find that faith that fuels belief. And at national level, there has to be considerable soul-searching to clean the springs of political co-operation and self-restraint, to identify the homogeneous fundamental interests upon which reliance and voluntary collaboration must be based and to seek that common consent without which federation is meaningless.

Under Abacha, Saro-Wiwa died for these ideas, for they resonated beyond the disaffected minorities to all victims of a ruinous oil economy held hostage by a kleptocratic regime. To grasp the underlying dialectic of Nigeria's particular form of immiseration, linking the plight of the Ogoni to the collapse of civil society, we can return to the forms of fetishized value under oil capitalism and the naturalized idioms of people and land—what Coronil (1997, 67–118) has called "the nation's two bodies"—which were so enriched and then polluted by an oil boom gone bust.

In terms of the model of the vampire state sketched in the previous section, in which the production of false value equals the consumption of human blood, the riverine context of rentier capitalism transposed blood into soil and water. It is historically appropriate that the Niger Delta area where the Ogoni reside is part of a historic complex of chiefdoms and trading networks known in the nineteenth century as the Oil Rivers, based on the extensive trade of palm oil that gradually supplanted the slave trade. As we saw in chapter 4, palm oil was sold domestically as a vitamin-rich source of cooking oil (rich in ritual properties as well), but also for export to overseas markets, primarily British, where it lubricated the growing cosmetics industry and the heavy machinery of the Industrial Revolution. So basic was palm oil as a measure and standard of social and economic value in the Delta that it actually served as a trading currency, in the form of containers or "puncheons of oil" (Jones 1963, 91). It was this type of exchange that has misled some scholars to characterize this trade as a barter system, in which a dominant commodity assumed a money form; but whatever technical economic description best applies, the palm-oil economy may well correspond to that period of greater abundance in the past when, as Batom Mitee, brother to one of condemned Ogoni activists would say, "in the old days . . . you could fish, farm, and survive without money" (quoted in Hammer 1996, 61). As a moral economy recalled with nostalgia, the palm-oil trade and the forms of "natural value" that it invoked—found in nature and sold together with such commodities as timber, ivory, and beeswax (Dike 1956, 57)—established a profound contrast with the immoral economy of petroleum, which pumps bad money from beneath the ground, only to pollute and destroy the productive base of the ecosystem.[9]

It is here, within this idiom of natural goods and value forms, that the *unproductive* relations of oil capitalism were ecologically expressed. As Harvey (1982), rereading Marx, explains, ground rent produces specific forms of fetishized value in which land is perceived as the source of value itself (a perspective refined in economic terms by the physiocrats). When Nigeria's oil boom took off and the good times rolled, the nation was naturalized as one blood and territory, blessed by God, heritage, and natural resources, in the heady words of FESTAC. Was it not in 1976 that Shell-BP, in partnership with the Nigerian Oil Corporation, published *Nigerian Heritage*, a large, glossy book narrating within one singular category—oil—Nigeria's land and people, arts and culture, trade and industry, power and mineral resources, as if to ground the wealth of nationhood itself beneath the very soil? Did not the head of state, Lieutenant General Olusegun Obasanjo, personally launch the book amid much media fanfare? Whether or not the book received much popular attention is not the point; for it is the underlying logic motivating its publication and launching that so accurately captures how the indigenization of foreign capital—oil rents, to be specific—naturalized the nation. Nigeria, after experiencing the oil boom and FESTAC, was no longer a colonial or neocolonial entity, but could boast a long and valuable singular heritage extending deep beneath the ground and back into the precolonial past.[10]

It followed from this ideological baseline that as the contradictions of oil capitalism developed and as the nation, with its currency, declined, the soil and waters of the oil-producing regions were sullied. These contradictions, we have seen, follow an "alienated" form of false value and bad wealth, conjured by the state through nefarious means to promote illusory growth while eroding the very foundations of citizenship and civil society. As the oil economy imploded and collapsed, the signs of wealth and development became increasingly estranged from their referents, infusing the value forms of everyday exchange with ghostly simulacra—food that did not satisfy, clothes and uniforms that disguised, financial instruments that had no legitimacy, banks lacking capital, hospitals without medicine, and finally a democracy that had no *demos*. As the condition of the Niger Delta waterways converged with the collapse of the nation, the Ogoni autonomy option became a movement for the survival of the entire nation.

CONCLUSION

If the plight of the Ogoni and all Nigerians raises political issues of considerable urgency, it also points to broader conceptual issues within the anthropology of what Appadurai (1996) has dubbed "the global cultural economy." Oil capitalism after OPEC has produced specific economies of meaning and power as well as specific modalities of hyperexpansion and underdevelopment (like the so-called Dutch disease) that acquire a distinctively ecological salience, not only in terms of contamination and deforestation but also in struggles over citizenship and civil society. To be sure, oil in Nigeria has undermined riverine ecosystems and weakened the nation's agricultural base when imported staples and the lure of easy money drew Nigerians away from the land and into the urban undertow of the petro-naira. But it also had less-material effects that belong to an economy of representation and value forms, and it is here that Saro-Wiwa's struggle conveys lessons he may not have anticipated.

If the false wealth of oil ruined the nation, polluting its land and waterways, ecopolitics attacked a mode of rentier oil capitalism that violated the natural foundations of real wealth and legitimate commerce. Compared with the "natural" economy of the Ogoni, the money and wealth of the national economy was unrelated to productive labor, intensifying circulation while actually undermining the nation's productive base. As the "natural" relation between wealth and hard work became more obscure, the pollution of the environment became more apparent. And Nigerians rallied to Saro-Wiwa's cause. Thus Soyinka (1996, 110) wrote, "The Ogoni predicament has provoked, sometimes in the most unexpected quarters . . . open debates that increasingly posit the assumptions of nation being—be it as an ideal, a notional bonding, a provider, a haven of security and order, or an enterprise of productive co-existence—against the direct experience of the actual human composition within the nation." I would extend this national identification with the Ogoni struggle to the erosion of citizenship and civil society, not only in terms of unrealized ideals to be achieved or minimal standards to be maintained—as expressed in the language of activists today—but in more abstract terms of the civic breakdown itself as the oil economy melted down.

In an immediate sense, MOSOP's reclamation of Ogoni land and waterways represents an appeal to the very ground of civil society itself, as adumbrated by the autonomy option that the organization pursued. The state, we recall, had quite literally taken possession of all mineral-rich land, extending its sovereignty into the earth according to the 1979 Land Use Decree and appropriating its oil according to the mysterious mathematics of derivation, by which oil revenues were nationally "chopped" and redistributed. And what the state seized, the oil companies destroyed, polluting the farmland and fishing creeks with spills and runoffs while filling the air with noxious gas and acid rain. As MOSOP invoked the language and iconography of secession, boycotting the 1993 elections and rallying around an Ogoni national anthem and flag (Welch 1995, 643), it set the stage for a more-inclusive "war of position" against the vampire state and transnational capital. From this perspective, Ogoni activism suddenly resonated with the general struggle for a civil society by a country robbed—in Soyinka's words—of its nationhood. Stripped of its social base and its representative mechanisms, Nigerian democracy proved to be a politics of illusion, depriving civil society of its president-elect and any effective participation or collective voice in national affairs. After June 12, as citizens took to the streets in defense of their citizenship, the Ogoni struggle joined hands with a larger national cause. Thus the ecological destruction of creeks and waterways in the remote areas of the Niger Delta epitomized the pollution of the public sphere by an invasive and extractive petro-state.

But what is this sphere of civil society that functions rhetorically in the language of liberal political economy as the "natural" ground of effective democracy through a free market of interests and preferences? In a larger sense, the extended crisis in Nigeria today sheds light on the location of civil society in postcolonial Africa, where, following Kunz (1995, 181–82), two dominant perspectives compete. The more-Lockean position "posits [civil] society as a self-regulating realm, the ultimate repository of individual rights and liberties, and a body that must be protected against incursions of the state" (ibid.). This vision concurs with the American constitutional separation of powers and protection of civil rights and liberties, such as free speech, assembly, et cetera, that are ultimately grounded in a market mechanism with its own assumptions of natural law. It also presupposes norms of sincerity, trust, and accountability in the representation of individual and collective interests. A second, more-"Hegelian" understanding of civil society presents "an integrationist or holistic picture of civil society and the state" (ibid., 182) where the former functions more as a sphere of communication and interaction within the nation-state as a whole. There is no question that as African states have liberalized in the late 1980s and early nineties, pursuing uneven paths of structural adjustment and democratization, the liberal model has reestablished itself in Africanist scholarship, particularly among political scientists focusing on "weak states" and predatory regimes. The Ogoni situation and the Nigerian crisis appear to support this perspective in that natural ecosystems have provided the moral framework of a civil society besieged by the state. As a strategic essentialism of political activism, moreover, such an organic idiom of civil society makes instrumental sense.

The dialectics of Nigerian rentier capitalism, however, and the forms of commodification that it has entailed, suggest a more-Hegelian or even Marxian approach to civil society in Africa, not as a natural and autonomous domain to be protected and reclaimed but as a fetishized sphere of circulation within the national economy. We have seen how notions of citizenship and national culture were animated by the logic of the commodity form in idioms of reciprocal equivalence and commensurate value. As oil boosted the national economy, accelerating the circulation of money and commodities through what were primarily political relations of distribution, the nation was naturalized as one blood and soil beneath a benevolent state rising above. But as the oil economy burned out and the dollar dropped out of the Nigerian naira, the illusory basis of the bonanza became apparent, draining the very blood of the nation and its citizens. Within the sphere of circulation, the arteries of the nation were blocked by irrational shortages until even oil disappeared from the service stations. As inflation soared, arbitrary exchange values destabilized the very phenomenology of exchange itself, giving rise to the era of the "419"—of fraud, con artistry, deception, and desperate survival. From this perspective, the breakdown of civil society and of the intersubjective norms governing accountable interaction and political representation in Nigeria can be attributed not only to the rapacious appetites of predatory rulers and multinational companies but to the collapse of a sphere of circulation whose previously obscure relation to "the hidden abode of production" (Marx 1976, 279; quoted in Postone 1993, 272) has almost literally disappeared.

Looking back on festac '77, one is struck by how much has changed in Nigeria since the euphoric marriage of oil and culture, when the future, burning bright, appeared like a mirage on the horizon. The Nigerian truism that "no condition is permanent" (Berry 1993) perfectly captures the trials and tribulations of the nation's postcolonial experience. Failed elections, military coups, windfall profits, petrol shortages, even tragic pipeline explosions are now familiar features of a nation that seems to be in endless transition. Oil, the precious commodity that initially centralized the state, is now the catalyst of devolution and division as new states and coalitions compete for shares of allocated revenues. If historic regional tensions have persisted between north and south, east and west in response to shifting configurations within the military and the new political class, the resurgence of religious violence, Sharia law, and born-again Pentecostalism mark a growing trend in what appears to be a postnational consciousness, turning away from a polluted past and toward a purified Mecca or New Jerusalem (Peel 2000, 317).[1]

No condition is permanent. Consider the extraordinary career of Olusegun Obasanjo, a Sandhurst-trained military man who rose quickly through the ranks; became head of state—and festac's Grand Patron —when Murtala Mohammed was killed (1976); distinguished himself as one of the few military rulers in Africa to oversee a return to civilian rule (1979); retired to his farm; was arrested by Sani Abacha, sentenced to death, had his sentence commuted to life, and was released after Abacha's disreputable demise; and reemerged as Nigeria's president, winning two national elections while somehow surviving the entrenched opposition between a disaffected northern oligarchy and ethnic chauvinism bordering on secessionism in the south. Indeed, Obasanjo has been born again, not only politically but in religious terms as well, like so many Nigerians who have endured debilitating hardships since the oil boom went bust. In this respect, Obasanjo embodies the very transformations I have explored through FESTAC, from the commanding heights of state-sponsored development to the dislocations of neoliberal reform.

To grasp the political economy of oil as distilled, we could say fetishized, by FESTAC's culture, I deployed two temporal frames that illuminated the festival's broader historical and anthropological significance. The first focused on the actual festival as celebrated from January 15 to February 12, 1977. A complex "event," to be sure, with its own embedded temporalities that range from the planning of exhibits and performances to the *longue durée* of early coastal trade, the historical ethnography of FESTAC as such developed two related arguments. One, emphasizing cultural production as a symbolic mode of commodification, related the "invariant substance" of the nation form (Balibar 1991, 86), conceived genealogically as one destiny and blood, to the general equivalent of the money form as animated by oil. In this respect, FESTAC highlights what may well be a crucial relationship between money and blood in the emergence of modern nations, abstracting identity out of difference through the production and circulation of value.[2] In the postcolonial context of an oil-rich Nigeria, however, the objectification of national culture—and its projection throughout the Pan-African world —revealed a second general process, specific to "third world" nationhood, of indigenizing, and thus nationalizing, colonial culture. With particular emphasis on the regatta and the durbar, we saw how central mechanisms of ceremonial exchange between Europeans and Africans, colonizers and colonized, were recuperated by FESTAC as precolonial traditions, thereby absorbing the "imprint" of colonialism under the sign of its erasure. My goal in tracing such erasures and revisions was not to correct a form of collective amnesia but to grasp the process itself as a significant transformation, a making and refashioning of nationhood out of colonialism's culture (Thomas 1994). Indeed, this "erased" past belongs to the congealed history of cultural production, one so embedded in the African postcolony that it must be acknowledged and embraced rather than rejected or ignored. If there is one obvious lesson from FESTAC's cultural project, it is that precolonial national traditions in Africa belong to myth rather than history, and any decolonization paradigm that seeks a return to such mythic origins is pursuing an illusion. The less obvious corollary of this negated pristine past is that European influences in the making of Nigeria—from breaking trade and saving souls to the colonial mediations of native administration—are no less African today for their "exogenous" origins.

The second dominant temporal frame looked forward, treating FESTAC not as the endpoint of an ambitious cultural project but rather as the beginning of the end. Whereas FESTAC occluded an eviscerating pattern of class involution by inverting the symbolic economy of *deficit production* by the Nigerian petro-state, the crises of the 1990s erupted when the contradictions of the oil economy played themselves out. Thus the electoral charade of June 12, 1993, and the brutal hanging of Ken Saro-Wiwa represent dramatic episodes within a larger trajectory of neoliberal reform, in which privatization, devaluation, inflation, and unemployment marked the collapse of the state and the erosion of civil society. The increased violence and pervasive insecurity were more than symptoms of difficult times, however, and the broader shift triggered by structural adjustment in Nigeria can be grasped more abstractly as one of general symbolic dislocation. If the 1993 elections inaugurated the dissimulative era of the "419," and the death of Saro-Wiwa transformed black gold into toxic waste, when placed in relation to the boom years of 1970s, they represent part of a larger drama unfolding throughout Africa and the global margins of the postcolonial (and postsocialist) world. Let us turn briefly to the economic and political dimensions of this drama.

The most compelling characterization of globalization in the African postcolony is that of Comaroff and Comaroff (1999), whose reflections on what they aptly call "occult economies" illuminate the consuming logics of market forces where rapid neoliberal reform has occurred.[3] Noting a resurgence of magical, nefarious, and even satanic idioms in which wealth is believed to be conjured and accumulated, ranging from various modalities of organ, blood, and fat extraction to pyramid schemes, ritual murder, and zombification, the Comaroffs show how the hidden hand of the market doubles as a severed body part for moneymaking medicine, no more or less intelligible than the invisible forces and flows of flexible accumulation and financial speculation of what they call "millennial capitalism" (see also Comaroff and Comaroff 2000). Focusing primarily on post-apartheid South Africa, where a deracialized state has embraced a deregulated economy, but extending their observations throughout Africa, to East Asia, Latin America, and the shadowy markets of the former eastern bloc, they argue that the occult signifiers of illicit accumulation emerge when "an optimistic faith in free enterprise encounters, for the first time, the realities of neoliberal economics: of unpredictable shifts in sites of production and the demand for labor; of the acute difficulties inherent in exercising stable control over space, time, or the flow of money; of an equivocal role for the state; of an end to old political alignments . . . of uncertainty surrounding the proper nature of civil society" (Comaroff and Comaroff 1999, 294). Clearly occult idioms emerge in a tangle of local registers and unifying translocal themes, but whether vampires, zombies, or derivative futures activate the moneymaking magic, a pervasive sense of false value, of surplus accumulated without proper production, accounts for its sordid and evil tinge.

In a similar vein, but with a more explicit focus on specific forms of domination, Mbembe (2001) explores the complex relationships between representation and violence through those figures of the *potentate* and the *commandement* that characterize the African postcolony. Central to Mbembe's analysis of power—its forms of excess, discharge, transgression, and conviviality—is a historical argument about colonial overrule based on patterns of subjection and subjecthood that have devolved into simulacra of governance. Taking "obscene" dictatorships as his paradigm cases—Mobutu's Zaire, Eyadema's Togo, Cameroon under Ahidjo and Biya, with material from Kenya as well—Mbembe tracks trajectories from colonial statehood, with its unequal social contracts and terms of exchange, to postcolonial regimes of arbitrary domination, in which power plays as much on the arbitrariness of the sign as on the sovereign's frivolous dispositions over life and death. Based on the politics of gift-giving and allocation, postcolonial African economies have been carving up the public sector and privatizing the state, generating political rather than economic capital and thus low productive capacity. In place of the goods, rights, guarantees, and freedoms promised by its ministries and national campaigns, the postcolony produces signs: "[The postcolony] is a specific system of signs, a particular way of fabricating simulacra or re-forming stereotypes . . . the postcolony is characterized by a distinctive style of political improvisation, by a tendency to excess and lack of proportion, as well as by distinctive ways identities are multiplied, transformed, and put into circulation" (Mbembe 2001, 102).

Like the occult economies described by the Comaroffs, Mbembe's postcolony has its share of zombies and bloodsuckers; the political zombies of leaders and soldiers, and vampires like the autocrat who consumes the blood of his acolytes (ibid., 160–61, 171n33). And like Fanon's "zone of occult instability," the signs of these times are fluid and unfixed, proliferating both at the top, where the carnivalesque flourishes within baroque court societies, and at the bottom, doubling as the potentate's orifice and popular laughter, in both cases manifesting the power to transgress official boundaries and produce surplus meanings. Within this profusion (and perfusion) of somewhat hallucinatory signs—the terrain of the contractor, the *sapeur,* and the criminal as well as the minister and the gendarme—state power sustains its tenuous coherence by generating a "master code," its own world of meanings through administrative and bureaucratic practices: stamps, insignia, forms, titles, but also styles of recognition and humiliation. What Mbembe foregrounds here as the organizing framework of power and violence is nothing less than the political economy of the sign.

And here is where I would bring the occult economies and the *commandement* of the postcolony together, in light of Nigeria's rather exceptional experience. In many ways, Nigeria's dramatic rise and fall, expanding and then imploding under the influence of oil, resonates with the occult signifiers of magical money and the excessive depredations of the self-arrogating potentate. During the boom years, when money flowed through a state that served as the locus of distribution, stories of child abductions and organ stealing for moneymaking magic appeared in tabloid newspapers and magazines, popular theater, literature, and film. As oil rents circulated throughout the body politic, unevenly and with no clear relationship to work, the occult dimensions of national prosperity were registered in what I have called "Nigerian nervousness," pervasive enough to generate uneasy laughter as the good times rolled, but submerged deeply enough beneath the veneer of abundance to be tolerated and overlooked. I have even suggested that the initial phenomenology of oil-fueled development—the new highways, hotels, heavy industries, and agricultural schemes—generated a visual ontology of the modern that demanded a direct denotational ratification, as in the UNILAG professor's flat bearing the names of each room affixed to its door (chapter 6). On a national scale, we can see FESTAC itself as a Nigerian campaign of Pan-African ratification, assimilating the revolutionary expansion of the oil boom to a legislated system of harmonized categories and to a narrative of progress in the FESTAC Colloquium. If ever there was a state-sponsored master code, it was FESTAC's reduction of surplus meanings to the official discourse of the Nigerian state. Just as Richards (1990) has argued that London's Crystal Palace Exhibition of 1851 assimilated the new Victorian commodity culture to an imperial hierarchy of races and classes, so we can appreciate FESTAC's spectacle of culture as a stabilizing conversion of sudden wealth into blackness.

But unlike the commodity boom of Victorian England which was generated by the Industrial Revolution, Nigeria's bonanza was fueled by oil, reversing the historic relationship between spheres of production and circulation. As we have seen, the visual ontology of "seeing is believing" and the signs of development that refashioned the nation represented a virtual productive sphere that was actually a hoax, producing at losses that could never be recouped. And here, in such reversals, lies the origin of the occult economies that have emerged so clearly under neoliberal reform, but were already reflected in FESTAC's mirror of cultural production, when signs became the basis of generating value rather than the media of its accumulation through exchange. Ironically, when FESTAC's commodification of culture converted ethnic difference and particularism into an exalted, blood-based Pan-African nation, the blood of Nigerians was already being extracted in sordid accounts of moneymaking sorcery, prefiguring with fearful symmetry the beginning of the end.

If the principles of occult economy were already in place in the 1970s, as the Nigerian case suggests, what happened when the petrostate withered away into the private domains of the Babangida and Abacha regimes? Here, *pace* Mbembe, is where the state's master code deconstructed, jettisoning the "mirage of the referent" into the social space of dissimulation and con artistry, giving rise to the era of the "419." But here also, following Mbembe, is where the postcolony's specific system of signs and distinctive regime of violence combined into a modus operandi for the new potentates and a modus vivendi for desperate Nigerians struggling to get rich or survive by their wits. If Babangida was known to coerce through gifts, Abacha distinguished himself as a killer, and died—in the arms of two prostitutes, the story goes—when the inner circle realized he had gone too far and had him poisoned.[4]

And if government became a grand theater of the absurd, with increasing repression masquerading as patriotic duty, business as usual fell increasingly at risk. The proliferation and ambiguity of social and professional identities in ornately decorated business cards; the circulation of fake logos, letters of credit, and bank drafts; "neon" money from mysterious chemicals; and the impersonation of oil ministers, military officers, and police were among the pervasive means of generating wealth from official insignia and symbolic fetishes of state. *Placed in a broader continental perspective, the Nigerian case recasts Mbembe's condition of postcoloniality as a generalized condition of semiotic suspension, in which signs, stripped of their referential moorings, are almost literally up for grabs.*[5] If the symptoms of such semiotic suspension vary, the condition itself results from two closely related trends: the collapse of national currencies when deregulated by the state, and the collapse of the state when "reformed" by the market and privatized from within—that is, when money scarcely "refers" to things, and the state's imprimatur and legislative categories have lost credibility and institutional backing.[6]

What is illuminating about this symbolic perspective is not that it applies uniformly to everyday life but that it captures a profound epistemological rupture with serious consequences throughout the continent, ranging from virtual democracies and demonic vampires to child soldiers and genocidal campaigns. Like their fallen counterparts in the former socialist bloc, the neoliberal regimes of Africa, whether clothed in fatigues or civilian dress, are struggling with the tyranny of the market, the imperatives of democracy, and the arbitrariness of the sign. In Nigeria today, if the trend away from national tradition and toward intolerant forms of Christianity and Islam represents the wave of the future, perhaps FESTAC should be revisited—not as a cultural project that failed but as a secular model of citizenship to be pursued.

NOTES

INTRODUCTION

1. For a representative sample of this scholarship, see Benedict 1983; Çelik and Kinney 1990; Greenhalgh 1988; Hinsley 1991; Lebovics 1992; Leprun 1986; Morton 2000; Richards 1990; Rydell 1984, 1993; Silverman 1977; and Stocking 1987.

2. However, Cosentino (1991, 251) could say of FESTAC: "Few contemporary cultural events can have affected the life of a great nation more dramatically."

3. See also the important works by Watts (1984, 1991, 1992, 1994, 1996, 1997, 2003), whose critical studies of the Nigerian oil boom have developed many of the issues upon which I draw, such as prebendalism, money fetishism, expenditure, circulation, and urban violence.

4. See Barber (1982, 436 passim), who describes the impact of the oil boom as a "spectacle of easy commercial profit."

5. As Coronil (1997, 10) explains in his study of the Venezuelan petro-state, the illusory spectacle of oil-based development stems from the "social dominance of rent circulation over the production of value."

6. In this respect, FESTAC's politics of signification resembled the Crystal Palace Exhibition of 1851, which, as Richards (1990) has so effectively demonstrated, responded to the dislocations of Victorian commodity culture by establishing clear codes of hierarchy and value. In Nigeria, FESTAC addressed the dislocations of the oil economy.

7. For a dazzling discussion of FESTAC's culture as a harbinger of national Afrokitsch, see Cosentino 1991.

8. For a rigorous theorization of the symbolic properties of valuation through copyright, see Coombe 1998.

9. For an excellent critical discussion and synthesis of this tradition, see Graeber 2001.

1. For a rigorously theorized Marxist analysis of the impact of oil rents on oil capitalism in Venezuela, see Coronil (1997, 21–66), who resituates labor in the exploitation of nature to relate the materiality of value to its manifold forms.

2. Accounts of the Magic Barrel are featured in "Petroleum—World Consumption Trends," *Nigerian Herald* (Ilorin), October 3, 1975, p. 5; and in "Lagos Oil Seminar," *Sunday Sketch* (Ibadan), October 12, 1975, pp. 3–4.

3. Upaka, B. J., "Oil: Most Important Commodity in International Commerce," *Nigerian Tide* (Port Harcourt), June 25, 1976, p. 9.

4. Randall, Jonathon, "Nigeria, Major Oil Companies Are Locked in Test of Wills," *Washington Post*, February 1, 1977; Osunde, Austin, "Evolution of Nigeria's Oil Industry," *Daily Times* (Lagos), September 9, 1975, p. 10.

5. For increased money supply figures, see "Nigeria Records Increase in Oil Revenue," *Nigerian Standard* (Jos), April 12, 1977. For GDP figures, see Darnton, John, "Oil Riches Unleash a Major Boom in Nigeria," *New York Times*, January 30, 1977.

6. For example, agriculture's 61.2% of GDP in 1962 dropped to 23.3% in 1976/77. In Akpan, Louis, "Gov't Measures to Destroy Dependence on Oil," *Sunday Punch* (Ikeja), October 30, 1977.

7. Ogunsanwo, Femi, "Electorate Must Get Value for Votes," *Daily Times* (Lagos), January 6, 1977, p. 3.

8. Obudu, John I., "Who Should Occupy Former Residents' Quarters: Secretaries or Chairmen?" *Nigerian Chronicle* (Calabar), May 12, 1977, p. 5.

9. On the exclusion of traditional chiefs, see "Awo Decries Exclusion of Emirs, Chiefs," *New Nigerian* (Kaduna), December 12, 1976. On their inclusion, see Ayede, Charles, "Benue Announces Traditional Councils," *Nigerian Standard* (Jos), May 2, 1977, p. 16.

10. Given that the naira was worth $1.60 US at the time, this amount was considerable. Although the allocation formula of 75% based on population and 25% based on the equality of states stipulated that 50% of the latter must be met by state matching grants, it should be noted that those matching funds were initially allocated to the states by the federal government in the first place.

11. The Udoji wage increases also generated an aesthetic wave that Cosentino had dubbed "Udoji kitsch," including "Udoji Hairstyles . . . gold colored plastic bric-a-brac from Hong Kong," and fantastical villas with fake Benin bronzes portraying "modern" themes, such that "everything became a commodity in this superhot market, including traditional culture and art" (1991, 247).

12. Both quotes are taken from "Is This an Oil Boom or an Oil Doom?" *Nigerian Herald* (Ilorin), March 26, 1977, p. 7.

13. "Oil Boom Is 'Killing' Nigeria," *Daily Times* (Lagos), July 27, 1977, p. 18.

14. Oriero, S. B., "The Reverse Side of the Oil Industry," *Sunday Observer* (Benin City), August 8, 1974, p.13; "Villagers Cry Out against Oil Company," *Nigerian Tide* (Port Harcourt), May 15, 1974, p. 1; Talor, Mohamed, "Pollution and Oil Industry," *Nigerian Tide* (Port Harcourt), May 28, 1977, p. 3.

15. Figures quoted from Col. M. Buhari, who was at that time Federal Commissioner for Petroleum Resources, in "Why the Fuel Crisis," *Nigerian Herald* (Ilorin), May 4, 1977, p. 1.

16. "Petroleum Production and Distribution (Anti-Sabotage) Decree 1975," News Release no. 1364, Federal Ministry of Information, Lagos, November 10, 1975. Delivered by special military tribunals, such sentences were beyond appeal, although they could be commuted to twenty-one years' imprisonment as a "compassionate alternative."

17. "Protecting Nigeria's Oilfield Installations," *Business Times* (Lagos), October 14, 1975.

18. "AFAM Well Repairs to Cost One Million Naira," *Daily Times* (Lagos), November 2, 1974, p. 1; "AFAM Oil Fire under Probe," *Daily Times* (Lagos), November 19, 1974.

19. "Protecting Nigeria's Oilfield Installations," *Business Times* (Lagos), October 14, 1975.

20. Ibid.

21. According to the official report, "Evidence of petrol fire disaster at Umuahia in Imo State, Ilesha in Oyo State, and the quantity of petrol discovered in hide-outs in places like Ilorin in Kwara State, Owerri in Imo State and Ibadan in Oyo State, all confirm nationwide hoarding and the diversion of fuel from the normal distribution channels to black markets." In Usoro 1977, 69.

22. "Col. Magoro Presents 90 New Petrol-Tankers to State Governments," Late News Release no. 712, Federal Ministry of Information, Lagos, June 10, 1976. The ninety new tankers supplemented twenty-four allocated earlier in the year to the former twelve states.

23. Ibid.

24. The Petroleum Equalisation Fund (Management) Board Decree of 1975 not only established uniform pricing throughout the country, but also provided for the reimbursement of oil marketing companies for any losses sustained as a result of the pricing measures. See Akinmoladun, Olu, "Knowing about Your Oil," *Business Times* (Lagos), September 10, 1977, p. 9.

25. "Petrol Smuggled out of Nigeria," *Daily Times* (Lagos), March 29, 1975, p. 28. The article highlights the fact that petrol was smuggled "in drums" that were sent by road, adding another valence to the drum as money form (in addition to its conjuring and explosive properties), and equating the transportation of oil with the flow of value throughout the national body. See also "Oil Politics and National Security," *Nigerian Observer* (Benin City), April 10, 1975, p. 3.

26. "Address by His Excellency General Yakubu Gowon on the Occasion of the Formal Launching of the Third National Development Plan 1975–80," in Oyediran 1977, 166.

27. The Adeosun Commission's "Report of the Industrial Enterpises Panel," cited in Biersteker 1987, 144.

28. For a discussion of Nigerian indigenization policy as a catalyst for class consolidation, see Sklar 2002, 136–38.

29. John Hollis, an American expatriate who lived in Nigeria from 1966 until his death in 2000, described one party during the oil boom where each table had a fifth of White Horse whiskey and tethered goats for the guests to take home.

30. On another occasion, I returned to Nigeria without the required reentry visa. When I dashed the official to help me through, he requested more, explaining that the

amount was not only for him but for his superiors as well. I begged him to have mercy, and we reached a compromise.

31. Interviews in Lagos with actor and director Lari Williams (September 24, 1993) and with the president of FESTAC's National Participation Committee, Dr. Garba Ashiwaju (November 7, 1993).

32. "Program of Events," Formal Opening of the National Theatre, Lagos, by His Excellency, Lt.-General Olusegun Obasanjo, Head of the Federal Military Government, Commander-in-Chief of the Armed Forces, Federal Republic of Nigeria, September 30, 1976, p. 8.

33. Ibid.

34. "Gov't to Build 144m Theatre for African Culture, Arts Festival," *New Nigerian* (Kaduna), July 17, 1973, p. 12.

35. "Life in the Village," *Festival News*, vol. 1, no. 11, 1977, p. 4.

36. Interview with Dr. Chibogu, principal social development officer and deputy director, Ministry of Social Development, Youth, Sports and Culture, October 26, 1993.

37. *Festival News*, op. cit.

CHAPTER TWO

A note on documentation for chapters 2 through 6: I obtained International Festival Committee (IFC) minutes and reports from the Centre for Black and African Arts and Civilization (CBAAC), housed in the National Theatre building, Lagos. At the time of writing, National Participation Committee (NPC) and National Participation Secretariat (NPS) minutes and reports were temporarily (?) stored in the Cultural Library, also housed in the National Theatre but separate from the CBAAC. NPC and NPS minutes are organized in subcommittee Folders (Dance, Arts and Crafts, etc.), and although the document pages are numbered, the folders themselves are not.

1. Text of Olusegun Obasanjo's opening speech for FESTAC '77, reproduced in the *Nigerian Standard* (Jos), January 17, 1977, p. 14.

2. As Nigerians were proud to joke, "When Nigeria sneezes, the West catches cold."

3. Technically, Guinea-Bissau, which gained independence from Portugal as the planning of FESTAC unfolded, is a lusophone country, but no separate lusophone category was formed. Although Angola and Mozambique later joined FESTAC as nations, they were still Portuguese colonies when the International Festival Committee first charted its zones, and were thus initially included with Liberation Movements.

4. The eight zones were Northeast (ME, RI, NH, VT, CT, MA), Mideast (NY, northern NJ), Southeast (PA, southern NJ, DE), Upper South (MD, VA, NC, WV, KY, TN, DC), Lower South (SC, GA, FL, AL, MS, LA), Southwest (AR, TX, OK, KS, NM, CO, AZ), Midwest (OH, IA, MI, IL, IN, MO, MN, NE, WI, ND, SD), and Far West (WA, ID, MT, UT, WY, OR, NV, CA, HI, and AK). This information comes from *The NAZ Report to the 7th Meeting of the Vice Presidents of the International Festival Committee of the 2nd Black and African Festival of Arts and Culture, Lagos, Nigeria. Nov. 27–Dec. 2, 1975.* CBAAC.

5. Jeff Donaldson, quoted in West, Hollie I., "African Arts Festival: Offer Refused," *Washington Post*, November 24, 1976.

6. The NAZ Report to the 7th Meeting of the Vice Presidents of the International Festival Committee of the 2nd Black and African Festival of Arts and Culture, Lagos, Nigeria. Nov. 27–Dec. 2, 1975. Loose folder, CBAAC.

7. Letter to Commander Fingesi from the National Black Coalition of Canada, December 2, 1975, Minutes of the Seventh Meeting of the International Festival Committee. Loose folder, CBAAC.

8. Minutes of the Second Meeting of the International Festival Committee, 26–31 March, 1973, p. 2, "Creation of More Zones." CBAAC.

9. Debayo, Jumoke, "Visit to Australasia from 5th Oct–15 Oct, 1976. Report to the President of the IFC, 22 Oct. 1976." CBAAC, loose file.

10. See, for example, Osikomaiya, Jiya, "A Reunion of Black Families," Daily Times (Lagos), January 15, 1977, p. 15.

11. Quoted in Lahey [1977?].

12. The Soviet proposal is mentioned in the Minutes of the 6th Meeting of the International Festival Committee of the 2nd Black and African Festival of Arts and Culture, 26 June 1975, document 093, p. 2. Loose folder, CBAAC. The Middle East discussion is drawn from minutes of a meeting between the president of FESTAC and the vice president of the North Africa zone, November 29, 1975. The document also notes Tunisia's withdrawal from FESTAC.

13. "FESTAC '75 at World Fairs," in Festival News, vol. 1, no. 1, May 1, 1975, p. 3. At this time FESTAC was still targeted for 1975, although it would be postponed twice until 1977.

14. To consecrate the building sites for housing festival participants and visitors in Lagos and Kaduna, Nigeria's Head of State laid the foundation stone of the project in both state capitals.

15. Diop's quotation is taken from a loose document in the minutes of the third IFC meeting, called " Allocution Delivered By the Secretary General, Monsieur Alioune Diop, Before the International Festival Committee at the Hoisting of the Festival Flag Ceremony, Held at the International Secretariat, 13 Hawksworth Road, Ikoyi on Thursday November 8, 1973 at 7:30 pm." Enahoro's festival toast was on an unnumbered entry. Loose folder, CBAAC.

16. Article 17 in the Agreement Between the Federal Military Government of the Federal Republic of Nigeria and the International Festival Committee of the 2nd World Black and Africa Festival of Arts and Culture (as amended), first IFC meeting. CBAAC.

17. "Committee Members Granted Diplomatic Immunity," Daily Times (Lagos), February 4, 1974, p. 2.

18. For a brilliant analysis of the Benin sculptures as "fetishes" of colonial knowledge, power, and desire, embodying contradictory attitudes of revulsion and respect while supporting "scientific" theories of degeneration, see Coombes 1994, 7–28 passim.

19. Robinson, Alma, "The Controversial Mask of Benin," Washington Post, February 11, 1977.

20. Ahmed, Mahmoon. "FESTAC: Time to Re-Assess Our Culture." New Nigerian (Kaduna), January 15, 1977, p. 1.

21. Robinson, "The Controversial Mask of Benin."

22. See Cosentino (1991, 250–52), who was quick to perceive in the FESTAC emblem

the simulacral quality of commodification under oil, thus becoming "an unwitting metaphor for other cultural transformations, visible and ideological, at FESTAC" (252).

23. Regarding stamps, "Ministry Issues FESTAC Stamps," *New Nigerian* (Kaduna), January 14, 1977, p. 14; the FESTAC handkerchief, Efeyini, Sunny, "Guy Who Designed FESTAC Hankies," *The Punch* (Ikeja), January 17, 1977, p. 11; and in the Minutes of the First IFC Meeting, 3–7 October, 1972, document 010: "It is hoped that the motif will be reproduced on the Flag and on various mementos (such as buttons, pens, coins, etc.)." CBAAC.

24. "The Black Frenchman," *New Nigerian* (Kaduna), June 3, 1976, p. 5.

25. See Irele 1990, 89–116 for a brilliant synthesis of both traditions.

26. In an interview about his experiences at the Dakar festival, black journalist Frederick O'Neal described the colloquium with the following linguistic economy: "There was a great discussion on Negritude and the meaning of Negritude, etc." He also notes the impressive participation of Langston Hughes. "Recorded Remarks by Frederick O'Neal," p. 15, in "First World Festival of Negro Arts, 1966," box 1, folder "Post-Festival Reports," Schomburg Center for Research in Black Culture, The New York Public Library.

27. The walkout is attributed by Nzekwu to the play's lack of a French synopsis (Nzekwu 1966, 87).

28. Explanatory Notes on Draft Agenda, no. 3, Second IFC Meeting, 26–31 March, 1973. CBAAC.

29. Ibid. The Francophone I zonal vice president was none other than Alioune Sene, Senegal's minister of cultural affairs.

30. Artist Ibou Diouf, quoted in Nzekwu 1966, 84.

31. "Address By The Federal Commissioner for Special Duties, Commander O. P. Fingesi, at the First Meeting of Intellectuals and Artistes at Lugard Hall, Kaduna, on 6th February, 1976." p. 10. Loose folder, CBAAC.

32. Aba, Andrew, "FESTAC 77 and Senghor's Negritude," *Sunday Standard* (Jos), July 11, 1976, pp. 5–6.

33. "Opening Remarks by Commander O. P. Fingesi, Federal Commissioner for Special duties of the Federal Republic of Nigeria and President of the 2nd World Black and African Festival of Arts and Culture to the Ninth Meeting of the I.F.C., held in Lagos on 6th to 9th July, 1976," Doc. IX/148/162A CBAAC.

34. Fingesi also finessed the reorganization of the Cultural Council in charge of the Colloquium into three separate bodies, thereby replacing its Cameroonian president— Father Mveng, who had directed the Dakar colloquium—with an anglophone African counterpart. The paper trail reveals the bureaucratic skullduggery deployed, in that Mveng's air ticket was never sent to ensure his absence at the meeting at which he was replaced.

35. Minutes of the 8th IFC Meeting, Doc. VIII/136, appendix A, p. 3. CBAAC.

36. Mveng's commitment to negritude is well established in his *Les sources grecques de l'histoire négro-africaine depuis Homère jusqu'à Strabon* (Paris: Présence Africaine, 1972).

37. "FESTAC and the Senegalese Boycott Threat," *Nigerian Observer* (Benin City), December 12, 1976, p. 5.

38. In 1977, 1 CFA franc was equal to 0.02 French franc (Falegan 1984, 218n12).

39. The specified convertible currencies were the pound sterling, French franc, US dollar, German mark, and Swiss franc (Falegan 1984, 207).

40. The 30% was determined by a coefficient—applying to all member states—calculated as "one half of the ratio of the gross domestic product of each member state to the total per capita income of all the member states" ("ECOWAS Takes Off," special correspondent, *Afriscope*, January 1977, p. 58).

41. Although the decree was specifically designed to reconcile foreign capital with the imperatives of entrepreneurial indigenization in Nigeria (see Biersteker 1987, 159–98), it reveals how global capital and citizenship became intimately linked.

42. "Nigeria in African Affairs," *Nigerian Observer* (Benin City), October 1, 1974, p. 70.

43. The Angola issue was particularly charged, dividing OAU member states between supporters of the Movimiento Popular de Libertação (including Nigeria), who pushed for inclusion in the OAU, and detractors (including Senegal), who favored a government of national unity. "Federal Military Government's Statement on the OAU Meeting," Federal Ministry of Information, News Release no. 48, January 14, 1976. OAU clip file, Nigerian Institute of International Affairs, Lagos.

44. Signed in February 1975, the Lomé Convention was triggered when Britain joined the EEC, as an African response to protective terms of trade. The agreement gave Africa "thirty-seven 'one-way free trade zones' to Europe and duty-free, quota-free access to the EEC markets" (Shepard 1991, 63). Senghor was virtually alone in criticizing Nigeria's leadership in shaping and rallying support for the agreement.

45. "Nigeria to Press for Restructure of the Organisation of African Unity (OAU)," Federal Ministry of Information, Late News Release no. 761, June 24, 1976. Speech by Brigadier Jospeh Garba, Commissioner for External Affairs, attached; delivered at the 27th Ordinary Session of the Organisation of African Unity Council of Ministers— Mauritius, 24th to 25th June, 1976. On Afro-Arab cooperation, he stated, "In the past, there were serious complaints about the patronising attitude of the Arabs towards the African states. Nigeria's position has always been in favour of Afro-Arab co-operation as long as the co-operation is mutually beneficial and Africa is not made to lose its identity."

46. Figueiredo, Antonio de, "The Power of Black Culture," *Guardian* (Lagos), February 4, 1977.

47. Figueiredo, Antonio de, "America Courts Black Africa." *Guardian* (Lagos), February 8, 1977.

48. "New Nations and World Economy," *Sunday Times* (Lagos), March 31, 1976, p. 2.

49. Famojuro, Biodu, "Agreement in Sight: Nigeria Joins Crucial Talks," *Daily Sketch* (Ibadan), March 30, 1977, p. 24.

50. "Nigeria Calls for New World Economic Order," *Daily Sketch* (Ibadan), October, 24, 1977, p. 13.

51. See, for example, July (1987, 20–44) and his discussion of the Second Congress of Black Writers and Artists (Rome), from March 26 to April 1, 1959.

52. Cuban delegate Geraldo Lastra, quoted in Agomo, K., C. Agufelo, and L. Lawal, "FESTAC 77 Opinion Poll," *Daily Star* (Enugu), February 14, 1977, p. 11.

53. Quoted in Lahey [1977?].

54. Quoted in Darnton, John, "Nigeria Evoking a Lost Past for U.S. Black Performers," *New York Times,* January 28, 1977, p. 2.

55. Ume, Bob. "It's Over to the OAU," *Daily Star* (Enugu), February 2, 1977, p. 3; my emphasis.

56. Okpei, Charles, "Lessons We Can Learn," *Nigerian Observer* (Benin City), February 21, 1977, p. 4.

57. Barrett, Lindsay, "Lead: Black World's Challenge," *Afriscope,* January 1977, p. 10.

58. Minutes of the Seventh IFC Meeting, 1 July, 1975, Doc. 109, p.5. CBAAC.

59. Abstract of a Colloquium paper submitted by U. P. Upadhyaya, "Dravidian and Negro-African Ethnic and Linguistic Affinities," quoted in *Festival News,* vol. 1, no. 11, 1976, p. 3.

60. Minutes of the Seventh IFC Meeting, 1 July, 1975, Doc. 109, p. 5. CBAAC.

61. At least as far as I know, the "subjective apparatus" was never built. I found no written evidence or eyewitness account of it, and the exhibit that remains in the National Theatre's Centre for Black and African Art and Culture did not have it.

CHAPTER THREE

1. " . . . It's All Fanfare!" *Sunday Tide* (Port Harcourt), January 16, 1977, p. 16.

2. Interview with Charlie Cobb in *All Things Considered,* National Public Radio, February 7, 1977.

3. See, for example, Gbenoba, Alex, "106 Injured at the Opening of FESTAC," *New Nigerian* (Kaduna), January 17, 1977, p. 15; and " . . . It's All Fanfare!" *Sunday Tide* (Port Harcourt), January 16, 1977, p. 16. See also the Minutes of the Special Meeting of the International Festival Committee, February 9, 1977, doc. XIV/176, p. 3 (iii) (CBAAC): "It should be included that the IFC advised the Security Men to be more lenient with the participants and guests in Nigeria during the Festival."

4. "Opinion," *The Punch* (Ikeja), January 17, 1977, p. 5.

5. "Fela Backs Out of FESTAC Panel," *Daily Times* (Lagos), January 21, 1976, p. 1.

6. Interview. In *FESTAC '77 Souvenir: An Encyclopaedia of Facts about Black Arts and Culture* (Lagos: Pioneer Pub. Co., 1977), pp. 103–6.

7. That Fela took his NPC role seriously is represented by his suggestion that the contents of the FESTAC Colloquium be distributed to students throughout the nation, which the committee positively endorsed. Minutes of the Meeting of the National Participation Committee for FESTAC: Baguda Lake Hotel, Kano 4th–6th July, 1976, p. 8. Cultural Library.

8. *Federal Military Government's Views on the Report of the Tribunal of Inquiry into the Finances of the Second World Black and African Festival of Arts and Culture* (Lagos: Federal Ministry of Information, 1976).

9. NPC Minutes, 4th–6th July, 1977, p. 4. Cultural Library.

10. Traditional chieftaincy was deemed too political by the predominantly francophone and socialist committee members, since chiefs in socialist one-party states were generally seen as conservative and reactionary forces better abolished than preserved.

11. *Kano Conference of Federal and State Officials of Information, Culture and Films, June 28–July 2, 1976,* p. 4. Cultural Library.

12. Ibid., p. 5.

13. Ibid., p. 6.

14. Ibid., p. 34.

15. Ibid., p. 7.

16. *Report and Recommendations of Kano Conference of Federal and State Officials of Information, Culture and Films, June 28–July 2, 1976*, p. 26. Note that this document is different although derived from that cited in notes 11–15. Cultural Library.

17. Ibid., p. 10.

18. *Kano Conference . . .* , p. 19. Cultural Library.

19. During the Kano Conference, a special subcommittee on culture recommended that state governors in Nigeria be encouraged to invite foreign participants at FESTAC to their capitals for performances, and that pavilions be erected to represent each state at Nigeria's national exhibition. That these plans never came to fruition does not detract from their significance in revealing the federal government's perspective on national culture as vertical integration. *Report and Recommendations of Kano Conference of Federal and State Officials of Information, Culture and Films, June 28–July 2, 1976*, pp. 26–27.

20. Thus Dr. Ekpo Eyo, director of the Department of Antiquities, was in charge of the entire Nigerian Exhibition at large.

21. For a compelling analysis of similar levels of articulation from the local perspective of Sulawesi in Indonesia, see Adams 1997.

22. NPS folder 2, p. 504 (handwritten letter). Cultural Library.

23. NPC Minutes, 9th–11th August, 1976, p. 9. Cultural Library.

24. For Nigeria's participation in the Leopold Senghor's First World Festival of Negro Arts, see Nzekwu 1966.

25. NPC Minutes, 9th–11th August, 1976, pp. 12–13. Cultural Library.

26. NPS Crafts Folder, p. 87. Cultural Library.

27. Letter from B.A. Bur, Permanent Secretary, Internal Affairs, Information & Research, Benue State, November 18, 1976. NPS Crafts Folder, p. 69. Cultural Library.

28. *Crafts Committee's Report,* doc. no. NPC.VI/005. Cultural Library.

29. NPS Crafts Folder, p. 112. Cultural Library.

30. This movement to the center is represented by the presence of some cultural officers at NPC meetings, and by letters like the following, addressed to the Ministry of Information in Niger State: "I am directed to inform you that your Chief Cultural Officer, Alhaji M. Saba arrived in Lagos to discuss your State's involvement in the national preparation for the 2nd World Black and African Festival of Arts and Culture. It was not possible to attend to him immediately owing to the preparation for the formal Opening of the National Theatre by his Excellency the Head of State and the subsequent public holiday marking the 16th Independent anniversary. Alhaji Saba has today held fruitful discussions with us and is returning to Minna immediately." October 4, 1976, doc. no. NPS.2/III/106. Cultural Library.

31. *Report by Sub-Committee on Crafts,* A. J. Udo Ema, Chairman, doc. no. NPC.V/003, p.3. Cultural Library.

32. Letter from National Insurance Corporation of Nigeria to Ministry of Internal Affairs and Information, Cultural Division, Jos, December 7, 1976. NPS Crafts Folder, p. 99. Cultural Library.

33. Minutes of the 1st Phase of the Meeting of the Sub-Committee (National Participation Committee) for FESTAC: Exhibition of Traditional Costumes, September 5, 1976,
p. 2. NPS Traditional Costumes Folder, p. 41. Cultural Library.

34. NPC Minutes, 9–10 August, 1976, p. 19. Cultural Library.

35. "Alafin Sues for Co-Operation," *Nigerian Herald* (Ilorin), September 21, 1976,
p. 27.

36. The Oba Oyekan of Lagos was unable to attend, but was represented by the Eletu
Odibo, who spoke for the entire assembly. *Reports Given by the Sub-Committee on Traditional Costume—2nd Phase of the Tour 12th to 28th October, 1972*, p. 1. Doc. no. NPS.VI/
010, NPS Traditional Costumes Folder, p. 90. Cultural Library.

37. Ibid., p. 2.

38. Ibid.

39. "One Nigeria" was a slogan of the federal forces against Biafran secessionism.

40. Letter from Clement Behora, Permanent Secretary, Ministry for Local Government and Social Development, Gongola State, November 25, 1976. NPS Traditional Costumes Folder, p. 107. Cultural Library.

41. NPC for FESTAC Itinerary of the Sub-Committee on Traditional Costumes (3rd
Phase). NPS Traditional Costumes Folder, p. 49. Cultural Library.

42. *Report of the Sub-Committee on Nigerian Traditional Costume Exhibition*, doc.
no. NPS.VII/007, February 27, 1976, p. 3. Cultural Library.

43. See Doortmont 1990; Law 1990; and Peel 1989. Ayorinde's projection of the
Western Region grid upon the north appears in his political lexicon as well, when he re-
ferred to the Emir of Kano as an "Oba" with a "crown." Minutes of the First Phase of the
Meeting of the Sub-Committee (NPC) for FESTAC: Exhibition of Traditional Costumes,
Sept. 5, 1976, p. 4. NPS Traditional Costumes Folder, p. 44. Cultural Library. Emirs are
not obas, and they have turbans, not crowns.

44. Hence the tainted underside of the African art market as cultural theft.

45. "Exhibition for Traditional Costume," letter of July 23, 1976, from A. J. Ayorinde
to the NPS, p. 4. NPS File 9, p. 8. Cultural Library.

46. Ibid., p. 3 (7).

47. See, for example, "Brief Explanatory Notes on Tapes of Plateau State Traditional
Music to Be Played during Exhibition of Traditional Costumes at FESTAC '77," noting
that "music on tape side one (Mandiang [male] flutes, Sombi [horns]) should go along
with exhibits numbering Jos 2–Jos 19, while music side two (xylophone music, Mandiang [female] voices and drums, Moll music [by C. dung], Jarawa-Asharuwa music)
should go along with exhibits numbering Jos 20–Jos 43; both to fit their cultural background." NPS Traditional Costume Folder, p. 13 (or 130; photocopy is smudged). Cultural
Library.

48. NPS Women's Popular Dressing Folder, p. 90. Cultural Library.

49. Women's Popular Dressing Subcommittee Minutes, 15th and 16th November,
1976, p. 3. Folder p. 43. Cultural Library. It is unclear whether the trip and purchases
were made.

50. Amagada, Bisi, "I Covered My Face in Shame," *Sunday Observer* (Benin City),
January 30, 1977.

51. National Participation for FESTAC Sub-Committee on Women's Popular Dressing,
NPS doc. no. VII/006, p. 2. Cultural Library.

52. "Complaints of Inhuman Treatment," letter from M. A. Mustapha for the permanent secretary, Ministry of Information, to the chairman, NPC, January 27, 1977. Women's Modern Dressing Folder, pp. 99–100. Cultural Library.

53. Ibid., p. 100. I have retained the "Nigerian English" used in the original. It is likely that the women recruited from the vicinity of Lagos were prostitutes, given the areas identified and their immediate availability, and that references to this profession were invoked in the insults delivered.

54. Interview with Dr. Garba Ashiwaju, Lagos, October 12, 1993.

55. Interview with Segun Ojewuyi, August 21, 1993.

56. Although these selections were technically made by state commissioners of culture, they selected from write-ups and recommendations provided by federal cultural officers who accompanied them to the villages during the initial performances. Thus the federal government was already involved at the most local levels of review.

57. Interview with Dan Awodoye, September 26, 1993. Needless to say, such sanitizing didn't always work. Awodoye described a famous case of an Olokun priestess who got possessed onstage and foretold the death of an assistant to the Oba of Benin—which then occurred. In a related story, he tells of a cultural officer who became possessed during his choreographic training, and later left to become a traditional priest of the deity.

58. Interview with Dan Awodoye, September 26, 1993.

59. Interview with Dr. Garba Ashiwaju, Lagos, October 12, 1993.

60. The entries were from North Central State, Rivers State, South Eastern State, and Western State. Letter to John Ekwere from F. O. Begho, December, 29, 1974. NPS Dance Folder, p. 188. Cultural Library.

61. It is likely that he was promoting Oyo State in this demand, since it was featured under "ritual" in Nafest. NPC minutes, August 9–11, 1976, p. 8. Cultural Library.

62. NPC minutes, October 7–8, 1976, pp. 14–15. Cultural Library.

63. Letter from H. Ogunde to Major General I. B. M Haruna, August 25, 1976. NPS File 2, Dance Folder, p. 45. Cultural Library.

64. Letter to Festus Adesanoye, Permanent Secretary, Ministry of Defence, from Alayeluwa Jisomosun III, Osamawe of Ondoland, February 26, 1977. NPS Dance Folder, p. 73. Cultural Library. The oba clearly had some kind of connection with the permanent secretary, based on kinship, locality, or ethnicity, which he was mobilizing for results.

65. Interview with Dan Awodoye, September 26, 1993.

66. IFC Minutes Progress Report of Events Division, June 23–25, 1976, doc. 151, pp. 2–3. CBAAC.

67. Interview with Dr. Garba Ashiwaju, Lagos, October 12, 1993.

68. However, their reproduced images were sold in brochures or as souvenirs, in what was a secondary sphere of economic commodification and circulation.

CHAPTER FOUR

1. The idea of transvaluation that I have in mind involves the mediation of economic and cultural oppositions through commodity exchange, whereby sign-values and exchange values, givers and receivers, sellers and buyers, achieve formal commensurability. In this sense, transvaluation resembles Fernando Ortiz's idea of transculturation—developed by Coronil (1995) into a critical method—as applied to sugar and tobacco,

and the broader dialectics of creolization in colonial Cuba. Thus Coronil (ibid., xxx) says of transculturation that it "breathes life into reified categories, bringing into the open concealed exchanges among peoples and releasing histories buried within fixed identities." The relevance of this critical perspective to the history of the Regatta is underscored by the fact that the slave and palm-oil trade in the Niger Delta was part and parcel of the black Atlantic economy that included Cuba (and the "West Indies") as well (see also Palmié 2002). Many of the "creole" themes in this chapter are also beautifully illustrated and developed further in Anderson and Peek (2002), an extraordinary book, with invaluable contributions, accompanying what was an extraordinary exhibition.

2. "Programme, National Traditional Boat Regatta, 25–6 January, 1977." 2nd World Black and African Festival of Arts and Culture, p. 5. Cultural Library.

3. "Seating Programme for Traditional Regatta," Major General I. B. M. Haruna, Federal Commissioner for Information and Chairman, National Participation Committee for FESTAC, to His Excellency, Head of Federal Military Government, Lt. Gen. Olusegun Obasanjo, January 19, 1977. NPS Regatta file, pp. 40–41. Cultural Library.

4. "Preliminary Regatta Sailing Programme," Chief H. J. R. Dappa-Biriye, Chairman, National Council for Arts and Culture, November 21, 1976. NPS Regatta file, p. 87. Cultural Library.

5. Benson, Precious, "FESTAC Viewing," *The Punch* (Ikeja), January 31, 1977, p. 5.

6. These characterizations are taken from Odafe, James, "Regatta Wins Ovation at FESTAC," *Nigerian Observer* (Benin City), January 26, 1977; "It's All Shipshape at the Regatta," *Daily Times* (Lagos), January 27, 1977, pp. 10–11; and Benson, Precious, "FESTAC Viewing," *The Punch* (Ikeja), January 31, 1977, p. 5.

7. The Cross River State contingent never showed up, for economic reasons that will warrant brief discussion toward the end of this chapter.

8. "Preliminary Regatta Sailing Programme," Chief H. J. R. Dappa-Biriye, Chairman, National Council for Arts and Culture, November 21, 1976. NPS Regatta file, p. 86; his emphasis. Cultural Library.

9. Jones (1963, 33–35) discusses this passage from the *Esmeraldo* in depth, speculating that the "village" might refer to Iyankpo instead of Bonny.

10. Jones (1963, 35) identifies these necklaces as "torques made from copper imported from Europe."

11. First published in Dutch in 1676, then popularized in a French edition of 1686. See Jones 1963, 36n8.

12. This is not to suggest that war prisoners were sold directly to the European slavers, since many were bought from inland markets and then resold to the European traders.

13. See also Hair, Jones, and Law 1992, 687–90 for Barbot's account of breaking trade with the "King of Bandy" (Bonny) in 1699, including a complex series of exchanges and negotiations over the price of slaves and the king's adoption of European clothes. See especially note 48 on the genealogy of the Pepple dynasty, a name most likely taken from an English captain, Nicholas Pepperell, who traded in Bonny in 1663 and 1679.

14. Supportive evidence comes from Oldfield (1837, 282), who provided bunting to Niger chiefs to identify them as privileged trading partners: "In order to secure the friendship of the traders, who dealt with me, I presented four or five of the most power-

ful (principally Abboka's sons) with pennants of different coloured bunting, about two yards long, for their canoes, and by this means they were easily distinguishable."

15. At least some of the rum would presumably be used to placate the spirit of the canoe: As Talbot (1932, 270) reports, "Kalabari chiefs used to consult with the canoe spirit before setting forth on any adventure. For an ordinary dug-out, on such occasions, a chicken was sufficient sacrifice, but for a war canoe nothing less than a bottle of rum must be poured over the bow before starting."

16. Thus James Barbot wrote in his 1699 *Abstract of Rio Real:* "Every time their small fleet of canoes goes up for slaves, and when they return, they blow their horns or trumpets for joy; and the king never fails . . . to pay his devotions to his idols, for their good success, and a short voyage." Quoted in Jones 1963, 41; his translation.

17. It is tempting to relate this ritual turning to the "U-turn" of the FESTAC canoes in Five Cowrie Creek, but such mythic correspondences are difficult to substantiate.

18. I would not be surprised if "Adumu" is the Adam of Genesis, since Christian and Muslim figures work their way into all sorts of myth-ritual complexes in West Africa.

19. I thus propose that the animated debate between Sahlins (1995) and Obeyesekere (1992) regarding the human/divine status of Captain Cook in Hawaii could be dialectically resolved as a case of "identity-in-difference," whereby "first-encounter" Europeans were both human and divine.

20. Allen and Thomson (1848, 1:18) referred to their capture as "a Providential circumstance; since, if they had passed unmolested, they might have selected a channel more promising in appearance than the Rio Nun; which would have led them by an unfrequented outlet, to the wide Atlantic Ocean; where they must inevitably have been lost, and their glorious achievement would have perished with them." It is interesting to compare this providential enslavement with that of Samuel Crowther (Apter 1992, 195–98).

21. For an account of an unusual American Niger expedition organized by the Providence Exploring and Trading Company of Rhode Island—an unqualified disaster in terms of human and financial loss—see Brooks and Talbot 1975.

22. The Benue was then called Tshadda or Chadda.

23. As Pietz (1988) has so clearly demonstrated in his genealogy of fetishism, commercial relations between Europeans and Africans on the coast gave rise to an ideological opposition between reason and faith on the one hand, as manifest in the contract of legitimate commerce, versus African ignorance and superstition on the other, as manifest in the fetishism of debased trade.

24. Note Mockler-Ferryman 1892, app. A, by Mr. John, "A Native's History of Lokoja" (282–85): "Dr. Baikie may be considered the founder of Lokoja, as well as the first English consul. After his death several naval and civil officers were appointed to act for a longer or shorter period, including the following—Lieutenant Bouchier, R.N., T.V. Robins, Paymaster Maxwell, W. Fell, and J. Edwards. The first real consul appointed by the English Government was, however, Lyons M'Leod, ex-consul for Mozambique, and W. Fell his vice-consul" (283).

25. Letter to the Foreign Office, September 1861, quoted in Marwick 1965, 13.

26. The constabulary was equipped with Martini rifles, Gatling guns, mountain guns, and sword bayonets (Mockler-Ferryman 1892, 29–30).

27. Is it historical irony or an overdetermining logic which placed this campaign at

the site—the so-called "Kirree market"—where the Landers were seized nearly sixty years earlier?

28. Kirk, Sir John, "Report on the Disturbances at Brass." Presented to both Houses of Parliament by Command of Her Majesty, March 1896. Africa, No. 3. London: Her Majesty's Stationery Office. Rhodes House Library, 600.17 s. 1/1896(3), Oxford University.

29. As a result of the Company prohibition, the chiefs were unable to bury their king, blocking the installation of his successor. The case shows how in addition to its naked economic exploitation, the Niger Company disrupted local political relations and procedures.

30. The final regatta with the Obi's then elderly sons provides tragic closure to the cycle of gifts and countergifts first set into motion by the seizure of Lander in "Kirree." After their arrival in state canoes "with bunting of every colour," the chiefs fought over gifts distributed by the Commissioner, providing an "amusing sight" which had to be controlled by the constabulary. Involved in the fray, the Obi's sons are described as "a ragged-looking pair" (Mockler-Ferryman 1892, 234).

31. Johnston (1888, 753) reports that in 1888, Old Calabar had "150 British subjects who are foreigners, of whom over fifty are whites."

32. Falk, Edward Morris, "Report on Native customs in Aba Division . . . 1920." In his Papers as D.O., Nigeria, 1910–33. Box. 1, p. 56. MSS. Afr. s., Rhodes House Library, Oxford University.

33. See Jones 1963, 127–32; Dike 1956, 182–202; Baker 1996, 76–113.

34. See Grier, S. M., *Report on the Eastern Provinces by the Secretary for Native Affairs.* Lagos: Government Printer. Rhodes House Library, 723.12 2. 43(12), Oxford University; Palmer, H. R., "Report of a tour in the Southern Provinces in 1914," Rhodes House Library, MSS Lugard 58/7, Oxford University; Lethem, G. J., "Impressions of a Tour in the Eastern Provinces," written June 1928. Rhodes House Library, MSS Brit Empire s 276, G. J. Lethem 6/8, Oxford University.

35. Logan, Robert, "Souvenir of the Coronation Celebrations at Minna on the 12th of May, 1937." From Papers as D.O., Nigeria, 1928–1937, Rhodes House Library, MSS Afr. s. 1033, Oxford University.

36. "Coronation Celebrations, 1953," Rhodes House Library, Barwick Box 1, file 1, MSS Afr. S, Oxford University. The chiefs and their captains were as follows:

Name of Chief	Name of Canoe Captain
Chief Obanikoro	Lawal
Chief Eletu-Odibo	S.S. Rahman
Chief Onilegbale	Lamidi
Chief Olorogun	Lati Disu
Chiefs Onitolo and Modile	Abudy Rahim
Chief Asajon	M. Y. Oduntan
Chief Aromire	Langus
Chief Olumegbon and Omitane	Saaka Alawo

37. These were (1) Aponron Dance (Ladies), Yoruba dancers and drummers; (2) Togo Society Tugba Dance, mixed dancing; (3) Warri Ladies Club, Itsekiri dancers and drummers; (4) Aponron Dance (Men), Yoruba dancers and drummers; (5) Hausa Dance (Ladies), Northern Nigerian dancers and players; (6) Fanti Dance, Gold Coast dancers

and drummers; (7) Atilogu Dance (Men), dancers and drummers of the Eziagu Clan in the Onitsha Province; and (8) Agere Dance, Yoruba dancers, drummers, and stilt walkers. Organized by Mr. Ayodele Williams and assisted by Dr. C. C. Adeniyi-Jones. "Coronation Celebrations, 1953," Rhodes House Library, Barwick Box 1, file 1, Mss Afr. S. 2127, Oxford University.

38. Anthony Kirk-Greene, personal communication, May 2000.

39. For a similar ancestral figure from Brass (Nembe Ijo), belonging to King Ockiya and influenced "by the figureheads of European ships," see Alagoa 2002, 67, fig. 2.1.

40. See Jones 1984, 114 on commissioned imports.

41. For two fascinating discussions of "snag-busting," in which the removal of obstacles from riverine waterways expands and facilitates the regional flow of value, see Sinclair n.d. and Trinick 1939.

CHAPTER FIVE

1. Pemberton (1994) provides a brilliant historical and ethnographic analysis of cultural objectification as it occurred under Dutch colonialism and became manifest in routine appeals to tradition in a number of marked and everyday practices. He is concerned "less with official policies of the Indonesian Department of Education and Culture than with the Javanese culture that this department would find most recognizable as an object for preservationist attention" (ibid., 10). My interest is to bring together both levels of "culture" in critical perspective.

2. "FESTAC's Triumphant End," West Africa no. 3110, February 14, 1977, p. 311.

3. The former Northern Region was reorganized into six and later ten states. The ten states represented at the FESTAC Durbar were Borno, Sokoto, Kano, Kaduna, Gongola, Bauchi, Plateau, Benue, Niger, and Kwara.

4. Estimates varied from 200,000, to 100,000 in the Nigerian press, while the New York Times (Darnton 1977) offered the more conservative figure of 40,000.

5. The African leaders were Presidents Ahmadu Ahidjo of Cameroon, Aghostino Neto of Angola, Mouktar Ould Daddah of Mauritania, Seyni Kountche of Niger, Mobutu Sese Seko of Zaire, Gnassingbé Eyadema of Togo, and Sangoule Lamizana of (then) Upper Volta.

6. "Durbar Recaptures Our Identity." Nigerian Chronicle (Calabar), February 10, 1977, p. 15.

7. Quoted in "FESTAC's Triumphant End," West Africa no. 3110, February 14, 1977, p. 3111.

8. The passage reads, "And hold in readiness against them all your strength, and of horses tether as many as you can, that the enemies of God and your enemies may be put in fear" (8:62).

9. See Bohannan 1952 for the clearest statement of how politics structures genealogical reckoning.

10. Quoted from the dust jacket of the first edition. We should note that C. K. Meek, the Anthropological Officer of the Administrative Service in Nigeria, placed the Jukun "tribe" within another dubious genealogy of Hamites coming from Egypt. I thank Richard Fardon for this information (personal communication).

11. See also Kramer 1993. For an Indian parallel to this ironic inversion, whereby an

indigenous native symbol derives from a colonial source, see Cohn's treatment of the Sikh turban (Cohn 1989, 305).

12. See also Madauchi 1968, 38–39.

13. Although Nadel made no specific mention of a "cavalry charge" as such, we can see a subordinate chief galloping with his retinue, with one footman and one rider brandishing a sword and a lance as they approach Nadel's camera, in the lower plate opposite p. 144.

14. Not all gifts were political. Distinguishing collective gifts such as a brass tray sent by the brass smiths from personal gifts sent by individuals, Nadel (1942, 273–74) showed how the former marked occupational status while the latter was an investment to attract the king's custom.

15. As Cohn (1983, 169) explains, "In durbars there were well-established rules for the relative placement of people and objects. The spatial order of a durbar fixed, created and represented relationships with the ruler."

16. In 1948, for example, the Emir Lamido of Yola (Adamawa) was still installed with "the Lugard Sword" as his staff of office in an elaborate durbar, replete with "jinjina" salute (Duckworth 1948, 181–293).

17. For a marvelous elaboration of this colonial philosophy, see Temple ([1918] 1968), particularly chapter 2, "On the Relations between Dominant and Dependent Races." See also Lugard 1965, 198: "The Fulani of Northern Nigeria are, as I have said, more capable of rule than the indigenous races, but in proportion as we consider them an alien race, we are denying self-government to the people over whom they rule, and supporting an alien caste—albeit closer and more akin to the native races than a European can be"; and again (ibid., 210): "Their traditions of rule, their monotheistic religion, and their intelligence enable them to appreciate more readily than the Negro population the wider objects of British policy."

18. As F. D. Lugard (1902, 84) wrote in the early days of the Protectorate, "in my view the tradition of British rule has ever been to arrest disintegration, to retain and build up again what is best in the social and political organisation of the conquered dynasties, and to develop on the lines of its own individuality each separate race of which our great Empire consists. That has been our policy in India; and Northern Nigeria, though but a third the size, and many centuries behind the great Eastern dependency, still presents to my imagination many parallel conditions. I believe myself that the future of the virile races of this Protectorate lies largely in the regeneration of the Fulani."

19. Although Lugard served as High Commissioner of the Protectorate of Northern Nigeria from 1900 to 1905, a title which changed to Governor in 1907, it is not clear that he was the man Kisch referred to simply as "H.E." (His Excellency) in this account. According to *Nigeria Handbook 1924* (1924, 221), Sir E. P. C. Girouard was Governor, while Sir W. Wallace served as Acting Governor, in 1908. It is possible that either of these men, rather than Lugard himself, received the Sarikin in Kisch's photograph.

20. This was what Haruna undoubtedly referred to as the "first" colonial durbar in Nigeria, in his speech quoted above. For a discussion of visual fields and the dialectics of recognition in this 1913 durbar, see Apter 2002, 573–76.

21. The Acting Governor at the time was C. L. Temple.

22. In this respect, the durbar was a classic ritual of rebellion (Gluckman 1954).

23. Six photographs of this durbar taken by William C. Fitz-Henry, chief architect and engineer of the Baro-Kano Railway, are reproduced in Apter 2002, 570–82, figs. 10–15. The original photo album is in the Rhodes House Library, Oxford University, Ms. Afr. S. 369.

24. For example, the Sultan of Sokoto became the Patron of the Northern People's Congress in 1954.

25. Thus in a Nigerian Legislative Council session of 1948, the Mallam and future Prime Minister Abubakar Tafawa Balewa went on record as saying, "The Southern tribes who are now pouring into the North in ever increasing numbers, and are more or less domiciled here do not mix with the Northern People . . . and we in the North look upon them as invaders." Quoted in Coleman 1958, 361.

26. See the unpaginated section of Adock [1925?] called "Nigeria, and Crossing the Line."

27. The riots were sparked by the proposed Action Group tour headed by Akintola. See the *Report on the Kano Disturbances, 16th, 17th, 18th, and 19th, May 1953* (Northern Regional Government: Government Printer, Nigeria, 1953). Many northern newspaper editorials blamed the riots on resident southerners, while even the *Report* cites fundamental cultural differences between northerners and southerners as a general cause.

28. Actually, there were only eight police bands from Sokoto, Bornu, Gwandu, Kano, Bauchi, Katsina, Ilorin, and Katagum native authorities.

29. John Smith (1968, 105), an assistant district officer and provincial marshal for the royal durbar, described how nearly the *jafi* charges led to a fight between Bornu horsemen and pagan Piti "at the feet of the Queen and notables." Sitting with the royal couple on the dais, Sir Bryan Sharwood Smith (1969, 322–23), Governor of the Northern Region, was also clearly worried during this *jafi* salute: "But as the first waves of horsemen came thundering toward us . . . spears aloft to draw up in a cloud of dust and spatter of stones, I glanced a little anxiously at the Queen. This was a little more realistic than had been planned."

30. *Queen's Tour of Nigeria,* Commemorative Pamphlet, p. 13.

31. One of the major goals of Ironsi's coup of 1966 was to break up the regions and consolidate the central military government, as proposed by his Unification Decree of May 1966, to which the northerners were bitterly opposed (Joseph 1987, 77).

32. "We Should Participate," *Washington Star,* December 26, 1976.

33. Personal communication, interview May 19, 1993, Quadrangle Club, University of Chicago.

34. The state contingents proceeded in the following order: Bauchi, Borno, Gongola, Kaduna, Kano, Kwara, Niger, Plateau, and Sokoto, with dancers representing Benue State. The Tor Tiv was supposed to represent Benue, but it is not clear that he arrived.

35. The rank order was (1) Sultan of Sokoto, (2) Shehu of Borno, (3) Emir of Kano, (4) Emir of Katsina, (5) Lamido of Adamawa, (6) Emir of Bauchi, (7) Etsu of Nupe, (8) Emir of Ilorin, (9) Tor Tiv, (10) Chief of Jos. From "Proposed Program for the Durbar at Kaduna, 8th February, 1977," NPS folder 19, vol. 2, p. 40. Cultural Library.

36. Minutes of Meeting of Emirs and Chiefs in Borno State Held in the Council of Chambers of the Borno Local Authority, NPS folder 19, vol. 2, p. 65. Cultural Library.

37. Official allocations for the durbar event and its commemorative hotel totaled nearly 20 million naira, which at the time equaled $32 million US. From NPS folder 19, EC 75. Cultural Library.

38. For a vivid description of the 1913 durbar in Kano, taken from Lugard's own dispatch to London, see Kirk-Greene 1959, 19. For descriptive fragments of independence durbars held in honor of Princess Alexandra in 1960, see "The Princess and the Premier," *West Africa* no. 2264, October 22, 1960, p. 1187.

39. Richard Rathbone (personal communication) has suggested that the colonial durbars of India and Nigeria played into the contemporaneous remaking of the British monarchy as well, adding an extremely important dimension of domestic politics and iconography at the metropole which I have not addressed.

40. For a variety of perspectives on the so-called Kaduna Mafia, see Takaya and Tyoden 1987.

41. For a useful background to Nigeria's state and national councils of art and culture, and the festivals that they organized, see Fasuyi 1973.

42. See for example Nkrumah 1970; Ngugi 1986; Senghor 1964.

43. See Austen 1992 for an interesting francophone African variation on this theme, in which the Ngondo Assembly among the Duala of Cameroon, an institution largely "invented" under colonialism, was commemorated as a venerable precolonial festival, and even incorporated aspects of "canoe races held on colonial and national holidays" (p. 305).

CHAPTER SIX

1. Ezeani, C. O., "FESTAC? Never Again in Our Lives," *Daily Times* (Lagos), February 24, 1977, p. 13.

2. "Awolowo Condemns FESTAC," *New Nigerian* (Kaduna), December 9, 1975, p. 20. See also Ola Rotimi's response, "I Beg to Disagree Sir," *Sunday Times* (Lagos), December 21, 1975, p. 11.

3. "The Second Black Re-Union," *Nigerian Chronicle* (Calabar), January 10, 1977, p. 3.

4. See, for example, "FESTAC Scandal Probe," *Daily Sketch* (Ibadan), May 25, 1977, p. 3.

5. Letter from Fubara David-West of *Nigerian Tide* to the Commissioner, Federal Ministry of Information, March 15, 1978. NPS folder 2, p. 255. Cultural Library. See also "Whitewash Job," *New Nigerian* (Kaduna), July 1, 1978 (editorial); and "Tell It to the Marines," *Nigerian Chronicle* (Calabar), July 7, 1978, p. 3.

6. *Federal Military Government's Views on the Report of the Tribunal of Inquiry into the Finances of the Second World Black and African Festival of Arts and Culture* (Lagos: Federal Ministry of Information, 1976), p.10.

7. "The Cost of FESTAC," *Afriscope*, January 1977, p. 41.

8. "Probing FESTAC," *Nigerian Tribune* (Ibadan), pp. 1, 13.

9. *Federal Military Government's Views . . .* , p. 16. The offending companies were Worldwide General Development Corporation (Nig.) Ltd., Warner and Warner International Associates (Nig.) Ltd., ARK Urban System, Inc., Condotte-Garboli & Nigtog (Nig.) Ltd., Daas Piling & Construction Co., Ltd., and Mesteron (Nig.) Ltd.

10. Ibid., p. 15.

11. Bonuola, Lade, "45 FESTAC Guides Stranded in France?" *Sunday Times* (Lagos), October 12, 1975, p. 20.

12. "Quit Order Notice on FESTAC Artistes," *The Punch* (Ikeja), February 24, 1977, p. 3.

13. The figure comes from IFC box 8, no. 137 (CBAAC), "Finance," based on an internal audit completed July 31, 1975. The auditor qualified the dollar equivalent as low, based on a 1.51 rate of exchange that was really 1.60 to the naira.

14. "The Cost of FESTAC," p. 40.

15. The IFC minutes reveal that officers on pay-grade levels G.S. 3 to G.S. 5 were entitled to car loans of 2,400 naira, and officers on P.1 to P.6 were entitled to loans of 4,800 naira. IFC box 8, no. 136, app. A. CBAAC.

16. "120 FESTAC Cars Stolen—Police Smash Syndicate," *Nigerian Observer* (Benin City), January 24, 1977, p. 1; "39 FESTAC Cars Feared Stolen," *New Nigerian* (Kadum), January 21, 1977.

17. The officials were Mr. Mallam Adamu Cirona, former Governor of the Central Bank, and Dr. Sola, Saraki, a member of the Constituent Assembly. See "FESTAC Bus Scandal," *Nigerian Herald* (Ilorin), May 26, 1977, p.5; "FESTAC Scandal Probe," *Daily Sketch* (Ibadan), May 25, 1977, p. 3; "FESTAC Probe," *Nigerian Standard* (Jos), May 27, 1977, p. 3; "Inconclusive Probe," *Daily Sketch* (Ibadan), November 30, 1977, p. 3.

18. In the end, Mr. Ciroma was merely assessed for tax on an estimated 50,000 naira of undeclared income.

19. The notion of Nigerian nervousness echoes Lutz (1991), who studied anxieties of turn of the (nineteenth) century America and their sociocultural conditions.

20. Quotations in this and the next two paragraphs were taken from IFC box 8, no. 137, "Finance" (CBAAC), based on an internal audit completed July 31, 1975.

21. Three of the restaurants were purchased from a subsidiary of Grand Metropolitan Group in England at a cost of 2.5 million pounds sterling. The entire order was airlifted to Lagos over a three-week period to meet deadlines. "Nigeria Contract for Grand Met. Subsidiary," *The Daily Telegraph* (London), October 11, 1976.

22. "Hundreds Hungry in the Midst of Plenty," *Daily Times* (Lagos), January 17, 1977, p.10.

23. *FESTAC '77* (London: African Journal and the International Festival Committee, 1977), p. 152.

24. IFC box 9, no. 159, p.2. CBAAC.

25. Oriere, Oje, "The Long and Winding Road to the Festival," *Daily Times* (Lagos), January 15, 1977, p. 26. That BON journalists and personnel were given woefully inadequate resources by the state is reported in "BON: Neglected and Miserable," *Daily Times* (Lagos), March 12, 1977, p. 13. The remarkable success of its FESTAC coverage is illustrated by its impressive list of 537 inventoried video recordings (and 390 audio recordings) at the Centre for Black and African Arts and Culture.

26. "No Private Filming: FESTAC Details Outlined," *Nigerian Herald* (Ilorin), January 14, 1977, p. 1.

27. To control rights of mechanical reproduction, IFC rules for FESTAC events stipulated that "the participating countries/communities shall have the right to film, tape-record and photograph only their own Events and not those of any other country. For the

coverage of the shows of other countries/communities, all rights are exclusively reserved by the International Festival Committee." *Festival News,* vol. 1, no. 7 April/May 1976, p. 7.

28. The FESTAC Emblem Decree of August 3, 1976, stipulated a fine of 1,000 naira or two years' imprisonment for offenders and their accomplices using the emblem for private purposes, without granted permission. "Decree on FESTAC Emblem," Federal Ministry of Information, Late News Release no. 996, August 17, 1976. Second World Black and African Festival of Arts and Culture clip file, Nigerian Institute of International Affairs, Lagos.

29. Letter from F. Bola Giwa for Brigadier Chief of Staff to the Commissioner, Federal Ministry of Information, May 12, 1978. NPS file p. 86. Cultural Library.

30. Ogun, Sam, "Memories of FESTAC," *Daily Express* (Lagos), January 13, 1978, p. 10.

31. Efeyini, Sunny, "Guy Who Designed FESTAC Hankies," *The Punch* (Ikeja), January 17, 1977, p. 11.

32. Ogun, "Memories of FESTAC."

33. Coronil (1997, 178) has noted how Venezuela under Pérez Jiménez promoted "a fetishistic vision of modernity" in its national development projects, which "had in common the quality of spectacular displays."

34. See Watts (1991), who first saw the relevance of Bataille, and used his phrase "visions of excess," to characterize the paradoxes of Nigerian oil prosperity.

35. "SMC Decisions on the Reports of Cement and FESTAC Tribunals," Federal Ministry of Information, News Release no. 583, Lagos, May 13, 1976. Second World Black and African Festival of Arts and Culture clip file, Nigerian Institute of International Affairs, Lagos.

36. "Nigeria's Modern Pirates," *West Africa,* no. 3106, January 17, 1977, p. 95.

37. This "tour" refers to Benjamin's "One-Way Street: A Tour of German Inflation," reprinted in Benjamin 1996.

38. Obasanjo, Olusegun, Opening Remarks at the Lagos International Trade Fair, November 27, 1977. In Oyediran 1977, 221–23.

39. See Coronil 1997, 190–99 for an earlier example of oil-funded steel production in Venezuela, which in the end remained productive despite kickbacks and inflated costs.

CHAPTER SEVEN

1. See, for example, Buchi Emecheta's *Naira Power* (1982), a novel that captures the spirit of the era. For a discussion of this and other novels and plays dealing with the dubious and deadly powers of oil wealth, see Watts 1994, 425–27.

2. In keeping with our semantic perspective, we could say that this truth-functional "meaning" of the naira denotes its "extension" rather than its "intension," its reference in dollars and commodities rather than its "sense" as constituted by a formal code.

3. See, for example, Shiner, Cindy, "Scamming Gullible Americans in a Well-Oiled Industry in Nigeria," *Washington Post,* August 30, 1994, p. A15; and Schiller, Bill, "Crooks and Con Men Stain a National Image," *Toronto Star,* May 10, 1992, p. F3.

4. "Singapore Weary of Nigerian Businessmen," *Daily Times* (Lagos), September 5, 1991.

5. Shiner, "Scamming Gullible Americans in a Well-Oiled Industry in Nigeria," p. A15.

6. "The Great Nigerian Scam," *The Economist* (London), January 7, 1995, p. 36. Since the late 1990s, these "419" letters have proliferated on the Internet, focusing on the illicit fortunes of deposed dictators like Sani Abacha and others (like Mobutu Sese Seko) beyond Nigeria. Curiously, their figures of wealth have shifted from oil barrels and revenues to material forms of bullion buried in safe boxes, and thus taken out of circulation.

7. "Much Ado About 419," *Daily Times* (Lagos), February 27, 1992, p. 18.

8. Lohr, Steve, "Nigerian Scam Lures Companies," *New York Times*, May 21, 1992, p. D1.

9. Shiner, "Scamming Gullible Americans in a Well-Oiled Industry in Nigeria."

10. See Dunkel, Tom, "Charlie's Hustle," *Washington Post*, February 27, 1994, p. F1.

11. "Beware of Scam, Hotel Owner Says," *Gazette* (Montreal), February 20, 1994, p. A6.

12. McGreal, Chris, "Victims Caught in a Web of Corruption," *Guardian*, September 4, 1993 (Foreign Page), p. 11.

13. "The Great Nigerian Scam," p. 36.

14. For a marvelous window into the world of this first elite, see Bola Ige's autobiographical *Kaduna Boy* (1991).

15. "Do Something about Certificate Racketeering," *Nigerian Observer* (Benin City), January 11, 1976, p. 3.

16. Haliechuk, Rick, "Nigeria Bank Scam Dupes Broker," *Toronto Star*, December 31, 1994, p. A1.

17. Dunkel, "Charlie's Hustle," p. F1.

18. For this story, see McCreal, "Victims Caught in a Web of Corruption."

19. See Lohr, "Nigerian Scam Lures Companies."

20. Faul, Michelle, "Dangerous Fraud in Nigeria," *Chicago Tribune*, June 1, 1992, p. 8.

21. Schiller, "Crooks and Con Men Stain a National Image," p. F3.

22. Ibid.

23. For the BCCI scandal, see Truell and Gurwin 1992; Beaty and Gwynne 1993; for the Kaduna Mafia, see Takaya and Tyoden 1987.

24. Decree no. 25 of 1987 banned all former and current public officeholders from campaigning in party politics.

25. For a general definition of governmentality, see Foucault 1991; for discussion of colonial governmentality, see Thomas 1994, 105–42 and D. Scott 1995; also Bayart 1993, 249, for its relevance to the postcolonial state in Africa.

26. Reuter Library Report, December 11, 1987, Friday AM cycle.

27. These were All Nigeria People's Party (ANPP), Ideal People's Party (IPP), Liberal Convention (LC), National Unity Party (NUP), Nigerian Labour Party (NLP), Nigerian National Congress (NNC), Nigerian People's Welfare Party (NPWP), Patriotic Nigerian Party (PNP), People's Front of Nigeria (PFN), People's Patriotic Party (PPP), People's Solidarity Party (PSP), Republican Party of Nigeria (RPN), and United Nigeria Democratic Party (UNDP); from Oyediran and Agbaje 1991, 225.

28. From National Electoral Commission, *Report and Recommendations on Party Formation* (Lagos, 1989), pp. 8–9; quoted in Oyediran and Agbaje 1991, 225.

29. Reuters, December 7, 1989, BC cycle, "Nigerian Elections Put Back to End 1990," Money Report. Energy News.

30. Noble, Kenneth, "Cynicism Clouds Nigerian Election," *New York Times,* November 8, 1990, p. A17.

31. Ibid.

32. Noble, Kenneth, "Nigeria Ends Ban for Ex-Officials," *New York Times,* December 20, 1991, p. A7.

33. Of 89 senatorial seats, 52 went SDP and 37 NRC; of 589 seats in the House, 314 went SDP, 275 went NRC. Two outstanding Senate and four outstanding House seats were held in later by-elections. "Nigerian Elections SDP Wins Majorities in Senate and House of Representatives," British Broadcasting Corporation, Summary of World Broadcasts, July 13, 1992. WEST AFRICA; ME/1431/B/1.

34. Maier, Karl, "Nigerians Contemplate the Price of Democracy," *The Independent,* August 1, 1992, p. 11.

35. Babalola, Kole, "Nigeria: Voting System Needed 'Nigerian-Factor' Proof," Inter Press Service, December 21, 1992 (electronic bulletin).

36. Tensions ran so high during these days of suspense that when the director of United States Information Service-Lagos, Michael O'Brien, declared any further postponement of the elections to be "unacceptable to the United States government," he was expelled from the country for his "blatant interference" with Nigeria's internal affairs. "Nigerian Election Still Set for Today," *San Diego Tribune,* June 12, 1993, p. A13.

37. The constitution stipulated that the winning candidate needed one-third of the vote in at least 20 of the 30 states. Sources for voting figures are from "Complaint Delays Release of Vote Results," Agence France Press, June 15, 1993; and Faul, Michelle, "Candidate Declares Victory in Nigerian Election," Associated Press, June 18, 1993, Friday, AM Cycle.

38. At this time, noted singer and critic Gbenga Adewusi produced an underground recording in the Yoruba Oro chanting mode that circulated widely in shops and on the airwaves. The artist, who was jailed and released, is credited with bringing IBB down with the song "Babangida Must Go!" and for influencing events with the power of his curse.

39. Cited in "Nigeria Election Scam," *Newsday,* July 17, 1993, Nassau and Suffolk Edition, p. 8.

40. It would be interesting to see if the old method of covering one's misappropriation—by burning down the government buildings where the records were kept— actually decreased after the "reforms."

41. Videotaped interview with Mama Juwe, Ayede Ekiti, September 8, 1990.

42. This popular revision of an official appellation or acronym provides an example of what Mbembe (1992, 8), no doubt following de Certeau (1988, 168), calls the "poaching" of meanings, as when Cameroonians renamed the Rassemblement Démocratique du Peuple Camerounais (RDPC) *redépécer,* as a gloss for "Cut it up and dole it out!" Nigerians sometimes jokingly refer to NEPA, the National Electric Power Authority, as Never Expect Power Again because of its long and frequent power failures.

43. Interview with Bisi A., November 29, 1993, in Ibadan.

44. I owe this information to a telephone conversation with Craig Spraggins of the U.S. Secret Service, who specializes in uncovering "419" operations in Nigeria.

45. See Barber 1982; Bastian 1991; and Matory 1994, 123–24 for discussions of moneymaking magic. When Major General Muhammadu Buhari changed the currency notes after his 1983 coup (in an effort to regulate the money supply and to determine the amount that the Shagari government printed to buy votes), a rash of kidnappings was reported because—like everybody else—rich wizards (*oso*) using money magic also needed new bills.

46. J. Haynes (1994, 3) describes a scene in Baba Sala's first film, *Orun Mooru/ Heaven Is Hot* (1982), in which Baba Sala is defrauded by a herbalist who "tricks him into believing he could magically fill oil drums with money, casting the magic of oil wealth in the idiom of 'traditional' money magic."

47. As part of the Structural Adjustment Program, the Central Bank abolished all controls on interest rates on July 31, 1987, which pushed prime lending rates up to more than 40% in some banks (Anyanwu 1992, 13).

48. Midas Merchant Bank Ltd., advertised in *Financial Post* 5, no. 22, June 19, 1993, p. 4.

49. I thank Robin Derby for this firsthand observation.

CHAPTER EIGHT

1. This chapter does not offer an in-depth account of the Ogoni movement or Delta oil politics, but merely frames Saro-Wiwa's struggle within a broader crisis of Nigerian citizenship and civil society. For a discussion of how access to Shell transformed relations between Ogoni chiefs and youth groups, and how Ogoni became "indigenous," see Watts 1997, 2003, 18–24. See also his bibliographies, which include references to Ikein 1990, Ikelegbe 2001, Obi 2001, Okonta 2002, and Osaghae 1995. See also Okonta and Douglas 2001.

2. For a masterful synthesis of this political and social history, see Coleman 1958.

3. For an extensive discussion of the history and politics of derivation and "fiscal federalism" in Nigeria, see Ikein and Briggs-Anigboh 1998. See also Adebayo 1993.

4. For a sophisticated discussion of prebendalism in the Second Republic, see Joseph 1987.

5. Nigeria reorganized its regions into 12 states in 1967, expanding to 19 states in 1969, 21 in 1987, and 30 in 1991 (Gundu 1991, 9). The proliferation of states involves complex agendas, including a more-"equitable" distribution of federal resources, the breaking up of entrenched political "mafias," and the buying off of disaffected factions by expanding the spread of administrative spoils.

6. This story is recounted and analyzed in Apter 1998, 84–86.

7. Soyinka (1996, 151–52) argues convincingly that the Ogoni elders were murdered by Abacha's hired hands.

8. Watts (1996) makes the case that the dislocations of oil capitalism in the north provoked reactions that were framed within dissident Islamic movements, such as Maitatsine. See also Watts 2003.

9. It is interesting how the European trade for Delta oil was based on a credit system called "trust," whereby English goods were trusted to Delta middlemen for periods from six months up to two years (Dike 1956, 102–4) in exchange for palm oil, establishing a normative contrast with the violation of trust endemic to the petroleum economy. On a

more abstract and theoretical note, Pietz (1993, 146), following Marx, reminds us that "[w]hen a given type of useful thing comes to function as a general-equivalent exchange object in trade activities, it comes to be recognized as embodying a new quality: that of a general form, the very medium of exchange (money)." It is possible that palm oil as a general equivalent of exchange came to signify a general form of trust and value associated with that exchange, almost as the moral substance of good economic faith.

10. The naturalization of nationhood by the political economy of oil in Venezuela is a major theme in Coronil (1997), one that he further relates to enclave economies more generally.

CONCLUSION

1. Watts (2003, 24–26) argues that the allocation of oil revenues to constituent states and local government areas (incorporated along "indigenous" ethnic lines) undermined the possibility of a national imaginary. Yet what was FESTAC but the production of just such a "national symbolic"? The question is not whether Nigeria could imagine a national community after independence, but why such figments of the imagined nation advanced and retreated with the oil boom and bust.

2. Although the voluminous literature on nations and nationalism does engage the symbolic dimensions of money, it is often as one factor among many rather than the motivating or generative principle of nationhood. My privileging of this constitutive relation between substances of monetary and national value suggests a rereading of Adam Smith's *Wealth of Nations* as one its earliest expressions. See Lemon 1998 for a post-Soviet variation on this theme.

3. See also Piot 1999 for a sustained analysis from the Togolese periphery, and Buggenhagen 2003 for the impact of trade remittances on Wolof domestic reproduction within the Senegalese Murid diaspora.

4. Abacha was allegedly poisoned for ordering the death of Yar'Adua while he was serving a trumped-up prison sentence. His death was a blow to the northern oligarchy and broke the rules of protecting one's own. Rumors circulated that Abacha's first son was actually fathered by Yar'Adua, establishing the real motive of Abacha's revenge. True or not, the rumors represent the phallocratic figures and anxieties of Abacha's dictatorship and the dangers of intimacy at the top.

5. One of the most tragic and poignant examples is how the child soldiers of Liberia and Sierra Leone have affixed wigs, toys, Disney T-shirts, and Rambo icons to their armed and dangerous bodies.

6. See Blunt 2003 for a satanic variation on this theme in Kenya.

REFERENCES

Abalogu, U. N. 1980. The regatta. In Enem 1980, 96–102.

Adams, Kathleen. 1997. Nationalizing the local and localizing the nation: Ceremonials, monumental displays and national memory-making in upland Sulawesi, Indonesia. *Museum Anthropology* 21 (1): 113–30.

Adebayo, Akanmu G. 1993. *Embattled federalism: History of revenue allocation in Nigeria, 1946–1990*. New York: Peter Lang.

Adock, St. John. [1925?] *The Prince of Wales' African book*. London: Hodder & Stoughton, Ltd.

Ahy, Molly. 1980. African dance in the diaspora: The example of Trinidad and Tobago. In Enem 1980, 8–30.

Akinkoye, 'Jibs. 1983. *Time, Naira, politics: An imaginative socio-economic analysis of a new nation-state*. Ibadan: B. I. O. Educational Services Ltd.

Akinyemi, A. B., S. B. Falegan, and I. A. Aluko, eds. 1984. *Readings and documents on ECOWAS*. Lagos: Nigerian Institute of International Affairs.

Alagoa, E. J. 2002. From middlemen to missionaries. In Anderson and Peek 2002, 67–79.

Allen, William. 1840. *Picturesque views of the river Niger, sketched during Lander's last visit in 1832–33*. London: John Murray, Hodgson & Graves, Ackerman.

Allen, William, and T. Thomson. 1848. *A narrative of the expedition sent by Her Majesty's government to the river Niger in 1841*. 2 vols. London: Richard Bently.

Anderson, Benedict. [1983] 1991. *Imagined communities: Reflections on the origin and spread of nationalism*. London: Verso.

Anderson, Martha, and Philip Peek, eds. 2002. *Ways of the rivers: Arts and environment of the Niger Delta*. Los Angeles: UCLA Fowler Museum of Cultural History.

Anyanwu, John C. 1992. President Babangida's structural adjustment programme and inflation in Nigeria. *Journal of Social Development in Africa* 7 (1): 5–24.

Appadurai, Arjun. 1996. *Modernity at large: Cultural dimensions of globalization*. Minneapolis and London: Univ. of Minnesota Press.

Apter, Andrew. 1987. Things fell apart? Yoruba responses to the 1983 elections in Ondo State, Nigeria. *Journal of Modern African Studies* 25 (3): 489–503.

———. 1992. *Black critics and kings: The hermeneutics of power in Yoruba society*. Chicago: Univ. of Chicago Press.

———. 1996. The Pan-African nation: Oil-capitalism and the spectacle of culture in Nigeria. *Public Culture* 8 (3): 441–66.

———. 1998. Discourse and its disclosures: Yoruba women and the sanctity of abuse. *Africa* 68 (1): 68–97.

———. 2002. On imperial spectacle: The dialectics of seeing in colonial Nigeria. *Comparative Studies in Society and History* 44 (3): 564–96.

Ashiwaju, Garba. 1974. Foreword. *Official Programme, 4th National Festival of the Arts, Kaduna 14th–21st December, 1974*, 9. Lagos: Federal Ministry of Information.

Augi, Abdullahi Rafi. 1978. *The history and performance of the Durbar in northern Nigeria*. Lagos: Nigeria Magazine, Cultural Division, Federal Ministry of Information.

Austen, Ralph. 1992. Tradition, invention and history: The case of the Ngondo (Cameroon). *Cahiers d'Études Africaines*, 126 (32-2): 285–309.

Baikie, William Balfour. 1856. *Narrative of an exploring voyage up the rivers Kwo'ra and Bi'nue in 1854*. London: John Murray.

Baker, Geoffrey L. 1996. *Trade winds on the Niger: The saga of the Royal Niger Company, 1830–1971*. London: Radcliffe Press.

Balibar, Etienne. 1991. The nation form: History and ideology. In *Race, nation, class: Ambiguous identities*, by Etienne Balibar and Immanuel Wallerstein, 86–106. New York: Verso.

Barber, Karin. 1982. Popular reactions to the Petro-Naira. *Journal of Modern African Studies* 20 (3): 431–50.

———. 1995. Money, self-realization, and the person in Yoruba texts. In *Money matters: Instability, values and social payments in the modern history of West African communities*, ed. Jane Guyer, 205–24. Portsmouth, NH: Heinemann.

Bastian, Misty. 1991. My head was too strong: Body parts and money magic in Nigerian popular discourse. Paper presented at "Meaningful currencies and monetary imaginations: Money, commodities and symbolic process in Africa," Univ. of Chicago.

Bataille, Georges. 1985. *Visions of excess: Selected writings, 1927–1939*. Ed. Allan Stoekl, trans. Allan Stoekl, with Carl R. Lovitt and Donald M. Leslie Jr. Minneapolis: Univ. of Minnesota Press.

———. 1991. *The accursed share: An essay on general economy*. Vol. 1. Trans. Robert Hurley. New York: Zone Books.

Baudrillard, Jean. 1975. *The mirror of production*. Trans. Mark Poster. St. Louis: Telos Press.

———. 1981. *For a critique of the political economy of the sign*. Trans. Charles Levin. St. Louis: Telos Press.

———. 1988. Symbolic exchange and death. In *Jean Baudrillard: Selcted writings,* ed. Mark Poster, 119–48. Stanford, CA: Stanford Univ. Press.

Baudrillart, M. H. 1884. Lectures choisies d'économie politique. Paris: Guillaumin Libraires.

Bayart, Jean-François. 1993. *The state in Africa: The politics of the belly.* Trans. Mary Harper. London: Longman.

Beaty, J., and S. C. Gwynne. 1993. *The outlaw bank: A wild ride into the secret heart of* BCCI. New York: Random House.

Becroft, John. 1841. On Benin and the upper course of the river Quorra, or Niger. *Journal of the Royal Geographical Society* 11:184–202.

Bello, S. 1992. Introduction. In *Nafest '90: National creativity fair,* ed. S. Bello, 1–2. Lagos: National Council for Arts and Culture.

Benedict, Burton, ed. 1983. *The anthropology of world's fairs: San Francisco's Panama Pacific International Exposition of 1915.* Berkeley and Los Angeles: Scolar Press.

Benjamin, Walter. 1976. The work of art in the age of mechanical reproduction. In *Illuminations,* ed. Hannah Arendt, 217–251. New York: Schocken Books.

———. 1983. *Charles Baudelaire: A lyric poet in the era of high capitalism.* London: Verso.

———. 1996. One-way street: A tour of German inflation. In *Walter Benjamin: Selected writings,* vol. 1, *1913–1926,* ed. Marcus Bullock and Michael Jennings, 444–88. Cambridge, MA: Harvard Univ. Press, Belknap Press.

Bennett, Tony. 1996. The exhibitionary complex. In *Thinking about exhibitions,* ed. R. Greenberg, B. W. Ferguson, and S. Nairne, 81–112. London: Routledge.

Berry, Sara. 1982. Oil and the disappearing peasantry: Accumulation, differentiation, and underdevelopment in western Nigeria. Working papers no. 66, African Studies Center, Boston Univ.

———. 1985. *Fathers work for their sons: Accumulation, mobility and class formation in an extended Yoruba community.* Berkeley and Los Angeles: Univ. of California Press.

———. 1993. *No condition is permanent: The social dynamics of agrarian change in Sub-Saharan Africa.* Madison: Univ. of Wisconsin Press.

Bhabha, Homi. 1994. *The location of culture.* London: Routledge.

Biersteker, Thomas. 1987. *Multinationals, the state, and control of the Nigerian economy.* Princeton, NJ: Princeton Univ. Press.

Blackwood's Magazine. 1912a. The Durbar, from the crowd. 191 (1156): 289–98.

———. 1912b. The Durbar at Zaria. 191 (1157): 352–58.

Blunt, Robert. 2003. Satan is an imitator: Kenya's recent cosmology of corruption. M.A. thesis, Univ. of Chicago.

Bohannan, Laura. 1952. A genealogical charter. *Africa* 22 (4): 301–15.

Bourdieu, Pierre. 1977. *Outline of a theory of practice.* Trans. Richard Nice. Cambridge: Cambridge Univ. Press.

———. 1991. *Language and symbolic power.* Cambridge, MA: Harvard Univ. Press.

———. 1993. *The field of cultural production: Essays on art and literature.* New York: Columbia Univ. Press.

———. 1999. Rethinking the state: Genesis and structure of the bureaucratic field. In Steinmetz 1999, 53–75.

Bridges, A. F. B. 1990. *So we used to do.* Edinburgh: Pentland Press.

Brooks, George E., and Francis K. Talbot. 1975. The Providence Exploring and Trading

Company's expedition to the Niger River in 1832–1833. *The American Neptune* 35 (2): 77–96.

Buck-Morss, Susan. 1993. *The dialectics of seeing: Walter Benjamin and the Arcades Project.* Cambridge, MA: MIT Press.

Buggenhagen, Beth Anne. 2003. At home in the black Atlantic: Circulation, domesticity and value in the Senegalese Muslim trade diaspora. Ph.D. diss., Univ. of Chicago.

Callaway, Helen. 1987. *Gender, culture and empire: European women in colonial Nigeria.* Urbana: Univ. of Illinois Press.

Canetti, Elias. [1960] 1988. *Crowds and power.* Trans. Carol Stewart. New York: Farrar, Straus & Giroux.

Çelik, Zeynap, and L. Kinney. 1990. Ethnography and exhibitionism at the expositions universelles. *Assemblage* 13:35–59.

Certeau, Michel de. 1988. *The practice of everyday life.* Trans. Steven Rendall. Berkeley and Los Angeles: Univ. of California Press.

Cohn, Bernard. 1983. Representing authority in Victorian India. In Hobsbawm and Ranger 1983, 165–209.

———. 1989. Cloth, clothes, and colonialism: India in the nineteenth century. In *Cloth and human experience,* ed. Annette Weiner and Jane Schneider, 303–53. Washington, DC: Smithsonian Institution Press.

Coleman, James S. 1958. *Nigeria: Background to nationalism.* Berkeley and Los Angeles: Univ. of California Press.

Comaroff, Jean, and John L. Comaroff. 1991. *Of revelation and revolution: Christianity, colonialism, and consciousness in South Africa.* Vol. 1. Chicago: Univ. of Chicago Press.

———. 1992. *Ethnography and the historical imagination.* Boulder, CO: Westview Press.

———. 1999. Occult economies and the violence of abstraction: Notes from the South African postcolony. *American Ethnologist* 26 (2): 279–303.

———. 2000. Millennial capitalism: First thoughts on a second coming. *Public Culture* 12 (2): 291–343.

Cooke, N. F. 1956. Bauchi Province. In *Provincial Annual Reports 1956, Northern Region of Nigeria,* 11. Kaduna: Government Printer.

Coombe, Rosemary. 1998. *The cultural life of intellectual properties: Authorship, appropriation and the law.* Durham, NC: Duke Univ. Press.

Coombes, Annie E. 1994. *Reinventing Africa: Museums, material culture and popular imagination in late Victorian and Edwardian England.* New Haven, CT: Yale Univ. Press.

Coronation Durbar, Delhi, 1911: Official directory with maps. 1911. Calcutta: Superintendent Government Printing, India.

Coronil, Fernando. 1987. The black El Dorado: Money fetishism, democracy and capitalism in Venezuela. Ph.D. diss., Univ. of Chicago.

———. 1995. Transculturation and the politics of theory: Countering the center, Cuban counterpoint. Introduction to *Cuban counterpoint: Tobacco and sugar,* by Fernando Ortiz, trans. H. de Onís, ix–lvi. Durham, NC: Duke Univ. Press.

———. 1997. *The magical state: Nature, money, and modernity in Venezuela.* Chicago: Univ. of Chicago Press.

Corrigan, Philip, and Derek Sayer. 1985. *The great arch: English state formation as cultural revolution.* Oxford: Basil Blackwell.

Cosentino, Donald. 1991. Afrokitsch. In *Africa explores: 20th century African art,* ed. S. Vogel, 240–55. New York: The Center For African Art.

Curtin, Philip, et al. 1978. *African history.* Boston: Little, Brown.

Darnton, John. 1977. Young attends a vast pageant in Nigeria. *New York Times,* Feb. 9, p. 13.

Debord, Guy. 1994. *Society of the spectacle.* New York: Zone Books.

Dike, Kenneth O. 1956. *Trade and politics in the Niger Delta, 1830–1885. An introduction to the economic and political history of Nigeria.* Oxford: Clarendon Press.

Doortmont, Michael. 1990. The invention of the Yorubas: Regional and Pan-African nationalism versus ethnic provincialism. In de Moraes Farias and Barber 1990, 101–08.

Duckworth, E. H. 1948. Over the hills to Yola. *Nigeria* 29:181–222.

Emecheta, Buchi. 1982. *Naira power.* London: Macmillan.

Enem, E. U., ed. 1980. *Pageants of the African world.* Lagos: Nigeria Magazine Special Publication.

Euba, Akin. 1990. *Yoruba drumming: The Dùndún tradition.* Bayreuth: E. Breitinger, Bayreuth Univ.

Ezeani, A. O. N. 1984. Community tariff treatment and indigenization policies in some ECOWAS countries. In Akinyemi, Falegan, and Aluko 1984, 504–16.

Fadahunsi, Akin. 1993. Devaluation: Implications for employment, inflation, growth and development. In Olukoshi 1993, 33–53.

Fagunwa, D. O. 1950. *Ogboju Ode Ninu Igbo Irunmale.* Lagos: Nelson.

———. 1961. *Aditu Olodumare.* Lagos: Nelson.

Falegan, S. B. 1984. Clearing and payments arrangement within the West African sub-region. In Akinyemi, Falegan, and Aluko 1984, 197–218.

Falusi, Abidoun O. 1981. Agricultural development: Operation Feed the Nation. In Oyediran 1981, 55–68.

Fanon, Franz. 1997. On national culture. In Grinker and Steiner 1997, 637–52.

Fasuyi, T. A. 1973. *Cultural policy in Nigeria.* Paris: UNESCO.

FESTAC '77. 1977. London and Lagos: Africa Journal Ltd. and the International Festival Committee.

Foucault, Michel. 1991. Governmentality. In *The Foucault effect: Studies in governmentality,* ed. Graham Burchell, Colin Gordon, and Peter Miller, 87–104. Chicago: Univ. of Chicago Press.

Fox, Richard. 1990. Introduction. In *Nationalist ideologies and the production of national cultures,* ed. R. Fox, 1–14. Washington, DC: American Anthropological Association.

Geertz, Clifford. 1980. *Negara: The theatre state in nineteenth-century Bali.* Princeton, NJ: Princeton Univ. Press.

Geisler, Gisela. 1993. Fair? What has fairness got to do with it? Vagaries of election observations and democratic standards. *Journal of Modern African Studies* 31 (4): 613–37.

Gell, Alfred. 1999. *The art of anthropology: Essays and diagrams.* London: Athlone Press.

Gellner, Ernest. 1998. *Language and solitude: Wittgenstein, Malinowski and the Hapsburg dilemma.* Cambridge: Cambridge Univ. Press.

Gilroy, Paul. 1993. *The black Atlantic: Modernity and double consciousness.* Cambridge, MA: Harvard Univ. Press.

Gluckman, Max. 1954. *Rituals of rebellion in south-east Africa*. Manchester: Manchester Univ. Press.

Goffman, Erving. 1974. *Frame analysis: An essay on the organization of experience*. New York: Harper and Row.

Goux, Jean-Joseph. 1990. *Symbolic economies: After Marx and Freud*. Trans. Jennifer Gage. Ithaca, NY: Cornell Univ. Press.

Graeber, David. 2001. Toward an anthropological theory of value: The false coin of our dreams. New York: Palgrave.

Greenhalgh, Paul. 1988. *Ephemeral vistas: The expositions universelles, great exhibitions, and world's fairs, 1851–1939*. Manchester: Manchester Univ. Press.

Grinker, Roy R., and Christopher Steiner, eds. 1997. *Perspectives on Africa: A reader in culture, history, and representation*. Oxford: Blackwell.

Gundu, M. 1991. Federalism and state creation in Nigeria. *The Nigerian Interpreter* 5 (5): 8–11.

Guss, David. 2000. *The festive state: Race, ethnicity, and nationalism as cultural performance*. Berkeley and Los Angeles: Univ. of California Press.

Habermas, Jürgen. 1992. *The structural transformation of the public sphere: An inquiry into a category of bourgeois society*. Cambridge, MA: MIT Press.

Hair, P. E. H., Adam Jones, and Robin Law, eds. 1992. *Barbot on Guinea: The writings of Jean Barbot on West Africa, 1678–1712*. London: The Haklyut Society.

Hallett, Robin. 1965. Epilogue. In *The Niger journal of Richard and John Lander*, ed. Robin Hallett, 290–97. New York: Praeger.

Halttunen, Karen. 1982. *Confidence men and painted women: A study of middle-class culture in America, 1830–1870*. New Haven, CT: Yale Univ. Press.

Hammer, Joshua. 1996. Nigeria crude: A hanged man and an oil-fouled landscape. *Harper's Magazine*, June, 58–68.

Handler, Richard. 1988. *Nationalism and the politics of culture in Quebec*. Madison: Univ. of Wisconsin Press.

Hart, Christopher. 1993. The Nigerian elections of 1983. *Africa* 63 (3): 397–418.

Haruna, I. B. M. 1977. Meaning and significance of the Durbar. *New Nigerian* (Kaduna), February 7, p. 18.

Harvey, David. 1982. *The limits to capital*. Chicago: Univ. of Chicago Press.

———. 1989. *The condition of postmodernity: An enquiry into the origins of cultural change*. Oxford: Blackwell.

Haynes, Douglas. 1990. Imperial ritual in a local setting: The ceremonial order in Surat, 1890–1939. *Modern Asian Studies* 24 (3): 493–527.

Haynes, Edward S. 1990. Rajput ceremonial interactions as a mirror of a dying Indian state system, 1820–1947. *Modern Asian Studies* 24 (3): 459–92.

Haynes, Jonathan. 1994. Structural adjustments of Nigerian comedy: Baba Sala. Paper presented at the Conference on Media, Popular Culture and "the Public" in Africa, Institute for Advanced Study and Research in the African Humanities, Northwestern Univ., April 30.

Helleiner, G. 1966. *Peasant agriculture, government, and economic growth in Nigeria*. Homewood, IL: Richard D. Irwin.

Hinsley, Curtis. 1991. The world as marketplace: Commodification of the exotic at the World's Columbian Exposition, Chicago, 1993. In *Exhibiting cultures: The poetics and politics of museum display*, ed. Ivan Karp and Steven Lavine, 334–65. Washington, DC: Smithsonian Institution Press.

Hirschmann, A. 1976. A generalized linkage approach to economic development with special references to staples. *Economic Development and Cultural Change* 56:134–59.

Hobsbawm, Eric. 1983. Introduction: Inventing traditions. In Hobsbawm and Ranger 1983, 1–14.

Hobsbawm, Eric, and Terence Ranger, eds. 1983. *The invention of tradition*. Cambridge: Cambridge Univ. Press.

Hogben, S. J., and A. H. M. Kirk-Greene. 1993. *The emirates of northern Nigeria: A preliminary survey of their historical traditions*. Hampshire, UK: Gregg Revivals.

Ibrahim, Jibrin. 1993. The transition to civilian rule: Sapping democracy. In Olukoshi 1993, 129–39.

Idrees, Aliyu A. 1988. The Patigi Regatta Festival: Its origin, historical significance and tourism prospects. *Présence Africaine* 147:63–70.

Ige, Bola. 1991. *Kaduna boy*. Ibadan: NPS Educational.

Ijewere, F. A. 1984. Multilateral monetary cooperation in West Africa. In Akinyemi, Falegan, and Aluko 1984, 219–37.

Ikein, Augustine. 1990. *The impact of oil on a developing country*. New York: Praeger.

Ikein, Augustine, and Comfort Briggs-Anigboh. 1998. *Oil and fiscal federalism in Nigeria: The political economy of resource allocation in a developing country*. Aldershot, UK: Ashgate.

Ikelegbe, A. 2001. The perverse manifestation of civil society. *Journal of Modern African Studies* 39 (1): 1–24.

Imoko, Dave. 1991. An overview of structural adjustments in Nigeria. *Nigerian Interpreter* 5 (4): 4–7.

Irele, Abiola. 1990. *The African experience in literature and ideology*. Bloomington: Indiana Univ. Press.

Ivy, Marilyn. 1995. *Discourses of the vanishing: Modernity, phantasm, Japan*. Chicago: Univ. of Chicago Press.

Johnston, H. H. 1888. The Niger Delta. *Proceedings of the Royal Geographical Society* 10, no. 12 (December): 749–63.

Jones, G. I. 1963. *The trading states of the oil rivers: A study of political development in eastern Nigeria*. London: Oxford Univ. Press for the International African Institute.

———. 1984. *The art of eastern Nigeria*. Cambridge: Cambridge Univ. Press.

———. 1989. *From slaves to palm oil: Slave trade and palm oil trade in the bight of Biafra*. Cambridge: African Studies Centre.

Joseph, Richard A. 1987. *Democracy and prebendal politics in Nigeria: The rise and fall of the second republic*. Cambridge: Cambridge Univ. Press.

July, Robert. 1987. *An African voice: The role of the humanities in African independence*. Durham, NC: Duke Univ. Press.

Karl, Terry. 1997. *The paradox of plenty: Oil booms and petro-states*. Berkeley and Los Angeles: Univ. of California Press.

Kemp, Alexander. 1987. *Petroleum rent collection around the world*. Halifax, UK: The Institute for Research on Public Policy.

The king emperor and his dominions: Souvenir of the Coronation Durbar of H. I. M. George V, Delhi, December, 1911. 1911. London: Burroughs Wellcome & Co.

Kirk-Greene, Anthony. 1959. Breath-taking Durbars. In *Advancing in good order*, 15–20. Kaduna: Government Press.

Kisch, Martin. 1910. *Letters and sketches from northern Nigeria*. London: Chatto and Windus.

Kramer, Fritz. 1993. *The red fez: Art and spirit possession in Africa*. Trans. Malcolm Green. New York: Verso.

Kunz, Frank. 1995. Civil society in Africa. *Journal of Modern African Studies* 33 (1): 181–87.

Lahey, J. [1977?] *Celebration: The Second World Black and African Festival of Arts and Culture*. Lagos: United States Information Service.

Laird, MacGregor. 1837. *Journal*. In *Narrative of an expedition into the interior of Africa, by the river Niger, in the steam-vessels Quorra and Alburkah, in 1832, 1833, and 1834*, by MacGregor Laird and R. A. K. Oldfield. Vol. 1. London: Richard Bentley.

Lander, Richard, and John Lander. [1832] 1965. *The Niger journal of Richard and John Lander*. Ed. Robin Hallett. London: Routledge & Kegan Paul.

Law, Robin. 1990. Constructing "a real national history": A comparison of Edward Blyden and Samuel Johnson. In de Moraes Farias and Barber 1990, 78–100.

Lebovics, Herman. 1992. *True France: The wars over cultural identity, 1900–1945*. Ithaca, NY: Cornell Univ. Press.

Lemon, Alaina. 1998. "Your eyes are green like dollars": Counterfeit cash, national substance, and currency apartheid in 1990's Russia. *Cultural Anthropology* 13 (1): 22–55.

Leprun, Sylviane. 1986. *Le théâtre des colonies: Scénographie, acteurs et discours de l'imaginaire dans les expositions, 1855–1937*. Paris: L'Harmattan.

Letchworth, T. E. 1956. Bornu Province. In *Provincial annual reports 1956, Northern Region of Nigeria*, 29–30. Kaduna: Government Printer.

Leton, G. B. 1990. Ogoni bill of rights: Presented to the government and people of Nigeria. Movement for the Survival of the Ogoni People (MOSOP).

Lloyd, P. C. 1961. Sallah at Ilorin. *Nigeria Magazine* 70:266–78.

Lugard, Flora Shaw. [1906] 1964. *A tropical dependency: An outline of the ancient history of the western Sudan with an account of the modern settlement of northern Nigeria*. London: Frank Cass.

Lugard, Frederick D. 1902. Colonial reports—Annual, no. 409. *Northern Nigeria, 1902*. In *Annual Reports: Northern Nigeria, 1900–1911*. London: Her Majesty's Stationery Office.

———. 1906. *Instructions to political and other officers on subjects chiefly political and administrative*. London: Waterlow and Sons Ltd.

———. [1922] 1965. *The dual mandate in British tropical Africa*. London: Frank Cass.

Lutz, Tom. 1991. *American nervousness, 1903: An anecdotal history*. Ithaca, NY: Cornell Univ. Press.

MacRow, D. W. 1956. The Nupe of Pategi. *Nigeria Magazine* 50:260–80.

Madauchi, Ibrahim. 1968. *Hausa customs*. Zaria: Northern Nigeria Publishing Co.

Marwick, Ernest W. 1965. *William Balfour Baikie: Explorer of the Niger*. Kirkwall, Scotland: W. R. MacKintosh: The Kirkwall Press.

Marx, Karl. 1976. *Capital: A Critique of political economy*, vol. 1. Trans. Ben Fowkes. Harmondsworth, UK: Penguin.

———. 1978. Capital, volume one. In *The Marx-Engels Reader*, ed. Robert C. Tucker, 294–442. New York: W. W. Norton and Co.

Matory, J. Lorand. 1994. *Sex and the empire that is no more: Gender and the politics of metaphor in Oyo Yoruba religion.* Minneapolis: Univ. of Minnesota Press.

Mbembe, Achille. 1992. The banality of power and the aesthetics of vulgarity in the postcolony. *Public Culture* 4 (2): 1–30.

———. 2001. *On the postcolony.* Berkeley and Los Angeles: Univ. of California Press.

Meek, C. K. 1931. *A Sudanese kingdom: An ethnological study of the Jukun-speaking peoples of Nigeria.* London: Kegan Paul, Trench, Trubner.

Mitchell, Timothy. 1991. *Colonising Egypt.* Berkeley and Los Angeles: Univ. of California Press.

———. 1999. Society, economy, and the state effect. In Steinmetz 1999, 76–97.

Mockler-Ferryman, A. F. 1892. *Up the Niger: Narrative of Major Claude MacDonald's mission to the Niger and Benue rivers, West Africa.* London: George Philip & Son.

———. 1902. British Nigeria. *Journal of the African Society* 1 (2): 151–73.

Moraes Farias, P. F. de, and K. Barber, eds. 1990. *Self-assertion and brokerage: Early cultural nationalism in West Africa.* Birmingham: Centre of West African Studies, University of Birmingham.

Morton, Patricia. 2000. *Hybrid modernities: Architecture and representation at the 1931 Colonial Exposition, Paris.* Cambridge, MA: MIT Press.

Nadel, S. F. 1942. *A Black Byzantium: The kingdom of Nupe in Nigeria.* London: Oxford Univ. Press for the International African Institute.

Needham, Rodney. 1983. *Against the tranquility of axioms.* Berkeley and Los Angeles: Univ. of California Press.

Ngugi wa Thiong'o. 1986. *Decolonising the mind: The politics of language in African literature.* Portsmouth, NH: Heinemann.

Nigeria handbook: Containing statistical and general information respecting the colony and protectorate. 1924. 5th ed. Lagos: Chief Secretary's Office.

Nkrumah, Kwame. 1970. *Consciencism: Philosophy and ideology for decolonization.* Rev. ed. New York: Monthly Review Press.

Northern Regional Government. 1953. *Report on the Kano disturbances: 16th, 17th, 18th and 19th May, 1953.* Kaduna: Government Printer.

Nuckolls, Charles W. 1990. The Durbar incident. *Modern Asian Studies* 24 (3): 529–59.

Nwankwo, Nkem. 1975. *My Mercedes is bigger than yours.* New York: Harper & Row.

Nzekwu, Onuora. 1966. Nigeria, Negritude, and the World Festival of Negro Arts. *Nigeria Magazine* 89:80–94.

Obeyesekere, Gananath. 1992. *The apotheosis of Captain Cook: European mythmaking in the Pacific.* Princeton, NJ: Princeton Univ. Press.

Obi, Cyril. 2001. *The Changing forms of identity politics in Nigeria.* Uppsala: Africa Institute.

Ofeimun, Odia. 1989. Democracy by fiat. *West Africa,* December 18–24, 2091–93.

Ogbonna, A., and E. Udo. 1993. Face to face with failure. *Financial Post* 5 (22): 1, 6 (June 6–19).

Okonta, Ike. 2002. The struggle of the Ogoni for self-determination. Ph.D. diss., Oxford Univ.

Okonta, Ike, and Oronto Douglas. 2001. *Where vultures feast: Shell, human rights, and oil in the Niger Delta.* San Francisco: Sierra Books.

Oldfield, R. A. K. 1837. *Journal.* In *Narrative of an expedition into the interior of Africa, by the river Niger, in the steam-vessels Quorra and Alburkah, in 1832, 1833, and 1834,* by MacGregor Laird and R. A. K. Oldfield. Vol. 2. London: Richard Bentley.

Olorunyomi, Dapo. 1993. The Giwa affair. *The News,* October 25, 13–18.

Olukoshi, A. O., ed. 1993. *The politics of structural adjustment in Nigeria.* London: James Currey.

O'Malley, Michael. 1994. Specie and species: Race and the money question in nineteenth century America. *The American Historical Review* 99 (2): 369–95.

Osaghae, Eghosa E. 1995. The Ogoni uprising: Oil politics, minority agitation, and the future of the Nigerian state. *African Affairs* 94:325–44.

Osofisan, Femi. 1981. FESTAC and the heritage of ambiguity. In Oyediran 1981, 32–46.

Oyediran, Oyeleye, ed. 1981. *Survey of Nigerian affairs 1976–77.* Lagos: Nigerian Institute of International Affairs.

Oyediran, O., and A. Agbaje. 1991. Two-partyism and democratic transition in Nigeria. *Journal of Modern African Studies* 29 (2): 213–35.

Oyegoke, Lekan. 1981. *Cowrie tears.* London: Heinemann.

Pacheco-Pereira, Duarte. 1937. *Esmeraldo de situ orbis.* Trans. and ed. George H. T. Kimble. London: The Hakluyt Society.

Pal, Pratapaditya, and Vidya Dehija. 1986. *From merchants to emperors: British artists and India, 1757–1930.* Ithaca, NY: Cornell Univ. Press.

Palmié, Stephan. 2002. *Wizards and scientists: Explorations in Afro-Cuban modernity and tradition.* Durham, NC: Duke Univ. Press.

Peel, J. D. Y. 1989. The cultural work of Yoruba ethnogenesis. In *History and ethnicity,* ed. E. Tonkin, M. O. McDonald, and M. Chapman, 198–215. London: Routledge.

———. 2000. *Religious encounter and the making of the Yoruba.* Bloomington: Indiana Univ. Press.

Pemberton, John. 1994. *On the subject of "Java."* Ithaca, NY: Cornell Univ. Press.

Perham, Marjorie. 1937. *Native administration in Nigeria.* Oxford: Oxford Univ. Press.

———. 1960. *Lugard: The years of authority, 1898–1945.* London: Collins.

Pietz, William. 1988. The Problem of the fetish, IIIa: Bosman's Guinea and the enlightenment theory of fetishism. *Res* 16:105–23.

———. 1993. Fetishism and materialism: The limits of theory in Marx. In *Fetishism as cultural discourse,* ed. Emily Apter and William Pietz, 119–51. Ithaca, NY: Cornell Univ. Press.

Piot, Charles. 1999. *Remotely global: Village modernity in West Africa.* Chicago: Univ. of Chicago Press.

Poster, Mark. 1988. Introduction. In *Jean Baudrillard: Selected writings,* ed. Mark Poster, 1–9. Stanford, CA: Stanford Univ. Press.

Postone, Moishe. 1993. *Time, labor, and social domination: A reinterpretation of Marx's critical theory.* Cambridge: Cambridge Univ. Press.

Queen's tour of Nigeria: Commemorating the visit of H. M. Queen Elizabeth II and H. R. H. the Duke of Edinburgh. 1956. London: Pitkin Pictorials.

Rabinow, Paul. 1989. *French modern: Norms and forms of the social environment.* Cambridge, MA: MIT Press.

Ranger, Terence O. 1980. Making northern Rhodesia imperial: Variations on a royal theme, 1924–1938. *African Affairs* 79 (316): 349–73.

————. 1983. The invention of tradition in colonial Africa. In Hobsbawm and Ranger 1983, 211–62.

Richards, Thomas. 1990. *The commodity culture of Victorian England: Advertising and spectacle, 1851–1914.* Stanford, CA: Stanford Univ. Press.

Riddell, J. Barry. 1992. Things fall apart again: Structural adjustment programmes in Sub-Saharan Africa. *Journal of Modern African Studies* 30 (1): 53–68.

Rydell, Robert W. 1984. *All the world's a fair: Visions of empire at American international expositions, 1876–1916.* Chicago: Univ. of Chicago Press.

————. 1993. *World of fairs: The Century of Progress expositions.* Chicago: Univ. of Chicago Press.

Sahlins, Marshall. 1972. *Stone Age economics.* Chicago: Aldine Publishing Co.

————. 1985. *Islands of history.* Chicago: Univ. of Chicago Press.

————. 1995. *How "natives" think: About Captain Cook, for example.* Chicago: Univ. of Chicago Press.

Sani, Habibu A. 1976. An ex-insider's overview of the civil service (1966–1977). *Nigerian Journal of Public Affairs* 6 (2): 77–96.

Saro-Wiwa, Ken. 1989. *On a darkling plain: An account of the Nigerian civil war.* London: Saros International Publishers.

————. 1990. Introduction. In G. P. Leton et al. 1990.

————. 1991. *Similia: Essays on anomic Nigeria.* London: Saros International Publishers.

————. 1992. *Genocide in Nigeria: The Ogoni tragedy.* London: Saros International Publishers.

————. 1995. *A month and a day: A detention diary.* New York: Penguin Books.

Schatz, Sayre P. 1984. Pirate capitalism and the inert economy of Nigeria. *Journal of Modern African Studies* 22 (1): 45–57.

Scott, David. 1995. Colonial governmentality. *Social Text* 43: 191–220.

Scott, James C. 1998. *Seeing like a state: How certain schemes to improve the human condition have failed.* New Haven, CT: Yale Univ. Press.

Senghor, Léopold S. 1964. *Liberté I: Négritude et humanisme.* Paris: Éditions de Seuil.

Shepard, Robert B. 1991. *Nigeria, Africa, and the United States: From Kennedy to Reagan.* Bloomington: Indiana Univ. Press.

Shipton, Parker. 1998. Bitter money: Forbidden exchange in East Africa. In Grinker and Steiner 1997, 163–89.

Silverman, Debora L. 1977. The 1889 exhibition: The crisis of bourgeois individualism. *Oppositions* 8:71–79.

Simmel, Georg. 1978. *The philosophy of money.* Trans. Tom Bottomore and David Frisby. London: Routledge & Kegan Paul.

Sinclair, D. n.d. The history of the Nigeria marine. Mss. Afr. s.809, Bodleian Library, Univ. of Oxford.

Sklar, Richard L. 2002. The nature of class domination in Africa, 1979. In *African politics in postimperial times: The essays of Richard L. Sklar,* ed. T. Falola, 129–51. Trenton, NJ: Africa World Press.

Smith, Bryan Sharwood. 1969. *Recollections of British administration in the Cameroons and northern Nigeria 1921–1957: "But always as friends."* Durham, NC: Duke Univ. Press.

Smith, John. 1968. *Colonial cadet in Nigeria*. Durham, NC: Duke Univ. Press.

Smith, M. G. 1956. On segmentary lineage systems. *Journal of the Royal Anthropological Institute* 86 (2): 39–80.

———. 1957. The social function and meaning of Hausa praise-singing. *Africa* 27:26–45.

———. 1960. *Government in Zazzau, 1800–1950*. London: Oxford Univ. Press for the International African Institute.

Soyinka, Wole. 1977. The scholar in African society. In *Colloquium Proceedings of the Second World Black and African Festival of Arts and Culture*, ed. A. U. Iwara and E. Mveng, 1:44–53. Lagos: Federal Military Government of Nigeria.

———. 1996. *The open sore of a continent: A personal narrative of the Nigerian crisis*. Oxford: Oxford Univ. Press.

Steinmetz, G., ed. 1999. *State/culture: State-formation after the cultural turn*. Ithaca, NY: Cornell Univ. Press.

Stocking, George. 1987. *Victorian anthropology*. New York: Free Press.

Takaya, Bala, and S. G. Tyoden, eds. 1987. *The Kaduna mafia: A study of the rise, development and consolidation of a Nigerian power elite*. Jos: Jos Univ. Press.

Talbot, Percy A. 1932. *Tribes of the Niger Delta: Their religions and customs*. London: The Sheldon Press.

Taussig, Michael. 1992. *The nervous system*. New York: Routledge.

———. 1993. *Mimesis and alterity: A particular history of the senses*. New York: Routledge.

Temple, C. L. [1918] 1968. *Native races and their rulers: Sketches and studies of official life and administrative problems in Nigeria*. London: Frank Cass.

Thomas, Nicholas. 1994. *Colonialism's culture: Anthropology, travel and government*. Princeton, NJ: Princeton Univ. Press.

Trevithick, Alan. 1990. Some structural and sequential aspects of the British imperial assemblages at Delhi: 1877–1911. *Modern Asian Studies* 24 (3): 561–78.

Trinick, G. W. 1939. Waterway clearing. *Nigeria* 18:127–30.

Trouillot, Michel-Rolph. 1990. *Haiti, state against nation: The origins and legacy of Duvalierism*. New York: Monthly Review Press.

Truell, Peter, and Larry Gurwin. 1992. BCCI: *The inside story of the world's most corrupt financial empire*. London: Bloomsbury.

Ukim, Utibe. 1994. Where is the money? *Newswatch*, October 24, 9–14.

Useh, Abraham. 1993. Babangida (Nigeria) unlimited. *Tell* 41, October 18, 7–13.

Usoro, Eno. 1977. Petroleum products supply crisis. In *Survey of Nigerian Affairs 1975*, ed. O. Oyediran, 57–70. Ibadan: Univ. Press Limited for the Nigerian Institute of International Affairs.

Vernon-Jackson, H. O. H. 1957. The Pategi Regatta, *Nigeria Magazine* 54: 289–92.

Waterman, Christopher A. 1990. *Jùjú : A social history and ethnography of an African popular music*. Chicago: Univ. of Chicago Press.

Watts, Michael. 1984. State, oil and accumulation: From boom to bust. *Society and Space* 2:402–28.

———. 1991. Visions of excess. *Transition* 51:124–41.

———. 1992. The shock of modernity: Petroleum, protest and fast capitalism in an industrializing society. In *Reworking modernity: Capitalism and symbolic discontent*, ed. A. Pred and M. Watts, 21–63. New Brunswick, NJ: Rutgers Univ. Press.

———. 1994. Oil as money: The devil's excrement and the spectacle of black gold. In *Money, power and space,* ed. Ron Martin, 406–45. Oxford: Blackwell.

———. 1996. Islamic modernities? Citizenship, civil society and Islamism in a Nigerian city. *Public Culture* 8 (2): 251–89.

———. 1997. Black gold, white heat. In *Geographies of resistance,* ed. S. Pile and M. Keith, 33–67. London: Routledge.

———. 2003. Development and governmentality. *Singapore Journal of Tropical Geography* 24 (1): 6–34.

Weiner, Annette. 1992. *Inalienable possessions: The paradox of keeping-while-giving.* Berkeley and Los Angeles: Univ. of California Press.

Welch, Claude Jr.. 1995. The Ogoni and self-determination: Increasing violence in Nigeria. *Journal of Modern African Studies* 33 (4): 635–49.

West Africa. 1960. The princess and the premier. No. 2264 (October 22): 1187.

West Africa. 1961. Ghana on parade. No. 2320 (November 18): 1267.

West African Review. 1956a. The Kaduna Durbar. 27 (343): 274–81.

West African Review. 1956b. The war canoes of Bonny. 27 (343): 282–85.

Williams, David. 1956. Nigeria today. *African Affairs* 55 (218): 109–19.

Abacha regime, 9–10, 16–17; arrest of Obasanjo, 272, 279; collapse of civil society, 257, 270–74; death, 283, 308n4; 419 scams, 255, 283; Ogoni activism, 259–67, 307n7; regional structures, 27–28; Saro-Wiwa execution, 254, 258, 270, 271–73; Saro-Wiwa trial, 258, 271–72
Abiola, Moshood, 10, 242, 244ff., 272
Abubakar, Alhaji, 236–347
Achebe, Chinua, 231
Ade, King Sunny, 2, 213
Adewusi, Gbenga, 306n38
administration of FESTAC, 54–65, 57ff., 82; Arab participation, 59, 67–70, 291n45; Australasian zone, 58–59; committee salaries, 69; control struggles, 59, 65–71, 82, 290n34; festival presidency, 66–67; International Festival Committee, 54–55, 61–62; marketing, 91–93; Nigeria's national mission, 91–95; North African zone, 67–70; North American zone, 56–58, 288n4; regional divisions, 15–16, 46–

47; zone framework, 55, 288nn3–4. See also cultural production; financial aspects of FESTAC
Adumu, 139–40, 140ff., 297n17
African Inland Commercial Company, 141, 144–45
Ahy, Molly, 77–78
Ajanaku-Araba, Fagbemi, 124
Ajaokuta Steel, 217
Ajuda, Fred, 230
Ake, Claude, 31
Albert, Prince Consort, of Great Britain, 145
Algiers Pan-African Cultural Festival of 1969, 70
Ali, Alhaji Tatari, 203
Allen, William, 141–48, 143ff., 297n20
Anambra State, 100
Anderson, Benedict, 7, 167
Angola, 74, 288nn3
Anikulapo-Kuti, Fela, 90, 292n7
Anyanwu, John C., 250
Appadurai, Arjun, 274
Arab participation in FESTAC, 59, 67–70

archeological presentations, 94
Ashiwaju, Garba, 109, 113, 116
Association for a Better Nigeria, 242–43,
    255
Atta, Alhaji Aliyu, 236
Australian aboriginals at FESTAC, 58–59,
    77, 79–80, 82
Awodoye, Dan, 112–13, 295n57
Awolowo, Obafemi, 200
Ayorinde, J. A., 99, 118; focus on chief-
    tains, 99–103; Yoruba favoritism,
    100–103, 105
Azikiwe, Nnamdi, 159, 262–63

Babalola, S. A., 95
Babangida, Maryam, 245–46. 246ff.,
    248, 252
Babangida regime, 9–10, 13, 16–17, 223–
    24, 226; accumulation of personal
    wealth, 236, 245–46. 246ff.; civil ser-
    vice reforms, 247–48, 306n40; civil
    unrest, 243, 244, 245, 276; creation
    of political parties, 238–40, 265,
    305n27; creation of states, 266–67,
    307n5; deregulation of the banking
    system, 228; directed democracy pro-
    gram, 237–40, 243, 255–56; drug
    trafficking, 252; economic crisis of
    value, 248–54; election manipulation,
    240–45, 255–56, 306nn36–38; 419
    scams, 230–36, 248–49, 254–56,
    283; inflation, 252–54; local elections,
    238–41, 306n33; maps, 246–47; na-
    tional census, 246; Ogoni autonomy
    movement, 266–67; political mur-
    ders, 252; regional structures, 27–28;
    resignation, 245–46, 272; women's
    programs, 248, 252
Baikie, William Balfour, 147–49
Baker, Corrine, 229
Baldwin, James, 76
Balewa, Abubakar Tafewa, 263
Balogun, Ola, 115
Bank of Credit and Commerce Interna-
    tional (BCCI), 236–37
Barber, Karin, 249, 269
Barbot, John and James, 131–32, 297n16
Bataille, Georges, 201

Bauchi State: costume representation,
    101; government subsidies, 247–48;
    Grand Durbar, 299n3, 301n34
Baudrillard, Jean, 201, 205, 218
Bayart, Jean-François, 266
BCCI. See Bank of Credit and Commerce
    International
Becroft, John, 134–35
Begho, F. O., 114
Bello, Alhaji Ahmadu, 190
Bendel State: costume representation,
    100; FESTAC Regatta, 126, 127;
    women's fashions, 107
Benin, 60, 72
Benin mask: British Museum, 62–63,
    193, 209; official symbol of FESTAC,
    61–64, 63, 64ff., 210, 289n18, 289–
    90nn22–23, 304n28
Benjamin, Walter, 51, 211
Benue State: costume representation, 101;
    Grand Durbar, 299n3
Biafra, 74, 193, 263–64
Biersteker, Thomas, 37–38
Black Heritage (film), 77
Blyden, Edward Wilmot, 65
Bongo, Oumar, 87
Borno State: government subsidies, 247–
    48; Grand Durbar, 194–95, 299n3,
    301n34
Botha, Pik, 230, 245
Bourdieu, Pierre, 162, 169–70
King Boy, 136–40, 142–43, 148, 164
Bradshaw, R. C., 170
Brazil, 55
Bridges, A. F. B., 157
Britain. See colonial contexts
British Museum, 62–63, 193, 209
Broadcasting Organisation of Nigeria
    (BON), 210–11, 303n25
Buhari, Muhammadu, 91, 195, 307n45
Buhari-Idiagbon regime, 226
King Burrow, 148

Callaway, Helen, 168, 179–80, 185
Campaign for Democracy, 245
Canetti, Elias, 253–54
canoes. See war canoe culture
Capital (Marx), 21

Carifesta, 60

Carr, Alfred, 147

Central Bank of Nigeria, 250, 255

Centre for Black and African Arts and Civilization (CBAAC), 10–11

The Children of Paradise (dance drama), 116–17, 260

Ciroma, Adamu, 242

Cobb, Charlie, 88–89

Cohn, Bernard, 168, 180, 181, 185

Coleman, James S., 188

colonial contexts, 3, 5, 6, 154–62; abolition, 145–47; Benin pectoral mask, 62–63, 193; commercial monopolies, 149; Coronation Durbars of George V, 185–87; crusade against fetishism, 151–52; dance festivals, 110; Delta "creole" culture, 161–66, 295–96n1; durbar practices, 170–72, 179–93, 197–98, 300nn16–21; inland colonization, 147, 148–49; invented traditions, 167–68; national culture, 45–46; nationalist movements, 188, 189–91; palm oil trade, 124, 136, 141, 144–46, 148, 151, 153, 155–56, 165, 273, 307–8n9; regattas, 157–62, 165–66, 298–99nn36–37; regional cultures, 15–16, 46–47, 198; regional organization, 27–28; riverine trade, 131–34; slave trade, 123–24, 130–32, 137, 145, 149, 155, 165, 273, 296n12; social hierarchies, 155–56; traditional costume exhibition, 103–6; war canoe culture, 123–24, 129–40; world's fairs and exhibitions, 4–5, 89, 105. *See also* war canoe culture

Colonising Egypt (Mitchell), 4

Comaroff, Jean and John L., 280–81

commodification of culture, 54, 94–95, 209–13; Benin pectoral mask, 63–65, 289–90nn22–23; broadcast rights, 210–11, 303n25; copyrights, 16, 210–12, 303–4nn27–28; ethnicity issues, 30–31, 108–9, 295n53; fetishism, 21–23, 36, 44, 51, 81, 118–20, 146–47, 150, 151; insurance valorizations, 98–99, 104, 113, 118, 119, 209, 294n44; modern war canoe fetish, 161–62;

photographs, 104, 295n68; reproductions and souvenirs, 16, 50, 64–65, 83, 89, 209–10, 211–13, 289–90nn22–23, 295n68; theme song, 2, 213. *See also* symbols of FESTAC; value of cultural production

Commonwealth Festival, London, 60

Congo, 74

Cooke, N. F., 191

The Coronation Durbar, Delhi, 1911: Official Directory with Maps, 185–86

Coronil, Fernando, 14, 268, 273, 308n10

Corrigan, Philip, 167

corruption: educational fraud, 231–32; FESTAC Tribunal of Inquiry, 201, 202–4, 206, 214; 50% rule, 40, 287–88n30; 419 scams, 12–13, 16, 226–36, 248–49, 277, 283; Kaduna Mafia, 38, 198, 203–4, 236–37; oil distribution interference, 287n25; prebendalism, 30–31, 39–40, 215, 252, 255, 266, 269. *See also* Babangida regime

Cross River State: costume representation, 100; creation, 237–38; FESTAC Regatta, 126, 296n7

Crowther, Rev. Samuel Ajayi, 148

cultural production, 3–4, 23–24, 45–51, 95–120, 299n1; administrative structures, 169–70; authenticity, 2, 4, 5, 8–9; blackness and oil, 83; colonial and postcolonial forms, 6–7, 45–46, 169; extensionist thesis, 103; federal model, 46–47; magic and work degree zero, 121–23, 162; marketing, 91–93; preservationist model, 94; search for commonality, 77–79; world's fairs and exhibitions, 4–5, 6, 89, 105. *See also* nationalization of culture; symbols of FESTAC; value of cultural production

Curtin, Philip, et al., 153

Da Costa, Pinto, 87

Dada, G. A., 203

Dahomey, 71

dance/choreography, 54, 82, 109–18; bare-breasted dance debate, 115–16, 117ff.; commonalities of culture, 77–

dance/choreography (*continued*)
79; cultural transmission role, 110;
filming, 112; Marx's commodity
fetishism, 119; modern dance drama,
109, 114–18; Nafest '74 (Kaduna),
109–14, 295nn56–57; national categories, 112; sanitization, 111–12,
295n57; secular dance, 110; traditional
dance, 109–14
Danjuma, Theophilus Yakubu, 87, 124,
195
Dappa-Biriye, H. J. R., 124, 129, 166
Dapper (Dutch explorer), 131
Dasuki, Alhaji Ibrahim, 236
Davis, Abimbola, 245
Davis, George, 229
Davis, Ossie, 56
Delta "creole" culture, 161–62, 164–66,
295–96n1
diaspora issues, 76–82; Australian aboriginals, 58–59, 77, 79–80; narratives
of black unity, 77–79
Dikko, Alhaji Umaru, 90–91, 203–4
Diop, Alioune, 61, 66–67, 68–69
Donaldson, Jeff R., 56
Duckworth, E. H., 45
durbar culture, 167–99; colonial contexts,
171–72, 177–93, 197–99, 300nn16–
21, 302n39; commodification, 177–
78; Coronation Durbars of George V,
185–87; Fulani roles, 184, 186–87,
300nn17–18; gift-giving, 177, 300n14;
Indian colonial version, 180–81, 197;
inspection durbars, 184–85; installation durbars, 182–83; invented traditions, 167–70, 188, 192–93, 198; Islamic connections, 168, 173–79, 197;
nationalization of culture, 193–99;
northern hegemony, 170, 195–96,
198, 299n3; origins, 168, 171, 173–79,
197; political dimensions, 169–73,
175–76; pre- and postcolonial contexts, 169, 171–73, 178–79, 197–99;
religious separation, 178; royal durbars, 168, 188–92, 301nn28–29; social and racial hierarchies, 180–88,
198, 300n15; stagecraft, 180, 182–83.
See also FESTAC Grand Durbar

Durbar Hotel, 91
Durbar Secretariat, 90–91

Economic Community of West African
States (ECOWAS), 3, 70–73, 82, 291n41
economic contexts: bank failures, 250; circulation economy, 41–44; crisis of
value, 248–54; currencies, 14, 71–72,
225–26, 228, 291nn39–41; globalization in Africa, 280–84; imports, 214–
15, 216; inflation, 215, 249–50, 252–
53, 277; magic and work degree zero,
121–23, 162; Marxian analyses, 44,
119; Marxian commodity fetishism,
21–23, 36, 44, 51, 81, 118–20, 268;
national renewal projects, 213–17,
304n33; New International Economic
Order (NIEO), 75–76; oil capitalism,
201, 268–70, 273–77; postcolonial
economies, 280–84; slavery, 123–24,
131–32, 137, 145, 149, 155, 165, 273,
296n12; trade, 70–74, 124, 136, 141,
144–45, 148–49, 151, 230–31,
291n44; transaction value of 419
scams, 231–36; transformation by
wealth, 8–9, 50–51, 254–55; transvaluations through exchange, 139–
41, 144, 147, 159–60, 164–65, 295–
96n1. *See also* colonial contexts; oil
boom economy of Nigeria; oil bust
economy of Nigeria
ECOWAS. *See* Economic Community of
West African States
Edward, Prince of Wales, 188–89, 192
Egungun spirits, 2
Ekwensi, Cyprian, 95–96
Ekwueme, Laz, 2
Elizabeth II, Queen of Great Britain, 103,
159–62, 168, 189–92
El-Yakubu, Alhaji, 96
Emo, Udo, 96
Enahoro, Anthony, 61, 91, 113, 204
Esmeraldo De Situ Orbis (Pacheco-Pereira),
130
ethnicity issues: commodification of eth-
nicity, 30–31, 108–9, 295n53; cultural
representation, 45–47; ethnic substi-
tution, 108; FESTAC Regatta, 127–29;

indigenization of industry, 37–38, 40, 44; minority movements, 260, 265–67; modern women's fashions, 118; segmentation around trade, 148. *See also* Ogoni movement

ethnographical presentations, 94

Euba, Akin, 2, 113

European Economic Community (EEU), 74

exploration of Nigerian rivers, 165; by Baikie, 147–49, 297n24; early impact of European culture, 132–38; by Laird and Oldfield, 141–45; by Richard and John Lander, 132–41; by MacDonald, 149–54; missionary activities, 146, 148; trade expansion, 144–45, 148–49; by Trotter and Allen, 145–47, 297n20

Ezeani, A. O. N., 72

Ezeani, C. O., 200

Falae, Olu, 242

Fanon, Franz, 281

Fawehinmi, Gani, 257

federal government of Nigeria: border security issues, 35; disbursement of oil revenues, 28–30, 286n11; expansion of the public sector, 29–30; indigenization of industry, 37–40; nationalization of oil, 32–37; national security system, 92–93; Oputa Inquiry report, 32; Petroleum Anti-Sabotage Decree of 1975, 32–33, 287n16; prebendalism, 30–31, 39–40, 215, 252, 255, 266, 269; reform and development projects, 28–31, 286n10; resistance activity, 32–33; Third National Development Plan, 25–26. *See also* corruption; political contexts; specific regimes

FESTAC '77, 2–9, 200–202; archives, 10–11, 288; black pan-African identity, 3–6; crowd control problems, 88–89; impact on Nigerian history, 8, 285n2; marketing, 60–61; modernity themes, 5–6, 50; national development, 213; National Theatre, 47–50; national unity, 45–46; opening ceremonies, 52–53, 76–79, 87–89,

292n3; police violence, 88–89; preliminary festivals, 59–61, 82; repossession of origins, 5, 54, 80–82; theme song, 2; triumph of oil, 50–51. *See also* administration of FESTAC; cultural production; financial aspects of FESTAC; visions of blackness

FESTAC Colloquium, 5, 48, 70, 94, 292n7; Arab members, 74; censorship issues, 95; Origin of Man exhibit, 80–82; theories of black migration, 80–81

FESTAC Grand Durbar, 168–73, 299nn3–4, 302n37; Borno contingent, 194–95; colonial aspects, 192–93, 302n39; committee expenditures, 202–4; concessions to northern power, 196; foreign dignitaries, 193–94; nationalization of culture, 193–99; participants, 193–94, 301nn34–35; pre- and post-colonial aspects, 171–73, 194–96

FESTAC Regatta, 121–30, 158, 166; hierarchical aspects, 125–26; historical commemorations, 129–30; mini-regattas, 159; nationalization of culture, 127–29, 166; offerings, 124; program, 125–30; ritual components, 138–39; values, 121–24. *See also* war canoe culture

FESTAC Village, 49; expenditures, 91, 202–3, 206; food shortages, 201; revenues, 209, 303n21

field research, 9–13

financial aspects of FESTAC, 200–219; arts and crafts purchases, 98; audit of the International Festival Committee (IFC), 206–7; awards and contracts, 201; cars and buses, 201, 204–5, 218; committee salaries, 69; debates about value, 200–202; expenditures, 202–8; fraud and embezzlement, 90–91; graft and mismanagement, 202–9; imports and the cement armada, 214–15; insurance valorizations, 98–99, 104, 118, 294n44; Nigerian control, 82, 91–92; North American zone, 56, 288n4; photography, 213; revenues, 208–9, 212, 213, 303n21; traditional costumes, 104; Tribunal of Inquiry, financial aspects of FESTAC (*continued*) 201, 202–4, 206, 214. *See also* corruption; value of cultural production

Fingesi, O. P., 68–69, 129, 290n34

First World Festival of Negro Arts, 65–67, 290n26, 290n36

King Forday, 138, 142

419 scams, 12–13, 16, 226–36, 277, 283; Babangida regime, 248–50; Internet circulation, 305n6; religious versions, 250–51; technology, 251; transacting value, 231–36

Fox, Richard, 7

the Gambia, 71

Garba, Joseph, 87, 195

Gell, Alfred, 121–23, 162–64

gender issues, 4; bare-breasted dance debate, 115–16, 117ff.; modern women's fashions, 105–9, 118, 119; traditional male garments, 105, 118

Genocide in Nigeria: The Ogoni Tragedy (Saro-Wiwa), 259–61, 267

George VI, King of Great Britain, 157–62

Ghana, 60, 71, 74

Gilroy, Paul, 123–24

Giwa, Dele, 13, 252

Giwa, F. Bola, 213

Goffman, Erving, 228

Goldie, Sir George, 149, 179

Gongola State: costume representation, 101; Grand Durbar, 299n3, 301n34

Gowon (Yakubu) regime, 25; coup, 195, 263; deposition, 81; establishment of twelve states, 46, 307n5; FESTAC Tribunal of Inquiry, 202–3; indigenization decrees, 38; National Theatre, 47; regional structures, 27–28; role in FESTAC, 61, 66–67; spending on FESTAC, 90–91

The Great Arch (Corrigan and Sayer), 167

Greenpeace, 271

Guinea, 55, 60, 70, 72, 77

Guinea-Bissau, 288nn3

Gulf Oil Company Nigeria Limited, 24

Haley, Alex, 76

Handler, Richard, 7

Harper, Peggy, 2, 113

Haruna, I.B.M.: bare-breasted dance debate, 116; FESTAC Regatta, 129; Grand Durbar speech, 171–73, 192, 299n8, 300n20; Kano conference speech, 91–92

Hausa-Fulani State, 27; costume representation, 100; language issues, 96; women's fashions, 107

Hawan Dawaki. *See* durbar culture

Haynes, Douglas, 199

Hegel, Georg, 7, 21

historical aspects of Nigeria: Biafran civil war, 21–22, 27, 263–64; exploration, 132–49; First Republic, 262, 264; Ogoni activism, 259–67; Second Republic, 265, 270; Third Republic, 270; war canoes, 130–32. *See also* colonial contexts

Hobsbawm, Eric, 167–68

Hollis, John, 287n29

Houphuet-Boigny, Félix, 87

Hughes, Langston, 76

Ibo State, 27, 96

iconography. *See* symbols of FESTAC

Idubor, Felix, 62–63

Imo State: costume representation, 100; FESTAC Regatta, 126, 127

Instructions to Political and Other Officers (Lugard), 184

International Festival Committee (IFC), 54–55; contract rights, 210–12; diplomatic VIP treatment, 61–62; internal audit, 206–8. *See also* administration of FESTAC

Ironsi, Thomas, 262

Islamic festivals. *See* Sallah celebrations

Ivory Coast, 71

Ivy, Marilyn, 7

King Jaja of Opobo, 155, 156ff.

Jibrin, Usman, 195

Johnson, John H., 56

Johnson, Pini, 240

Johnston, H. H., 153–54

Jones, G. I., 155, 164

Joseph, Richard A., 30, 196

Jos Museum, 45–46
Jukun kingdom, 174–75, 176, 299n10

Kaduna Mafia, 38, 198, 203–4, 236–37
Kaduna State: costume representation,
    100; creation, 237–38; FESTAC partici-
    pation, 90; Grand Durbar, 170–73,
    299n3, 301n34; Royal Durbar of 1956,
    191–92
Kalabari canoes, 163, 297n15
Kano State: costume representation, 100;
    Grand Durbar, 299n3, 301n34
Kaunda, Kenneth, 75, 87
Kenya, 60
Kettler, Rev. Don, 229
The King Emperor and His Dominions,
    185–86
Kirk-Greene, Anthony, 173–74, 192–93
Kisch, Martin, 184
Kongi's Harvest (Soyinka), 66
Kula canoes, 121–22, 162–63
Kunz, Frank, 276
Kwara State: costume representation,
    100–101; FESTAC Regatta, 126, 127;
    Grand Durbar, 299n3, 301n34

Lagos State: costume representation, 100;
    FESTAC Regatta, 126, 127
Laird, MacGregor, 141–45, 164
Lake, Captain, 136, 140
Lambodo drama, 48–49
Lander, John, 132–41
Lander, Richard, 132–44, 143f, 146
language use, 5, 65–68, 96
Lapido, Duro, 113
Lebovics, Herman, 89
Leton, G. B., 202
Leyland Bus scandal, 201, 205, 218,
    303nn17–18
Libya, 77
literature events, 95–96
Lloyd, P. C., 178
Local Government Authorities (LGAS),
    28–29, 286n10
Lugard, Flora Shaw, 182
Lugard, Frederick, 154; on colonizing role,
    300n18; first colonial durbar, 179–80;
    Governor-General appointment, 185,

300nn19–20; inspection durbar, 184–
    85; military operations, 181–82; rules
    for durbars, 184, 188
Lumumba, Patrice, 74
Lytton, Lord Edward Bulwer, 180

M. V. Oloibiri (supertanker), 35
MacDonald, Claude, 149–52
MacRae, Sir Christopher, 243
Madame Tussaud's Wax Museum, 103,
    105
marketing of FESTAC, 91–93
Marxian analyses, 44, 119; civil society,
    276–77; commodity fetishism, 21–23,
    36, 44, 51, 81, 118–20, 268, 276–77
Matory, J. Lorand, 269
Mauritania, 71
Mbembe, Achille, 237, 270, 281–83
Mbia, Ambroise, 69–70
McIntosh, Warren, 77
media of Nigeria, 91–93
Meek, C. K., 174, 299n10
Mid-Western State, 27, 111
Mitchell, Timothy, 4, 89, 161, 169, 268
Mitee, Batom, 273
Mobutu Sese Seko, 55, 74, 281
Mockler-Ferryman, A. F., 149–52, 184
Mohammed (Murtala) regime, 26–27,
    39–40, 278; coup, 195; FESTAC
    finances, 90–91
A Month and a Day: A Detention Diary
    (Saro-Wiwa), 259–60
Moriarty, John, 59
Moshoeshoe, King of Lesotho, 87
Movement for the Survival of the Ogoni
    People (MOSOP), 260, 266, 270–71,
    275–76
Mozambique, 74, 288nn3
museum presentations, 94
Mveng, Father Englebert, 70, 290n34,
    290n36
My Mercedes Is Bigger Than Yours
    (Nwankwo), 215

Nadel, S. F., 176–77, 300n13
Nafest, 60
Nafest '74 (Kaduna), 109–14, 295nn56–
    57; bare-breasted dancing, 116; cor-

Nafest '74 (Kaduna) (*continued*)
  porate sponsorship, 111–12; filming,
  112
Namibia, 74
National Black Coalition of Canada, 58
National Colour Television, 41–42, 42*f*
National Council of Arts and Culture, 46,
  47, 124
National Exhibition, 95–120; arts and
  crafts, 96–99, 118, 119; centralized
  process, 97–98, 110, 293n30, 295n56;
  chieftaincies, 99–103, 292n10;
  dance/choreography, 109–19,
  295nn56–57; Kano Conference, 90–
  95, 103–4; literature events, 95–96,
  118; marketing of FESTAC, 91–93; nationalization of culture, 47–51, 83,
  89–95, 103–5, 112, 118, 293n19; traditional costumes, 99–109, 118, 119,
  294n44; women's fashions, 105–9,
  118, 119; Yoruba favoritism, 100–103
National Festival of the Arts, 46
National Insurance Company of Nigeria
  (NICON), 98–99, 104, 113, 118, 119,
  209
nationalization of culture, 7–8, 15, 274,
  279–80, 282, 308n1; colonial contexts, 45–46; FESTAC Grand Durbar,
  193–99; FESTAC Regatta, 123, 125,
  127–29, 166; language use, 5, 65–68,
  96; National Exhibition, 47–51, 83,
  89–95, 103–5, 112, 118, 293n19; regional festivals, 46–47
National Participation Committee (NPC),
  89, 116; Grand Durbar, 170, 196; Kano
  Conference, 90–95, 293n19
National Republican Convention (NRC),
  238, 241
National Secretariat, 90
National Theatre, 5, 47–50, 288, 288n32;
  costs, 91; expenditures, 202–3
National Theatre Library, 11
Neto, Agostino, 55
New International Economic Order
  (NIEO), 75–76, 82
News Agency of Nigeria (NAN), 92
NICON. *See* National Insurance Company
  of Nigeria

Nigeria Magazine, 45
Nigerian Department of Antiquities, 93–
  94
Nigerian exhibitions and events, 94–95
Nigerian Heritage, 274
Nigerian Institute of International Affairs,
  11
Nigerian Ministry of Information, 91–94
Nigerian National Museum, 46
Nigerian National Petroleum Corporation
  (NNCP), 28, 35–36, 225–26, 255
Nigerian Oil Corporation, 274
Nigerian Task Force on Trade Malprac-
  tices, 230
Niger State: costume representation, 101;
  Grand Durbar, 299n3, 301n34
Nkrumah, Kwame, 65, 74
No Longer At Ease (Achebe), 231
Northern People's Congress, 188
NPC. *See* National Participation Com-
  mittee
Nuckolls, Charles W., 180
Nupe kingdom, 176–77
Nwankwo, Nkem, 215
Nwoko, Demas, 114–17, 260
Nwosu, Humphrey, 243
Nzekwu, Onuora, 66, 290n27
Nzeribe, Arthur, 230, 241, 243–45, 255

Obasanjo, Olusegun: on election financing, 241; election to presidency, 279;
  FESTAC Grand Durbar, 170–71, 195;
  FESTAC opening ceremonies, 87–89;
  FESTAC Regatta, 123, 124, 126, 127,
  129; on FESTAC's role, 213; origins, 126;
  prison term, 272, 279; vision of Black
  and African world, 52–53, 76, 87
Obasanjo (Olusegun) regime, 27, 47,
  288n32; concessions to northern
  power, 195–96; economic policies,
  216; Nigerian Heritage book launch,
  274; Operation Feed the Nation, 216;
  return to civilian rule, 278–79; spending on FESTAC, 91
Obi Assai, King at Aboh, 135–36, 142–47,
  164
O'Brien, Michael, 306n36
Ogoni Bill of Rights, 266–67

Ogoni movement, 17, 254, 258–77, 307n7; Autonomy Option, 266–67, 275–76; Biafran civil war, 263–64; demise of civil society, 270–75; history, 259–67; Ogoniland infrastructure, 265; oil company promises, 263; oil revenue distribution, 264–67; pollution, 252, 256, 258–67, 271, 275; violence, 271–74. *See also* Saro-Wiwa, Ken

Ogun, Sam, 213

Ogunde, Hubert, 115, 211

Ogun State: costume representation, 100; FESTAC Regatta, 126

Ogunwale, Wale, 2

oil boom economy of Nigeria, 2, 3, 14–31, 50–51, 254–55; agriculture, 27, 216, 269, 275; centralization of the state, 193, 265; circulation of capital, 41–44; commodity fetishism, 35–39, 41–44, 51, 119–20, 225, 232, 268, 286n11, 287n24, 287n29; control of FESTAC, 73–75; costs of culture, 16, 50–51, 73–75; development projects, 25–31, 213–17, 286n10, 304n33; distribution of oil, 31–34, 44, 287n22, 287n24; distribution of revenues, 264–67; Economic Community of West African States (ECOWAS), 70–73; education, 231–32; labor laws, 216; Magic Barrel gimmick, 24–25; manufacturing, 27, 216–17, 286n6; money magic anxieties, 231–32, 268–69, 282; *naira* power, 225, 304n2; national grid map, 36ff.; nationalization of foreign business, 22–23, 76; new bourgeoisie, 231–32; pollution, 31, 254; production and consumption, 25, 215–19; transformative aspects, 8–9, 14–15, 285nn5–6; the vampire state, 267–70, 273; war canoe symbols of value, 124. *See also* corruption; economic contexts; value of cultural production

oil bust economy of Nigeria, 10, 14, 16–17, 223–57; Babangida regime fraud, 236–37; collapse of civil society, 270–74; counterfeit money, 248–50, 251ff., 307n45; crisis of value, 248–54; deregulation of the banking system, 228; drug trafficking, 252, 253ff.; 419 scams, 226–36, 249–50, 254–56, 277, 283; high-risk speculation, 250, 307n47; illusions of wealth, 204–6, 225–26; inflation, 252–53, 256, 277; 1993 election, 224, 236–48, 255–56; petroleum dependency, 226; pollution, 252, 256, 258–67, 271, 275; religious aspects, 250–51, 307n8; shortages, 250–52, 256, 274, 277

Ojukwu, C. Odumegwu, 263–64

Okpei, Charles, 79

Okwesa, Fidelma, 113

Oldfield, R. A. K., 141–45, 296–97n14

Omatshola, Emmanuel, 24

On a Darkling Plain: An Account of the Nigerian Civil War (Saro-Wiwa), 263–64

Ondo State: costume representation, 100; dance performances, 115–16; FESTAC Regatta, 126, 127, 128ff.

OPEC, 15, 21–22, 264

Operation Feed the Nation (OFN), 28, 30

Organisation of African Unity (OAU), 3, 68, 82; Algiers Pan-African Cultural Festival of 1969, 70; Arab member states, 74; Nigeria's role, 74–75, 291n45

Organization of Petroleum Exporting Countries. See OPEC

Oshun Festival, 2

Osofisan, Femi, 211

Oyo State, 100

Pacheco-Pereira, Don Duarte, 130–32

palm oil economy: colonial contexts, 273, 307–8n9; social class issues, 155–56; war canoe culture, 124, 136, 141, 144–46, 148, 155–56, 165

Pan-African Cultural Festival of 1969, 70

Park, Mungo, 132

Pascale, Charlie, 233–35

Pategi Regatta, 158–59

Pemberton, John, 168

Perham, Marjorie, 179

Petroleum Anti-Sabotage Decree of 1975, 32, 287n16

Petroleum Equalisation Fund, 287n24

Philip, Duke of Edinburgh, 159
Plateau State: costume representation,
    101; Grand Durbar, 299n3, 301n34
political contexts, 3; Algiers Pan-African
    Cultural Festival of 1969, 70; Biafran
    war, 193, 263–64; centralization of the
    state, 23–31, 45–46, 193, 264, 275–
    76, 301n31; citizenship, 9, 73–74, 92,
    291n41; colonial hierarchies, 188;
    coups, 26–27, 226; creation of politi-
    cal parties, 238–40, 265, 305n27; cre-
    ation of states, 46, 266–67, 307n5;
    draft constitution of 1989, 238–39,
    240; Economic Community of West
    African States (ECOWAS), 70–73; elec-
    tion funding, 241–42; FESTAC admin-
    istration, 54–75, 61, 92–95; FESTAC
    participation, 90–95; 419 scams, 12–
    13, 16, 230–36, 249–50, 254–56, 277,
    283; independence, 189, 193, 262;
    Kano riots of 1953, 191, 301n27; lan-
    guage issues, 5, 65–68, 96; liberation
    movements, 55, 288n3, 291n43; Local
    Government Authorities, 28–29; na-
    tionalist movements, 188, 189–91,
    199; 1979 elections, 195–96; 1983
    elections, 224; 1993 election, 9–10, 13,
    16–17, 223–24, 230, 236–48, 270,
    306nn36–38; northern hegemony,
    170, 188, 195–96, 198, 259–60, 272,
    299n3, 301n25, 301n27; Organisation
    of African Unity (OAU), 74–75; re-
    gional structures, 27–29; resistance
    activities, 32–33; Richards Constitu-
    tion of 1945, 189; South African apart-
    heid, 193; Supreme Military Council,
    28. See also economic contexts; federal
    government; Ogoni movement
pollution, 31, 252, 256, 258–67, 271, 275
Port Harcourt Regatta, 159–62
Procession to Ibu (Allen), 143ff.
production of culture. See cultural pro-
    duction
Public Enlightenment Units, 92–93

racial classifications, 4, 59. See also visions
    of blackness

Ranger, Terence, 167–68, 188
Regatta State, 15–16; FESTAC participation,
    90; Secretariat, 90–91
Rhodes, Cecil, 75
Rhodesia, 74–75
Rivers State: costume representation, 100;
    FESTAC Regatta, 126, 127; Nafest dance
    presentation, 111; oil revenue distribu-
    tion, 265–66; women's fashions, 105.
    See also Ogoni movement
Roots (Haley), 76
Royal Dutch Shell, 258. See also Shell-BP
Royal Niger Company: consolidation of
    British control, 123; discovery expedi-
    tions, 141, 149–54, 297–98nn26–27,
    298n29; surrender durbar, 179
Russell, Lord John, 145

Sahlins, Marshall, 131, 139
Sallah celebrations, 168, 175–78, 197. See
    also durbar culture
Saro-Wiwa, Ken, 252–53, 258–77; auton-
    omy demands, 266–67, 275–76;
    death, 17, 31, 254, 258, 270; environ-
    mental activism, 258–59, 270–74;
    oil revenue allocations, 261, 264–67;
    trial, 258, 271–72; the vampire state,
    267–70, 273; writings, 259–67
Sayer, Derek, 167
Schön (missionary), 146
Second World Black and African Festival
    of Arts and Culture. See FESTAC '77
Selassie, Haile, 197
Sene, Alioune, 70, 290n29
Senegal, 55, 61; on Arab participation in
    FESTAC, 68–70; Economic Commu-
    nity of West African States (ECOWAS),
    70–73; FESTAC control, 59, 65–75,
    82; Senghor's First World Festival,
    65–67
Senghor, Léopold: on Arab participation
    in FESTAC, 70; Economic Community
    of West African States (ECOWAS), 70;
    First World Festival of Negro Arts, 65–
    67; role in FESTAC, 60–61, 66–67;
    vision of blackness, 65, 70, 77. See also
    Senegal

Shagari's Second Republic, 224, 228, 307n45

Sharwood-Smith, Sir Bryan E. and Lady, 192

Shell-BP, 260, 263, 271, 274

Shonekan, Ernest, 9, 247, 272

Sierra Leone, 71

Similia: Essays on Anomic Nigeria (Saro-Wiwa), 252–53

Simmel, Georg, 121–22, 162

slavery: Baikie's visionary communities, 149; Delta region, 273; Society for the Extinction of the Slave Trade, 145; war canoe culture, 123–24, 131–32, 137, 155, 165, 296n12

Smith, Ian, 74–75

Smith, Jerry, 229

Smith, M. G., 175

Smithsonian Institution, 57–58

social class issues: crowd control, 88–89; Delta trading states, 132, 136; oil boom bourgeoisie, 30–31, 231–32, 252; oil bust leveling, 252–53; palm oil trade, 155–56; political class, 347; slave trade, 155; transformations, 3, 8, 31

Social Democratic Party (SDP), 238, 241

Society for the Extinction of the Slave Trade, 145

Sokoto State: costume representation, 100; Grand Durbar, 299n3, 301n34

Sorgi, Terry, 229

South African apartheid, 55

Soyinka, Wole, 65, 66, 95–96, 271, 275, 307n7

Stevens, Siaka, 87

Sultan of Sokoto: durbars, 182–83, 184–85, 189, 192; FESTAC Grand Durbar, 193–94, 195, 196ff., 301n35; regional government role, 187–88, 190, 242, 301n24

symbols of FESTAC, 218; Benin mask motif, 62–64, 67, 193, 209–10, 289n18, 289–90nn22–23, 304n28; building-site rituals, 289n14; copyright issues, 16, 210–12, 303–4nn27–28; FESTAC Regatta, 126; flag, 61–65, 67; inverted

value production, 212; name change, 67–68; theme song, 2, 213

Talbot, Percy, 139–40, 163, 297n15

Taussig, Michael, 268

T.B. Can Be Cured (film), 211

Third National Development Plan, 25–26

Tito, Josip, 60

Tofa, Bashir, 10, 242

Togo, 71

Touré, Sekou, 60, 70

Townson, Captain, 142

trade. *See* economic contexts

Trotter, H. D., 145–47, 148, 297n20

Tshombe, Moise, 74

Twins Seven-Seven, 2

2000 Years of Nigerian Arts (film), 211

Udoji Commission reforms, 29, 69, 286n11

Ume, Bob, 78–79

Unipetrol, 34

Universal Primary Education (UPE), 28

Upper Volta, 71

Up the River (Mockler-Ferryman), 149–52

U.S. Bicentennial Celebration, 57–58

U.S. participation in FESTAC: Ambassador Young, 75, 170, 193–94, 195; parade delegation, 77, 78ff.; State Department role, 56–59

value of cultural production, 7–9, 14–15, 63, 73–75; conversion of money into culture, 2, 50–51; debates about FESTAC, 200–202; inverted value of signs and symbols, 212–19; transvaluations through exchange, 139–41, 147, 159–60, 164–65, 295–96n1; war canoe magic, 122–24, 156, 162–63. *See also* commodification of culture

Vanderburg, Ben, 233–34

Victoria, Queen of Great Britain, 179–80

visions of blackness, 52–83; beyond negritude, 65–76, 82, 290n34, 290n36; diaspora issues, 76–82; FESTAC administration, 54–65; measurements of blackness, 81–82,

visions of blackness (*continued*)
292n61; narratives of black unity, 77–
79; Nigerian national culture, 83; symbols, 61–65, 67–68; worldwide participation, 54–61

war canoe culture, 121–54; administrative
hierarchies, 155–56; aesthetics, 163–
64, 165; armaments, 163; colonial consular authority, 153–54, 297n24; colonial regattas, 157–62, 165–66, 298–
99nn36–37; Delta "creole" culture,
161–62, 164–65, 166, 295–96n1; European impact, 132–38; flag use, 133–
34; gift giving, 132, 135, 144, 164–65,
296–97nn14–15; historical functions,
125, 130–40; Kalabari canoes, 163;
Kula canoes, 121–22, 162–63; Landers' journey, 132–41; last regatta, 152–
53, 298n30; modern canoe fetish, 161–
62; palm oil trade, 124, 136, 141, 144–
46, 148, 155–56, 165; processions, 138;
rituals and fetishism, 137–41, 146–47,
151–53, 163–65, 297nn16–17, 297n23;
riverine trade, 131–34, 136–38, 144–
45; role of leaders, 129; Shrine of Adumu, 139–40; slave trade, 123–24,
131–32, 137, 145, 149, 155, 164–65,
296n12; value as magic, 122–24, 156,
162–63. *See also* exploration of Nigerian rivers; FESTAC Regatta
Watts, Michael, 249, 251–52, 268–69,
307n8, 308n1
Wenger, Suzanne, 2
Williams, David, 191–92
women's issues: bare-breasted dance debate, 115–16, 117ff.; harassment problems, 108, 295n53; modern fashions,
105–9, 118, 119
world's fairs and exhibitions, 4–5, 6, 89,
105
Wright, Richard, 76

Yar'Adua, Shehu Musa, 87, 124, 195,
196ff.; death, 272, 308n4; presidential
election, 242
Yoruba drum language, 1–2
Yoruba ethnicity, 27; involvement in
FESTAC, 96; women's fashions, 107
Young, Andrew, 75, 170, 193–94, 195

Zimbabwe, 74–75